Shawn T. Wahl // **Jake Simmons** // **Jeffrey Q. McCune, Jr.** //
Missouri State University   Missouri State University   Washington University

Second Edition

Kendall Hunt
publishing company

Intercultural Communication
in Your Life

Cover image © Shutterstock, Inc.

www.kendallhunt.com
Send all inquiries to:
4050 Westmark Drive
Dubuque, IA 52004-1840

Copyright © 2014, 2018 by Kendall Hunt Publishing Company

Text only ISBN 978-1-5249-5220-4
PAK ISBN 978-1-7924-2060-3

Published in the United States of America

brief contents

contents

CHAPTER 7: Intercultural Issues in Group Communication 175

CHAPTER 8: Intercultural Communication and Conflict 205

preface

THE ELEPHANT IN THE ROOM

Where groups of people gather, there is always an elephant in the room: **difference**. In a desire for sameness, too often how some communities do culture differently is made invisible. Difference matters. All around the world, there are folks living differently than you, whose culture and community have little familiarity. Somehow little snapshots of individuals and groups, have made us feel as if we are more knowledgeable than we are; new media—from Facebook to Instagram—produces an imagined connectedness which deemphasizes the huge disconnect between us and others. The true elephant in the room is that we live in a world which connects us by device, but divides us by creating a feeling that our differences are smaller than they are. Elephants are huge creatures. No elephant is small, or simple. The truth: elephants are remarkable, complex creatures which take up much space. Likewise, matters of race, culture, and difference require creative and complicated conversations—which moves us beyond "we are all alike" or "we all matter"—to understanding the significance of difference, as both a gift and a challenge.

Like elephants, differences can't be simply ignored or walked around with anticipation that we can operate without confronting them head on. Race, Religion, Gender, Class, Sexuality, and Geography matters. *Intercultural Communication in Your Life* is an opportunity to teach readers the essential nature of difference, what to do with difference, and how to see difference beyond deficiency. This text provides a lens for understanding the complex networks of communication in which we dwell. For what we know in our two decades in the field, is that the ability to understand cultural difference and diversity requires careful study, critical generosity, and some undoing of accepted meanings and cultural myths. Of course, this is complicated when communication sites such as social media offers us snapshots, suggesting that knowing people is possible through an engagement with pictures. Pictures are not people. And even when we are presented with a cacophony of diverse pictorial images, we often rely on age-old myths of communities to interpret them. Many of these readings, or interpretations, have always been limited, while others are just plain wrong.

We, as authors, want students, faculty, university agents, and community leaders, to get it more right. Using our textbook, we hope readers will take seriously the importance of connecting one's individual experience with understandings of intercultural communication. It is our belief that intercultural knowledge and behaviors are not "common sense," but rather a site of global deficiency. Through engagement with new approaches to communication, culture, and everyday life, we are able to better facilitate richer and real relationships with different people, communities, and perspectives. It is only through study and interaction that we develop better modes of communication which help dispel faulty and dangerous perceptions.

In this book, the author team is going to take you on a journey through many rooms, personal and professional. You will see many critical topics, theories, and dialogue embedded within this text—providing concrete and complex, but accessible approaches to studying and thinking seriously about culture and everyday life. Our hope is that the elephant will remain in the room; but, the room will not be empty of conversation, careful listening, collaborative connections, and critical reflexivity.

—Jeffrey Q. McCune, Jr.

ORGANIZING FEATURE: IN YOUR LIFE

We believe that developing an organizing feature lends clarity to a textbook. The **organizing feature** running throughout the text is IN YOUR LIFE, a feature to develop students' application of intercultural communication theory and research to their lived experience.

The IN YOUR LIFE FEATURE appears as follows:

OVERVIEW OF THE BOOK

In this text, we provide 11 focused chapters in which the best material—drawn from the research bases of communication and other disciplines—is explored with relevance to the study of intercultural communication. This book doesn't attempt to cover the entire world of intercultural communication—we had to make difficult choices regarding the content, based on teaching communication in higher education, consulting with experts in the discipline, and experimenting with texts written by friends and colleagues across the nation. What emerged is a representation of the cutting-edge work in the field, combining rhetorical/critical and social science research on intercultural communication with applications to students' everyday lives to help them develop cultural competency through the study of communication applied to their life and career—without overwhelming them.

Chapter 1 provides an introduction to the foundations and key concepts important to the study of intercultural communication, as well as a preview of the contexts covered in the text. The first topic included in the book connects the study of communication and culture to ethics in **Chapter 2** ("Ethical Dimensions of Intercultural Communication"). **Chapter 3** ("Culture and Identity") helps students explore the issue of identity and connect how their communication and identity are linked.

The text then explores the rewards and challenges of traveling abroad—or sojourning—as well as the ways people adapt to their new environments, which we describe in the chapter as acculturation. **Chapter 4** ("Sojourning, Assimilating, and Acculturating") also explores virtually any situation where we might try to fit in and adapt to a group or culture to which we want or expect to belong. We refer to this process as assimilation. **Chapter 5** ("Intercultural Dimensions of Verbal and Nonverbal Communication") looks at the different properties of verbal and nonverbal communication and how they relate to the topic of intercultural communication. The following chapters explore interpersonal and small group communication with **Chapter 6** ("Conversing and Relating in Intercultural Contexts") and **Chapter 7** ("Cultural Issues in Group Communication"). **Chapter 8** ("Intercultural Communication and Conflict) and **Chapter 9** ("Communicating Social Class and Understanding the Culture of Poverty") look at culturally based conflict as well as the class struggles and the implications of poverty and inequality.

The next two chapters review communication and culture in applied contexts such as health and business and professional situations in **Chapter 10** ("Intercultural Issues in Health, Wellness, and Medicine") and **Chapter 11** ("Intercultural Communication in Business and Professional Contexts").

PEDAGOGICAL FEATURES

This book includes nine pedagogical features. Each chapter contains two opening features to help instructors deliver course content and enhance student learning.

- *Chapter Outlines* detail the organization of each chapter.

- *What You Will Learn* helps students prioritize and personalize information so that they can learn more efficiently.

- An opening *Ripped From the Headlines* feature connects students to the primary chapter content—a brief example to gain attention from readers as they move into a new topic. In all chapters, the opening chapter feature represents actual events and real experiences intended to resonate with students.

- Themes from the opening feature appear throughout each chapter and are applied to and evaluated with the *In Your Life* feature that appears in each chapter.

- Communication ethics is emphasized in all chapters with a feature called *Ethical Connection,* which connects the topic to an ethical perspective—because it's the foundation of studying communication and culture.

- Chapters contain a *Self-Assessment* feature designed to help students inventory their intercultural communication skills.

- Discussion questions, the *Reflect* section of each chapter, are also included so that instructors can use them as a means of generating class discussions about chapter content, as actual assignments, or as thought-provokers for students to consider on their own time.
- *Key Terms* at the end of each chapter are defined in the full *Glossary* at the end of the book.

Finally, complete *References* to the research base cited within the text appear at the end of the book and are organized by chapter. Students might find these references useful as they prepare assignments and/or conduct their own research projects. Instructors might use references to gather additional material for their own research or to supplement instruction.

INSTRUCTIONAL SUPPLEMENTS

On adoption of the text, an online Instructor's Manual (IM) is provided on the book's accompanying website. Designed for both community colleges and 4-year universities, the IM contains chapter outlines that can serve as class notes for instructors or students, PowerPoint slides containing outlines and graphics for each chapter, and activities/exercises to enhance instruction and stimulate class discussion. An online Test Bank that includes multiple-choice and short-answer questions is available for instructors' use. Materials from the IM support **distance education**, making them useful to **traditional**, **online**, and **hybrid delivery formats**. The IM can support **large courses** and departments using graduate teaching assistants or adjunct instructors—both the textbook and IM support departments needing either instructional flexibility or consistency in the way intercultural courses are delivered across sections.

ACKNOWLEDGMENTS

This project has been both exciting and challenging. Thus, there are many people we would like to acknowledge. We wish to thank the team at Kendall Hunt, with whom it's been a pleasure to work, and who offered great assistance, feedback, and encouragement: Paul Carty, Angela Willenbring, Lynne Rogers, and Jen Wreisner.

ABOUT THE AUTHORS

Shawn T. Wahl, Ph.D., Professor of Communication and Interim Dean of the College of Arts and Letters at Missouri State University, has authored six other textbooks, including *Business and Professional Communication: KEYS for Workplace Excellence*, *Public Speaking: Essentials for Excellence*, *Persuasion in Your Life*, *Nonverbal Communication for a Lifetime*, and *The Communication Age: Connecting and Engaging*. He has published articles in a variety of national communication journals, including *Communication Education*, *Communication Research Reports*, *Communication Teacher*, *Basic Communication Course Annual*, and *Journal of Family Communication*. He is an active member of the National Communication Association and the 2016 President of the Central States Communication Association. In addition, Shawn has worked across the nation as a corporate trainer, communication consultant, and leadership coach in a variety of industries.

Jake Simmons, Ph.D., Assistant Professor of Communication, Director of The Master of Arts in Communication Graduate Program at Missouri State University, has published articles in a variety of national and international academic journals, including *Communication Education*, *Text and Performance Quarterly*, *Communication Teacher*, *Departures in Critical Qualitative Research*, *Technoculture: A Journal of Technology and Society*, and others. Jake serves on the editorial board for a number of National Communication Association journals. He is co-editor of *Digital Horizons*, a recurring section in *Liminalities: A Journal of Performance Studies*. He is an active member of The National Communication Association, Central States Communication Association, and The International Congress of Qualitative Inquiry. In addition, Jake has presented to various groups on the importance of intercultural communication and diversity and inclusion on college campuses.

Jeffrey Q. McCune, Jr., Ph.D., Associate Professor of African & African American Studies and Women, Gender, and Sexuality Studies at Washington University in St. Louis, is the author of the award-winning book *Sexual Discretion: Black Masculinity and the Politics of Passing*. He is presently completing two book projects. The first, *Read!: An Experiment in Seeing Black*, and the other *On Kanye: A Philosophy of Black Genius. He* has published in a variety of journals, which include *Text and Performance Quarterly* and *QED: A Journal in GLBTQ Worldmaking*. Jeffrey serves on the editorial board of numerous journals, while being an active member of the National Communication Association and the American Studies Association. He has directed several initiatives which advance diversity and inclusion within and outside college communities. For his work at the intersections, of race gender, and sexuality, Jeffrey has been featured on *Left of Black*, *Sirius XM's Joe Madison Show*, *HuffPost Live*, *NPR* and as a guest expert on *Bill Nye Saves The World*.

CHAPTER ONE
Intercultural Communication in Your Life

CHAPTER OUTLINE

WHAT YOU WILL LEARN

After studying this chapter, you should be able to

1. define culture;
2. identify examples of diversity across communication contexts;
3. apply ethics to your study of intercultural communication;
4. define cultural competence; and
5. identify barriers to communication, culture, and diversity.

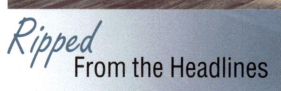

Ripped From the Headlines

Justin Flitter, a New Zealand–based customer advocate for Zendesk, has noted several benefits of using the social media application Twitter for his cross-cultural communication. General cultural communication issues such as accents, tone, body language, and other variables are reduced whenever there is only text on screen (Carter, 2010). Also, applications such as Twinslator, Tweettrans, and Twanslate allow users to tweet in other languages as well as translate other people's tweets into a language of the user's choosing. Flitter also notes that Twitter features such as the "Trending Topics" section allow users to focus their communication on shared interests, without separators such as cultural context and jargon alienating different users from one another.

In the United States, Twitter has played a major role in political discourse and political coverage. President Barack Obama made history in 2010 when he became the first Commander in Chief to use Twitter in office (Henry, 2010). President Trump used Twitter throughout his election campaign and continues to utilize it during his presidency. President Trump has said that Twitter allows him to put out an honest and unfiltered message to his followers (Nelson, 2017). It is not uncommon to see major news stories break on Twitter before other traditional media (such as radio and television) can report to the public.

Twitter is only one example of technology opening up new communication opportunities across the globe. However, this increased reach of interpersonal and intercultural communication requires people to be more culturally considerate and competent. As you navigate this chapter, continue to be reflexive about the ways you communicate across cultures in your everyday life. Continue to ask yourself whether you are being both an effective and an ethical communicator and feed that knowledge back into your communication practice.

Welcome to your study of intercultural communication. This is a fascinating topic essential not only for students of communication, business, health, cultural competency, diversity, rhetoric and culture, and media studies but also for a variety of other disciplines. Let us introduce ourselves as your textbook authors. We have years of experience teaching and researching communication—and our students know that studying communication and culture is the foundation of human decency, mutual respect, civility, and cultural competency across personal and professional contexts. We will serve as your tour guides and coaches in the learning process. Connected to our passion for teaching in the college classroom and for communication research is our focus on explaining technical information and putting it into words you can understand and apply in your personal and professional lives. We have consulted with other communication scholars across the nation in the process of writing a textbook that will assist you in connecting to important learning objectives and skill development related to communication and culture. Our belief is that we can learn more about communication and culture by grounding it in lived, everyday experiences. That's why the title of this textbook (*Communication and Culture in Your Life*) serves as a driving theme of every chapter. This title and theme were selected with you, the student of communication and culture, in mind. So throughout the book you will notice references to everyday experiences, with attention given to a variety of face-to-face and mediated contexts that serve as awesome examples to assist you in your study of this important topic. Coupled with the driving theme of the book are important principles that encourage critical thinking, analysis, ethics, and application of knowledge related to communication and culture present in personal, social, political, and professional contexts.

This introductory chapter explores the importance of communication, culture, and diversity in everyday contexts—the relation of self to other in your life. Let's begin by defining several important terms.

COMMUNICATION, CULTURE, AND DIVERSITY DEFINED

This section defines culture and diversity as connected to your study of communication. Consider your transition to college (e.g., first-year freshmen, working professionals returning to school, students facing a change in career/life goals) as a reference point in your study of intercultural communication in your life. As you grow more familiar with this topic, think about issues you associate with culture and diversity.

COMMUNICATION

As you begin your study, it's important to define what communication means. This term has been defined in many ways, but here's the definition we prefer: **Communication** is the collaborative process of using messages to create and participate in social reality. The most important aspects of our lives—our individual identities, relationships, organizations, communities, and ideas—are accomplished through communication. Communication enables us to actualize possibility, realize human potential, and achieve change and growth, both for ourselves and for our communities (Edwards, Edwards, Wahl, & Myers, 2016).

Communication in your everyday experiences is the essential process and skill that helps you make sense of things across life contexts. Because communication is so much a part of your everyday life, you probably think of it as a simple process. Communicating comes so naturally to us that we rarely feel the need to give communication a second thought. When was the last time you really stopped and examined your communication skills? Do you pause to analyze your communication regularly? Indeed, as you will learn in this course, communication is clearly shaped by culture. The next sections make an important connection between these two concepts.

Communication

the collaborative process of using messages to create and participate in social reality and to achieve goals. The most important aspects of our lives—our individual identities, relationships, organizations, communities, and ideas—are accomplished through communication.

CULTURE

From Day 1, your parents, siblings, relatives, friends, teachers, and even strangers have been working to socialize you into the **culture**(s) that make up their experiences—that is, the rules of living and functioning in a particular society (Jandt, 2010; Samovar, Porter, & McDaniel, 2009; Ting-Toomey & Chung, 2005). Put in a different way, think about culture as the set of shared attitudes, values, goals, and practices that characterizes an institution, organization, or group (Edwards et al., 2016). The way you talk, behave, dress, and think have all been shaped by the way others have socialized you into various cultural groups. There are a number of things to consider that will help you start thinking carefully about culture. For example, Joel is a gay high school student who has recently "come out" to friends and family. He is being bullied at school and is unsure how to share this difficult time with others. An experience such as Joel's emphasizes the need for communication competence and sensitivity related to diverse groups of people.

Culture

the set of shared attitudes, values, goals, and practices that characterizes an institution, organization, or group. The way you talk, behave, dress, and think have all been shaped by the way others have socialized you into various cultural groups.

DIVERSITY

Diversity is a term used to describe the unique differences among people. These differences are based on a variety of factors such as ethnicity, race, heritage, religion,

Diversity

a term used to describe the unique differences among people. These differences are based on a variety of factors such as ethnicity, race, heritage, religion, gender, sexual identity, age, social class, and the like.

Many college campuses offer a rich, in-depth environment in which to engage in co-cultural communication.

© Amir Ridhwan/Shutterstock.com

gender, sexual identity, age, social class, and the like. When *culture* and *diversity* are discussed in the United States, the terms are often understood in relation to **co-cultural communication**, which refers to interactions between underrepresented and dominant group members. Examples of co-cultures include, but are not limited to, people of color, women, people with disabilities, gays and lesbians, and members of low-income communities. Do you identify with any of the co-cultures listed here? Many students describe culture by referencing national borders and language, but a person can be a member of many different cultures, most of which have nothing to do with boundaries or nationalities.

If you take a moment to think about your own college or university campus, there is likely a sense of culture. How would you describe it? Obviously, some groups are more distinct than others. For instance, athletic teams have their own distinct culture: Athletes have a common interest in their sport, engage in team-specific rituals, support one another, and share a sense of community. Athletes may use certain phrases or expressions that people outside of the athletic team do not recognize or understand. Some interesting nonverbal rituals athletic teams practice are butt slaps, body bumps, and high-fives, to name a few. Nonverbal behaviors (specifically, various forms of touch) are ways for athletic teams to celebrate winning or to convey the message "good job" or "nice try." Outside of the team environment, butt slaps and body bumps might be viewed by others as strange

Co-cultural communication
refers to interactions between underrepresented and dominant group members.

Sports teams often practice various nonverbal cultural behaviors such as chest bumps to celebrate.

© Aspen Photo/Shutterstock.com

or even inappropriate. Clearly, one must be a part of this team culture to truly understand it.

Consider Daniel's experience. Daniel came from a traditionally conservative small town, and college was his first introduction to a culturally diverse environment. Daniel experienced some heavy culture shock his first few weeks at school and felt alienated from his peers on campus. Noting his lack of socialization during classes, Daniel's English professor, Dr. Klie, suggested that Daniel try to join one of the school's fraternities. During his pledge period, Daniel was introduced to new friends he would never have approached on his own, and he became more and more comfortable with (and excited about) the college lifestyle. Through membership in his fraternity, Daniel learned more about not only his campus but also his community and peer network. Daniel would later cite his involvement with the fraternity as a major factor in his success in future professional and social interactions.

CULTURAL RITUALS

Cultural rituals

practices, behaviors, celebrations, and traditions common to people, organizations, and institutions.

As a new student, you learned **cultural rituals**—practices, behaviors, celebrations, and traditions common to people, organizations, and institutions. Rituals include things such as professors' passing out syllabi on the first day of class and rush week for Greek organizations. Graduation is the most important ritual at a college or university and one you most certainly aspire to participate in someday. What are some other rituals on your campus? What do they tell you about the culture?

As an entering freshman, you also had to learn the language of higher education. For example, students trying to get into college learn acronyms such as SAT and ACT. Every organization and profession has its own language or jargon that you must learn to communicate effectively in your chosen field (Quintanilla & Wahl, 2016). Part of your education will be learning that jargon so you can communicate with other professionals once you graduate. Can you think of any examples of miscommunication that occurred as you were learning specific jargons? What is some of the jargon you have learned as part of your major? What jargon is used on your college campus?

High school and college graduation are major cultural rituals and milestones in U.S. culture.

Communication scholar Walter Fisher (1984) argues that all humans are storytelling creatures. Using narratives or stories, we as communicators come to understand the cultural context and one another. Paying attention to stories is central to understanding any cultural context. Many of you have probably used stories to determine which courses to take and from which professors. All of you have heard the good and bad rumors about various faculty members on your campus. In fact, today's high-tech world has taken storytelling to a whole new level, with programs such as Pick-a-Prof and RateMyProfessor.com allowing students to hear stories from other students they have never met (Edwards, Edwards, Qing, & Wahl, 2007). Listening to what criteria students use to deem a professor good or bad will tell you a lot about your campus culture. What are the criteria on your campus? What stories helped you learn the culture on your campus? Indeed, the terms *culture*, *diversity*, and *cultural rituals* are important to your study of intercultural communication in your life. The section that follows focuses on connection, engagement, cultural awareness, and several other important concepts.

CONNECTING AND ENGAGING INTERCULTURAL COMMUNICATION

The process of studying intercultural communication is all about connecting and engaging. **Connection** refers to the power of communication to link and relate you to people, groups, communities, social institutions, and cultures (Edwards et al., 2016; Wahl & Morris, 2018). Modern technology and mobility seem to

Connection
power of communication to link and relate you to people, groups, communities, social institutions, and cultures.

make connecting with others easier than ever. Social networking sites link you effortlessly with an extended network of family, friends, and acquaintances. Mobile phones keep your contacts available at the touch of a button. Day or night, you can reach and be reached by virtually anyone you desire. News and information from around the world arrive with a few keystrokes or screen taps. Such connections are at the heart of communication as a process of creating and participating in social reality. We communicate in a dynamic and intricate system of personal and social relationships, and each of us is linked to all others by fewer degrees of separation than ever before. Yet connecting alone is not enough to fully realize the potential of communication in transforming our identities, relationships, communities, and social realities (Edwards et al., 2016).

Your study of intercultural communication also requires engagement (Edwards et al., 2016; Wahl & Morris, 2018). Simply "connecting" to the Internet or a social networking site fails to fully realize the possibilities of what we can achieve. You must also engage those with whom you connect; you must engage in your study of intercultural communication. **Engagement** refers to the act of sharing in the activities of the group (Edwards et al., 2016). In other words, engaging is participating. It requires an orientation toward others that views them always as potential partners in the creation and negotiation of social reality. In this way, being engaged in your study of intercultural communication is like being "engaged" in a close relationship. The idea of a promise to join and act together serves as an appropriate and uplifting metaphor for the attitude we can take when communicating with others (Edwards et al., 2016).

In almost every aspect of your life, you're presented with both opportunities and challenges to connect and engage. You're encouraged to be an engaged citizen, engaged community and group member, engaged member of a workforce, and engaged relationship partner (Edwards et al., 2016). One of the ways you can do so is by engaging in **communication activism**, or direct energetic action in support of needed social change for individuals, groups, organizations, and communities (Frey & Carragee, 2007).

CULTURAL AWARENESS

Cultural awareness is more important than ever before (DeAndrea, Shaw, & Levine, 2010). Specifically, being culturally aware improves communication, makes you an educated citizen, and promotes ethical communication across life contexts. Having cultural awareness across communication contexts is important for the following reasons: (1) For you to succeed in any personal, social, or professional context, you

Engagement
the act of sharing in the activities of the group.

IN YOUR *life*

Each chapter in this book will remind you to connect your study of intercultural communication to lived experience.

Communication activism
direct energetic action in support of needed social change for individuals, groups, organizations, and communities.

must be aware of and sensitive toward differences between yourself and others; and (2) your ability to communicate effectively when encountering differences of ethnicity, race, language, religion, marital status, or sexual identity is essential to being an educated citizen. You will be interacting with people who may present you with differences you have never encountered before, and your communication choices will shape these experiences as either positive or negative (Cruikshank, 2010; Quan, 2010). We will now explore a few important concepts related to the study of intercultural communication in your life.

CULTURAL COMPETENCE

Awareness of diversity across communication contexts is crucial to navigating a globalized world (Cruikshank, 2010; DeAndrea et al., 2010). One way to prepare for diverse social situations and environments is to improve your cultural competence. **Cultural competence** refers to the level of knowledge a person has about others who differ in some way in comparison with him or herself. A culturally competent person is sensitive to the differences among people and strives to learn more. A person with a high level of cultural competence is usually good at **perception checking**—the practice of asking others to gain a more informed sense of understanding of a communication event. Remember to pay attention to cultural differences across contexts, make your own interpretation of those differences, and then consider the following direct or indirect approach: (1) Check your interpretation with others to get a different perspective before you draw a conclusion, or (2) use a more direct approach, in which you ask the people with whom you're communicating about their cultures.

Cultural competence
the ability to interact effectively with people of different cultural or ethnic backgrounds.

Perception checking
the practice of verifying our perceptions with others to gain a more informed sense of understanding.

Consider this example: Coming from a traditional Central Texas background, Travis did not have much exposure to people with a European background. During his first few years in college, Travis began to take classes with more and more people from overseas. Realizing his need to develop cultural competence and to check his perceptions, Travis decided to try to interact with a classmate named Ivana. While working on a class project, Travis simply asked Ivana where she was from. Ivana not only disclosed that she was from Serbia but also talked about her family history and experiences in the United States in relation to her Serbian background. Her openness persuaded Travis to ask her for more information about her cultural background and gave him some valuable insight about different cultural perspectives of college and everyday life.

In this example, Travis asked Ivana some simple introductory questions that led to a more detailed and in-depth conversation about each other's cultures. Travis practiced cultural competence by asking for basic information without relying on stereotypes to frame his questions. This led to a more honest and comfortable communication dynamic for both Travis and Ivana to learn more from each other. Now that you have reviewed the connection between cultural competence and perception checking, it is time to examine the importance of mutual respect.

MUTUAL RESPECT

You develop positive personal and professional relationships with people who are different in terms of race, ethnicity, religion, gender, and sexual identity by coming to understand those differences. When individuals and groups communicate with the goal of perception checking—also known as mutual understanding—cultural tensions, misunderstandings, and conflict can be avoided (Christian, Porter, & Moffit, 2006; Jandt, 2010). Mutual respect develops when a person seeks to understand another with an open attitude and dialogue; doing so encourages others to respond in a similar way.

Practicing mutual respect is critical to both your social and professional interactions.

When cultural competence and mutual respect are absent, conflict usually follows. Consider this example: Tara recently became the new Human Resources supervisor for her company. As part of her team-building initiative, Tara began to schedule out-of-office lunches during the workweek for the members of her department to socialize and become acclimated with one another. For the first two lunches, Tara began by talking about particular issues or goals for their department, and once the food arrived she had everyone bow their heads for a prayer to bless the food before eating. Before the third scheduled lunch, however, Tara was called into her supervisor's office. She informed Tara that she had received several complaints from Tara's staff regarding the pre-meal prayer. Several of Tara's employees were Jewish, and one employee was an atheist who was offended by having to take part in a religious ritual before a company meal. Tara was informed she would have to remove the prayer from the meetings or cancel the lunches entirely. Tara was greatly offended and admonished her employees at the next team meeting to "be open-minded" and "thankful for the blessings you have."

©WPA Pool/Getty Images News/Getty Images

Self-Assessment:
Intercultural Effectiveness

The following assessment will help you gain a better understanding of your skills related to intercultural communication. Answer each question thoughtfully, and then reflect on your response to each item. Consider how this information can help you be a better communicator.

Directions: Below is a series of statements concerning intercultural communication. There are no right or wrong answers. Please work quickly and record your first impression by indicating in the blank before each statement the degree to which you agree or disagree with that statement.

5	4	3	2	1
Strongly agree	Agree	Uncertain	Disagree	Strongly Disagree

_____ 1. I find it is easy to talk with people from different cultures.
_____ 2. I am afraid to express myself when interacting with people from different cultures.
_____ 3. I find it is easy to get along with people from different cultures.
_____ 4. I am not always the person I appear to be when interacting with people from different cultures.
_____ 5. I am able to express my ideas clearly when interacting with people from different cultures.
_____ 6. I have problems with grammar when interacting with people from different cultures.
_____ 7. I am able to answer questions effectively when interacting with people from different cultures.
_____ 8. I find it is difficult to feel my culturally different counterparts are similar to me.
_____ 9. I use appropriate eye contact when interacting with people from different cultures.
_____ 10. I have problems distinguishing between informative and persuasive messages when interacting with people from different cultures.
_____ 11. I always know how to initiate a conversation when interacting with people from different cultures.
_____ 12. I often miss parts of what is going on when interacting with people from different cultures.
_____ 13. I feel relaxed when interacting with people from different cultures.
_____ 14. I often act like a very different person when interacting with people from different cultures.
_____ 15. I always show respect for my culturally different counterparts during our interaction.
_____ 16. I always feel a sense of distance with my culturally different counterparts during our interaction.
_____ 17. I find I have a lot in common with my culturally different counterparts during our interaction.
_____ 18. I find the best way to act is to be myself when interacting with people from different cultures.
_____ 19. I find it is easy to identify with my culturally different counterparts during our interaction.
_____ 20. I always show respect for the opinions of my culturally different counterparts during our interaction.

Sources: Ruben (1976, 1977) and Ruben and Kealey (1979).

The preceding example illustrates that you need to be aware of problems that can emerge when there is an absence of mutual respect. While mutual respect and cultural competence are important in all facets of life, organizations are implementing workforce training programs to increase cultural sensitivity, tolerance, and appreciation of diversity in the workplace (Burkard, Boticki, & Madson, 2002; Quintanilla & Wahl, 2016). Positive communication cannot occur in a diverse context without cultural competence, perception checking, and mutual respect.

CULTURAL IMPERATIVES

There are many different reasons to study communication, culture, and diversity. On any given day, you come into contact with people from different cultures. The foundations of communication, culture, and diversity are located in five imperatives. These include peace, economic, technological, self-awareness, and ethical. The sections that follow examine each imperative in more detail and relate them to your study of communication, culture, and diversity.

Peace Imperative

Peace imperative
essential in understanding the foundations of communication, culture and diversity.

As a global community, we are dependent on one another to maintain peace. As the 9/11 terrorist attacks and other acts of war indicate, select countries have the ability to inflict mass destruction with advanced weapons technology, while others pose terroristic threats with car bombs, airline hijacking, mass transit sabotage, and the like. Many of the tensions seen globally today are brought on by strong cultural differences that evolve into war and acts of terrorism. This is why the **peace imperative** is essential in understanding the foundations of communication, culture, and diversity (Wahl & Morris, 2018). While conflict exists between various cultures, maintaining overall peace is a top priority.

Economic Imperative

Economic imperative
associated with the economic needs of all nations in matters of trade relations, international business ventures, and the like.

Also connected to intercultural communication is an understanding of the **economic imperative**. Countries are becoming more and more interdependent in shaping a global economy. Importing and exporting are important to countries around the globe. Clearly, intercultural communication is associated with the economic needs of all nations in matters of trade relations, international business ventures, and the like (Wahl & Morris, 2018).

Technological Imperative

Techological imperative
technological advances make the world more accessible and continue to gain more importance in today's society.

The **technological imperative** continues to gain more importance in today's society as technological advances make the world more accessible (Wahl & Morris, 2018). Because of the Internet alone, people are able to communicate with others across oceans and beyond mountains—something not possible in the past without first taking a long journey. In our globalized world of information and connection, you can buy something from Japan and receive it in just a few days. You can drive to the airport and find yourself on the other side of the planet within 24 hours. Consider your online relationships with friends, classmates, family, and so on. If not for this technology, how well would you be able to stay in contact with others? Not only are you able to stay in contact, but you are also more likely to come across people from other cultures with access to these same technological advances.

Self-Awareness Imperative

The **self-awareness imperative** is particularly important because it is essential for communicators to learn about other cultures (Wahl & Morris, 2018). Not only do you learn about other cultures, but in doing so, you learn more about your own culture. People never truly understand their own culture until comparing it with others. Have you ever found yourself in an encounter with a person from a different culture and suddenly realized something about your own?

> **Self-awareness imperative**
> communicators learning about other cultures.

Ethical Imperative

The **ethical imperative** is also important to understand. The ethical imperative should guide you in doing what is right versus wrong in various communication contexts (Wahl & Morris, 2018). It is also important to understand why some cultures value different things. You may find someone else's cultural norms unusual, but remember that this could be a sign of culture shock.

> **Ethical imperative**
> guides you in doing what is right versus wrong in various communication contexts.

While all the cultural imperatives are important in our study of intercultural communication, the next section explores specific examples of diversity across contexts.

EXAMPLES OF DIVERSITY ACROSS COMMUNICATION CONTEXTS

The previous sections reviewed some important concepts related to intercultural communication in your life. This section surveys a number of examples of diversity you may encounter. Gender, ethnicity and race, language differences, religion, people with disabilities, and sexual identity are just a few examples of the areas of diversity you will experience across communication contexts.

GENDER

The first example of diversity across communication contexts focuses on gender. Scholars have found that men and women communicate in different ways (Wood, 2009). However, an important distinction exists between people of different sexes and people of different gender identities. **Sex** is biological; it's about the chromosomal combinations that produce males, females, and the other possible, but rarer, sexes. **Gender** is social. When individuals refer to the behaviors associated with a particular sex, they are really referring to gender. Gender is about culturally constructed norms associated with biological sex. So whereas sex refers to male and female, gender refers to masculinity, femininity, and/or androgyny (Edwards et al., 2016). Commonly, these characteristics are associated with masculinity or the cultural signifiers associated with being a man in a specific culture; femininity, what it means culturally to be a woman; or **androgyny**, a blend of both feminine and masculine traits (Ivy, 2017; Ivy & Wahl, 2014) For example, you may have heard that "women always have to go to the bathroom together" or "men never want to talk about emotions or relationships." These statements are derived from perceived patterns of social behavior shown by men and women, but they are not biological traits. Rather, these tendencies arise from differences in what a society expects from women and men—differences in how men and women may be taught to speak, act, dress, express themselves, and interact with others (Edwards et al., 2016).

You may not think of men and women as being part of different cultures, but communication scholar Deborah Tannen (1990) argues that indeed they are. Further, according to communication and gender scholar Julia Wood (2009), women have a different way of knowing and communicating than do their male counterparts. As a result, consider practicing cultural competence with gender diversity as you would with any other form of diversity. Women are more likely to use communication to establish relationships, resulting in something known as rapport talk (Tannen, 1990). If asked, "How was your weekend?" a woman is likely to give a detailed description of events. Furthermore, women often add tag questions to their statements to invite conversation and help develop rapport. So a woman might say, "That is an excellent opportunity for the sorority chapter, isn't it?" By adding the tag question—"isn't it?"—she has invited a response from the other party. Conversely, men are more likely to communicate in a style know as report talk (Tannen, 1990). If asked, "How was your weekend?" a man might reply, "Great. The guys got together for poker night." He reports what occurred without much detail. Men are also more likely to talk in statements and commands, excluding tag questions. "That is an excellent opportunity for the department." Understanding the cultural differences in the ways men and women communicate can help you avoid miscommunication and false stereotypes. For example, a woman who uses tag questions does not lack confidence. Rather, she is simply developing rapport and inviting conversation. Similarly, a man may still consider rapport and relationships important even if he communicates using report talk.

Gender Influences

Like culture, gender influences cannot be avoided in interpersonal relationships. Gender, culture, and communication are all inextricably bound (Edwards et al., 2016; Ivy, 2017; Wood, 2009). A great deal of research has examined the communication differences between men and women. Some scholars assert that men and women differ greatly in their relational needs and communication behaviors, while others contend that men and women are more alike than they are different (Ivy, 2017). In general, communication scholars have shifted their focus from communication differences that stem from sex (being born male or female) to focus on the ways gender socialization (being raised as male or female) may create distinctive communication tendencies in interpersonal relationships (Edwards et al., 2016; Ivy, 2017).

Gender-fluid actress Ruby Rose practices an androgynous fashion style where she is neither explicitly feminine nor masculine.

Gender may influence communication in numerous ways, but let's focus on the different purposes for which men and women may use communication in their relationships. These differences arise from gendered socialization practices that teach women and men distinct ways of engaging in and evaluating communication (Edwards et al., 2016; Ivy, 2017). For many women, talk is used as the primary means to establish closeness and intimacy in a relationship (Ivy, 2017; Riessman, 1990). By self-disclosing personal information and sharing their lives through conversation, women show their relational partners they are trusted and cared for. Communication is encouraged as a way to spend time together and build the relationship. For that reason, it may not matter to women whether they have discussed "important" issues or accomplished a goal. What matters is keeping the dialogue going.

Men, on the other hand, may not be raised to view relationships in the same way. Many men enjoy doing things together to build their relationships (Ivy, 2017). Participating in joint activities creates a sense of belonging with many men, and talk is used in primarily functional ways, such as to solve problems and accomplish tasks. According to Tannen (1991), women engage in a greater degree of rapport talk, or cooperative messages used to establish connection. Men engage in a greater degree of report talk, or information-based messages used to establish status and gain power. Several scholars have pointed to similar gender differences in spoken communication (Coates, 1993; Ivy, 2017; Lakoff, 1975; Tannen, 1994).

Consider this example: Skyler and Nicole have been dating for 3 years. While they have always been intimate and committed to their relationship, Nicole is alarmed by the fact that Skyler has never talked seriously with her about marriage. They live together and have been in an exclusive relationship, but Nicole is worried that Skyler does not want to marry her at all. Whenever Nicole asks him about the future of their relationship, Skyler becomes worried that there is a problem Nicole is not telling him about. This has led to several arguments that neither of them wanted in the first place.

Have you ever experienced a relationship issue like this? Nicole simply wanted to develop and further their relationship, but Skyler assumed that Nicole had a problem with him that needed to be solved. Knowing both the gender and sex differences in communication styles is essential for both romantic and platonic relationships.

Gender differences in the general purpose of communication filter down to affect the nature of specific interactions in a number of ways. Because women are socialized to build and maintain relationships through talk, listening is often an active and responsive activity for them. For many women, eye contact and frequent verbal and nonverbal responses indicate that they are paying close attention to what their companion is saying. Cooperative overlap, or talking over someone to encourage him or her to go on, is also common among women (Tannen, 1991). Men, however, might see talking over someone as a blatant interruption—a power move or an attempt to control the conversation. Because men view talk as a tool to solve problems, they might listen to everything a companion has to say before responding at all. These differences do not indicate that one gender is better at listening than the other; they simply show that men and women have been socialized to listen differently, and these differences will affect communication between them.

Early research on gender and interpersonal communication focused mainly on face-to-face interactions (Edwards et al., 2016). With the growth of computer-mediated communication, scholars have begun to explore differences in the ways men and women communicate online (Ivy, 2017; Quan, 2010). Several studies have demonstrated that when communicating online, women tend to use language that is more hesitant, polite, and supportive in comparison with men, who tend to use language that is more certain, assertive, and competitive (Guiller & Durndell, 2007; Herring, 1993; Thomson & Murachver, 2001). Among teens, females tend to present themselves as emotional, friendly, good listeners, sexually available, and eager to please males. On the other hand, young males tend to present themselves as more assertive, manipulative, initiating, visually dominant, and distant (Kapidzic & Herring, 2011; Magnuson & Dundes, 2008). These studies demonstrate that gender differentiation occurs in both mediated and unmediated communication environments.

In your discussions of gender and communication, it is important to avoid stereotyping, or applying the traits of one member of a group to that entire class of people. Gender differences do not apply to *all* women and *all* men. It may be helpful to consider how women and men communicate distinctively in relationships, but gender is only one of many influences on communication behavior.

ETHNICITY AND RACE

When you think of diversity in the world, you probably most often think of differences in *race* or *ethnicity*. Although the terms race and ethnicity are often linked, when it comes to communication competence, people focus on differences based on ethnicity, not race. **Race** is the categorization of people based on physical characteristics such as skin color, dimensions of the human face, and hair. The old typology categorized people into one of three races, but those typologies are no longer deemed useful and have been replaced with ethnic identification or classification. **Ethnicity** refers to a social group that may be formed factors such as shared history, shared identity, shared geography, and shared culture. If you rely on nonverbal cues to detect someone's ethnic background, you do so without taking into account that what you see may not always be accurate. In other words, a person's physical qualities may lead you to perceive them as being a part of one particular ethnic group, when in fact they identify with a different ethnic group. Unfortunately, people across the globe are categorized, stereotyped, and discriminated against based on physical appearance, specifically the color of their skin (Bloomfield, 2006; Ivy & Wahl, 2014).

Race
a generalized categorization of people based on physical characteristics such as skin color, dimensions of the face, and hair texture and color.

Ethncity
a social group that may be joined together by factors such as shared history, shared identity, shared geography, and shared culture.

Thus, as you get to know the people around you, it is important to remember that what you see through nonverbal dimensions of physical appearance does not always shape accurate perceptions of another person's ethnicity. The same sensitivity and awareness for cultural competency is important in your life, as issues of race, gender, sexuality, health, and more are topics fostered in online and social networking communities (Cruikshank, 2010; DeAndrea et al., 2010; Quan, 2010). Now that you have considered the importance of race and ethnicity in your study of communication, culture, and diversity, the next section explains the importance of language differences.

LANGUAGE DIFFERENCES

Globalization will continue to present emerging professionals with the challenge of language differences as encountered in a variety of industries and career choices (Quintanilla & Wahl, 2016). According to intercultural communication scholars Samovar et al. (2009), the impact of globalization is an unstoppable process that will continue to emphasize the need for an international orientation that impacts your personal and professional life. Consider your own future goals and realize the likely impact of diversity and globalization on your academic major and occupation.

Globalization exposes people to new and different accents, dialects, and languages. For example, a person's accent may provide you with clues as to where that person is from. If someone in your class speaks with a German accent, she probably hails from a German-speaking country in Europe. If someone else speaks with an accent as well as using different vocabulary and syntax, that person has a different dialect. You may encounter a coworker or classmate who speaks an entirely different language. Despite the lack of shared language, you will still need to communicate with each other through the use of verbal and nonverbal communication. Clearly, accent, dialect, and lack of a shared language impact communication effectiveness in professional settings, both with coworkers and customers. Language differences will compound other cultural differences that are sure to exist.

When you encounter language barriers, be prepared to ask and answer many questions to ensure a clear understanding. Try to avoid the common mistakes of losing patience and giving up or speaking to the person as if they cannot hear you. Speaking louder or, even worse, yelling at another person when a language barrier is present can often lead to frustration and further misunderstanding.

In addition to language differences, language preferences can also create language barriers. For example, all students in one dorm can speak English, but three of the students prefer to speak Spanish. When they are speaking to one another in Spanish, other students in the dorm are unable to understand what is being said and often get annoyed. If the resident assistant (RA) tells the Spanish-speaking students to stop using their language, is she discriminating against them or violating their rights? Think critically about this example. Consider alternatives the RA could use to promote cultural competence. She could also consider asking the English speakers to learn Spanish. As a counter-example, consider English students studying abroad in Italy. What would these students do if their Italian dorm leader told them to stop speaking English to one another outside of class or organized functions? Remember that speaking in one's own language is a matter of choice and a fact of life.

RELIGION AND SPIRITUALITY

Religion and spirituality are other areas of diversity among people (Driscoll & Wiebe, 2007). Consider how religion or spirituality comes into play with people in your social environment. Review the following example: Brent was getting to know his new college campus. One guy whom Brent really related to in his new dorm was Sawyer. Brent had observed that several of the guys from his floor got together for poker night once a week, and he thought it would be fun if he and Sawyer joined the group. Brent invited Sawyer out for poker several times, but Sawyer always declined. After the third rejection, Sawyer took the time to explain to Brent that he and his family were members of The Church of Jesus Christ of Latter-Day Saints. Sawyer further explained that he had moral concerns with playing poker and being around people who chose to drink alcoholic beverages. Think of other ways religion and spirituality impact various communication contexts; in addition to Christianity, keep in mind world religions (e.g., Buddhism, Judaism, Islam).

PEOPLE WITH DISABILITIES

In addition to religion and spirituality, people with disabilities are another example of diversity. The verbal and nonverbal cues of a person with a disability can lead to disrespectful or insensitive communication (Braithwaite & Braithwaite, 2009; Braithwaite & Thompson, 2000; Ivy & Wahl, 2014; Quintanilla & Wahl, 2016).

Physical appearance is normally a signal that a person is living with a disability, but remember that some forms of disability are invisible (Ivy & Wahl, 2014). Be aware of the communication challenges that a person with a disability deals with every day (e.g., Tourette's syndrome, a stutter). For example, Philip Garber, Jr., a student taking classes at the County College of Morris, kept his hand raised for an entire class period before his professor informed him that he would not call on him because his stutter was disruptive. Regardless of the type of disability, people can develop cultural competence in this area and support fair treatment and respect. Communication scholar Dawn Braithwaite (1991) examined how people with disabilities are challenged when it comes to managing private information about their disabilities, because able-bodied people tend to ask personal, often embarrassing questions (e.g., how a person became injured, how difficult it is to live with a disability).

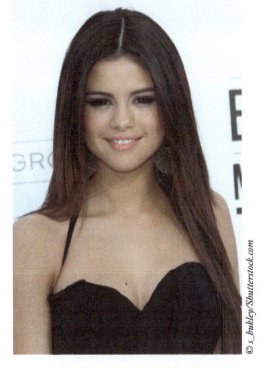

Some disabilities cannot be seen; celebrity Selena Gomez has struggled with anxiety and depression as a result of her battle with lupus.

© s_bukley/Shutterstock.com

People with disabilities have a major presence in everyday social settings today, and it is important for you to strive for respectful communication. Thus, keep in mind several of the tips that follow to guide competent communication with and among people with disabilities: (1) Avoid staring at a person with a disability; (2) try not to call too much attention to someone's disability by being overly helpful; and (3) focus on the person, not the disability.

SEXUAL IDENTITY

Nick is a single college student. When his friends ask about his relationship status, he answers, "I don't want to talk about it," and tries to change the topic. One of his friends, Jason, goes on to ask invasive questions about any women he might be talking to or whom he finds attractive in his classes. While some people are open about their relationship status and enjoy sharing information about their personal lives in everyday situations, it is important to realize that not everyone feels the same way about the disclosure of personal information.

Sexual identity
refers to one's identity based on whom one is attracted to sexually.

Since coming out publicly in 1997, TV show host Ellen DeGeneres has put LGBTQ-IA+ issues in the spotlight.

© Joe Seer/Shutterstock.com

In Nick's case, he wishes to maintain privacy around his relational status and sexual identity. **Sexual identity** refers to one's identity based on whom one is attracted to sexually. Like Nick, lesbian, gay, bisexual, transgender, queer, asexual, and other individuals whose identities differ from the majority (LGBTQIA+) often find themselves speaking an entirely different language of ambiguous pronouns. Recognize the choice you will have to make regarding being open or private about your sexual identity. Being "out" is easier for some LGBTQIA+ people than others. Regardless of your own sexuality, it is critical to recognize that LGBTQIA+ communication and culture are present across communication contexts (Eadie, 2009). A couple of things to keep in mind related to communication with and among LGBTQIA+ individuals are (1) do not inadvertently "out" someone, and (2) avoid being **heterosexist**, which means assuming that everyone is heterosexual.

Heterosexist
assuming that everyone is heterosexual.

FIGURE 1.1 Sexual Identity: Some Important Terms

Lesbian	Physical and romantic attraction to people of the same sex (women).
Gay	Physical and romantic attraction to people of the same sex (men).
Bisexual	Physical and romantic attraction to people of both sexes.
Transgender	The state of an individual's gender identity not matching biological male/female assignment at birth.
Questioning	People who are exploring or questioning their sexual identity.
Asexuality	Having little, if any, interest in sex.
Queer	An umbrella term often used to describe LGBTQIA+ people in general; used by some as an activist term and by others to refer to an identity that does not conform to common labels and terms of sexual identity.
Intersex	A term used to describe people born with reproductive/sexual anatomy that does not seem to align with strictly male or female anatomy.

This section focused on gender, ethnicity and race, language differences, religion, people with disabilities, and sexual identity as examples of diversity across communication contexts. Now that you have studied specific examples, the next section explores the types of common barriers to communication, culture, and diversity.

BARRIERS TO COMMUNICATION, CULTURE, AND DIVERSITY

Dealing with differences may seem like an overwhelming task; however, you can come to understand fellow classmates, friends, and others—even if they have views and practices different from your own—if you practice cultural competence, perception checking, and mutual respect. To begin your study of intercultural communication in your life, it is important to understand several barriers, including stereotypes, prejudice, discrimination, ethnocentrism, and hate speech.

STEREOTYPES

While the term tends to have a negative connotation, **stereotypes** are merely popular beliefs about groups of people. These preconceived notions can be positive, neutral, or negative, but when it comes to individuals, each one forms an incomplete picture and

Stereotypes

popular beliefs about groups of people. These preconceived notions can be positive, neutral, or negative, but when it comes to individuals, each one forms an incomplete picture and is potentially harmful.

is potentially harmful. For example, gay men are often stereotyped as being feminine and flamboyant, while lesbian women are believed to be aggressive and masculine. When developing your skills related to cultural competence, it is important to take a personal inventory. Also, pay attention to the communication context. You can do this by researching a culture to increase your understanding of difference. You can also ask questions of the person with whom you are communicating in a particular situation. Often coupled with stereotypes are the terms *prejudice* and *discrimination*. Focus on these concepts to gain a more detailed understanding of barriers to communication and acceptance of cultures and diversity.

PREJUDICE AND DISCRIMINATION

Prejudice

the dislike or hatred one feels toward a particular group.

Discrimination

the verbal and nonverbal communication behaviors that foster prejudiced attitudes, including the act of excluding people from or denying them access to products, rights, and services based on race, gender, religion, age, sexual identity, or disability.

You may have heard these two terms previously, but do you know the distinction between them? Many confuse the two and think they are one and the same. **Prejudice** is the dislike or hatred one feels toward a particular group. **Discrimination**, however, refers to the verbal and nonverbal communication behaviors that foster prejudiced attitudes, including the act of excluding people from or denying them access to products, rights, and services based on race, gender, religion, age, sexual identity, or disability (Jandt, 2010; Ting-Toomey & Chung, 2005). Discrimination can be carried out in obvious ways, such as burning a cross in someone's yard, or it can be so subtle that one may not know it is there unless one is a member of the group being discriminated against.

Consider this: Maurice and April were having a housewarming party to celebrate the new home they had recently purchased. They wanted to invite both sides of the family as well as their mutual friends to the party. As Maurice and April were creating the invitations, they identified several family members and friends they wanted to exclude from the housewarming. April's sister, Gina, was a lesbian, and they didn't want to offend Maurice's traditionally conservative family by having Gina and her partner at the event. Also, they didn't want to invite their friend Tyler, because his son suffered from Down syndrome, and they didn't want members of the family to feel awkward around him. This example illustrates the presence of two types of discrimination, since Maurice and April refrained from inviting particular people based on sexual identity and disability.

Ethnocentrism

placing your own cultural beliefs in a superior position, which leads to a negative judgment of other cultures.

ETHNOCENTRISM

Another barrier to communication, culture, and diversity is **ethnocentrism**—placing your own cultural beliefs in a superior position, which leads to a negative judgment of other cultures (Jandt, 2010). Severe ethnocentrism impedes cultural competence, because a person will reject the uniqueness of other cultures. People who view their culture as dominant are unwilling to learn about and are not open to the ideas of other cultures.

HATE SPEECH

Hate speech is another barrier to communication, culture, and diversity that is still a problematic force in society today. The term **hate speech** refers to insulting discourse, phrases, terms, cartoons, or organized campaigns used to humiliate people based on age, gender, race, ethnicity, culture, sexual identity, social class, and more (Edwards et al., 2016). Hate speech has been associated historically with—but is not limited to—racist groups such as the Ku Klux Klan and other white pride groups that argue that white people are superior to African Americans and other ethnic groups.

Hate speech is clearly persuasive communication used to intimidate and segregate based on gender, sexual identity, race, and ethnicity (Wahl & Morris, 2018). In contrast, the newer forms of hate speech have been revised to focus on "us" (white people) versus "them" (ethnic minorities, gays, and women). New forms of hate speech are more about how the authenticity of being white is somehow reinforced by religiosity. Put simply, hate speech uses the Internet and new media to disseminate messages of fear and intimidation (Edwards et al., 2016).

Hate speech
insulting discourse, phrases, terms, cartoons, or organized campaigns used to humiliate people based on age, gender, race, ethnicity, culture, sexual identity, social class, and more.

© Boston Globe/Getty Images

In June 2017, Michelle Carter was found guilty of involuntary manslaughter after she encouraged her boyfriend, who suffered from mental illness, to commit suicide via text and phone call (Seelye & Bidgood, 2017).

School Bullying

The use of hate speech is also a troubling aspect of school bullying. Hate speech targeting gay and lesbian youth led to a 2008 advertising campaign titled "Think Before You Speak"—sponsored by Ad Council, ThinkB4YouSpeak.com, and the Gay, Lesbian and Straight Education Network to address the homophobic phrase, "That's so gay," popular among young Americans (Wahl, & Morris, 2018). The campaign was designed to discourage use of this slur. Each advertisement featured people in various situations stating that something they did not like was "so gay." Then a popular celebrity, such as Wanda Sykes or Hilary Duff, would walk out and tell them that they should not use the word gay to describe something they do not like. Each advertisement ended with text and a voiceover saying, "When you say 'that's so gay,' do you realize what you say? Knock it off." This campaign won the Ad Council's top award for "Best Public Service Advertising Campaign" and received much attention across the nation for taking on the issue of homophobia.

More recently, websites such as itgetsbetter.org have sought to encourage gay teens experiencing a difficult time. The website features a collage of videos posted by people across life experiences, reminding viewers that everyone should be respected for who they are. The website invites people to take a pledge to advocate against hate speech, violence, and intolerance toward lesbian, gay, bisexual, transgender, and other people who are bullied and attacked. Inspirational videos assure viewers that "It Gets Better."

This section focused on several barriers to communication, culture, and diversity, including stereotypes, prejudice, discrimination, ethnocentrism, and hate speech.

Moving past labeling other people is a crucial step in becoming an effective communicator.

© Amir Ridzuan/Shutterstock.com

AN OVERVIEW FOR YOUR STUDY OF INTERCULTURAL COMMUNICATION

Before you begin your study of this important topic, it's important to understand the concepts that receive specific attention in this book. Your study of intercultural communication will explore the following: identity and dimensions of cultural variability; ethics; assimilation, acculturation, and sojourning; verbal and nonverbal communication; interpersonal communication; group communication; conflict; social class; new media; health; and business and professional contexts. These topics are all important to the study of intercultural communication in your life. Let's take a look at each in more detail.

ETHICS

Chapter 2 connects your study of intercultural communication to an ethical perspective. **Ethics** is the general term for the discussion, determination, and deliberation processes that attempt to identify what is right or wrong, what we and others should or should not do, and what is considered appropriate in our individual, communal, and professional lives (Japp, Meister, & Japp, 2005; Johannesen, Valde, & Whedbee, 2008; Wahl & Morris, 2018). What considerations or factors help shape your ethical decisions when communicating with others? **Ethical considerations** are the variety of factors important to consider across communication contexts (Japp et al., 2005). Ethical considerations vary from person to person and are not always as simple as right or wrong. For example, you may experience **ethical dilemmas**, situations that do not seem to present clear choices between right and wrong or good and evil. Our increasingly technological, global, and multicultural society requires us to be ever more sensitive to the potential impact of the words we choose, images we portray, and stereotypes we uphold.

So what counts as ethical communication? How do we determine whether or not our communication conduct respects self, others, and surroundings? Communication philosopher and ethicist Jurgen Habermas (1979) maintains that ethical communication is that which promotes **autonomy** (freedom) and **responsibility**. To be ethical, communication should provide a sense of choice and empowerment, while simultaneously acknowledging and encouraging a sense of social responsibility. Communication that limits the free will and self-determination of ourselves or others, or strips people of their power, is not ethical. Likewise, communication without regard for our shared responsibility to one another and our communities is not ethical.

Ethics
a system of accepted principles that make up an individual's or group's values and judgments as to what is right and wrong.

Ethical considerations
the variety of factors important when considering what is right or wrong.

Ethical dilemmas
situations that do not seem to present clear choices between right and wrong or good and evil.

Autonomy
freedom.

Responsibility
the elements of fulfilling duties and obligations, being accountable to other individuals and groups, adhering to agreed-on standards, and being accountable to one's own conscience.

ETHICAL CONNECTION

Rafael was a graduate assistant for the English department at his university. His responsibilities included grading undergraduate papers for several of his professors. While grading for one particular class, Rafael noticed the paper he was grading belonged to one of his friends. As Rafael graded the paper, it became clear that the work had been plagiarized from some of Rafael's earlier work. However, since this was Rafael's friend and he did not want to see him kicked out of school, he turned a blind eye and gave the paper a good grade. A few weeks later, Rafael was called into his supervisor's office and told he was being relieved of his position in the department. Rafael's boss showed him the paper he had graded and told him there was no place for cheating in their department. Rafael was told he was ineligible to work for the university and was lucky not to be kicked out of the graduate program.

Questions to consider:

1. What ethical boundary did Rafael cross by giving his friend's paper a good grade?
2. How should Rafael have handled the situation? Should he have given his friend a chance to resubmit the work?
3. Why is academic honesty so important to the college experience? Why is academic dishonesty so harshly punished?
4. Would this situation have been resolved differently if it took place in a business environment? Does the context of the situation ever allow for plagiarism or copying?

IDENTITY AND DIMENSIONS OF CULTURAL VARIABILITY

Chapter 3 explores the issue of identity and perhaps gets you to think more closely about how your communication and your identity are linked. The first section in this chapter describes what an identity is, as well as what influences one's identity construction. You will also learn that your identity serves several functions, and that certain factors impact how you communicate your identity to others. Next, you will read about face theory and how the concept of face is tied closely with identity. Third, you will be exposed to various theories that explain the nature, purpose, and influences of identity. Finally, you will be encouraged to think about the issues and implications related to various ways we construct our identities, particularly those based on ethnicity, age, and gender and sex.

ASSIMILATION, ACCULTURATION, AND SOJOURNING

Chapter 4 explores almost any situation where we might try to fit in and adapt to a group or culture to which we want or expect to belong. We refer to this process as assimilation. This does not necessarily occur only outside of the United States; rather, many cultural groups in our country feel like outsiders and perceive many pressures to act in certain ways to fit in more. Furthermore, some cultural groups have endured much prejudice, hatred, and discrimination in the process of assimilation. This chapter examines the process of assimilation in a variety of contexts, as well as recognizing the influences on one's ability to adapt culturally.

VERBAL AND NONVERBAL COMMUNICATION

Chapter 5 explores the basic principles of verbal and nonverbal communication and makes a direct connection to the influence of culture. **Verbal communication** includes both our words and our verbal fillers (e.g., *um*, *like*). Verbal messages are created through the use of our respective languages. Effective communication involves accurate interpretations of others' verbal messages as meaning is co-created (Quintanilla & Wahl, 2016). Along with verbal communication, nonverbal communication can vary greatly from culture to culture. **Nonverbal communication** encompasses all the ways we communicate without the use of words (Ivy & Wahl, 2014). You will explore messages communicated through nonverbal codes (e.g., your environments and surroundings, use of space, physical appearance, body movements and gestures, facial and eye expressions, touch). In all, this chapter will help you understand how culture influences the ways we perceive both nonverbal and verbal communication.

Verbal communication
both our words and our verbal fillers (e.g., *um*, *like*).

Nonverbal communication
all the ways we communicate without the use of words.

CONVERSATIONS

Chapter 6 explores interpersonal communication, particularly the influences on our ability to engage in conversation with diverse others. This will be accomplished by exploring the nature of conversations and how we coordinate them, especially within intercultural settings. We move on to discuss the role of language and its variations, as well as how norms vary in terms of emotional expression. The latter part of the chapter will progress to relationship issues—particularly, the challenges and rewards of intercultural relationships, as well as matters associated with romantic relationships and friendships. Finally, we discuss relational dialectics and their influence on intercultural interactions.

GROUP COMMUNICATION

Chapter 7 reviews the basics of small-group communication and discusses how cultural variability affects the group dynamic. It will also prepare you with skills to negotiate all kinds of differences in groups. This chapter opens with an explanation of small-group communication and differentiates groups and teams. The functional perspective of group communication is also discussed by highlighting the importance of task and relationship functions. Next, the chapter discusses different types of diversity characteristics, particularly those that are psychological in nature. Other types of diversity include dimensions of cultural variation (e.g., individualism and collectivism), as well as ethnicity, gender, and generation or age group. In the final section, the chapter presents theoretical and practical implications for appreciating and overcoming differences in the group communication context.

CONFLICT

Chapter 8 explores what conflict truly is and how it can contribute to productivity and effectiveness. Also, we will discuss conflict styles and the cultural factors that affect differences in the choice of style. Finally, this chapter reveals positive ways to introduce and engage in conflict, with special emphasis on principled negotiation.

SOCIAL CLASS

Chapter 9 explores social class and poverty to get you to think more critically about these issues from a communication perspective. The chapter defines social class, as well as what influences your own view and communication about social class. You will also learn why social class is important to your study of intercultural communication. Next, you will read about the presence of social class across communication contexts, such as in the workplace, education, media, and more. Third, you will engage the definition of poverty and understand it from a cultural perspective. Finally, you will be encouraged to think about the issues and implications of communication about social class and the culture of poverty.

HEALTH

In Chapter 10, you will be exposed to a variety of health care issues that are affected by cultural differences. First, it will be important for you to understand how health can be defined, as well as what health communication is and how it is studied. Once these terms are addressed, you will learn different perspectives with which health and health care are approached, particularly the biomedical and biopsychosocial models of health care. You will also understand Eastern and

Western approaches to medicine and how they complement each other. Next, you will explore interpersonal issues of health, especially how cultural differences influence how we talk to our doctors and important others about our health. In addition to issues of access to care and marginalization, this chapter will expose you to health literacy and the problems associated with low health literacy.

BUSINESS AND PROFESSIONAL CONTEXTS

Chapter 11 explores the importance of cultural recognition and inclusion across business and professional contexts. Applying communication and cultural competency across business and professional contexts is important because (1) discrimination produces unproductive work environments, (2) diversity is a positive aspect of the workplace and can even improve productivity, and (3) using cultural competency makes you a more valuable employee in the modern workplace. This chapter also reviews discrimination laws and how power and corporate colonization affect both the workplace and the employee.

WHAT YOU'VE LEARNED

In this chapter, you learned fundamental information to begin your study of intercultural communication and how it impacts your life. You began by learning the definition of communication preferred by this text and the definition of cultural competence. You were then given examples of diversity across various communication contexts, including gender, ethnicity, and race; language differences; religion and spirituality; people with disabilities; and sexual identity. You then learned that ethical communication promotes both autonomy and responsibility. Finally, barriers to communication, culture, and diversity were discussed; these barriers include stereotypes, prejudice and discrimination, ethnocentrism, and hate speech.

Chapter 1 concluded with an overview of the topics you will learn in your study of intercultural communication. Each of these topics have a chapter dedicated to them and to your understanding of each topic. In Chapter 2, you will explore ethics as a core component in your study of intercultural communication.

REVIEW

1. _____ is defined as the collaborative process of using messages to create and participate in social reality.

2. _____ is defined as the set of shared attitudes, values, goals, and practices that characterizes an institution, organization, or group.

3. _____ refers to the power of communication to link and relate you to people, groups, communities, social institutions, and cultures; _____, on the other hand, refers to the act of sharing in the activities of the group.

4. The difference between *sex* and *gender* is that _____ is social, whereas _____ is biological.

5. The categorization of people based on physical characteristics is referred to as _____, while a social group that is joined together by factors such as shared history, shared identity, shared geography, and shared culture is referred to as _____.

6. Define *sexual identity*, and discuss what it means to be *heterosexist*.

7. What is the difference between *prejudice* and *discrimination*?

8. Define *hate speech* and discuss the tools newer forms of hate speech use.

9. What does it mean when a person is experiencing an *ethical dilemma*?

10. Define *verbal communication* and *nonverbal communication*.

Review answers are found on the accompanying website.

REFLECT

1. Write down your own definition of *culture* and compare it to the one in the chapter. Do you think all communication is influenced by culture?

2. Discuss the advantages of engaging in perception checking during your social and professional interactions. Can you think of any instances when this practice might be problematic and/or offensive?

3. Why do you think it is important to distinguish between *sex* and *gender*? Have you ever felt at odds with culturally constructed gender norms? Explain.

4. Mark has been asked to train Nina, a new employee. Nina seems quiet, and Mark would like to get to know her better. He notices a wedding ring on her finger and decides to ask her what her husband's name is. Using the terminology from the book, discuss what is potentially problematic about Mark's question. Then, discuss any suggestions you might have that would address those problems.

5. Greg—your classmate and friend—has dyslexia and sometimes has trouble reading and taking notes off your professor's projected slides. You notice Greg seems embarrassed because your professor often stares at him while teaching and pauses her lessons to ask him if she is moving too quickly. What is problematic about your professor's actions toward Greg?

KEY TERMS

communication, 4
culture, 4
diversity, 4
co-cultural communication, 5
cultural rituals, 6
connection, 7
engagement, 8
communication activism, 8
cultural competence, 9
perception checking, 9
peace imperative, 12
economic imperative, 12
technological imperative, 12
self-awareness imperative, 13
ethical imperative, 13
sex, 14
gender, 14

androgyny, 14
race, 17
ethnicity, 17
sexual identity, 20
heterosexist, 20
stereotypes, 21
prejudice, 22
discrimination, 22
ethnocentrism, 22
hate speech, 23
ethics, 25
ethical considerations, 25
ethical dilemmas, 25
autonomy, 25
responsibility, 25
verbal communication, 27
nonverbal communication, 27

CHAPTER TWO
Ethical Dimensions of Intercultural Communication

CHAPTER OUTLINE

WHAT YOU WILL LEARN

After studying this chapter, you should be able to

1. define the term *ethics*;
2. identify the importance of ethics in your study of intercultural communication;
3. discuss ethical responsibility across communication contexts;
4. apply ethics to political persuasion and adapting to the audience; and
5. explain the different perspectives of ethics in persuasion and how each of them can be applied to real-life situations.

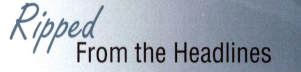

Ripped From the Headlines

Currently, immigration reform is one of the major political issues facing the United States. There are numerous standpoints and positions on how to address this issue but no consensus as of yet. Roughly half a million U.S. citizen children experienced the deportation of at least one parent between 2011 and 2013, based on estimates using Immigration and Customs Enforcement (ICE) data (American Immigration Council, 2017). Undocumented children and children of such undocumented parents often face the challenge of whether to discuss and/or how to discuss their family's immigration status.

While speaking as class valedictorian at her high school graduation, Larissa Martinez made the bold decision to share that she is one of 11 million undocumented immigrants living in the U.S. Martinez fled Mexico to Texas with her mother and sister, and she has waited seven years for her immigration application to even be processed. Martinez said she chose to share her status because "this might be my only chance to convey the truth…that undocumented immigrants are people, too" (Richmond, 2016).

Undocumented immigrants who have children in the United States present a difficult ethical question concerning immigration reform: Is it OK to deport an illegal parent if the child can remain in the United States? But the issues go beyond being able to stay in the United States; access to education, health care, and work are also closely tied to this debate. The ethical ground becomes muddy once you cannot separate legitimate U.S. citizens from their undocumented immediate families.

In this chapter, you will address the issues of ethics as they relate to intercultural communication. It is important to note that ethical intercultural communication involves not only following your own code of ethics but also being sensitive to your communication partner's. Although your day-to-day intercultural communication may not be as drastic as the previous example, it is important to learn good practices to ensure ethical communication throughout your professional and social life.

Islam is discriminatory toward women!
Some Asian cultures are so barbaric!
We can say whatever we want about those foreign exchange students;
they can't understand us anyway!
If people come to the United States, they should be required to learn English!

What do the above statements all have in common? The correct answer can be articulated in two words: **ethical communication**. Each of you encounters ethics and ethical choices in your life. Your values, beliefs, and morals help evolve your understanding of ethics. Many ethics, or codes of ethics, are universal, while others are strictly meant for particular individuals or cultures. However, you will inevitably encounter particular situations where your ethics will be contradicted by those of another culture. You must be careful not to judge the cultural ethics of others, since your own cultural understanding of ethics may seem just as alien or harsh to them. Think about it: Where do your ethics come from?

Let's face it. Understanding ethics is complicated. However, ethics is critical to your study of intercultural communication. This chapter explores the connection between ethics and intercultural communication. In both your personal life and your professional career, you will be confronted with ethical issues and dilemmas concerning sensitivity and understanding of another culture. How do I interact with a coworker who has different religious beliefs than mine? Is it OK to speak a language my coworkers do not understand? Should I file a grievance against my supervisor for racial slurs or keep my mouth shut?

To study the effectiveness of intercultural communication in your life, it's important to place ethics at the core of your critical evaluation practice. The process of critically evaluating intercultural messages is connected to ethical perspectives. You can think about ethical perspectives as a unique set of lenses you may want to use to critically evaluate your intercultural communication. Many different lenses

Ethical communication

symbolic verbal and nonverbal behavior that reflects perceptions and attitudes about what is right or wrong.

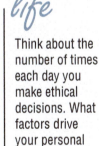
IN YOUR *life*

Think about the number of times each day you make ethical decisions. What factors drive your personal ethics? Make a list of the things that inform your own system of ethics.

Moral Judgment

Moral Rules

Ethical System

Code of Ethics

© Kheng Guan Toh/Shutterstock.com

are available, and each one will allow you to see the world of intercultural communication from different points of view. Similarly, each of the lenses covered in this chapter will encourage you to evaluate intercultural messages from different ethical points of view. Let's get more familiar with the term as connected to your study of intercultural communication.

A code of ethics is the foundation for your intercultural interactions.

Ethics

a system of accepted principles that make up an individual's or group's values and judgments as to what is right and wrong.

Codes of ethics

all different sets of principles that people hold themselves to or are held to by multiple organizations or groups.

Distinguish

the ability to decide what's right and wrong.

Dedication

committing to do what is right no matter the situation.

DEFINING ETHICS

When you hear the word *ethics*, what do you think of? Words such as *right*, *wrong*, *values*, and *principles* may come to mind. Put simply, **ethics** is a system of accepted principles that make up an individual's or group's values and judgments as to what's right and wrong. These "principles" can change from culture to culture or from group to group. Maybe you've heard of a **code of ethics**. Codes of ethics are sets of principles that people hold themselves to or are held to by multiple organizations or groups. Take a moment to review the code of ethics held by the National Communication Association (NCA). This code establishes the importance of ethics in the study of communication across contexts (see Figure 2.1).

Think for a moment about something you're a part of, perhaps a group or an organization. For example, maybe you belong to a religion, fraternity, sorority, sports team, or academic institution that provides a daily code of ethics for you. To understand ethics properly, you must have two abilities: The first is the ability to **distinguish**. To distinguish, you need to be able to decide what's right and wrong. The second ability is **dedication**. Dedication means committing to do what is right no matter the situation.

Think about this scenario: You're supposed to meet with your professor to make up an exam due to an absence. You arrive at his or her office just a bit early, and the answer key is lying on the desk. Perhaps you're part of a church or religious organization that provides you with a code of ethics that assists you in choosing the right option. Maybe you signed an agreement with the university to honor the academic honesty policies. Regardless of the ethical code or codes you decide to honor or reject, ethics seem to play a role in almost every decision made throughout the day. In assessing this situation, you must use the two abilities we just listed. In your mind, you distinguish what is right and what is wrong; after completing the distinguishing process, you then decide to dedicate or commit yourself to the ethical decision or to reject it.

FIGURE 2.1 NCA Credo

NATIONAL COMMUNICATION ASSOCIATION
CREDO FOR ETHICAL COMMUNICATION
(Approved by the NCA Legislative Council in 1999)

Questions of right and wrong arise whenever people communicate. Ethical communication is fundamental to responsible thinking, decision making, and the development of relationships and communities within and across contexts, cultures, channels, and media. Moreover, ethical communication enhances human worth and dignity by fostering truthfulness, fairness, responsibility, personal integrity, and respect for self and others. We believe that unethical communication threatens the quality of all communication and consequently the well-being of individuals and the society in which we live. Therefore we, the members of the National Communication Association, endorse and are committed to practicing the following principles of ethical communication:

- We advocate truthfulness, accuracy, honesty, and reason as essential to the integrity of communication.
- We endorse freedom of expression, diversity of perspective, and tolerance of dissent to achieve the informed and responsible decision making fundamental to a civil society.
- We strive to understand and respect other communicators before evaluating and responding to their messages.
- We promote access to communication resources and opportunities as necessary to fulfill human potential and contribute to the well-being of families, communities, and society.
- We promote communication climates of caring and mutual understanding that respect the unique needs and characteristics of individual communicators.
- We condemn communication that degrades individuals and humanity through distortion, intimidation, coercion, and violence, and through the expression of intolerance and hatred.
- We are committed to the courageous expression of personal convictions in pursuit of fairness and justice.
- We advocate sharing information, opinions, and feelings when facing significant choices while also respecting privacy and confidentiality.
- We accept responsibility for the short- and long-term consequences for our own communication and expect the same of others.

The value of having good grades can create an ethical dilemma with regard to cheating and plagiarism.

Values

beliefs and attitudes we hold about what is important or worthwhile.

The definition of ethics includes the word *values*. **Values** are beliefs and attitudes we hold that can actually conflict with our ethical decisions. For instance, in the previous example, you may not be prepared for the test, and perhaps a low grade will cause you to fail the class or drop below the GPA you need to get accepted into graduate school. One of your values may be success, and a low grade on this exam could cause you to be unsuccessful. Thus, you may choose to violate your code of ethics to honor your values.

Ethical communicator

one who values truthful information and cultural sensitivity.

Unethical communicator

one who is an insensitive, insulting, and ultimately ineffective communicator because of a lack of understanding and caring for other or cultural differences.

Now that you have a general understanding of ethics, let's not forget to connect this term to intercultural communication. What comes to mind when you think of intercultural communication? How do you communicate effectively and ethically with someone who might not share your cultural values? What ethical criteria do you use when evaluating intercultural communication? Do you consider ethics when you're crafting an intercultural message? Would you consider yourself an **ethical communicator** or an **unethical communicator**? Ethical communicators value truthful information and cultural sensitivity. They want to communicate effectively and fairly with people of different cultures and beliefs. Unethical communicators will be insensitive, insulting, and ultimately ineffective communicators because of their lack of understanding and caring for the differences of other cultures.

THE IMPORTANCE OF ETHICS IN INTERCULTURAL COMMUNICATION

Ethics in intercultural communication are critical to creating shared meaning and understanding among different cultures. A major area involving ethical intercultural communication pertains to the way the U.S. government (and modern Western democracies in general) communicates with other nations in the world. In the United States, democracy has achieved an almost sacred status and is generally considered a "universal" right. However, in some nations around the world, the transition to and acceptance of modern democracy have been difficult, hostile, and even violent. Also, countries such as China reject Western democracy entirely, indicating that not all cultures hold democracy in the same esteem as the United States does. Scholar Monica Riccio (2011) discusses the evolution of democracy as a cultural ideal:

> The process of transformation and exaltation that the concept of democracy went through in the 20th century was punctuated and "promoted" by crucial historical steps. These led it to be a form of government which from "better" eventually turned into the only thinkable and feasible one. This process was accompanied by the progressive loss of the political weight of the concept, the concealment of its complexity and aporia, and finally its crystallization as a "universal value." (p. 74)

Ethics can often give us a broad internal government that keeps everyone accountable. However, this internal government must not be overthrown at any price. Many people are likely to remain ethical until it comes to the loss of their jobs or until they have a chance to gain money or favor. This might make us wonder, what good is an ethical system anyway?

The United States is known for valuing freedom; therefore, it's important that we respect the rights of all citizens. If we're all so diverse in our religious perspectives or values, then we must have a common code of conduct that doesn't tie directly to a religion or doctrine but, instead, relies on human decency. In this way, the United States tries to set guidelines for intercultural ethics. No doubt, there's an ethical presence at your college or university. Think about your student handbook and review the current syllabus for this course you are taking related to intercultural communication. What statements can you find that address special needs or cultural sensitivity? How does your university handle cultural or religious holidays with respect to intercultural students? Something as simple as looking at your class syllabus or student handbook can give valuable insight into how critical ethics are with regard to intercultural communication.

Many cultures have strict rules regarding what they will and will not eat. It is important to avoid taking an ethnocentric view of another culture based on their eating practices.

© Alexander Narraina/Shutterstock.com

IN YOUR
life

How do you respond to people who belittle or attack your culture? Do you perceive other cultures as having either right or wrong ethics and values?

One of the central issues facing ethical intercultural communication involves negative cultural transfer. Negative cultural transfer occurs when people take an ethnocentric view when engaging in intercultural communication, thereby measuring or assessing their communication based on their own cultural understanding of truth, morality, and values. Intercultural communications scholar Xiaohong Wei (2009) discusses the impact our cultures have on our communication:

The reasons why negative cultural transfer is one of the greatest obstacles to successful intercultural communication mainly lie in two aspects: (1) culture is deep-rooted; (2) culture is characterized by ethnocentrism. Culture is deep-rooted because most of culture is in the taken-for-granted realm and below the conscious level. Usually, the content of culture is consciously or unconsciously learned and transmitted from generation to generation. From birth, people are deeply influenced by their native culture. How they think and behave is guided by their native culture. With the development of economy and society, great changes may occur in such surface-structure cultural aspects as dress, food, transportation, housing, living habits and laws, etc., through innovation, diffusion and acculturation, but the deep structure of a culture such as values, ethics and morals, religious beliefs and ethics often resists major alterations.

As you can see, removing the ethnocentric viewpoint from your intercultural communication is central to becoming an ethical communicator. Often, the media we consume (television, books, newspapers, Internet, etc.) are biased toward this idea that our particular culture is the pinnacle of truth, morality, and ethical behavior. This way of thinking can often lead to cultural misunderstandings and mistrust. Your first step as an intercultural communicator should be to open your mind to the beliefs and practices of other cultures and not to judge them based on your own culture's understanding of ethics.

ETHICAL CONSIDERATIONS

Many of you are probably thinking that by now you have a pretty good sense of ethical perspective. You probably understand the groundwork and many of the components. However, being ethical in intercultural situations can become problematic if you do not have a proper understanding of the culture. Take a look at this example, known as the Teddy Bear Story, published by John Oetzel (2009):

> Gillian Gibbons is a British woman who was working in a Sudanese school as a teacher of young children. As part of the mandated government curriculum to learn about animals, Gibbons asked one of her students to bring a teddy bear to class. She asked the predominantly Muslim students to identify some names for the bear and then to vote on their favorite names. The voting was a way to introduce the students to democracy. The students, all around 7 years old, identified Abdullah, Hassan, and Muhammad as possible names. Ultimately, the vast majority chose Muhammad. The students took turns taking the teddy bear home and writing a diary, which was labeled "My name is Muhammad."
>
> Gibbons was arrested in November 2007 and charged with inciting religious hatred—a crime that is punishable by 40 lashes and 6 months imprisonment. The Prophet Muhammad is the most sacred symbol in Islam and to name an animal Muhammad is insulting to many Muslims. (p. 2)

In the previous story, many people would not consider Gibbons's classroom activity to be unethical; it was simply a cultural misunderstanding. However, being ethical in intercultural communication requires a person to be sensitive to the customs and traditions of the other culture. Use this story as a reminder that while your intentions may be good, it is important to assess and be sensitive to the other culture before you begin your communication.

Ethical considerations can help walk you through the process of what you must ask yourself when trying to communicate with someone from a different culture, or when you are trying to analyze the intercultural communication of another person. You must always consider your motives, attitudes, integrity, and cultural values. You probably feel as though you're a fairly ethical person. Perhaps you don't cheat, steal, or lie, and you speak politely and courteously to others. However, the interesting thing about intercultural communication is that you often don't recognize when you are being insensitive or contradictory to another person's beliefs, but you more than likely recognize when someone is doing it to you. Therefore, the only thing you can do to stay on top of ethics is educate yourself on what you are doing and when you are doing it. Think about every conversation you've had in the past 24 hours. What questions were asked? Did you withhold information? Did you gossip? Did you tell the truth? At some point during the day, many of you have used an unethical tactic to get something from someone else (it could be as simple as exaggerating a story). Can you apply this **reflexive ethics cycle** to intercultural communication? What are some ways you can be unethical when communicating across cultures?

Reflexive ethics cycle

using an unethical tactic to get something from someone else.

Ethical considerations can save you time and stress. Think about these key elements to ethics at the beginning and end of each day. Hold yourself accountable regarding ethics. Check each conversation you have against your reflexive cycle to achieve ethical conversations and cultural sensitivity. You'll be surprised at the level of respect others will have for you when you consider their feelings and needs by holding yourself accountable to doing what's right.

THE ETHICS OF ELECTRONIC COMMUNICATION

Think about your communication choices related to electronic communication. How can electronic communication be used to communicate interculturally with others? What forms of electronic communication do you use to communicate across cultures? The preceding questions can be explored by assessing the presence of electronic communication in your life. Think about how you use social networking sites such as Facebook and Twitter to communicate, and how your communication can be perceived across cultures from an ethical perspective.

Earlier, when you were asked to use the reflexive ethics cycle, many of you probably considered just your face-to-face conversations. However, if you consider the strong reliance on technology today, it's important to apply the same ethical principles to electronic communication. Consider the following scenario about Jennifer and Daniel.

Daniel was having a bad day. One of his coworkers, Jennifer (a native Colombian), whom he had a pleasant relationship with, reported him to his boss for forwarding insensitive e-mails! Needless to say, Daniel was upset—the e-mail was only an innocent joke about the current immigration law debate. They both worked in the human resources department at a large automotive factory. Daniel and Jennifer socialized with a nice group of coworkers on Saturday nights—a clear social network existed outside of work. To get back at Jennifer, Daniel wanted to make a statement. To put it mildly, the bad feelings escalated quickly. Daniel decided not to text Jennifer to figure out what the problem was and also didn't want to confront her face-to-face at work. Instead, he used the workplace e-mail list (the same list used to organize the Saturday night coworker gatherings) to go on the attack. Daniel sent a "reply all" to one of Jennifer's old e-mail messages and told the entire story about the joke and subsequent disciplinary action. Not only that, but Daniel continued to write about Jennifer, using the "F word" and spreading rumors that Jennifer was ratting out other coworkers to their superiors. As you can see, this is an example of someone using e-mail to attack another person.

Electronic communication allows people like Daniel the opportunity to sit safely behind their computer screens or other digital devices and promote confrontation. While Daniel's motivation to behave the way he did via e-mail was personal, he acted it out in a professional setting. Daniel was insensitive to the fact that Jennifer was a native Colombian and might find jokes about immigration reform insulting and demeaning.

People across cultural contexts take topics in need of discussion, or controversial topics, and place them in electronic formats often termed **e-mail dialogues**—exchanges of messages about a particular topic using e-mail, blog space, and other electronic tools to encourage participation that will ideally lead to new ideas, planning, and sound decision making. These electronic exchanges are, at first glance, supposed to contain rational arguments for or against policies, proposals, and the like. E-mail dialogues can be useful and should not be avoided; however, they have a drawback that many of you have already experienced. The dark side of these electronic exchanges is **electronic aggression**—a form of aggressive communication in which people interact on topics filled with emotionality and aggression (Quintanilla & Wahl, 2016). Topics that begin in an appropriate spirit can get nasty when people don't agree with the direction of the discussion or if particular language is used to disagree about a program or idea others support. People engaged in electronic aggression think their responses are persuasive. Unfortunately, these electronic exchanges filled with emotionality serve as daunting examples of incivility and unethical intercultural communication today.

E-mail dialogues
exchanges of messages about a particular topic using e-mail, blog space, and other electronic tools to encourage participation that will ideally lead to new ideas, planning, and sound decision making.

Electronic aggression
a form of aggressive communication in which people interact on topics filled with emotionality and aggression.

The great thing about advances in new media is that you can send messages instantly and communicate at faster and faster rates each day. The downfall is that people often don't take the time to think before they "speak," or hit *send*. If you take some time to calm down during a heated conversation or electronic debate, you'll establish rational discussion rather than an aggressive dispute. However, you probably have heard of situations where hurtful or inappropriate electronic messages were forwarded to tens of hundreds of people to make a statement. In the above example with Daniel, it's reasonable to believe that had he taken time to "cool off" before constructing the e-mail message that embarrassed Jennifer, there might have been a different outcome. It's important to be mindful when speaking to or about others in an electronically mediated message, because once you say it, or type it, it doesn't go away.

Celebrities read mean tweets about themselves on Jimmy Kimmel Live to make light of the electronic aggression that plays out against them online.

@Supa_Ram
Robert Deniro is too old to be making gangsta movies still.....dude needs to start playing grandfather roles or something

© Mark Ralston/AFP/Getty Images

IN YOUR *life*

Have you ever sent an electronic message in high distress or anger and immediately regretted it? How do you respond to an aggressive e-mail message?

How do you use electronic communication as intercultural communication in your life? Have you ever experienced a situation like the one between Daniel and Jennifer? Think about how people use their cell phones or e-mail to communicate with others. Perhaps you've sent your significant other or friends text messages worded to initiate some sort of response. Maybe you've called someone and hidden your number. We often use technology to communicate with others for our own benefit—for instance, convincing your boss that you're sick through a text message or messaging others during a test to persuade them to share the answers. Whatever the cause, new media are often used in disturbing ways. It's important that before you press the *send* button on any message, you apply the same ethical considerations when using new media as you do in face-to-face communication. Take a moment to evaluate your electronic communication from an ethical perspective (e.g., text messages, e-mail, Facebook, Twitter). Ask yourself if you're sensitive and ethical with people when you use electronic communication. Think about your communication motives. Does anything need to change? Perhaps these ethical considerations could save you and others some grief and hurt. Each time you pick up your cell phone or turn on your computer, be mindful of how you go about getting your way when using electronic communication.

A recent example of unethical use of electronic communication occurred after the nuclear reactor meltdown in Japan that sent contaminated water into the sea. In 2011, rumors began circulating around the Internet that sea salt was no longer safe for consumption since it was contaminated by radiation. The rumor triggered panicked purchases of iodized salt in the United States and other countries, notably China. Supermarkets in many major Chinese cities soon found themselves with a salt shortage. In Korea, rumors spread that "radiation rain" could impact the country, and fake news stories encouraged the mass buying of iodized salt, seaweed, and other products to "resist radiation." This points to a similarity between Western and Asian cultures, in that the United States and other European countries have also had their fair share of Internet hoaxes. Scholar Xiaochi Zhang (2012) discusses this similarity:

> Especially from the above cases, the peoples from different cultural backgrounds, both the Asian people including Chinese people, Korean people and the Americans, appeared a confusing phenomenon that under the conditions of excessive "presses freedom," a large amount of false information has been spread while the information reflecting the truth cannot be communicated. Why? This is because the instinct to prevent potential danger has made people choose to accept more information that is closely related with their personal interests while the other information has been neglected. (p. 14)

The above passage indicates a fundamental need to be ethical and consider the repercussions of our communication. Regardless of whether we mean it as a joke or are actively trying to spread false information (please don't!), using electronic communication irresponsibly can have dire effects on countless people. Try to place yourself in the shoes of someone in the previous reactor meltdown example; it can be easy to fall for a story like that, but such misinformation obscures clear, useful information and can cause irreparable harm to people's lives.

ETHICAL RESPONSIBILITY

Responsibility

the elements of fulfilling duties and obligations, being accountable to other individuals and groups, adhering to agreed-on standards, and being accountable to one's own conscience.

Now that you've covered the basics of ethics, let's focus on ethical responsibility. According to communication ethics scholar Richard L. Johannesen and his colleagues, **responsibility** includes the elements of fulfilling duties and obligations, being accountable to other individuals and groups, adhering to agreed-on standards, and being accountable to one's own conscience (Johannesen, Valde, & Whedbee, 2008). In every intercultural interaction you encounter in life, there's at least one sender and receiver. While you have reviewed many responsibilities of the sender of a message, do you think the receiver of the message has ethical responsibilities, too?

With regard to ethical responsibility during intercultural communication, it is important not to make judgments about another culture based on your own cultural ideas of ethics, morals, and values. When we discuss using ethics in intercultural communication, it does not necessarily mean you are trying to persuade cultural others to join your way of thinking. Rather, it refers to the need to be considerate and understanding during your intercultural communications. Scholar Stella Ting-Toomey (2010) discusses this situation:

> Many problematic cultural practices perpetuate themselves because of long-standing cultural habits or ignorance of alternative ways of doing things. Education or a desire for change from within the people in a local culture is usually how a questionable practice is ended. From a metaethics social ecological framework, making a sound ethical judgment demands both breadth and depth of culture-sensitive knowledge, context specific knowledge, and genuine humanistic concern. (p. 349)

From the above passage, it should be apparent that the goal of ethical communication in intercultural interactions is not persuasive in nature; it involves having knowledge of and concern for people of different cultures. That is not to say that people do not make the mistake of trying to persuade. Many people can be deceiving or "shady" when participating in intercultural communication. When you think of such people, politicians might come to mind. Many of you have probably heard jokes or quotes comparing politicians to used-car salesmen or lawyers. In general, politicians aren't viewed as the most honest individuals in society. From Watergate to the Clinton sex scandal, Americans have seen their share of "dirty politicians." However, instead of focusing on the individual, focus on the ethical process of politics with respect to culture. One of the many political processes is campaigning. Barack Obama didn't become the president of the United States on his own. It took a team of people representing him and constantly working on

ETHICAL CONNECTION

Alisha is an editor for her university's school newspaper. One of her major job functions is to write a weekly article that highlights the cultural backgrounds of the university's extensive foreign-exchange student body. Because she was swamped with exams one week, Alisha decided to base her article about the university's Korean exchange students on a recent documentary she watched on TV. When the article was published, the newspaper saw a severe backlash of criticism from the Korean student body. The documentary had been edited to appeal to an American audience, but the "cultural norms" it displayed were actually perceived by native Koreans as stereotypical and racist. Had Alisha actually talked with some of the Korean students, she would have realized that the documentary was biased and unfair from a Korean standpoint.

Questions to consider:
1. Why was it irresponsible for Alisha to base her article on a television show?
2. Do you believe media have a tendency to portray different cultures inaccurately?
3. What should Alisha have done differently to create a more accurate article?
4. How can effective intercultural communication enable us to better understand other cultures?

his public persona to get him into the White House. Sadly, appealing to the largest possible group of voters can lead to the repression of minority opinions and cultures. U.S. citizens who come from different cultures may have their deeply held beliefs thrown in their faces during elections. Campaigns are normally run through commercials that point out flaws in opposing candidates and their values. Because of this vicious format, people from different cultures or religious backgrounds may suddenly find themselves demonized or ridiculed based on their beliefs.

© Ryan Rodrick Beiler/Shutterstock.com

Gun ownership/safety is a subject that brings up major ethical issues in U.S. culture.

With so many types of communication and so many communicators in a campaign, it is almost impossible to monitor this notion of intercultural ethics. Outside of the media, think of all the people involved with the campaign team—candidates, representatives, consultants, reporters, editors, and more. Each of these people who impact the campaign should be held responsible for following a strict code of ethics. However, they're all held responsible for portraying the candidate's image in an appealing manner in hopes of winning the election, which can sometimes encourage them to be insensitive or demeaning toward cultures different from the U.S. mainstream. This idea of ethics within politics or campaigns is difficult to enforce due to special interest and political action committees (e.g., Swift Vote Veterans, Human Rights Campaign, National Rifle Association), known for funding negative political campaign ads.

ADAPTING TO THE AUDIENCE

Many of you taking this course will probably have taken public speaking by now. Think back to the generic speeches some of your peers may have given. Often when people speak to an audience, they consider only their own personal opinions or values. However, at the extreme opposite end of this spectrum, other people try to please everyone in the audience. Questions about how far persuaders should go in adapting their message to particular audiences should also be associated with ethical responsibility (Johannesen et al., 2008).

Many politicians and business professionals struggle when they try to please everyone in the audience. You may sometimes have to step on a few toes or fall short of some people's expectations to remain ethically responsible in front of an audience. Some degree of adaptation in language choice, evidence, value appeals, organization, and communication medium for specific audiences is a crucial part of successful and ethical cultural communication. As a communicator, always be mindful of others' spiritual perspectives (if any), values, personal experiences, families, and the like. You've probably seen speakers who are completely heedless of their audiences, as well as those who are willing to say anything to win their audiences' favor. Both of these extremes are unethical and irresponsible.

Earlier in the chapter, we discussed how the ideal of democracy may not necessarily be shared across all cultures. China was used as an example of a country where Western-style democracy has not gained much popularity. Many politicians and media personalities make the unfair and inaccurate assertion that the Chinese government and people do not want freedom or the ability to speak freely. This is another example of unethical intercultural communication. Scholar Rafael Capurro (2011) discusses this misunderstanding and what we can learn from it:

What is the goal of this kind of analysis for intercultural debates on information ethics? First of all, to learn from each other. Western information societies can learn from Taoism and the spirit of the "Far East" not only on how to deal with blocking processes based on fixed moralities, exacerbating the primacy of direct speech. Information societies in the "Far East" might learn from direct speech, individual freedom and autonomy as correctives of an idealized harmony that might block social changes. In both cases we should be careful not to oversee the complexity and richness of our traditions including the difference itself between "Far East" and "Far West" that is nothing but a starting point for intercultural information ethics that should be both theoretical and empirical. (p. 43)

After reading the previous passage, it should be apparent that "intercultural information ethics" goes hand in hand with our discussions of ethics in intercultural communication. The following section delves more into the ways we can use different ethical perspectives to become more effective intercultural communicators.

ETHICAL RESPONSIBILITY STRATEGIES

Integrating ethical practices is critical to your daily interactions with others, and there are a few strategies you can use to incorporate ethical behavior in your daily routine. In intercultural communication, it is critical that ethical standards remain flexible and open to discussion (Guilherme, Keating, & Hoppe, 2010). Basically, you should always be developing new ways to interpret a situation. One strategy is mindful reframing. **Mindful reframing** is described as "the mindful process of using language to change the way each person or party defines or thinks about experiences" (Ting-Toomey & Chung, 2005). Keep in mind that this practice is meant to be reciprocal; both parties should take an active role to keep the communication from becoming fragmented and ineffective. Think of mindful reframing as a reflexive practice, something you should be actively critiquing as your communication interaction occurs. A good way to practice might be to watch a television show or movie that involves communication between two or more cultures and to attempt to reframe the dialogue from several different perspectives with respect to intercultural sensitivity.

> **Mindful framing**
> "the mindful process of using language to change the way each person or party defines or thinks about experiences."

Another ethical intercultural communication strategy involves the use of **sustained dialogue**. The goal of sustained dialogue is to promote change in intercultural group relationships by moving the communication dynamic from negative to positive (Mollov & Schwartz, 2010). Basically, sustained dialogue is a method of relationship building that attempts to restructure the relationship from the ground up. Typically, this strategy is used whenever two different cultural groups are

> **Sustained dialogue**
> promotes change in intercultural group relationships by moving the communication dynamics from negative to positive.

in conflict. Critical to this strategy is the **contact hypothesis**. Scholars M. Ben Mollov and David Schwartz describe the contact hypothesis this way:

> The contact hypothesis developed initially by Allport (1954) and later enlarged upon by Amir (1969) maintains that contact in itself is not necessarily a means of bringing about perception change among groups in conflict, which can be a pre-requisite to relationship building. The contact hypothesis maintains that for such contact to have a positive impact several main conditions must be met: (1) equal status between the parties; (2) intimate as opposed to merely formal relations between the parties; (3) cooperative as opposed to competitive interactions; and (4) institutional support. (pp. 211–212)

© ArtisticPhoto/Shutterstock.com

For a global intercultural organization such as the United Nations, how important is the idea of reframing in creating a healthy international dialogue?

As you can see, the principles of sustained dialogue and the contact hypothesis involve moving beyond formal dialogue and into a more intimate communication setting. Commonly, this strategy has been forwarded as a method to ease tensions in the current Israeli–Palestinian conflict, but this can easily be applied to your intercultural interactions as well. Instead of using formal communication to hammer out an agreement, it is sometimes better to change the relationship dynamic itself before working out a problem. Sustained dialogue enables two intercultural communication partners to develop empathy for and understanding of the other that would otherwise not be possible.

SOME ETHICAL PERSPECTIVES

To get more familiar with ethics and its connection to your study of intercultural communication, let's review a few different perspectives concerning ethics. These perspectives can be used alone or in combination with one another to help seek out the best ethical solution in certain situations. Think of these perspectives like a shelf full of eyeglasses at the eye doctor. Each different pair you try on causes you to see things around you a bit differently. As you read through these perspectives, try to see yourself in previous social situations from a different point of view.

RELIGIOUS PERSPECTIVE

At one time or another, we have all landed on a television program or read a newspaper article that appealed to our beliefs. Many religious leaders have the reputation of appealing to people's psychological needs in hopes of gaining money or power. The **religious perspective** examines the relationship between us as humans and a higher power. Throughout the history of religion and media, there have been instances when spiritual leaders have stated that another religion is wrong or that its teachings and beliefs go against God's will. Florida pastor Terry Jones publicly encouraged followers to burn the Koran (the holy book of Islamic faith) on the 2010 anniversary of the 9/11 terrorist attacks.

Many times in life, we have to question the ethics of those who are communicating to us about another culture or belief. Is it acceptable to burn another faith's holy book? What are this pastor's motives? To assess Jones's appeal from an ethical perspective, let's consider Emory Griffin's ethics for Christian evangelism, established in 1976. To what degree could Jones's message be criticized as that of a "rhetorical rapist" who uses psychological coercion to force a decision to act (Johannesen et al., 2008)? This perspective is not to say that we should reject our religious views or values. However, in every communication situation, we have an ethical responsibility as senders and receivers. Therefore, we must be sure to notice when others may be appealing to our emotions with the goal of deceiving us. Are there other ethical standards of religious doctrine you may be able to use to evaluate Jones's entreaty to burn the Koran?

Religious perspective examines the relationship between us as humans and a higher power.

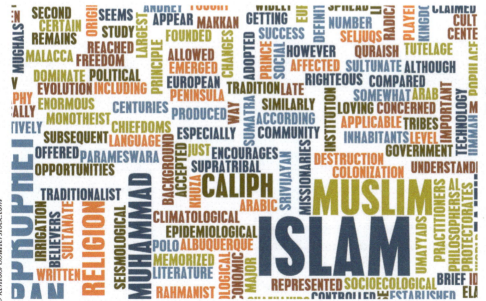

Religions such as Christianity and Islam can be better understood by analyzing them from several different perspectives.

© kentoh/Shutterstock.com

Developing positive intercultural communication practices with respect to religion involves realizing some of the shortcomings inherent in using only one ethical perspective to view the world. Part of becoming an effective intercultural communicator is understanding other ethical or religious perspectives and using them to help frame your interactions. Scholar Satoshi Ishii (2009) offers two inherent weaknesses in using only a Euro–U.S.-centric viewpoint in regard to religion:

> The first weakness is that their views and concepts of communication ethics supposedly derived from Ancient Greek philosophy, Judeo-Christianity, and the Western Enlightenment are academically Euro-US-centric, hegemonic, and imposedetic in nature. They commonly neglect to pay due respect to non-Euro-US-centric, particularly Asian, concepts and thoughts of communication and human relationship ethics. Their second weakness is that they ignore the traditionally latent impact of religion upon the foundation and development of ethical beliefs, values, and worldviews. Hence in promoting more interculturally trustworthy and sustainable communication ethics, it is crucial to complement and enhance these two scholarly weaknesses with Asian religio-ethical philosophies and thoughts. (pp. 49–50)

As you can see from the above passage, we generate the most effective intercultural communication practices when we give ourselves the ability to understand communication from more than one cultural viewpoint. Whenever we are exposed to other cultural practices that might seem backward or barbaric, it is important to realize that many different cultures frame their concepts of morals and values from an entirely different religious perspective. The next time you come across an international news story that leaves you appalled or angry, remember to be critical about the ethical and moral lessons inherent to different religious beliefs. Can you think of any morals or values you hold that could seem alien or brutal to someone from a different religious background?

HUMAN NATURE PERSPECTIVE

Human nature perspective

states that our ability to judge, reason, and comprehend far exceeds that of any other species. Therefore, we hold ourselves accountable to make good judgments and decisions.

What makes us human? This is a question many people ponder. Perhaps you've heard someone say, "I'm only human." What does this mean? Most often, when people say this, they are stating that they are prone to making mistakes and are declaring their imperfection. However, as humans, we are often held accountable for our mistakes. We are judged or face consequences. Other mammals do not face trial or risk going to prison; so what is it about the human race that sets us apart? The **human nature perspective** states that our ability to judge, reason, and comprehend far exceeds that of any other species. Therefore, we hold ourselves accountable to make good judgments and decisions. This is where our ethics come into play. You often hear parents tell their children that they are old enough to know right from wrong. These parents feel that they have taught their children the ability to distinguish between good and bad; the children are expected to make good judgment calls from that point onward. Parents and guardians attempt to instill in their children values and morals similar to those you reviewed earlier in the chapter.

Throughout the past decade, we have seen leaders of our country and of the world commit unethical acts or fail to make ethical decisions. Perhaps this was going on all along, or perhaps social media platforms such as Facebook and YouTube have just made footage of and information about such events more widely accessible. We've seen the terrorist acts of 9/11, the hanging of Saddam Hussein, and even a shoe thrown at President George W. Bush during a press conference. We've seen companies shut down for discrepancies between the way they've handled their money and the information they gave customers about their practices. We've seen the Federal Communications Commission tell musicians that their music cannot be played on the radio due to explicit and vulgar content. In each of these situations, humans have failed to make ethical decisions. The human nature perspective is both a gift and a curse. We are distinguished from other species, however, in that we are liable for our mistakes and misjudgments as humans.

© Hasloo Group Production Studio/Shutterstock.com

As your individual global presence continues to increase, how important is the need for reflexive dialogue in your everyday interactions?

DIALOGICAL PERSPECTIVE

Dialogical perspectives emerge from current scholarship on the nature of communication as dialogue rather than monologue (Johannesen et al., 2008). **Monologue** is normally looked at as a performance or speech by a single person. **Dialogue,** on the other hand, is a conversation between two or more people. Think about the way you handle yourself in a conversation with someone you like. You may be attentive and interested, even if the subject matter doesn't necessarily pertain to you; you have a general interest because you care about that person. For instance, try to think of your most recent conversation with a person whom you aren't so fond of. How did you handle yourself in this conversation? In the dialogical perspective, we think of communication as a dialogue by considering the different attitudes we emit in a conversation. These can be attitudes of hatred, prejudice, jealousy, inequality, or manipulation. On the other hand, they may be attitudes of tenderness, compassion, interest, or love. Although we've just examined a few extreme ends of the spectrum, there are many different attitudes in each dialogue we encounter throughout the day. These dialogues are important because we must consider how to treat others ethically. In each social situation we encounter, we must consider our audience, even if it is an audience of one. This consideration of others and their feelings will help us remain ethical as we engage in conversations.

Let's take this same idea of communication as dialogue and apply it to intercultural communication. If we engage in conversations with others and seek to manipulate them based on their misunderstanding of our culture, we are being unethical. People who have a hidden agenda or desire to initiate a reaction through intercultural communication are also acting unethically. It is important as we attempt to communicate with cultural others in our dialogues that we do so by being sensitive and aware of their cultural differences, and also by carefully assessing what meaning our words and nonverbal communication can convey. This act of intercultural communication should not be manipulative or misleading.

SITUATIONAL PERSPECTIVE

The **situational perspective** examines every situation we encounter related to intercultural communication. When we think of scenarios where intercultural communication is involved, we often think of international business meetings, study-abroad programs, vacations, or perhaps politics. However, think about the different cultures represented in your classroom, dormitory, or job. Simply being from the same country does not mean that everyone shares the same culture. Do you think you ever violate any ethical codes when talking to people from different cultures? Consider the concrete contextual factors to make a purely situational ethical evaluation.

Dialogical perspectives

those that deal with sense making that occurs through cognition and communication.

Monologue

typically a performance or speech by a single person.

Dialogue

a conversation between two or more people.

Situational perspective

examines every situation we encounter related to intercultural communication. This perspective involves being critical of your everyday communication.

Self-Assessment: Ethical Choices

Put a check by each item that reflects your choices related to ethics.

____ 1. I think it is OK to lie in certain situations.
____ 2. I think it is best to make a decision that helps the most people.
____ 3. My religious perspective guides my choices in personal and professional situations.
____ 4. I can distinguish between right and wrong based on what my parents taught me.
____ 5. I think it is important to consider the feelings, attitudes, morals, and values of others.
____ 6. My ethical decisions are always driven by the situation.

WHAT YOU'VE LEARNED

In this chapter, you have learned that *ethics* is a system of accepted principles that make up an individual's or group's values and judgments as to what's right and wrong. You then learned ethics are important in the study of intercultural communication because understanding various codes of ethics are needed in order to create shared meaning and understanding among different cultures. Next, you were taught that your ethical responsibility with regard to intercultural communication is to not make judgments about other cultures based on your own cultural ideas of ethics, morals, and values. The importance of adapting to various audiences was then discussed, and, finally, the various ethical perspectives—religious, human nature, dialogical, and situational—were defined and discussed.

Each of the aforementioned topics in Chapter 2 are important to keep in mind while in intercultural contexts in order to help you communicate both ethically and competently. Consider everything you have learned and will learn in this course as you evaluate information and make communication choices in your life. In Chapter 3, you will learn about both culture and identity and the role they have in the study of intercultural communication.

REVIEW

1. A system of accepted principles that make up an individual's or group's values and judgments is to what is right and wrong is referred to as _____.

2. _____ is a form of aggressive communication in which people interact on topics filled with emotionality and aggression.

3. _____ value truthful information and cultural sensitivity, while _____ are insensitive, insulting, and ultimately ineffective communicators.

4. _____ occurs when people take an ethnocentric view when engaging in intercultural communication, thereby measuring or assessing their communication based on their own cultural understanding of truth, morality, and values.

5. Constantly assessing your communication with others by reflecting on what questions were asked, if any information was withheld, and if the truth was told is a process called the _____.

6. Explain what *ethical responsibility* means in regard to intercultural communication.

7. Define "mindful reframing" and discuss its importance in intercultural communication.

8. According to the contact hypothesis, what are the four main conditions that must be met to have a positive impact in intercultural communication?

9. Which perspective examines every situation we encounter related to intercultural communication and involves being critical of everyday communication?

10. Which dialogue strategy has the goal of promoting change in intercultural group relationships by moving the communication dynamics from negative to positive?

Review answers are found on the accompanying website.

REFLECT

1. You learned from the text that values are beliefs and attitudes that can actually conflict with ethical decisions. Can you think of a time when your own values made it difficult for you to make an ethical decision?

2. Jimmy and Tara were in a romantic relationship, but the relationship ended after Tara caught Jimmy cheating. After the breakup, Jimmy posted on social media that the reason they broke up was because Tara would become overly emotional when Jimmy spent time with female friends and was too clingy and controlling. He continually labeled her as being a "crazy ex-girlfriend." Use the reflexive ethics cycle to determine why Jimmy's choice to post this information was unethical.

3. Can you think of a time when you witnessed (or were part of) electronic aggression between people of different cultures?

4. Amala, a practicing Muslim woman, is walking across campus when she is stopped by a woman she does not know. The woman, Brittney, asks Amala why she would embrace her own oppression by wearing a hijab. Given Brittney's negative tone, how could Amala respond to promote sustained dialogue?

5. With which ethical perspective do you most closely align? Can you think of a challenge you faced when communicating with someone who aligns with a different perspective?

KEY TERMS

ethical communication, 35
ethics, 36
code of ethics, 36
distinguish, 36
dedication, 36
values, 38
ethical communicator, 38
unethical communicator, 38
reflexive ethics cycle, 42
e-mail dialogues, 43
electronic aggression, 43

responsibility, 46
mindful reframing, 49
sustained dialogue, 49
contact hypothesis, 50
religious perspective, 51
human nature perspective, 51
dialogical perspectives, 54
monologue, 54
dialogue, 54
situational perspective, 54

CHAPTER THREE
Culture and Identity

CHAPTER OUTLINE

WHAT YOU WILL LEARN

After studying this chapter, you should be able to

1. explain what identity is, describe its influences and functions, and discuss its impacts on communicating with others;
2. describe the connection between identity and face, and explain how facework helps shape and reinforce identity;
3. discuss and critique the various theories that explain the nature, purpose, and influences of identity; and
4. discuss the implications of identity related to ethnicity, age, and gender.

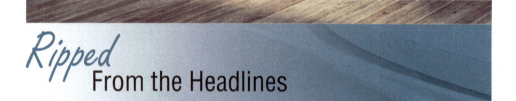

Ripped From the Headlines

© Mega Pixel/Shutterstock.com

With LBGTQIA+ rights becoming a central part of public discourse, new issues are being discussed that were previously not often discussed. A person's sense of identity is a complicated, multi-layered view of oneself, and this is especially prominent when a person's biological sex does not match their gender. Communication and identity are often linked, and the process of communicating one's gender can be a complicated process for transgender and gender non-binary people.

Everyday mundane activities, such as a day at the DMV, can pose a challenge to people who do not identify as being either male or female. For people like Nic Sakurai, being given only two options for gender on a driver's license does not accurately represent their true self. For the first time in the United States, residents of Washington D.C. now have the option to choose X as a gender marker as opposed to the traditional M (male) or F (female) options. This X marker signifies that they identify as being gender non-binary. LGBTQIA+ rights advocates assert that being given this option may reduce the risk of harassment and discrimination when a person's physical appearance does not match the label on their ID (Grinberg, 2017). This option is now spreading to other areas of the country, with Oregon becoming the first state to allow residents to choose "not specified" as the gender on their driver's licenses (Associated Press, 2017).

As we move through this chapter and discuss the importance of identity and its relationship with culture, reflect on how this new option impacts people and how they communicate their gender. People communicate various parts of their identity in ways we do not often actively think about. While learning about identity and its relation to communication, think about the ways in which you communicate your own gender in your everyday life.

Your **identity** is the representation of how you view yourself and how others might see you. Almost every word you utter in the presence of others, and virtually every way you express yourself nonverbally, is an expression of your identity. This chapter will explore the issue of identity and perhaps get you to think more closely about how your communication and your identity are linked. The first section in this chapter describes what an identity is, as well as what influences one's identity construction. You will also learn that your identity serves several functions, and that certain factors impact how you communicate your identity to others. Next, you will read about face theory and how the concept of face is tied closely with identity. Third, you will be exposed to various theories that explain the nature, purpose, and influences of identity. Finally, you will be encouraged to think about the issues and implications regarding various ways we construct our identity, particularly those based on ethnicity, age, and gender and sex.

Identity
the representation of how you view yourself and how others may see you.

THE NATURE OF IDENTITY

IDENTITY AS SELF

To understand identity and how it plays into intercultural communication, we first should explore the notion of self. According to Campbell, Assenand, and Di Paula (2000), the **self** is a complex set of beliefs about one's attributes, as well as memories and recollections of episodes that confirm such beliefs. These attributes and memories form a **schema** of oneself, or a mental structure that contains various bits of information that define who a person is and guides how he or she communicates with others (Trenholm & Jensen, 2013). For example, a 20-year-old male college student majoring in chemical engineering might see himself as energetic, someone's son, technical in how he approaches problems, and busy with schoolwork. These descriptors might form that student's schema. In communication encounters, part of this schema might compel him to be more task than relationship oriented in how

Self
a complex set of beliefs about one's attributes, as well as memories and recollections of episodes that confirm such beliefs.

Schema
a mental structure that contains various bits of information that define who a person is and guides how he or she communicates with others.

The self can be whatever the person believes.

he works with teammates on group projects. He might also see himself as somewhat dependent on his parents and might not yet possess the self-confidence to assert himself in certain situations.

One really cannot discuss the self without acknowledging the scholarship of George Herbert Mead, who wrote *Mind, Self, and Society* (1962) and other works that explore the self in relation to society. Mead talks about the distinction between the "I" and "me" in oneself, as well as the synthesis of the two. The "me" represents the self as learned through interactions with others. The insights gained through these interactions become internalized and become the "me." In contrast, the "I" is the attitude of the individual in response to society or the community. The "I" is akin to Freud's "ego," the aspect that is more self-serving. The "I" and "me" are integrated into an individual who understands himself or herself as he or she interacts with society. Mead explains that the "me" sometimes has to rein in the "I" to keep it in line with community norms and standards.

Suppose you think of yourself as a funny person because it seems easy to get a laugh from others when you make sarcastic remarks or tell jokes in social situations; this funny person might be considered your "I." But it can be easy for the "I" to use comedy and sarcasm to poke fun at others or even cause serious offense. This is where the "me" steps in, to remind the "I" that there are norms of empathy and politeness, and that one might lose friends if humor is always implemented at others' expense. This synthesis of "I" and "me" is a function of communication, which in turn helps develop one's self-concept. This process can be viewed as "self-shaped-by-society-shaped-by-self" (Tanno & González, 1998).

There is more than just one layer to the self, and this is especially true when we attempt to communicate aspects of our self to others. Brewer and Gardner (1996) and Hecht and colleagues (Hecht, 1993; Hecht, Warren, Jung, & Krieger, 2005) discuss three levels of self-representation: the individual, the interpersonal (relational self), and the group (collective self). The individual level reflects the personal self that includes the self-concept (e.g., funny, young, analytical). The interpersonal level is the relational self that derives from the relationships or connections with others (e.g., wife in a marriage, second oldest child in one's family of origin). Hecht et al. (2005) point out that not only is an individual identity developed from a relationship, but that very relationship eventually takes on its own identity, its own relational culture. The group level represents the collective self, which is reflected in group memberships (e.g., faith community, being the "analytical one" in most class group projects).

Gudykunst and Kim (1992) point to several cross-cultural differences in how the self is constructed and perceived. For instance, citizens of the United States generally view the self in more individualistic terms. An individualistic person might view the self as a composite of personality traits, character markers, and personal accomplishments. In addition, these individuals' self-esteem can be bounded by how independent they are or how well they stand on their own feet (Geertz, 1975). In particular, Akande (2008) differentiates academic and nonacademic self-esteem and finds that people from individualistic cultures have higher nonacademic self-esteem than do those from collectivist cultures; the opposite is true about collectivist individuals.

Continuing with the general view of self, the collectivistic self might be more likely to take into account ties to family or friends (Gudykunst & Kim, 1992). Rather than just viewing one's accomplishments as the results of one's own individual talent and hard work, the collectivist might see these accomplishments as a result of the support of parents, or collaboration with colleagues. The collectivist self might also be tied to one's workplace or school attended. The collectivist self might even deny the importance of the individual self. This is often the case in Japanese

© Eugenio Marongiu/Shutterstock.com

You may be known as the "funny one" in your group of friends, or your group may be known as the outgoing group of people in relation to other groups of friends.

culture, especially when one is interacting with someone of higher status (Doi, 1986).

Most of us can think of ways in which we identify with more than just one cultural group (Collier & Thomas, 1988). Chances are you do not think of yourself just in terms of country of origin but also in terms of your gender or sex, perhaps your religious affiliation, your academic major, and any other classification according to group membership or an aspect around which people share some common ground. This phenomenon might be especially noticeable to an individual who immigrates to another country and has to struggle to fit in, while at the same time maintaining his or her sense of cultural identity. To illustrate, Lu (2001) conducted an observational study of students in Chinese schools in Chicago, utilizing Collier and Thomas's definition of cultural identity, which is identifying with and gaining acceptance into a group that shares your values, belief systems, and norms of conduct. Lu concluded that the students generally worked hard to maintain their Chinese identity but, at the same time, put great effort toward establishing themselves as Chinese Americans. This struggle for dual identity at times seemed to imply tension for the students as they were assimilating.

FUNCTIONS OF IDENTITY

Understanding the personal, interpersonal, and collective levels of self can serve several functions (Simon, 2004; Spencer-Oatey, 2007). For one thing, identity can give us a sense of belonging, or even guide us to individuals and groups with whom we might feel community. Having a sense of who we are can help us find people with whom we might belong. This may be the case for a person graduating from high school and entering college. The new student is trying to find a sense of belonging and, thus, might find a student group that shares her or his attitudes or interests. Second, if we know where we belong, we might also figure out where we do not belong and, more important, how we see ourselves "anchored" in this world. Such might be the case for students who belong to political groups; belonging to a particular political group can remind them of which groups' philosophies or ideologies they do not agree with. Third, a strong sense of identity can build our self-esteem and confidence. If we can pinpoint positive aspects, we can feel good that those things help define who we are. Unfortunately, some people more quickly zero in on what they think are negative self-aspects, which can contribute to a negative self-esteem, especially if they belong to groups in which they feel they do not measure up (e.g., feeling academically inadequate in a group of honor students).

THE CONNECTION BETWEEN IDENTITY AND FACE

Understanding the nature of identity can be enhanced even further by examining the notions of face and facework (Spencer-Oatey, 2007). **Face** refers to the image of self that we project or show to others (Goffman, 1967). **Facework** includes the communicative actions we take to project our face, maintain the face of self and others, or even threaten another person's face (e.g., in criticism). Face is constructed through social interaction (Spencer-Oatey, 2007). For example, if you think you are a funny person (face), you might goof off or make funny remarks in front of your peers (facework), and if they laugh at your antics, then you are receiving affirmation of the face you are trying to project.

Face
the image of self that we project to others.

Facework
the portrayal of one's face is an inherently communicative act that is an extension of one's identity.

Moreover, the construction of face and the reinforcement or disconfirmation of face are social elements based on the judgments of others (Lim, 1994). This means that face is not just something we construct for ourselves; this construction also takes into consideration others' judgments of us so that we learn to project the very best aspects of ourselves that get positive confirmation from those with whom we interact. Other people's attempts to save or threaten our face can confirm or disconfirm the aspects of face we project, thus compelling us to continue to negotiate our projected identity. As in the previous example, suppose after many attempts to get laughs in social situations, people instead rolled their eyes or ignored you. This response might compel you to rethink your image of yourself as a funny person.

Identity is a negotiable concept. Whether or not we realize it, we decide which aspects of our identity to present to the world. Ideally, the aspects we think show us in a more positive light are part of our facework. Goffman (1967) claims that because of this tendency, face is primarily a compilation of positive attributes. Face is typically not associated with negative qualities, or the qualities we believe we do *not* own (Goffman, 1967). One caveat to this is the fact that people vary in their perceptions of what attributes are positive, negative, or neutral (Spencer-Oatey, 2007). For example, you might take pride in the fact that you are punctual for events and appointments, and you may

World leaders must understand one another's cultural differences when meeting so there are no misunderstandings.

© Drop of Light/Shutterstock.com

even lose patience with people who are chronically late. However, not all cultures value punctuality; rather, some view time as a fluid concept. Therefore, someone who holds the latter view of time might judge your punctuality negatively and even say you are punctual *to a fault*.

Face and identity are arguably social phenomena because, while we can make individual distinctions about what is and is not part of our identity, the projection of our identity in public is partially dependent on how that identity is received, accepted, affirmed, or rejected by the social world and, more important, by those in our social networks. For this and other reasons, in this textbook, we treat face as an interpersonal communication issue; the portrayal of one's face is an inherently communicative act (Scollon & Scollon, 1995).

Face and identity are not identical, but they are strongly linked. Imahori and Cupach (2005) contend that face is a social, interactional phenomenon, which is what makes it distinct from one's identity. In other words, identity is the individual occurrence, whereas face is relational and social. While this might help us make the distinction between these two constructs, we might also consider how the two are interrelated. Spencer-Oatey (2007) argues, "Certainly, face entails making claims about one's attributes that in turn entail the appraisal of others, so in this sense the notion of face cannot be divorced from social interaction" (p. 643). Spencer-Oatey explains that while face reflects positive attributes as deemed by the person, identity can include a person's negative as well as positive attributes, as judged by others during interaction.

Cultures often differ in the conception and utility of face. For instance, Ting-Toomey (1988) describes the individualistic face as focusing on the "I," whereas collectivistic cultures emphasize social connections in the presentation of face. Ting-Toomey argues that the more collectivistic view of face might encourage one to be more concerned about the face of the other person than would a more individualistic view.

THEORIES AND MODELS OF IDENTITY

We have already discussed what the self is in relation to identity, as well as the role of identity in facework. We now move on to more complex explanations of identity and its significance in culture and communication. The theories and models discussed below represent different approaches to understanding and capturing the nature and function of identity.

SELF-ASPECTS MODEL OF IDENTITY

We previously talked about how identity is inextricably linked with notions and portrayals of the self. Simon's (2004) **self-aspects model of identity** goes into more detail about how the self is conceptualized and identifies the different characteristics that make up one's self-concept, which really reflects beliefs and attitudes about the self. More specifically, according to the self-aspects model of identity, the self encompasses one's perceived abilities (or deficiencies), personality traits, physical features, behavioral characteristics, ideologies or belief systems, social roles, languages, and group memberships. Table 3.1 illustrates how various self-aspects can help a person make sense of who he or she is, and how to convey that self to the rest of the world.

Self-aspects model of identity
the self encompasses several different facets, including perceived abilities (or deficiencies), personality traits, physical features, behavioral characteristics, ideologies or belief systems, social roles, languages, and group memberships.

TABLE 3.1 Examples of a person's (Martha's) self-aspects, according to the self-aspects model of identity

Self-Aspects of Martha	Corresponding Attitudes of Martha	Corresponding Communicative Behaviors of Martha
Personality traits	"I'm rather shy."	Does not participate much in class; is quiet during classroom discussions
Abilities	"I'm an excellent cook."	Likes to have friends over for dinner
Physical features	"I'm too fat."	Wears large T-shirts to hide body features
Behavioral characteristics	Stays up late at night and finds it hard to rise early in the morning	Does not answer phone before 11:00 a.m.
Ideologies	Republican	Posts conservative memes on social media sites
Social roles	Project manager at work	Speaks to subordinates in terms of giving directions and orders
Language affiliation(s)	Fluent in English and Spanish	Speaks English at work and Spanish at home
Group	Member of local Baptist church	Wears a cross pendant

How do religious or ethnic affiliations relate to your identity, if at all? In other words, are there specific affiliations that help shape who you are?

Valence

positive and negative feelings.

Centrality

the extent to which a self-aspect is crucial or central to how we describe ourselves.

Core

central, most important aspect.

Peripheral

refers to an aspect of characteristic that appears unimportant or hardly noticeable.

Currency

a perceptual concept that refers to how we see certain aspects fitting in time.

Actuality

the distinction we make between characteristics we possess and those we aspire to have.

Not all self-aspects are pertinent or salient to each individual. In fact, some aspects carry more weight or importance than others. For instance, you might be able to speak both Spanish and English fluently, but you might not have a need to speak both languages a great deal of the time, especially if your first language is English and you speak it at home and with your closest friends. Individuals also vary in how much their self-aspects overlap or integrate with one another. For some people, their religious and ethnic affiliations are closely linked, and for others they might be seen as merely coincidental. For instance, Jewish people who practice Orthodox Judaism embrace not only their Jewish ethnicity but also the religious aspect, as opposed to other ethnic Jewish individuals who are not as religious.

According to Simon (2004), four concepts describe how we perceive and evaluate our self-aspects. One of those concepts is **valence**, or positive and negative feelings. Not all our attributes are held in the same esteem; rather, we might have positive valence (feelings) toward some and negative valence toward others. For example, Martha, the person described in Table 3.1, might feel good about her ability to cook and speak multiple languages but bad about being overweight.

Another way we view our self-aspects is **centrality**, which is the extent to which a self-aspect is crucial or central to how we describe ourselves. For instance, Martha might see her political affiliation or church membership as the most important aspect of her identity, rather than her ability to cook or her day-to-day schedule. Simon describes some aspects as **core** (central, most important) or **peripheral** (not as important, hardly noticeable). For instance, Martha's religious affiliation might be important enough to her that it comes out in the things she says to others (e.g., "God bless you") or in the cross pendant she wears around her neck. Her physical attributes, such as her curly hair, might not be something she thinks much about in terms of who she really is.

Currency, another perceptual concept, refers to how we see certain aspects fitting in time. In other words, some aspects that were important in the past are not so salient now; in the future, other aspects will take on more importance as we continue to define our identity. For instance, Martha might place a lot of personal emphasis on her personality traits while she is in college, but after graduation and upon entering the workforce, she might think more about how she spends her waking and evening hours (behavioral characteristics).

Finally, **actuality** is the distinction we make between characteristics we possess and those we aspire to have. Martha already holds some characteristics, such as being an late riser and knowing how to cook; however, there are others she wishes she had or would like to work on, such as being less shy and more outgoing. Martha might feel as though these desired aspects can help her more accurately convey her true personality.

SOCIAL IDENTITY THEORY

Social identity theory is sometimes called the social identity of intergroup relations, and it takes the perspective that identity is a function of one's social groups. Human beings are innately social beings, and they establish aspects of the self through social interactions with influential others. According to the theory, the social categories into which one falls help define that person and his or her characteristics (Hogg & Abrams, 1988; Tajfel & Turner, 1979). Moreover, those characteristics are based on the social groups.

Social identity theory
takes the perspective that identity is a function of one's social groups. Humans are innately social beings, and they establish aspects of the self through social interactions with influential others and self-categorization.

Society identity theory has two underlying mechanisms: categorization and self-enhancement. **Categorization** helps an individual decide which characteristics represent the group of which he or she is a member, and in turn reveals to that person the characteristics that can help define him or her on an individual basis. So, if a person wants to enhance her Hindu identity and heritage, she might seek out Hindu groups and notice how the members talk to one another, pray, and socialize. The specific characteristics attributed to this group might be what this person takes on to reaffirm her own Hindu identity. **Self-enhancement** assumes that people want to see the positive aspects of themselves in relation to their groups. Self-enhancement of these positive characteristics might encourage one to compare one's own group with out-group members who might not possess those

Categorization
helps an individual decide which characteristics represent the group of which he or she is a member.

Self-enhancement
assumes that people want to see the positive aspects of themselves in relation to their groups.

© AFP/Shutterstock.com

Women devotees applying sindhoor to each other's foreheads for a festival.

characteristics. The awareness of such positive attributes can be affirming to one's self-concept and self-esteem. For example, the Hindu woman in our example might perceive Hindu women to be very beautiful, even more beautiful than some other groups of women. This perception might feed into her self-esteem as a Hindu woman.

Self-categorization theory

an extension of social identity theory which takes a more psychological approach to capturing the self.

An extension of social identity theory is **self-categorization theory** (Turner, 1985, 1987, 1991; Turner, Hogg, Oakes, Reicher, & Wetherell, 1987), which takes a more psychological approach to capturing the self. Self-categorization implies that the self-concept is the cognitive element of the self that comprises several representations available to a person (Turner, 1987). Specifically, the self-concept contains some levels of abstraction, which include the over-arching level of self as human, the intermediary level of categorizations that help define an individual as a member of one or more groups (e.g., "woman," "middle class," "American"), and the individual level that differentiates a person from other members of a group (e.g., being the youngest of a group of professional, educated women). These levels of self-conception influence our choices of group membership and with whom we form relationships (Gudykunst & Kim, 1992).

We have explained that self-enhancement can make differences between the in-group and out-group more noticeable to the perceiver. Along the same lines, self-categorization can compel one to exaggerate the positive qualities of one's group membership and even amplify the negative qualities of out-group members. For example, if a woman who identifies as feminist believes that women are less aggressive than men are, she might hold an exaggerated view of men as generally aggressive. She might even go further to downplay the differences among women, particularly feminists, and overlook some instances in which women can also be aggressive. In general, categorizing people as in-group or out-group members reaffirms one's own identity (Hogg, Terry, & White, 1995).

COMMUNICATION THEORY OF IDENTITY

Communication theory of identity

illustrates how individuals make assumptions about each other based on their backgrounds, and helps explain how misunderstandings occur in the medical context. Identity is often communicated through *identity salience* and *identity intensity*

The **communication theory of identity** proposes, among other things, (1) that people maintain different, overlapping identities within one cultural group, and these may vary in salience and intensity, and (2) that there can be different ways of expressing or experiencing a single cultural identity (Hecht, 1993; Jung & Hecht, 2004). From the perspective of this theory, cultural groups are fluid and constantly changing because these groups are created through communication. It stands to reason, then, that people create their group memberships and their identities through communication.

One characteristic of communication theory of identity is **salience**, or the importance of one identity in relation to others. For example, a person might identify as Christian, Asian, and a resident of the West Coast but see the Asian self-aspect as the most important. Moreover, the importance of such identities varies from person to person (Collier & Thomas, 1988). This means that another person who is Christian, Asian, and from the West Coast might embrace his or her Christian self-aspect most.

Salience
the importance of one identity in relation to others.

Some people identify quite strongly with some self-aspects, but their **intensity**—the degree to which one expresses the identity—might vary. The expression of one's ethnic characteristics might not occur often or strongly, or might vary in how vocal one is in identity expression. For instance, Liesel is aware of her German heritage and has heard stories from her grandparents, but she does not talk about her German background to her friends, has no desire to learn German, and does not care if she never gets to sample a dish of schnitzel and spötzel.

Intensity
the degree to which one expresses their identity or the power, force, or concentration of bodily contact.

The communication theory of identity is based on three assumptions about how identities are communicated and created. First, people have multiple identities that overlap and even contradict one another. For instance, a person might identify strongly as a Democrat and, at the same time, hold views not typically associated with the Democratic party (e.g., being pro-life). The second assumption pertains to fluid identities. Because identities are created through communication, they can always change. As an example, you probably know a few people who started college with a particular political ideology; then, after interacting with others and discussing certain issues, their ideologies had changed by the time they graduated college. Third is the notion of emerging identities. Because we are constantly negotiating our identities through communication, just one conversation might compel someone to move between identities. For example, a heated discussion with your friend about immigration reform might compel you to pay more attention to your ancestral heritage and perhaps convey that aspect of your identity more in future interactions. A fourth important assumption is that there is a distinction between avowed and ascribed identities. An **avowed identity** is one you claim for yourself; an **ascribed identity** is one given or assigned by others. For example, the term *Hispanic* is often used to refer to people of Latin American origin. However, this term was originally used by the U.S. government for census purposes and has not been linked to any label used by members themselves, who might prefer *Latino/Latina*, *Chicano*, *Spanish*, or any other label. Therefore, the term *Hispanic* can be viewed as an ascribed identity (one assigned to an ethnic group). If, however, a Mexican national wants to use the term *Mexican American* as a self-label, then that term is an avowed identity because it was self-chosen.

Avowed identity
one you claim for yourself.

Ascribed identity
one given or assigned by others.

Identities can be ascribed to you, without your even knowing, based on appearances.

© arek_malang/butterstock.com

Personal frame

an identity construction based on how one views himself or herself.

Enactment frame

reflects the communicative behavior symbolic of one's identity.

Relational frame

represents the identity constructed through inter- actions with others.

Communal frame

reflected in identity shared with members of the group to which one belongs.

IN YOUR *life*

How, if it all, do you communi- cate your identity to others? Can you think of spe- cific examples from your life when others communicated their identities to you?

Identities have both content and relational dimensions, so two people who hold the same identity might have different feelings toward this identity. Also, identities manifest in one or more of four frames that overlap and emerge within the same interaction or situation (Hecht, 1993). The **personal frame** is an identity construction based on how one views himself or herself (e.g., funny, chronically late for events). The **enactment frame** reflects the communicative behavior symbolic of one's identity (e.g., assertive vs. introverted). The **relational frame** represents the identity constructed through interaction with others (e.g., sister, classmate), and the **communal frame** is reflected in identity shared with members of the group to which one belongs (e.g., Asian American; Hecht, 1993; Hecht, Collier, & Ribeau, 1993). We should not assume that these frames are constant, however. We sense and express our identities at many levels—personally, relationally, and in groups— but, ultimately, the communication theory of identity argues that identities are fluid and negotiated contextually through interaction.

There are practical implications to understanding how people construct their identities, especially in specific contexts, such as the doctor's office, where the patient and provider come from cultures that differentiate them professionally, on an educational level, and even in terms of power (with the doctor usually taking a more powerful role in the interaction). Scholl, Wilson, and Hughes (2011) applied the communication theory of identity to explore how patients and providers communicated with someone from another culture and the potential health- related consequences of their identity portrayals. Their findings suggested that both physicians and patients often tried to mask the importance of their ethnic identity in communication situations, frequently citing language as the only difference they experienced. More specifically, intensity of ethnic identity might have been diminished when patients' or providers' talk was used to mask their identities. At the same time, they still reported finding ways to portray their identities as important parts of who they were, either as patients or physicians.

Intercultural communication research on identity salience might reveal more detailed aspects of how we construct our identity. In their research examining the impact of ethnic identity on conflict styles, Ting-Toomey and colleagues' (2000) findings expanded the notion of identity salience. In particular, they discovered four dimensions of ethnic identity. **Ethnic belonging** refers to the level of comfort one has with one's ethnic group, as well as the sense of attachment. The **fringe** dimension describes the clarity (or confusion) one has about his or her ethnic identity. Another dimension is **intergroup interaction**, which reflects how much one is oriented toward communicating with members of other ethnic groups. Finally, **assimilation** refers to how much members of an ethnic group identify and blend in with the mainstream culture (e.g., U.S. culture).

Ting-Toomey et al. (2000) differentiate ethnic identity (self-described membership in a group characterized by a common language, nationality, or ethnic group) and **cultural identity** (identifying with the larger mainstream culture, such as the United States) among African Americans, Asian Americans, European Americans, and Latino(a) Americans. They found that African Americans were generally stronger in their ethnic identity than in their cultural identity; the opposite was true for European Americans. In terms of their findings on conflict styles, people who had a stronger cultural identity tended to compromise more and be more emotionally expressive than did those who had weak cultural identities. In addition, those with strong ethnic identities tended to use more integrating or collaborating approaches to conflict resolution.

Ethnic belonging
the level of comfort one has with one's ethnic group, as well as the sense of attachment.

Fringe
describes the clarity (or confusion) one has about his or her ethnic identity.

Intergroup interaction
reflects how much one is oriented toward communicating with members of other ethnic groups.

Assimilation
the process of adaptation that allows one to fit into or conform in some way to a group or culture.

Cultural identity
a dynamic production in and through intercultural contact and interaction with a cultural other.

IMPLICATIONS OF CULTURAL IDENTITY

ETHNIC IDENTITY

While uncertainty plays a prominent role in cultural encounters (Gudykunst & Hammer, 1987), another variable that affects the nature and progression of interpersonal interactions is **ethnic identity**, which is "the depth of commitment to certain shared patterns of communication, underlying beliefs, and philosophy

Ethnic identity
an individual's commitment to communication patterns, beliefs, and philosophies shared by a particular cultural group.

of life with a particular cultural group" (Ting-Toomey, 1981, p. 383). Commonly spoken language is another distinguishing characteristic of an ethnic group, perhaps the most important one in some instances. However, it is not enough simply to speak the language and "look like" those in one's avowed ethnic group. Because an ethnicity is something with which one can choose to identify, it is something into which one is usually socialized. As we have already explained, a great deal of one's identity is social (Gudykunst & Kim, 1992), and adoption of an ethnic identity is definitely a social experience. Use of certain symbolic behaviors, patterns of talk, and expressions of belief or ideas are a big part of fitting in or socializing into a group. Put another way, while race might be something you are born *with*, ethnicity is something you *become*. Once you start to act and talk like those in your ethnic group, you start to become more socially aware of who you are and your affiliation with such groups.

Individuals who highly identify with a particular ethnic group tend to utilize a communication style and belief system that strongly reflects that cultural group. To illustrate, Gudykunst and Hammer (1987) compared the communication styles of African American and white individuals, as well as their perceptions of communicated identities. They found that the ethnic heritages of African American people and white people had an influence on the use of question-asking, self-disclosure, nonverbal affinity seeking (i.e., seeking closeness), and behaviors conveying attraction or liking. This finding suggests that when people from two different cultures interact, they tend to communicate using styles that reflect their traditions.

It is understandable that preconceived notions and stereotypes come into play when people interact with diverse others, especially if they come from different cultural or ethnic backgrounds (Hughes & Baldwin, 2002a, 2002b). These cultural and ethnic stereotypes, which sometimes stem from faulty identity perceptions, can hinder cultural communication and the relationships that emerge from such encounters. Despite what we know about the harm and inaccuracies often associated with stereotypes, many people still seem to rely on them when making judgments of and engaging in facework with others. Such stereotypes are often grounded in perceptions of the other's identity, for better or for worse. Furthermore, such identity perceptions can shape the way we interact with the individuals we are stereotyping.

Even when stereotypes are not an issue, our ethnic identities can flavor the way we interact with others, especially when we perceive those others to be different. Collier (1988) examined the role of identity as it influences people's ability to communicate competently within and outside of their cultural groups. In her study, participants who identified as Mexican American were the least likely to use different sets of standards for communicating intraculturally and interculturally. This means that, according to the findings, Mexican Americans were the least likely to adapt their own interaction rules and communication expectations of others to different contexts. Instead, they basically expected the same kinds of behaviors whether they were talking with someone who was similar to or different from them. On the contrary, black Americans and white Americans tended to use different communication rules when interacting with diverse others. In other words, these individuals tended to have one set of communication expectations for those similar to them and a different set for out-group members.

Stereotypes can hinder communi-cation. *American Horror Story* actress Jamie Brewer often com-bats stereotypes related to ability and made history by being the first model with Down syndrome to walk the runway during New York Fashion Week (Stampler, 2015).

Adopting particular ethnic or cultural identities allows people to group themselves with people who face similar goals, beliefs, and challenges. Salience and intensity can help explain how and why people identify with certain groups (Hecht et al., 1993). When diverse individuals intermingle, they interact according to the prescribed ways people from their ethnic groups communicate. By acting according to these norms and adhering to the personal, enactment, relationship, and communal frames, interactants enact their identities with particular groups.

Adoption and expression of an ethnic identity is not always taken as authentic. In other words, the expressed identities of some ethnic minorities might be questioned by members of that culture. This is sometimes the case among American Indians. Pratt (1998) talks about instances in which the verbal and nonverbal cues of cultural members lead others to question whether they are truly members of that group. Pratt observes that identifying as American Indian can be troublesome for Indians who leave the reservation and make contact with members of other tribes, as well as with non-Indians; these individuals are referred to as contact Indians. When contact Indians interact with grassroots Indians (those who rarely leave the reservation and interact only with other tribal members), their experiences with getting an education or working outside the reservation make them more likely to be questioned about the authenticity of their Indian identity. It is often the case that, in an interaction between two American Indians, one interactant might not take the other's identity for granted and might even question his or her authenticity as an Indian.

When an American Indian's identity is called into question, **razzing** might be used to test the other person's legitimacy (i.e., his or her "Indianness"). According to Pratt (1998), razzing is similar to "sounding" or "playing the dozens," which is verbal dueling often done by African American youths in urban areas. Razzing assumes that both parties are skilled at humor and verbal sparring, that they have an audience, and that both parties know the rules involved. Razzing is a ritual with specific rules. For example, one can razz someone else about something done or said, but one should never razz someone about her or his family. Pratt describes one incident in which two Indians within the same university office were asked if they knew each other. One of them said, "I don't think we've met before, but I heard your name mentioned a lot. I guess you owe a lot of people money" (p. 70). As is typical of the Indian culture, "Indianness" is not something you simply are but something you eventually become (Pratt, 1998), and razzing is a ritualized form of humor that enables members to affirm and express their identities through interpersonal banter.

Judgment of the authenticity or realness of another person's identity might be tied to the tendency to impose labels or identities on others, which might not be accurate. As was mentioned with communication theory of identity, assigning a label to someone else is ascribing or assigning an identity to that person. Gudykunst and Kim (1992) warn that when we force labels on others, such labels might not be what those people wish to use to describe themselves. Not too long ago, the term *Oriental* was often used to refer to Asians or Asian Americans; however, this term is offensive to many individuals of Asian heritage. This term has not been traditionally avowed by members of this ethnic group, and it also goes back to the time of European explorers, who used it in reference to anything coming from the East or Asia, which was often viewed as "primitive" or "inferior" (Chan & Lee, 2009). Assigning a label to someone who does not accept that label is running the risk of offending.

AGE

Many cultural identities and self-aspects are more stable and not likely to change much throughout one's life (e.g., nationality, ethnicity, gender). Also, the boundaries between cultural groups are not very malleable, leaving little possibility for crossover (unless for transgendered individuals, for example). On the other hand, age group is a cultural category that is very fluid; all of us will pass through

ETHICAL CONNECTION

Brittany is a college graduate who just recently began her first job working as a pharmaceutical sales representative for a major corporation. After receiving splendid reviews through her orientation and training, Brittany began giving her own presentations to different hospital administrations and medical doctors. After several lackluster sales presentations, Brittany was approached by her superiors, who informed her that her personal appearance was offending potential customers; she was told either to change her hairstyle or to leave the company. Brittany, whose family comes from a North African background, has always worn a traditional hairstyle not commonly seen in the United States. After spending several days contemplating a decision, Brittany decided to leave the company and search for another job.

Questions to consider:

1. Were Brittany's superiors justified in demanding that she change her hairstyle? Could they have considered any other alternatives?
2. Do you agree with Brittany's decision to leave the company? How would you react in her position?
3. How does this scenario exemplify the conflicts that can arise between maintaining self-identity and still meeting a particular culture's or society's expectations?
4. Is it ever possible to maintain a completely honest self-identity when living or interacting within a different culture?

several age categories before we die. For instance, being 20-something has different implications than does being middle-aged or in later life.

Age identity is often driven by discussion of intergenerational differences, such as comparing baby boomers with Generation Xers or Millennials. Common stereotypes of age groups, particularly of older adults, also feed into communication with such individuals (Hummert & Ryan, 2001). Such instances involve talking to older adults in a patronizing tone or assuming that they are deaf or mentally incoherent.

Communication predicament of aging model

explains how age identity and perceptions of older adults can lead to communicated stereotypes.

The **communication predicament of aging model** (Ryan, Giles, Bartolucci, & Henwood, 1986) can help explain how age identity can lead to communicated stereotypes. The model proposes that perceived characteristics of an older adult can trigger stereotypes, even misconceptions, which lead to the kind of speech that might come across as patronizing or belittling (Hummert & Nussbaum, 2001; Hummert & Ryan, 2001). The harmful implications come in when an older adult avoids future interactions because of the desire to avoid further patronizing speech. This also can lead to the internalization of such stereotypes as being feeble-minded or childlike. In essence, receiving patronizing speech and avoiding future interactions as a result can feed into negative impressions of one's age-related identity.

People can also manage their age identity when engaged in interpersonal communication. One example might be the disclosure of one's exact age, which Coupland, Coupland, and Giles (1989) call disclosure of chronological age. This can serve a couple of functions. First, it fulfills what Coupland and colleagues call a disjunctive function, meaning that it might allow a person to present a physical or health status in contrast to that person's actual age. You might know someone who looks incredibly young for his or her age, and that person might even disclose his or

Ageism toward the elderly can perpetuate age-related stereotypes.

© Diego Cervo/Shutterstock.com

her actual age to affirm this youthful appearance. Second, disclosure of chronological age serves an accounting function, providing an excuse or explanation for a negative state. Perhaps you have taken walks with a grandparent and were told, "Hey, slow down, youngster. I'm not as young as I used to be." Although both these functions imply a decline in ability or function due to advanced age, they also both serve as a presentation mechanism, enabling older adults to assert that they are doing quite well despite their chronological age.

Our perceptions and stereotypes about age might also be influenced by media images. Robinson, Skill, and Turner (2004) note a lack of media representation of older people, which might contribute to the decreased value often attributed to this group. When individuals from this group are portrayed, it is often in a negative light, thus perpetuating stereotypes about older adults.

GENDER AND SEX

The terms *gender* and *sex* are often used interchangeably, both in normal conversation and even in academic writing. For purposes of clarification, we refer to **sex** as possessing the biological characteristics that make one male or female, or having the biological male or female sex organs. **Gender**, on the other hand, is a more fluid identification, implying not biological but socialized behaviors. Moreover, gender encompasses psychological, social, and cultural qualities that are generally associated with a particular sex (Canary, Emmers-Sommer, & Faulkner, 1997). In this sense, gender refers to being masculine, feminine, androgynous (exhibiting neither feminine nor masculine characteristics), or any other variation of these identities. For many people, gender is the most significant aspect that shapes who we are, or who we think we are (McCornack, 2013).

Unlike biological sex, which is something we are born with, gender is learned. Our sense of being female or male, or feminine or masculine, likely has been shaped from a very young age. For example, if you are a woman, as a child you might have been told to "act like a lady." Some boys have been warned to keep some of their emotions hidden and told that "boys don't cry." These notions of what it means to be a boy or a girl, a woman or a man, have been taught to most of us. The practice of teaching girls to be sensitive to their emotions and the feelings of others and nurturing and compassionate is well documented. Boys are discouraged from being so open with their feelings and are pushed to be more assertive and competitive (Lippa, 2002; Tannen, 1990). As a result of being taught how to be a girl or boy, each of us has been set on a long road of gender socialization, which has had a significant influence on our self-concept and how we continue to develop and express it to the world. For instance, for some men, taking on seemingly masculine characteristics in nonverbal cues and speech might enable them to view themselves more as men or to "perform" being a man in social life. The same can be said for many women. However, being a woman or man does not require one to be exclusively feminine or masculine, and not all men and women adopt identical masculine and feminine identities, respectively. In reality, many women and men "appreciate and embrace both feminine and masculine characteristics in their self-concepts" (McCornack, 2013, p. 46).

Another construct often linked with gender and sex is **sexual orientation**, which is a romantic or sexual attraction to others, whether of the same sex (homosexual), opposite sex (heterosexual), or both sexes (bisexual) (McCornack, 2013). Identifying as gay, lesbian, or bisexual can open one up to discrimination and prejudice, despite relatively recent advancements in civil rights for sexual minorities. The act of disclosing one's sexual orientation, or "coming out of the closet," can be a

Sex
biological; refers to the chromosomal combinations that produce males, females, and the other possible, but rarer, sexes.

Gender
a range of social behaviors that reflect biological, mental, and behavioral characteristics used to portray oneself as masculine, feminine, or any combination of the two. When individuals refer to the behaviors associated with a particular sex (e.g., male, female), they are referring to gender.

Sexual orientation
a romantic or sexual attraction to others.

defining moment for a person, and it usually happens not just once but several times throughout one's life as one comes out to family, various friends, and new acquaintances.

IN YOUR
life

What experiences, if any, have you had communicating with others about sexual orientation in your life?

Coming out of the closet can be a symbolic way for a person to align one's private self with one's public self or identity. However, some individuals engage in physical relationships in their private lives but do not publicly adopt the identity that would typically be associated with that private self. In some cases, this is out of fear of stigma, hate, or discrimination. In other cases, individuals draw a clear distinction between their private physical relationships and their expressed public identity. For instance, Boellstorff (2011) explores the history of "men who have sex with men but do not identify as gay" (p. 287). This particular type of self-concept might reflect a difference between a self-avowed straight identity and a behavioral pattern that some might not find consistent with a straight identity. However, others might view sexual activity as just one aspect of one's identity, thus supporting the notion that one's gay, straight, or other identity is a multifaceted identity that includes a variety of thoughts, choices, and cognitions that make up one's sexual preference.

NEGOTIATING BETWEEN IDENTITIES

What happens when a person feels compelled or pressured to manage two or more personal identities? How does one accomplish this in a society where one has to straddle the fence between two cultural identities? This situation is faced by many people who sojourn (defined further in the next chapter) or emigrate from one country to another. Upon arrival in the new culture, the person must balance the desire to fit into the mainstream culture with the desire to maintain certain aspects of the culture of origin. Hegde (1998) asserts that migrating individuals already see themselves as "other" just by being in a foreign land or culture, and they tend to cling to certain symbols and artifacts from their old culture to maintain a nostalgic connection with their past. Such symbolic behaviors might include keeping religious artifacts in the house, wearing some articles of traditional dress, or speaking their own language when around family or others of their ethnic group.

Hegde (1998) writes about the dilemma of Asian Indian women as they struggle to deal with the contradictions between their individual identity and the one they are expected to adopt in the United States. The choice of Asian Indian women to maintain and practice traditional female roles is a significant way members retain a connection to their heritage. In their traditional cultures, Asian Indian women follow their husbands to the new country; in fact, they usually have no say in the decision to emigrate. At the same time, many of these women face the challenge and pressure to conform to expectations for women in the United States, which include more independence for women, enacting more fluid gender roles, and even becoming more "Americanized." This clash makes many Asian Indian women feel conflicted between these two worlds: Dress more like the mainstream, but don't look too American or you won't attract a husband. Maintain strong expressions of the Hindu religion and culture, but if you do you might face racist comments and isolation. Hegde describes this as a "trapeze act replete with precarious swinging from the demands of one world to another" (p. 35).

This need to straddle the line between two identities is likely to be more salient to an individual who identifies as an ethnic minority in relation to the larger mainstream or host culture. It can be more pronounced when one is trying to claim one's culture after being deprived of it for years. Shaver (1998) describes a Cherokee family who, over the years, experienced a loss of their language, heritage, traditions, and identity to assimilate into U.S. culture. Family members' communication patterns revealed how they attempted to adapt to European American cultural demands, and how this created a great deal of internal conflict as they attempted to regain aspects of their lost culture years later.

WHAT YOU'VE LEARNED

In this chapter, you learned about the nature of identity and the ways in which your identity functions in your life. You then learned about face theory and its relation to identity and culture. Next, you learned about the various theories—self-aspects model of identity, social identity theory, and communication theory of identity—that explain the nature, purpose, and influences of identity. Finally, you overviewed the implications of cultural identity in relation to ethnicity, age, and gender along with learning about the struggle that comes with negotiating between multiple identities. As you reflect on what you've learned in this chapter, think about your own various identities and how the culture of those identities impacts your communication.

1. _____ is the representation of how you view yourself and how others might see you.

2. Self-representation of one's identity comprises three levels: the _____, the _____, and the _____.

3. This refers to the image of self that we project to others: _____.

4. _____ includes the communicative actions we take to project our face, maintain the face of self and others, or even threaten another person's face.

5. _____ is one you claim for yourself; an _____ is one given or assigned by others.

6. What are all of the different facets included in the self-aspects model of identity?

7. Discuss the difference between *ethnic belonging* and *assimilation*.

8. What are some of the harmful implications with regard to older adults as outlined by the communication predicament of aging model?

9. Discuss the difference between *sex* and *gender*.

10. Discuss some of the ways people negotiate between identities.

Review answers are found on the accompanying website.

REFLECT

1. List or describe some of the cultural groups with which you identify.
2. Discuss some of the face characteristics you project, and describe the facework strategies you use to project that face.
3. Nathan self-identifies as a man, though his biological sex at birth was female. Growing up, he was referred to by his family and peers as being female. Using the vocabulary from the text, discuss which two identity characteristics are at odds with one another.
4. Juanita comes from a Mexican family, though she was born in the United States. She speaks English as her primary language, and she speaks limited Spanish. Her limited Spanish causes a rift between her and her parents because they would like her to embrace her Mexican heritage by speaking Spanish more fluently. Discuss some of the other challenges Juanita might face when balancing ethnic belonging and assimilation.
5. Discuss some of the ways you can avoid some of the harmful implications as outlined by the communication predicament of aging model.

KEY TERMS

identity, 61
self, 61
schema, 61
face, 65
facework, 65
self-aspects model of identity, 67
valence, 68
centrality, 68
core, 68
peripheral, 68
currency, 68
actuality, 68
social identity theory, 69
categorization, 69
self-enhancement, 69
self-categorization theory, 70
communication theory of identity, 70
salience, 71
intensity, 71

avowed identity, 71
ascribed identity, 71
personal frame, 72
enactment frame, 72
relational frame, 72
communal frame, 72
ethnic belonging, 73
fringe, 73
intergroup interaction, 73
assimilation, 73
cultural identity, 73
ethnic identity, 73
razzing, 76
communication predicament of aging model, 77
sex, 79
gender, 79
sexual orientation, 79

CHAPTER FOUR

Sojourning, Assimilating, and Acculturating

CHAPTER OUTLINE

WHAT YOU WILL LEARN

After studying this chapter, you should be able to

1. describe the concept of sojourning, the reasons for sojourning, and its challenges and rewards;
2. define the process of assimilation and describe the assimilation process experienced by new members;
3. understand the process of acculturation and describe its relationship with cross-cultural adaptation;
4. describe the various models and theories that explain cultural adaptation; and
5. identify the factors that influence one's willingness and ability to acculturate.

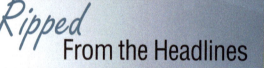
From the Headlines

© Lucky Business/Shutterstock.com

Today's classrooms are becoming increasingly multicultural, and an understanding of different cultural dynamics is important for adequate student learning to occur. For example, more and more Chinese students are pursuing education in Anglophone (English-speaking) countries, and they often practice various assimilation strategies to adapt to a new culture. Some of these students choose to be called by an English name in order to make their interactions with native English speakers easier (Diao, 2014).

The process of choosing a name for a child often carries cultural significance; parents may choose a particular name for various reasons like honoring someone important to the family or society, the name may have meaning that embodies qualities they want the child to have, or the way the name sounds (Kiang, 2004). Given the importance of names within a culture, the decision to use a new name in a new country can be a big step for some students. However, their decision to change their name could be seen as justified due to what some academic research has found. Researchers have found that people who have names that are difficult to pronounce are perceived less favorably than those with easy-to-pronounce names (Laham, Koval, & Alter, 2011).

As you move forward in this chapter, reflect on your own cultural norms, and think about how they would translate in another culture. Imagine being in a context where people could not pronounce your name. Would you choose to adopt a new one? If you have had the opportunity to travel abroad, think about the blunders you might have made and try to remember if you did any kind of research into the country's culture before visiting. In both your social and professional life, you will inevitably be thrust into communication situations that require you to practice some type of cultural sensitivity and etiquette. After reading this chapter, you should have the tools to be a more effective intercultural communicator and overall traveler.

Perhaps you have had the benefit of traveling to a foreign country, whether for vacation, business, missionary work, or study abroad. Many people look forward to the idea of going to another country to see someplace new, try the local cuisine, hear and dance to the music, meet interesting people, and see some beautiful sights. You might even be excited about an upcoming trip while reading this chapter.

Along with the excitement of traveling abroad are the occasional moments of uncertainty, anxiety, and frustration. Getting used to the local culture and language can be difficult at times, even in other English-speaking countries. These difficulties might take place during seemingly mundane situations—getting directions to the bus station from someone who does not speak English, deciding how or what to order at a restaurant, or following different traffic laws while driving the rental car. Whether you are in a foreign land for 2 weeks or 2 years, it is not always easy to make adjustments as you try to navigate your surroundings and learn to

© potowizard/Shutterstock.com

Traveling can be exciting and scary. What are some challenges you think you might face while traveling?

communicate with and relate to the locals. The rewards and challenges of traveling abroad—or sojourning—will be discussed in this chapter, as well as the ways people adapt to their new environments, which we refer to here as acculturation.

This chapter also explores virtually any situation where we might try to fit in and adapt to a group or culture to which we want or expect to belong. We refer to this process as assimilation. This does not necessarily occur only outside of the United States; rather, many cultural groups in our country feel like outsiders and perceive many pressures to act in certain ways to help them fit in. Furthermore, some cultural groups have endured much prejudice, hatred, and discrimination in the process of assimilation. We will explore assimilation in a variety of contexts, as well as recognizing the influences on one's ability to adapt culturally.

SOJOURNING

There is a chance that once you graduate from college or university, you will be faced with moving to a new region, country, or culture that is foreign to you. The move from one's own culture to a new one is referred to as **sojourning**, and it can be temporary or permanent. Regardless of the reason for sojourning or the length of time you spend in another location, your experience abroad will inevitably change you. In addition, the mere process of sojourning and subsequently adapting will be transformative in that you will likely learn to be more open-minded and come away with a wealth of insights and experiences.

Sojourning
the move from one's own culture to a new one.

People sojourn for a variety of reasons. Some are taking on a new job or making a career move, which often requires a major geographic change. Other sojourners move to another state or country to obtain an education or get a chance at a better quality of life. Still others sojourn for a variety of personal and social reasons, such as going on vacation or visiting families or friends. Regardless of the reason, any person who sojourns has to engage in some cultural adaptation, even if minimal. For instance, Gudykunst and Kim (1992) point out that international students' adaptation can be minimal if they plan to head back to their home countries upon completion of their educational goals. Nevertheless, moving to an unfamiliar and new environment requires some mindful adjustments.

For sojourners who are inexperienced or new to a setting, almost anything in the new culture—the food, people, city layouts, language, or even smells—can be viewed as an obstacle or difficulty. A new language, for example, can constitute an impediment one must navigate and figure out (Anderson, 1994). However, obstacles are not attributed just to the environment. The sojourner likely has assumptions and predispositions that can make adjustments easier or more difficult. Later on, we will discuss some of these assumptions, as they can serve as influences on one's ability to adapt.

As we said earlier, sojourning can have its rewards and challenges, particularly in the ups and downs many people experience. Lysgaard (1955) uses a U-shaped model to describe these ups and downs. According to this viewpoint, sojourners experience a "high" at first when they encounter the new culture. They are excited about being someplace new, curious about the music and food, and enjoying their discoveries. What follows, according to Lysgaard, is a "bottoming out" as individuals are confronted with the difficulties of not knowing how to cope with an unfamiliar situation, such as living in a village where no one speaks English or trying to locate a restroom. Eventually, sojourners move back up the U-shape, so to speak, becoming more acclimated to their surroundings as they have adapted more.

The U-shape or U-curve has been conceptualized as having four stages (Oberg, 1960): honeymoon, crisis, recovery, and adjustment. Consider this hypothetical experience of traveling to a foreign country. You get off the plane and settle into your hotel room. After a quick nap and some relaxation time, you feel excited and want to venture out. You head to the open-air market near the hotel. You delight in the live band playing local music, and you think the sandwich you purchased from the food cart on the corner is absolutely delicious. This could be viewed as the

IN YOUR *life*

Have you ever sojourned abroad? Reflect on your experience, both in how you enjoyed the trip and any instances where you had a misunderstanding or social blunder. How might those instances have been avoided?

© jonesyinc/Shutterstock.com

Navigating a new city where a different language is spoken can be a challenge for sojourners.

honeymoon, or the time of enjoyment or euphoria. A few days into your stay, you go down to speak to the concierge in the hotel lobby to get directions to a museum. Although she speaks your language relatively well, you seem to have a difficult time understanding her directions; you get frustrated and decide to give up. You thank her curtly and head out the front door to find your own way to the museum. You get lost and have trouble finding someone who speaks your language and can help you with directions. You never get to the museum and make your way back to the hotel feeling grumpy. At this stage, you experience a type of crisis, during which you feel hostility toward the environment and even harbor some stereotypes (e.g., "These people can't even give simple directions. What idiots!"). After a few more days of navigating your way around and making sincere attempts at speaking the language, you realize that it helps to write things down as you talk to the locals. This new idea represents a form of recovery, which is a flexible response to the environment that entails ways of working with the culture to embrace some of its aspects. When you try this approach, you unexpectedly strike up a conversation with a local who speaks your language. You have a great time talking to this person and make plans to meet later for dinner. Overall, despite your initial excitement and subsequent frustration, you find a way to adapt to your unfamiliar setting, have a great trip, and eventually return home with wonderful memories.

Not all adjustment periods resemble a U-shaped pattern; rather, many are marked by a series of up-and-down progressions. Gullahorn and Gullahorn (1963) use a W-curve to explain this phenomenon. As an extension of the U-curve, the W-shaped hypothesis first describes a honeymoon stage similar to that in the U-model, one that is marked by hope, enthusiasm, and the promise of new acquaintances and experiences, such as enrolling as a brand-new student at a university (Hoffenburger, Mosier, & Stokes, 1999). Eventually, the hopeful feelings give way to the first downturn, or culture shock (discussed in more detail later in this chapter), which is filled with self-doubt, discomfort, and confusion. This might happen to new students who have trouble finding their classrooms or who are not used to the customs of the student body. What follows is an initial adjustment period, during which the newcomer starts to adapt and obtains increased awareness of the new environment. For example, students adjusting to a new university might start to feel comfortable socializing with other students or be surprised at how much they enjoy their first on-campus social event. Eventually, though, the newcomer descends into another downturn. This time, it feel less like culture shock and more like mental isolation, in which the person recoils and wants to withdraw from others and the environment. For new students, this might occur after not doing well on midterm exams and can fuel additional feelings of self-doubt and search for meaning. Subsequently, this period gives way to a renewed feeling of integration and acceptance, during which the newcomer learns to adapt more effectively and even gains a renewed sense of belonging in the new environment.

The downturns reflected in the U-curve or W-curve models are often referred to as **culture shock** (Oberg, 1960), which describes the feeling of disorientation one experiences when entering a new culture. Culture shock can be quite distressing, even leading to physical symptoms, which is why this phenomenon was viewed as a medical condition in the 1950s (Anderson, 1994). Today, we typically talk about culture shock as an emotional, cognitive, and even psychological response to the unfamiliar or unpredictable. Culture shock can be experienced as a sense of loss or feeling of displacement, as well as a perceived rejection from members of the mainstream culture. To overcome culture shock, one has to learn the constraints of the new location and know what it means to respond appropriately to certain events. You might say that the key is simply to make the unfamiliar familiar. Moreover, Anderson (1994) argues that overcoming culture shock and adapting involves accepting what is unfamiliar, as well as losing familiar people and ways of doing things. In other words, it requires a combination of deculturation and adaptation to the new culture.

Culture shock
a state of confusion, anxiety, stress, or loss felt when one encounters a culture that has little in common with one's own.

Culture shock can also be described as a crisis in identity or personality (Lewis & Jungman, 1986; Stillar, 2007), implying that when one is in an unfamiliar place, one's own self and individual role in that new place can be called into question or must be renegotiated. For example, this might happen when gays or lesbians who enjoy relative freedom in their own cultures must be more secretive about their sexual identities in more repressive countries, out of fear of stigma or physical violence. As another example, a person of European descent might feel like a member of the majority in some parts of the United States but feel like a minority in Peru or another such country where the actual majority of citizens are people of color.

Malaysian devotee celebrating Thaipusam. Ceremonies vary greatly among cultures, and some may be shocking for outsiders to view.

© Amir Ridhwan/Shutterstock.com

Although most of us are somewhat familiar with the term, **culture shock** might not be an accurate way to describe all the difficulties sojourners face. Anderson (1994) argues that the "shock" might simply be frustration or irritation with the way things seem to be. In response, some frustrated persons resist adapting, while others eventually make a slow transition. Anderson explains, "It has long been known that some people never adapt; some slide inexorably into chronic alienation ...; others adapt in a slow and steady linear pattern, without discontinuities" (p. 297). The experience of and response to culture shock is not the same in degree or kind for everyone.

Although frustrating and even scary at times, sojourning is something one should not avoid, despite the challenges associated with it. Adler (1987) argues that the adaptation necessitated by sojourning can be an opportunity for personal growth. Seeing other places and learning what it is like to live in different settings can be rewarding and educational, as well as help you appreciate your own culture back home. The ability to adapt to new surroundings makes the difference between a rewarding and frustrating experience for the sojourner.

ASSIMILATING

Assimilation

the process of adaptation that allows one to fit into or conform in some way to a group or culture.

Socialization

how members learn the values, norms, and behaviors needed to fulfill their roles within a group or organization. Socialization can help one assimilate into a group.

Adapting to a new culture does not happen only when entering another country or region. We find ourselves adapting whenever we enter a situation as a new member. This type of adaptation is known as **assimilation**, which is the process of adaptation that allows one to fit into or conform in some way to a group or culture. Unlike sojourning and some instances of acculturation, assimilation does not necessarily require a geographical change (Gudykunst & Kim, 1992). In fact, many of us find ourselves engaging in assimilation when we take on a new job, join a new club or organization, or get married. To some individuals, adapting to a new technological or information system at work requires some assimilation.

© pixelheadphoto digitalskillet/Shutterstock.com

Assimilation involves learning as well as sense making (Eisenberg, Goodall, & Trethewey, 2010). The newcomer wants to know the written and unwritten rules of conduct and how not to break them. Assimilating is also about learning what other group members expect of the newcomer and what it will take to get their approval or acceptance. Assimilation implies that new members go through a socialization process to gain acceptance and full membership. During **socialization**, new members learn the values, norms, and behaviors needed to fulfill their roles within a group or organization, as well as to meet the expectations placed on them by other members and those in superordinate positions. Socialization is not the same as assimilation but is a related construct, such that socialization as a process can help one assimilate into a group (Cheney, Christensen, Zorn, & Ganesh, 2011) and become a successful and contributing member (Jablin, 1982).

Assimilation does not occur only in a cultural sense; even marriage is assimilation into a new family.

Keep in mind that not all socialized members remain with the group or even acquire full membership status. What can be difficult about fitting in is that groups and cultures do not remain static. Their expected behaviors, norms, and values change over time. For instance, a philanthropic group that starts out small might adopt an informal structure during meetings. As that group grows in size, however, members might decide to adopt parliamentary procedure during meetings and expect all members to adhere to it strictly. To accommodate the new rules and expectations, current members might find themselves going through socialization repeatedly to keep fitting in with an ever-changing group.

Some of the research on socialization identifies phases members might go through when becoming part of the group. Jablin (1982, 1987) writes about one such pattern, which includes the stages of anticipatory socialization, encounter, and metamorphosis. First, during **anticipatory socialization**, a newcomer will form expectations of what it is like to be a member of the group, as well as assumptions about how members of that group behave and communicate. For example, you might move to a different country to work for a company that you assume has loose expectations about being on time for meetings or events. You also assume that those expectations are different from yours, which reflect a strict adherence to schedules. The second stage is **encounter,** or organizational encounter, which involves learning more about the group and becoming more acquainted with the written rules and unwritten norms. For example, as a new member of the company, you could observe how other members behave with regard to being on time. When there is a meeting scheduled for 8:00, do other members generally show up before 8:00 or trickle in about 15 minutes after? During the encounter stage, one could also question other members about appropriate behaviors or break rules and see how others respond. The third stage is **metamorphosis**, which occurs when new members alter their behaviors and even come to accept such changes, especially if it means falling in line with the values and expectations of the group. For example, if you are used to showing up early for meetings, you might realize that other members do not hold to this rule and so allow yourself some flexibility when arriving to meetings in the future. In this three-phase process, the new member starts to feel like and become a regular member. The transitioning member can experience this when others ask her or him for opinions, allow that person to expand her or his role, and involve that person in decision making.

Presenting assimilation and socialization as linear processes might be limiting. Portraying assimilation as going through such distinct steps might not accurately reflect everyone's experiences. For instance, even if someone reaches the metamorphosis stage, he or she might violate an important rule, which might diminish that person's status as a "true" member and thus make that person feel excluded from or irrelevant to the group (Jablin, 1987). After such a transgression,

Anticipatory socialization
forming expectations of what it is like to be a member of the group.

Encounter
learning more about the group and becoming more acquainted with the written rules and unwritten norms.

Metamorphosis
new members alter their behaviors and even come to accept such changes.

© Tongake Ingkulanonda/Shutterstock.com

Socialization can result in engaging in new behavior, such as eating new foods you wouldn't normally eat.

IN YOUR *life*

Think about times you have experienced assimilation in your life. Was your resocialization painless or difficult? Think about the stages of transition and their effect on your understanding of social reality.

that person might lose some status with the rest of the group and have to work to regain his or her previous standing. In addition, to talk about assimilation as a person's morphing of self into another group or culture could undermine that person's original identity and culture, perpetuating the idea that aspects of her or his original identity should not be retained or even considered important.

In contrast to a linear view, we can also understand assimilation in terms of types or dimensions. In their effort to construct a measure of organizational assimilation, Myers and Oetzel (2003) present different dimensions of assimilation that might occur. The survey they tested in their study revealed that assimilation might be facilitated through familiarity with leaders and supervisors, organizational acculturation (i.e., how well members are acculturated), recognition for completion of tasks or accomplishments, involvement with the group, competency regarding one's tasks or roles, and the extent to which one has a say in one's own group role. Myers and Oetzel (2003) argue that understanding how new members navigate through these dimensions can help groups improve how they help new members assimilate. Organizations can help facilitate successful assimilation by holding orientations and training to familiarize newcomers with policies, resources, and behavioral expectations. Despite formal orientations, new members will often feel awkward and make mistakes until they reach a certain level of familiarity with the group (Eisenberg et al., 2010). Increasing familiarity implies making better sense of how things work in the organization, which includes understanding the unwritten rules (e.g., "Never let the boss see you go to lunch before noon") and what it takes to get along with other members (e.g., "Never pass up an invitation to happy hour; otherwise, you'll look like a snob").

As a newcomer to a group, organization, or culture, there are things you can do to make your transition easier (Eisenberg et al., 2010). Perhaps the easiest thing to do is just watch. Observe how other people interact with one another, and pay close attention to the kinds of behaviors that get praised or criticized. Second, certain people have valuable information about the culture, such as supervisors and leaders, long-time members, and outsiders (e.g., customers, vendors) who deal with the group on a regular basis. In the case of a workplace or professional organization, it is also a good idea to befriend people who provide administrative assistance or support for those in leadership positions. Third, do not be afraid to ask questions, even if they seem obvious or simple. For example, asking to whom you report to file a certain document can help you avoid a critical error or keep you from being passed over for other opportunities.

New members often engage in indirect or covert tactics to learn more about their cultures (Eisenberg et al., 2010). While some of these tactics might bring about negative consequences, they can help you make more sense of your group and thus facilitate assimilation. For instance, eavesdropping on or monitoring other conversations can be informative. Hearing other members' observations, complaints, or comments can reveal much about the group's culture and work climate. Additionally, one can test certain limits, such as wearing attire that is more casual and seeing how others respond. However, this tactic might backfire if violating a dress code brings about negative repercussions, such as not being taken seriously as an employee.

ACCULTURATING

A more focused way to look at assimilation is to acknowledge when it occurs across cultures. Fitting in with a new environment becomes even more of a challenge when that environment is in a different country, or even just a different region of the country. In such cases, acculturation becomes an inevitable and necessary process.

Acculturation is the progression through which individuals adapt their own cultural identities, norms, and patterns to fit into another culture, which is often the dominant or mainstream culture of a region or country (Gudykunst & Kim, 1992; Mainous, Diaz, & Geesey, 2008). We also point out that acculturation might happen when one moves to a different region of the same country or from a rural area to a large metropolitan one, although the transition might not be as challenging or difficult as international migration. The process of acculturation compels us to

Acculturation
the progression through which individuals adapt their own cultural identities and norms to fit into another culture, which is often the dominant or mainstream culture of a region or country.

appreciate both enculturation and deculturation. **Enculturation** refers to how we learn our own culture as we grow up, while **deculturation** occurs when we unlearn certain aspects of our culture to fit into a new one. We should not assume that the acculturating person completely gives up her or his culture during this process. Rather, a blending of the person's old and new cultures typically occurs, especially when sojourning individuals can find others from their home culture and develop close ties with them while living in the new culture.

Migration from one country to another requires a person to undergo major cultural changes, no matter how long one expects to reside in the foreign culture. The transition might be temporary or permanent, voluntary or involuntary. Involuntary migration can be especially difficult if it involves fleeing one's own country or region because of a natural disaster, political unrest, or economic difficulty. One can do very little to prepare for the distress that might result. Notwithstanding the emotional toll that natural and political disasters can take, the mere process of acculturating or adapting to the current culture can be difficult for most migrants. Part of the difficulty might result from the negative reactions of locals who experience the influx of migrant individuals. For instance, Hopkins (2012) observed that communities who took in evacuees from Hurricane Katrina appeared to be less supportive of efforts to help poor and African American individuals who had to relocate because of the storm. Hopkins hypothesized that drastic changes in the demographic makeup of the community, which resulted from the migration, brought about this effect.

How does one come to feel acculturated into the host or mainstream culture? One indicator is language competency (Cuellar, Harris, & Jasso, 1980; Mendoza, 1989; Padilla, 1980), which can be enhanced through frequent communication with members of the host culture. Young Kim (1979, 1994), who has researched and written extensively on acculturation, claims that a great deal of interpersonal communication with host members, as well as increased use of the mass media, helps the process. The reason these various forms of communication are helpful is that they enable newcomers to read, hear, and speak the language through which interpersonal and mediated messages are conveyed (Marin, Sabogal, Marin, Otero-Sabogal, & Paerez-Stable, 1987). Acquiring competency in the local language is crucial in gaining access to the host culture and its benefits, such as greater access to health care, work opportunities, and expanded social networks. The more one becomes acculturated, the more one will speak the host language in public, social, and professional settings (Kimbro, 2009).

CROSS-CULTURAL ADAPTATION

Adaptation requires paying attention to the way one communicates and understanding how one's communication patterns need to change or evolve to fit the new environment. This is why we devote a great deal of this section to cross-cultural adaptation. First, we need to be clear about what we mean by adaptation, as well as distinguish it from adjustment. **Adjustment** is a short-term state of reducing an uncertainty to meet a more immediate need, whereas **adaptation** is more of a long-term response or process that prompts someone to evolve to fit into an environment.

Adjustment
a short-term state of reducing an uncertainty to meet a more immediate need.

Adaptation
a long-term response or process that prompts someone to evolve to fit into an environment.

Keep in mind that adaptation does not always have to fall on the sojourner. Part of being culturally sensitive and competent means that members of the host culture need to learn to understand the communication of other cultures, be patient with those who are foreign to their culture, and even adapt their own behaviors to be more accommodating to those who visit or immigrate permanently. However, not all host cultures are patient, tolerant, or compassionate toward visitors, so it is probably in a sojourner's best interest to do what he or she can to adapt his or her own communication.

When moving from one's home culture into another one, the individual faces a new process of acculturation (Gudykunst & Kim, 1992). This means that the person becomes familiar with a new set of language patterns, a new system of nonverbal cues, a new process for engaging in symbolic behavior and interpreting the symbolic behavior of others, and different patterns of relating to others at social gatherings. To some extent, one has to adopt a sense of identification with that new culture and find significant or important others from whom one can learn these new patterns. Acculturation is indeed a learning process that requires good communication skills to adapt, detect the nuances of social interaction, and recover from verbal and nonverbal mistakes (Furnham & Bochner, 1986). Learning how to use one's communication skills can also mean coping with the vacillation between learning and recovery. As we

© lev radin/Shutterstock.com

First lady Melania Trump and former first lady Michelle Obama both drew criticism from the media for not wearing head coverings when visiting Saudi Arabia. Do you think they should have worn head coverings, or is it the responsibility of the host country to adjust to cultural differences?

discussed with the U-shaped and W-shaped models, an acculturating person can fluctuate back and forth between gaining a new sense of enlightenment about the culture and feeling frustrated and isolated because of the inability to understand or be understood.

Inherent in cross-cultural adaptation are occasional moments of tension and attempts to reduce it. Learning how to fit into a new culture can make one feel nervous or tense, and it is natural to want to reduce that tension to achieve balance or equilibrium (Anderson, 1994; Gudykunst & Hammer, 1988). More specifically, people—or organisms—are systems that typically operate in steady, even states until something happens to disrupt that arrangement (Kim, 2002). For example, you might come to an event over- or underdressed, say something offensive without intending to, or experience a breakdown when you can't seem to understand what someone else is saying. Cross-cultural adaptation is the process of bringing things back into balance. Therefore, if you are having trouble understanding a person who does not speak English as well as you do, you could start to get stressed out and feel at a loss. Instead of getting upset and leaving the conversation in a bad mood, you might look to that person's facial cues, hand gestures, or even the communication situation to get a better sense of what that person is trying to tell you. In using these skills, you might understand the message and thus reduce your tension and frustration.

Acculturation also implies a new way of thinking, because resocializing into a new culture means coming to terms with a new social reality. While acculturation is taking place, the individual will likely lose or discard some of his or her old cultural patterns or ways of thinking and socializing. This is deculturation, which we defined previously in the chapter. According to Kim (1979, 1988, 1989), acculturation and deculturation are in interplay during the period of transition, which feeds into a complex cultural adaptation process, with newcomers adopting new ways and shedding some old ones.

IN YOUR *life*

Think about specific cultures you have joined and adapted to throughout your life. What opportunities and resources have you gained throughout your life by moving to or sharing with another culture?

Acculturation takes time and usually occurs gradually in stages. One characteristic of this whole process is conflict, often between a person's old, familiar ways and those of the new environment. On the one hand, it is normal for a person to want to cling to familiar customs and traditions that bring comfort and affirm his or her identity; on the other hand, an acculturating person also wants to adapt to the new ways to maintain harmony with others and gain access to that culture's benefits and opportunities. Cross-cultural adaptation is often facilitated by social support, being "institutionalized" within a workplace or other organizational structure, or building relationships with people who end up having a great deal of interpersonal influence.

MODELS AND PERSPECTIVES OF CULTURAL ADAPTATION

A number of perspectives, theories, and models explain how individuals adjust and adapt to new cultures. While the perspectives described below share some common threads, you might see a few differences in terms of the effect of cultural adaptation on the individual, what best predicts the success of adaptation, and the trajectory or direction that can be used to describe one's "journey" into a new culture.

Kim's Cross-Cultural Adaptation

Young Kim's (c.f., 1988, 1989, 2002) work addresses cultural adjustment and the role of the person as a "system" who operates within the larger system of a cultural environment. According to Kim, when this person or "system" encounters a new culture or something unfamiliar about that culture, the "system" will go into **disequilibrium**, or a state of imbalance or disorder. This is in contrast to the sense of balance sought during cross-cultural adaptation, a notion we discussed earlier. To return to balance, the system (i.e., acculturating person) takes feedback from the environment, or host culture, to adapt. Ideally, the person uses this feedback to engage in corrective behaviors. Incorporation of this feedback is essential for maintaining equilibrium.

Disequilibrium
a state of imbalance or disorder.

While adjustment and adaptation can be stressful, Kim's (2002) model does not adhere to the U-shaped curve. Instead, she proposes a **stress-adaptation-growth model**, which describes a fluctuation between adaptation and stress over time, resembling the W-shaped model discussed earlier. When attending to and incorporating feedback from the environment, the person will periodically make progress toward acculturation and then flounder yet again, followed by another period of upward progress. Over time, this two-steps-forward–one-step-back trajectory will result in growth. Kim points out that stress or culture shock is not bad; it is necessary for personal and cultural growth. The outcome, according to Kim, is **intercultural transformation**, which involves learning a new set of behaviors, thoughts, and feelings about the culture. In this sense, adaptation means "transforming" into a more well-rounded person who is empowered to thrive in more diverse environments.

Stress-adaptation-growth model
a fluctuation between adaptation and stress over time.

Intercultural transformation
learning a new set of behaviors, thoughts, and feelings about the culture.

The incorporation of feedback to maintain balance makes this akin to a systems approach, which acknowledges an input-throughput-output process. More specifically, **input** includes the features a person brings to the new culture, such as his or her predispositions and knowledge. **Throughput** involves communication with members of the host culture, as well as those of the person's own culture. Interpersonal and mass communication are the means through which an acculturating person can learn what is appropriate and inappropriate in a given

Input
the features a person brings to the new culture.

Throughput
the symbols and cues that are exchanged during a communication process.

Output

resulting behavior that is learned and adopted by the new member.

Homeostasis

making adjustments and achieving conformity and adapting to a new culture.

culture (Kim, 1979, 1994). Finally, **output** implies resulting behavior that is learned and adopted by the new member.

This input-throughput-output process is shaped by such influences as pressure to toe the line and the extent to which host members accept new members. If members of the host culture are less than receptive—even hostile—to those adapting, it can be difficult to make the adjustments and thus achieve **homeostasis** in such an unfriendly environment. While the presence of conformity pressures and receptivity could explain one's desire to adapt, it might not be that easy. For example, newcomers could feel resentful about the perceived pressure they feel to adjust their own behaviors, especially if that pressure is coming from an inflexible and unsympathetic society. Adapting simply to protect oneself from retaliation or to avoid ridicule can be unsatisfying, and certainly would hinder any cultural transformation one might otherwise experience.

As previously discussed, degrees of ability and desire to acculturate will vary with the individual. Even when migrants come to a new country of their own free will (rather than to flee disaster or political turmoil), "international migrants differ in their motivation to adapt to the new environment and to make the host society their 'second home.' This motivation to adapt is dependent largely on the degree of permanence of the new residence" (Gudykunst & Kim, 1992, p. 214). Some people who acculturate into a host culture do not want to lose all their original culture. For others, total acculturation, or the complete merging into mainstream culture, is a lifelong goal (Kim, 1979, 1988, 1989).

Cross-cultural adaptation, from Kim's perspective, assumes that the burden of adaptation falls primarily on the newcomer (Gudykunst & Kim, 1992; Kim, 2002). It is far more likely that the host culture will have an influence on those acculturating, rather than the other way around. However, acculturation can also be seen as a two-way street, with the acculturating person both receiving and contributing to the culture to which he or she is adapting. Anderson (1994) explains it this way:

> Real-life adjustments involve working toward a fit between person and environment, regardless of how that fit is achieved. . . . It is a two-way interactive process. Individuals both give to and take from their environments: Environments make demands but also can be used to satisfy individuals' needs. (p. 301)

Many schools offer Spanish classes to children to accommodate the growing Spanish-speaking population.

© Photographbee.eu/Shutterstock.com

Anderson points out that people entering a new culture can make their own impacts, which can have altering influences.

Moreover, many instances demonstrate how host cultures adapt themselves to accommodate people from foreign cultures. This is evidenced by the increasing presence of Spanish in many facets of life in the United States. People who call into voice helplines often get to choose between Spanish and English before speaking to a service representative. In addition, increasing numbers of elementary schools offer Spanish-language immersion programs. Such changes arguably have resulted in part from the significant immigration of individuals from Mexico and Central and South America. While newcomers need to adjust some of their communication patterns, host cultures also change, which results in a transformed culture for both newcomers and hosts.

Bennett's Ethnorelativism Model

Becoming more acculturated is a journey of sorts from being closed-minded about what one sees and experiences to being more appreciative of the differences and willing to adapt accordingly. Bennett's (1993) developmental **ethnorelativism model** explains this progression. According to Bennett, as a person experiences a new culture and becomes more acclimated to it, he or she tends to move along an ethnocentric–ethnorelative continuum. At first, a person might feel closed-minded toward certain customs. For example, if you are in Jerusalem on a Saturday afternoon

Ethnorelativism model
the journey from being closed-minded about a culture to being more appreciative of the differences and willing to adapt accordingly.

and are craving falafel, you might feel frustrated about not being able to get a hot meal because many merchants observe the weekly Sabbath of Shabbat. On the Sabbath, Orthodox Jewish custom does not allow one to operate any machinery or use electricity, which is often required to prepare a hot meal. Someone who is not familiar with the Shabbat customs and restrictions might be angry about not being able to order falafel and might even think, "This is stupid! I'm not Jewish. Why do I have to go along with this restriction?!" Such an opinion might reflect **ethnocentrism**, which is the belief that one's cultural values and practices are superior to those of others.

placing your own cultural beliefs in a superior position, which leads to a negative judgment of other cultures.

Over time, however, one might understand more why a culture does what it does, and one can become more accepting and respectful of those customs. After being in Jerusalem for some time, one might become less frustrated over the Sabbath customs and even appreciate the reverence local Jewish people show for this time of the week. This change in thought might compel a person to become more culturally sensitive and even become used to different eating arrangements on this day. This shift in thinking might be described as **ethnorelativism**, or the ability to see behaviors as culturally bound and relative, rather than universal.

Ethnorelativism

the ability to see behaviors as culturally bound and relative, rather than universal.

Anderson's Cognitive Perspective

Anderson (1994) proposes a more cognitive approach to understanding cultural adaptation, one that acknowledges the ways we handle perceived obstacles and the tensions that arise. Part of this tension comes from a sense of bereavement in which acculturating individuals grieve over what they perceive they have lost in the transitional "journey." However, adapting does not always trigger a sense of loss. Part of dealing with the tension is to understand what one gains from the cultural transition and how this can be a transformative process. This transformation is made easier when one realizes one's interaction with the environment of the new culture and how one gives to and takes from it.

Anderson's (1994) cognitive view of adaptation is different from adjustment, something we discussed previously. Again, adjustment is more short-term, while adaptation is long-term. To facilitate the long-term process, Anderson argues that one must recognize the motivation or goal behind adapting to the new culture and handling the perceived hurdles. Furthermore, six principles drive successful adaptation: adjustment, learning, appreciating the stranger–host relationship, treating the process as interactive and cyclical, recognizing the relative nature of adaptation, and anticipating personal development. In general, these principles represent social skills necessary to adapt successfully to a new culture.

To summarize, it would be unrealistic to assume that one can make a complete transition from one culture to another. You might adopt new behaviors and meet some new social requirements, but your underlying values might not change much. For instance, suppose you are used to being prompt, even early, for social and work engagements. This is something to which you have been accustomed most of your adult life. However, if you go to a Latin American country for a study-abroad program, you might find that most people residing in that country do not adhere to the strict time standards you hold. To be accommodating, you might loosen your own behaviors with regard to arriving on time and decide to be patient with individuals who arrive late for social gatherings. While you outwardly adopt this new pattern, you might personally not like it and secretly look forward to resuming your normal relationships with time upon your return home.

INFLUENCES ON ADAPTATION

The degree to which one is able and/or willing to adapt to a new culture is influenced by a number of factors, one of which is the acculturating person's perceived physical appearance or characteristics, such as skin color and facial features (Kim, 1988). In other words, to what extent does the newcomer look like those in the mainstream culture? For example, Vazquez (1997) found that Mexican American college students who had a darker skin color appeared to have a more Mexican-oriented acculturation than did other students. In turn, their skin color had an effect on their interest in the Latino community at their university.

Some cultural and ethnic minorities in the United States, even those who were born here, might not feel a "part" of this culture, particularly if they happen to experience racial or ethnic discrimination based on their physical appearance. This can also be the case if such individuals perceive little to no representation of their culture in media or popular culture (Gudykunst & Kim, 1992), especially when it comes to seeing few representative people in television shows, in movies, and as newscasters.

Another adaptation influence is the perceived similarity between one's original culture and the host culture into which one is adapting (Gudykunst & Kim, 1992). It stands to reason that U.S. citizens who move to Canada might have an easier time adapting than if they were to move to Japan, partly because we are talking about a change from Western to Eastern perspectives. Compared with moving to Japan, the language adjustment from the United States to Canada is arguably minimal, unless you live in Montréal or another area that has more French speakers. In addition, the religious and social traditions, political structures, economic systems, and even national holidays can accentuate either similarities or differences, depending on which move you are talking about.

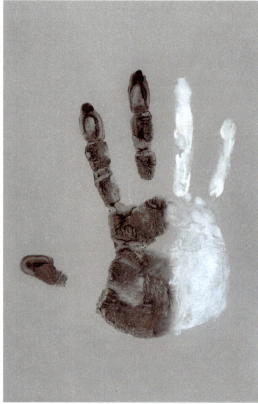

© Beror/Shutterstock.com

A third influence is personal disposition or personality. The ability or willingness to adapt can depend largely on a certain level of open-mindedness, patience, desire to learn, or a number of other personal characteristics. Predispositions such as cognitive complexity (Kim, 1977), resilience (Kim, 1988), attentiveness to change (Kim, 1988), tolerance for uncertainty or ambiguity (Ruben & Kealey, 1979), and orientation to learning (Ruben & Kealey, 1979) are correlated with the ability to adapt cross-culturally.

The ability or willingness to adapt can also depend on one's motivation. In fact, not everyone feels positive or enthusiastic about adapting to a new environment. Acculturating individuals do not adapt simply for its own sake; they often need a strong reason to adjust the way they behave or communicate. For example, an immigrant who does not yet speak English might not be motivated to learn the local language if he or she is surrounded by and lives in a community of fellow immigrants who speak his or her language of origin. On the contrary, that immigrant might be more motivated if it means a greater likelihood of employment or if there are few people from his or her own country. As Anderson (1994) puts it, "If a goal is not perceived as a goal and an obstacle as an obstacle, no purposeful (goal-directed) movement and no obstacle-related (coping) behavior will occur" (p. 302).

Another important influence on adaptation ability is communication competency, which is defined as exhibiting effectiveness (getting the message across so it is understandable) and appropriateness (fitting for the situation and the people involved) in one's communication (Wiemann & Backlund, 1980). Being able to adapt to another culture often hinges on your ability to pick up nonverbal cues and respond to those cues without offending or misunderstanding. For example, the American hand signal for "okay" might not go over well in other countries, where it is sometimes considered vulgar and offensive. A communicatively competent person would try to learn about such nonverbal patterns in anticipation of being in such cultural climates. Ruben and Kealey (1979) identify several interpersonal communication behaviors that are important to cross-cultural adaptation: empathy, respect, flexibility in role enactment, and posture when interacting.

© Stefano Garau/Shutterstock.com

Hand signals can have different meanings in different cultures. It is important to know what hand signals mean to specific cultures.

We can understand the importance of competence through Spitzberg and Cupach's (1984) competence model, which acknowledges motivation, knowledge, and skill as factors in competence. In terms of competence in cultural adaptation, one should have the motivation to learn as much about different social situations as possible, and to keep in check any tendencies to avoid settings that seem unfamiliar or potentially uncomfortable. Second, one can acquire knowledge about a new culture or setting to feel more prepared to communicate and generally know how to act. Finally, skill goes beyond merely thinking or talking about competent communicative behaviors and involves exhibiting them appropriately and effectively in certain situations. We might possess the desire or skill to be competent in our efforts to adapt, but that does not mean we have yet acquired the ability to do so.

ETHICAL CONNECTION

Clint is a vendor for his U.S.-based office-supply company. His recent promotion requires him to do business with their international partners—namely, their customers in China. Upon meeting his Chinese customer, Clint presented him with a clock he had bought at a gift shop in the United States. After setting a time to meet for lunch to discuss business, Clint warned his customer that he was still jet-lagged and might be a little late. During the meal, Clint applied the assertive deal-making tactics he had been taught in the United States, using direct and prolonged eye contact and offering an assertive handshake after the meal. Upon returning to the United States, Clint's boss informed him that their Chinese customers had decided to cancel their business relationship with Clint's company. When Clint detailed for his boss what happened on the business trip, he was informed that a clock is considered a rude gift in China; punctuality is critically important; and prolonged eye contact, handshakes, and aggressive—assertive behavior are frowned on in Chinese culture. Clint was reprimanded and taken off international vending duties.

Questions to consider:

1. How does this story emphasize the need to do research before traveling to a new country?
2. How should Clint have altered his communication style to accommodate his Chinese customer?
3. What are some resources available to people to improve their intercultural communication competency?
4. Why is it important in both business and pleasure to be a considerate traveler when visiting a new culture or country?

Adaptation or acculturation can influence a number of personal and everyday experiences, as well as communication behaviors and choices. In general, cultural adaptation can allow individuals to have greater access to another culture's resources, social networks, and opportunities, which is why many people choose to move from one culture to another. On the other hand, adaptation also means picking up the harmful aspects of the mainstream culture, such as the unhealthy lifestyles and counterproductive choices common to it. For instance, Heuman, Scholl, and Wilkinson (2013) interviewed Latino parents and children on their eating habits and histories of diabetes. Many of the first-generation Latinos interviewed described eating habits that involved more naturally grown produce and meats compared with foods typical of the American diet. These individuals reported less reliance on prepackaged and fast food compared with the second- and third-generation individuals, who described being more accustomed to the unhealthy food associated with the mainstream culture. While the participants in this study appeared to benefit greatly from increased acculturation (e.g., increased knowledge of health issues, higher health literacy, more financial means with which to purchase healthy food), there were drawbacks, such as a movement toward unhealthy eating habits that stood in contrast to the more healthy cuisine of the culture of origin.

WHAT YOU'VE LEARNED

In this chapter, you learned about the concept of sojourning, the various reasons for sojourning, and the challenges and rewards that come with traveling to a different country. You then learned about the process of assimilation experienced by those who immerse themselves in a culture different from their own, and you read about the acculturation process and its relationship with cross-cultural adaptation. Finally, you overviewed the various models and theories that explain cultural adaptation—Kim's Cross-Cultural Adaptation, Bennett's Ethnorelativism Model, and Anderson's Cognitive Perspective—along with the factors that influence one's willingness and ability to acculturate. In the next chapter, you will learn about the intercultural dimensions of both verbal and nonverbal communication.

REVIEW

1. The move from one's own culture to a new one is referred to as _____.

2. The second phase of the U-shape hypothesis—when a person feels hostility toward the new environment—is called _____.

3. _____ is the process of adaptation that allows one to fit into or conform in some way to a group or culture.

4. _____ refers to how we learn our own culture as we grow up, while _____ occurs when we unlearn certain aspects of our culture to fit into a new one.

5. _____ is a short-term state of reducing an uncertainty to meet a more immediate need, whereas _____ is more of a long-term response or process that prompts someone to evolve to fit into an environment.

6. Define *acculturation* and discuss some contexts when a person might need to acculturate.

7. Discuss the theory of Cross-Cultural Adaptation's concept of *intercultural transformation*.

8. Discuss the input-throughput-output process.

9. Explain the difference between *ethnocentrism* and *ethnorelativism*.

10. List the six principles that drive successful adaptation to a new culture.

Review answers are found on the accompanying website.

REFLECT

1. Mary, a college student, goes to Spain to finish up her degree. She knows she will need to engage in *adjustment* to help make her short stay more comfortable by meeting immediate needs. Discuss various ways in which Mary can engage in adjustment during her stay.

2. Give a detailed example of an individual who has a sojourning experience that reflects the U-shaped curve model. Be sure to include the four stages of the model.

3. Sam is an American who just moved in with her host family in Japan. Rui, her host mother, mentions possibly going to a restaurant for dinner. Sam responds that she would like to go to a seafood restaurant, and Rui seems taken aback by Sam's directness. Sam realizes she was too forward and made the situation uncomfortable, and she makes a mental note to be less direct in the future. Using terminology from the input-throughput-output process, explain what happened in this scenario.

4. Think of a time when you had to engage in assimilation when faced with a different culture. Discuss your experience and describe some of the challenges you faced while engaging in assimilation practices.

5. Use one of the models of cross-cultural adaptation presented in this chapter to explain a time when you had to adapt to a different cultural environment.

KEY TERMS

sojourning, 88
honeymoon, 90
crisis, 90
culture shock, 91
assimilation, 92
socialization, 92
anticipatory socialization, 93
encounter, 93
metamorphosis, 93
acculturation, 95
enculturation, 96
deculturation, 96

adjustment, 97
adaptation, 97
disequilibrium, 99
stress-adaptation-growth model, 99
intercultural transformation, 99
input, 99
throughput, 99
output, 100
homeostasis, 100
ethnorelativism model, 101
ethnocentrism, 102
ethnorelativism, 102

CHAPTER FIVE

Intercultural Dimensions of Verbal and Nonverbal Communication

CHAPTER OUTLINE

WHAT YOU WILL LEARN

After studying this chapter, you should be able to

1. define both verbal and nonverbal communication;
2. identify the importance of learning nonverbal cues that take place during intercultural communication;
3. discuss the relationship between verbal and nonverbal communication in your daily interactions;
4. apply the nonverbal codes outlined in this chapter to a personal experience with intercultural communication; and
5. explain why culture plays such an important role in the ways you communicate nonverbally with others.

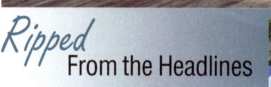

Ripped From the Headlines

© Christophe Archambault/AFP/Getty Images

Amazingly, something as small as a handshake can make headlines around the world. One thing that has taken the political world by storm has been President Trump's handshakes with leaders from other countries. The image shown here depicts French President Emmanuel Macron and his wife, Brigitte Macron, receiving one of the President's now infamous handshakes where he grabs the hand of the other person and pulls them in; this handshake has been dubbed the "tug and pull" by some media outlets (Cillizza, 2017).

Why does President Trump do these types of handshakes, and why do media outlets care so much about them? Nonverbal gestures, such as the way a person shakes another person's hand, can communicate many messages related to social and power status. International etiquette expert Jacqueline Whitmore and body language expert Chris Ulrich offer that grabbing and pulling in a person's hand, as President Trump does, asserts power and dominance over another person. Additionally, these experts assert that the pat that President Trump adds to the end of his handshakes can be seen as a friendly gesture, but in many professional contexts, it can be seen as belittling to the recipient (CNN, 2017).

While it is almost impossible to know everything about different cultures, there are certain techniques and studies to keep in mind to enhance your ability to navigate the cultural gaps throughout your communication, professional or otherwise. In this chapter, you will look at the different dimensions of verbal and nonverbal communication and how they relate to the topic of intercultural communication.

I ntercultural communication takes place all around us. We interact with different cultures while at school, work, the grocery store, the bar, and any other place where communication occurs. Also, with much of our social communication converging on popular social networking sites such as Facebook and Twitter, many people now find themselves exposed to more different cultures than ever before. With this increase in intercultural interaction, it becomes necessary to increase our understanding of how cultural issues affect communication (Scollon & Scollon, 2000).

To aid in the understanding of intercultural communication, it is critical to understand the roles of verbal and nonverbal communication. **Verbal communication** includes both our words and our verbal fillers (e.g., *um*, *like*). Verbal messages are created through the use of our respective languages. Effective communication involves accurate interpretations of others' verbal messages as meaning is co-created (Quintanilla & Wahl, 2016). This indicates that a certain level of cultural understanding is needed to create effective shared meaning with a cultural other; it is not enough simply to understand the word definitions and grammar of a particular language. Can you think of certain slang terms that are used in one area of the country but not in others? It becomes easy to see that simply sharing a language does not immediately constitute shared understanding. Along with verbal communication, nonverbal communication can vary greatly from culture to culture. **Nonverbal communication** encompasses all the ways we communicate without the use of words (Ivy & Wahl, 2014). Be critical of all the nonverbal cues you use in your everyday interactions: hand gestures to emphasize a point, a raised eyebrow to insinuate disbelief, or even a change in tone of voice to indicate anger or excitement. We communicate with others in numerous ways without using words, and oftentimes we are unaware of the nonverbal cues we send.

Verbal communication
both our words and our verbal fillers (e.g., *um*, *like*).

Nonverbal communication
all the ways we communicate without the use of words.

Our cultural background influences the ways we perceive both nonverbal and verbal communication. Especially with the convergence of business and social communications in an Internet format, it becomes necessary to increase our intercultural communicative competence. Scholars Larrea Espinar, Raigón Rodríguez, and Gómez Parra (2012) elaborate:

> Our daily routine reminds us that we live in a global world: technological advances, international media, the Internet, European rapprochement, international cooperation. . . . In this globalized society there is a pending necessity to interact with people from other cultures. Today's citizens must be able to communicate effectively with individuals from different cultures. However, this is a difficult ability to develop since "intercultural contact does not automatically breed mutual understanding.

© Simone van den Berg/Shutterstock.com

The ways you use both your verbal and nonverbal communication can have significant impacts on the relationships you develop.

Rather, it confirms the groups involved in their own identities and prejudices" (Gordon & Newburry, 2007, p. 254). (p. 116)

The goal of this chapter is to familiarize students with the basic principles of how verbal and nonverbal communication relate to intercultural communication. As Gordon and Newburry (2007) have stated, simple intercultural interaction does not guarantee shared understanding of communication. After reading this chapter, you will be better able to identify the verbal and nonverbal codes that make up interpersonal communication and to place them in an intercultural context.

VERBAL COMMUNICATION

Verbal communication includes both our words and our verbal fillers (e.g., *um*, *like*). Verbal messages are created through the use of our respective languages. However, sharing the same language with another person does not guarantee understanding. Have you ever traveled across the country and noticed different accents, slang, or jargon in the regions you visited? In the United States, there are many regional differences in the way people use language to convey meaning (Danesi, 2010). Basically, the ways we use language depend on a variety of factors such as region, culture, economic status, and function.

For an example of how language is constantly shifting and evolving, think about a movie you have seen that was released 10, 20, or even 50 years ago. You really don't have to go far back to see how significantly our verbal slang, etiquette, and mannerisms alter with the times. The social networking revolution is another example of how our cultural lexicon changes over time. Words that started off as nonverbal supplements in the online world (e.g., *lol*, *idk*, *omg*) have made their way into the general public's verbal communication. These examples underline the fact that verbal communication can still have different meanings for people who share the same language. Many different cultures can exist within a single language, and being an effective intercultural communicator involves understanding the different meanings verbal communication can have. After finishing this chapter, you should be able to identify some of the barriers to verbal communication and to learn some effective ways to combat these shortcomings.

THE RELATIONSHIP BETWEEN VERBAL AND NONVERBAL CODES

Verbal communication and nonverbal communication are closely related. We use each of the two forms to complement, reinforce, and add meaning to the other. Yet verbal and nonverbal communication are separate and distinct types of codes. Verbal communication (language) is a digital code, whereas nonverbal communication is an analogic code. A **digital code** represents things through the use of symbols. An **analogic code**, on the other hand, represents things through likeness or similarity. A good way to understand the difference between digital (verbal) and analogic (nonverbal) codes is to think about a favorite song. Have you heard the song performed live as well as recorded? The differences can be staggering. The version you hear on an MP3 file or CD has been digitally tuned, remastered, auto-tuned, and edited in the studio before it reaches your ears. It is, in its simplest form, a digital code that reflects only the language and symbols heard in the music. In a live performance, however, the music is in the moment, and you have the nonverbal communication of the crowd, performers, and environment to supplement the lyrics and instrumentals of the song. The live show feels much more real because it encompasses both the verbal and nonverbal codes to create a more comprehensive message.

> **Digital code**
> represents things through the use of symbols.

> **Analogic code**
> represents things through likeness or similarity.

The cultural desire to place both digital and analogic codes in the same environment can be observed on the popular video-streaming site YouTube. Any time you search for a song, you can easily choose either the studio version or live performance. The live videos can range from a professionally edited official release to a grainy amateur video pulled from a personal video camera or smartphone. Either way, the recurring theme is that many people want to enjoy their music in a broader capacity. Researchers Jessa Lingel and Mor Naaman (2012) examine this trend in relation to past cultures:

> If the enduring image of concert-going in the 1960s was enthusiastic attendees waving their lighters in approval of an acoustic guitar set, in the 2000s, the prevalent view of live music could very well be a sea of music lovers with their mobile phones raised to capture video for rapid uploading to a variety of social media sites. The infusion of personal technology at events like concerts points to a number of tensions related to the use of technology in social settings, with purposes that span the personal/private and the social/public. (pp. 332–333)

> **Symbol**
> an object that stands for something else. Symbols are arbitrary, which means there is no natural likeness between a symbol and what it represents. The symbol represents what a culture agrees it should mean.

As stated earlier, language (verbal communication) is a digital code, made up of symbols. **Symbols** stand for something else. Symbols are arbitrary, which means there is no natural likeness between a symbol and what it represents. The symbol represents what we as a culture have agreed it should mean. For instance, there's nothing particularly "dog-like" about the letters D-O-G that we string together to refer to that animal. The word doesn't *look* like a dog. Saying the word aloud doesn't *sound* like a dog. Our shared understanding of what *dog* means relies on social agreement, rather than likeness. The speakers of a language have agreed that the letters D-O-G will stand for a particular animal. The arbitrary nature of symbols means that we could just as easily have called a "dog" a "cat," as long as everyone used the same word to refer to the animal. Social agreement about what each word stands for is what makes the system work. It is also what makes the use of verbal communication, or language, highly intentional. Speakers must understand how the words are interpreted and use them in ways that reflect that shared understanding.

Nonverbal communication, on the other hand, is an analogic code. Instead of using symbols to create meaning, nonverbal messages get their meaning from similarity to the things they represent. Take a hug, for example. Hugs are generally understood to convey closeness, intimacy, and caring. Also, the act of hugging bears a close likeness to the things it conveys. Being brought near to another's body *literally* conducts warmth/heat, *literally* brings two people closer together, and *literally* enacts intimacy. Therefore, nonverbal behaviors are not arbitrary like language. They are chosen because of their likeness to what they are trying to convey. Furthermore, nonverbal communication appears somewhat less intentional and confrontational than verbal communication. We often assume that it's easier to lie with words than with the body. In fact, when a person's verbal communication contradicts his or her nonverbal behaviors (like saying one is happy when one's arms are crossed and posture is withdrawn, or saying one feels great when one's skin is pale and sweaty), we tend to believe the nonverbal message. We may interpret the sweating and fidgeting as **leakage cues**, or signs that information the speaker wishes to conceal verbally is spilling out nonverbally (Ekman & Friesen, 1969a).

Leakage cues
signs that information the speaker wishes to conceal verbally is spilling out nonverbally.

Think back to the differences between recorded songs and live performances. Like the smaller digital files, language is more compact and efficient than nonverbal communication. This is especially true when representing complex or abstract ideas. Take the concept of "liberty." That single word encapsulates the complexities of a historical concept, a way of structuring government, and a set of cultural ideals. Try expressing "liberty" nonverbally! It goes without saying that it's going to take you a while to get that message across. Language also offers greater clarity. Although there's always room for interpretation when we communicate verbally, words are less ambiguous than nonverbal behaviors.

LANGUAGE: AS BARRIER AND BRIDGE

Language has the ability both to hinder and to aid in understanding. Obviously, sharing the same language will aid in creating shared meaning much more than trying to communicate with someone who does not understand the language and symbols you are using. However, when language is not used in the proper context, or carries a different meaning across different cultures, it can have an unintentional or even negative effect on communication. Also, the way a certain culture perceives another language can hinder the communication process. Whether intentional or not, we make judgments about other people's culture based on their native language. Scholars Anna De Fina and Kendall King (2011) discuss the role language plays in intercultural communication and how we value language as a commodity:

> Language is an important form of cultural capital given that it has the potential to be transformed into symbolic capital and therefore into a tool for individuals and communities to ensure better social positions. These insights are crucial in analyzing the cultural and material processes of migration as immigrants' lives are profoundly influenced by the symbolic status of their native and new languages. Such symbolic status is established through social and discursive practices that attach certain values to languages and language users; these practices also serve as vehicles for the construction and circulation of language ideologies. (p. 164)

Currently in the United States, there is a heated debate over the issue of illegal immigration. The focus has been mainly on undocumented Hispanic workers, who some argue are driving the cost of labor down to a point that is hurting U.S. interests. An unfortunate side effect of this controversial issue is that many native Spanish speakers are being unfairly discriminated against based on their native language alone. We will discuss hate speech and racial slurs next, but suffice it to say that these perceptions are creating significant barriers to effective communication.

IN YOUR *life*

Have you ever interacted with someone when there was a language barrier present? How do you respond when verbal communication is difficult or impossible?

Hate speech and discrimination cause countless problems in both your intercultural communication and your everyday life.

© Juan Camilo Bernal/butterstock.com

HATE SPEECH

Hate speech is a significant barrier to intercultural communication and understanding. **Hate speech** is communication that vilifies a person or group on the basis of color, disability, ethnicity, gender, race, sexual orientation, religion, or any other characteristic that sets people apart. With respect to intercultural communication, hate speech severely fractures any chance of creating mutual understanding because it places the cultural other within a rigid stereotype that is often discriminatory and hostile. Basically, hate speech can turn off people's desire to communicate, causing them to rely on close-minded impressions that don't provide an accurate picture.

Some of the most common places for hate speech today include chat rooms, forums, and message boards on the Internet. The Internet offers individuals relative anonymity and safety from retaliation, which might explain why there is more hate speech in this medium than any other. There is also the trend of "trolling," where an Internet user writes an inflammatory statement to get the other commentators to move away from the subject at hand and focus exclusively on the controversial remark. While the original poster may not be an actual proponent of hate speech, the message is nonetheless there for everyone to see.

The United States in particular has major problems with online hate speech because of First Amendment concerns over freedom of speech (Henry, 2009). In fact, many hate groups base their websites in the United States as a way to avoid prosecution for disseminating hate mail in other countries. The issue of hate speech versus freedom of speech is a tricky one; it is important to try to curtail hate speech while not infringing on the right to open debate. Some Internet sites are trying to stem hate speech by having commentators assent to a "terms of use policy/agreement" that explicitly prohibits posters from engaging in hate speech, while other sites use moderators (real people who act as editors for message and comment boards) to personally remove speech deemed as hateful. It will be interesting to see how both technology and human resources continue to evolve to meet the threat of online hate speech.

RACIAL SLURS

Many types of hate speech contain racial slurs in their communication. **Racial slurs** are derogatory or disrespectful nicknames for racial groups. These slurs can make intercultural communication virtually impossible because of their inflammatory and belligerent nature. It is important to note that while language can be an indicator of a person's cultural or ethnic origins, it is easy to mistake languages and cultures you are not familiar with. To the untrained ear, many Eastern European languages may sound similar, when in actuality they are quite different and represent different regions, cultures, and ethnic groups.

Although racial slurs are generally meant to injure or insult, they can also be appropriated by the targeted group as a way of removing the negative meaning associated with the slur. Researcher Adam Croom (2011) elaborates on this phenomenon:

> The very taboo nature of these words makes discussion of them typically prohibited or frowned upon. Although it is true that the utterance of slurs is illegitimate and derogatory in most contexts, sufficient evidence suggests that slurs are not always or exclusively used to derogate. In fact, slurs are frequently picked up and appropriated by the very in-group members that the slur was originally intended to target. This might be done, for instance, as a means for like speakers to strengthen in-group solidarity. (p. 343)

THE CONNECTION BETWEEN LANGUAGE AND CULTURE

The connection between language and culture can be understood by the way we perceive our environment. **Perception** is the process of being aware of and understanding the world around us. Perception plays an important part in tying our language to our culture. Our perceptions help form, challenge, and reinforce our ideas, values, and beliefs, which then influence how we choose to interact with others. Because our perceptions are tied to cultural expectations and norms, it becomes impossible to separate language from culture. Researcher Cui-ping Han (2012) describes the need for a language/culture connection:

Perception
the process of being aware of and understanding the world around us. Perception plays an important part in tying our language to our culture.

> The relationship between language and culture determines that culture teaching must be included into foreign language education. Meanwhile, the culture teaching should cover both target culture and native culture due to the bidirectionalness and equality principle of cross-cultural communication. (p. 117)

When learning or speaking a foreign language, it is critical to have some type of understanding about its respective culture. In much the same way that different regions of the United States have their unique cultures and slang, new languages require you to immerse yourself in the culture to truly understand them. Think about common sayings in the United States such as, "The early bird gets the worm" or "You can lead a horse to water, but you can't make it drink." Someone new to English might find those phrases confusing or nonsensical; an understanding of the culture and origin of these sayings is required. If you have a friend who speaks a different language, try asking him or her about a few common sayings from his or her native culture. You might be surprised to find that these sayings make little sense to you as well!

A number of factors determine the conceptualizations we form from messages, other people, and social interactions. Specifically, we'll discuss the role of culture, personal fields of experience, and language in shaping perception. **Cultural influences** include the ways of understanding and interpreting the world that arise from the unique features of various social groups. We do not exist in a single cultural environment but, rather, blend with the different cultures we interact with on a daily basis (think about the culture of school versus that of work or your peer group). Each of us is a product of the multiple cultures we belong to. Those cultures may include religious communities, nationalities, ethnic heritages, social movements, or even gender.

Cultural influences

ways of understanding and interpreting the world that arise from the unique features of various social groups.

A second important influence on language and culture is an individual's field of experience. **Fields of experience** are collections of attitudes, perceptions, and personal backgrounds. As we interact with others in the world, we are not blank slates. We come with baggage that we've accumulated through years of living, learning, and interacting with others. While this point seems obvious, your past experiences do carry tremendous influence in your interactions with others. We look to our histories to determine how we should perceive new situations. Yet an important part of connecting and engaging with others, and truly realizing the potential of communication, is to maintain our openness to new situations—to stop and think critically about how our pasts may be constructing barriers to positive experiences.

Fields of experience

collections of attitudes, perceptions, and personal backgrounds.

A third major influence on perception is **language** itself. Languages are far from neutral. Words carry meanings that coordinate what we are able to think, imagine, and express. Languages enable us to perceive and interpret in certain ways while preventing us from perceiving and interpreting in others. As the philosopher Ludwig Wittgenstein (1922) phrased it, "The limits of my language are the limits of my world." A perfect example would be the new words and slang that have emerged in recent years. Think about words such as *defriend* and *tween*, or even the term *Facebook official*. Several years ago, these words and phrases had no meaning, but through the use of language, they have taken on cultural meaning. As the terms emerged and gained social usage, new ways of grouping people, relating with others, and behaving also emerged and gained social acceptance.

Language

words that carry meanings that coordinate what we are able to think, imagine, and express.

ETHICAL CONNECTION

John recently transferred to a supervisor position at an overseas branch of his company. While there, John received numerous complaints from his employees, ranging from poor understanding of communication to insensitivity regarding cultural holidays. John was also accused of using racial slurs and mimicking the native language in a derogatory way. John constantly asserted that his leadership method had worked for him in the past but that he felt his employees didn't fit into U.S. corporate culture. John was also frustrated that his employees had either poor or no understanding of the English language, and he demanded that his workers learn the language. After 6 months of dismal performance results and poor employee retention, John was called back to the corporate office in the United States and relieved of his supervisor position. John is at a loss as to why his overseas team performed so badly in comparison with his previous employees.

Questions to consider:

1. How could learning more about his employees' culture have helped John be a better leader?
2. Should employees have to adapt to the workplace culture of the corporation, or should supervisors be more sensitive to the local culture of their employees?
3. What intercultural communication rules did John ignore when confronted with his employee complaints? What steps should John have taken to alleviate his employees' concerns?
4. Why is it important to be sensitive when communicating across language barriers? What can result from misunderstanding or ridicule of another person's home language?

SAPIR–WHORF HYPOTHESIS AND OTHER LANGUAGE THEORIES

Language theories can offer valuable insight into how language relates to culture. Cultural anthropologists Edward Sapir and Benjamin Whorf presented the **linguistic relativity hypothesis** to refer to the view that language helps shape perception. In a particularly well-known example, Whorf (1956) contrasted the languages and cultures of the Hopi (American Indians residing primarily in Arizona) and English speakers. The Hopi language considers time as a single

Linguistic relativity hypothesis

the view that language helps shape perception.

process, whereas the English language treats time as a "line" that can be separated into numerable units such as days, months, or years. In the Hopi language, there are no verb tenses to differentiate between past, present, and future. According to Whorf, these differences in language correspond to different ways of being in and perceiving the world. How would your interactions change if you had no concept of countable time? Linguistic relativity hypothesis provides a perfect example of how language structure can impact culture and world perceptions.

Once we learn the ability to make the sounds of a language and combine them to form words and sentences, how do we use language to create and participate in our respective cultures and social settings? **Coordinated management of meaning** theory focuses on how we coordinate our actions with others to make and manage meaning (Pearce & Cronen, 1980). According to this theory, communication involves eight levels of interpretation. The first is **content**, or the actual information contained in a spoken or written message. Imagine you are walking through the mall and you see a coworker. You might wave and say something along the lines of, "Hey, Tim, good to see you!" At a content level, Tim probably heard what you said and will react to his name. The second level is the **speech act**, which refers to the various actions we perform through speech. Promises, threats, apologies, questions, and assertions are good examples of speech acts. In this case, Tim will recognize your message as the speech act of a "greeting." He'll realize that you are acknowledging his presence and expressing good will. However, Tim will also need to put this speech act into the context of a larger episode. An **episode** is a broader situation created by conversational partners. After Tim returns your greeting, you might say, "Hey, I just finished my shift. Want to grab a drink and hang out?" Tim can now form a larger picture of the interaction as a situation in which two coworkers would like to fraternize outside of work. Likely, he'll even realize that he has a "script" for this situation. He can use his former experiences to decide what to expect and how to behave. Yet he will also need to consider the **relationship** between the two of you. Whether two people are worker and coworker, teacher and student, romantic partners, or strangers has a significant impact on how they coordinate their actions and manage meanings. In this case, Tim may decide that the two of you are currently only casual acquaintances but have the potential to be friends. He may be inclined to accept your offer. However, Tim's view of **self** will also come into play. Each of us brings a "script for who we are" into every interaction. If Tim sees himself as outgoing and eager for new experiences, he may say, "Absolutely! Let's do it," because that response is in line with his self-concept. Culture also plays a role in how you and Tim navigate the context of the situation. Culture relates to a set of rules for acting and speaking that determines what we consider to be normal and acceptable in a given situation. Imagine a similar situation where Tim wants to invite out a woman who is engaged to be

Coordinated management of meaning

focuses on how we coordinate our actions with others to make and manage meaning.

Content

the actual information contained in a spoken or written message.

Speech act

the various actions we perform through speech.

Episode

a broader situation created by conversational partners.

Relationship

a complex set of beliefs about one's attributes, as well as memories and recollections of episodes that confirm such beliefs.

Self

a complex set of beliefs about one's attributes, as well as memories and recollections of episodes that confirm such beliefs.

married. It may occur to both Tim and the woman that U.S. culture can sometimes look down on cross-sex friendships, and this may give one or both of them a reason to question the suitability of making or accepting such an invitation.

As communication occurs, it requires a good deal of **coordination**, or the establishment of rules that help guide people through the interaction. To make and manage the meanings of an interaction, communicators rely on two distinct types of rules. **Constitutive rules** stipulate what counts as what and how our messages and behavior can be interpreted. For instance, your job may have a constitutive rule that texting during a shift counts as "rude" (or, most likely, intolerable). Or in your family, you may have a constitutive rule that incessant teasing counts as "affection." Likewise, you and Tim may coordinate an understanding that getting a drink counts as "friendly" rather than "romantic." **Regulative rules** guide how individuals respond or behave in interactions. For instance, you may recognize regulative rules such as "Always raise your hand before you speak in class" or "Don't turn your work in late" in the classroom context. You and Tim may rely on regulative rules such as "Take turns speaking," "Pay for your own drinks," and "Stick to topics that are appropriate for casual friends" once you get to the restaurant, bar, or coffee shop.

> **Coordination**
> the establishment of rules that help guide people through the communication interaction.

> **Constitutive rules**
> what counts as what and how our messages and behavior can be interpreted (i.e., texting at dinner can be considered "rude").

> **Regulative rules**
> guide how individuals respond or behave in interactions (i.e., "Always raise your hand before you speak in class").

In regard to the language and culture connection, standpoint theory offers an insightful view as to how language fits in with a culturally and socially constructed world. **Standpoint theory** asserts that our points of view arise from the social groups we belong to and influence how we socially construct the world (Wood, 1992). For instance, a young, white, Protestant woman raised in the United States may perceive a burqa as a marker of strangeness and a symbol of women's repression. She may react to seeing a woman in a burqa with confusion, anger, pity, fear, or any other drastic emotion. However, a religious Muslim woman of Arab heritage who lives in Saudi Arabia will likely see the burqa differently. She may associate it with respect for culture and tradition, as well as seeing it as a positive example of modesty. Understanding how culture can alter perception is indispensable when attempting to communicate effectively between cultures.

> **Standpoint theory**
> asserts that our points of view arise from the social groups we belong to and influence how we socially construct the world.

USING WORDS INCLUSIVELY AND WITH SENSITIVITY

Our language and words can powerfully influence our perceptions. Using sensitive, empowering, and inclusive language is especially important during intercultural communication. **Inclusive language** employs expressions and words that are broad enough to include all people and avoids expressions and words that exclude particular groups. For example, when referring to people, in general, gender-inclusive language replaces words such as *man*, *chairman*, and *mankind* with *human*,

> **Inclusive language**
> employs expressions and words that are broad enough to include all people and avoids expressions and words that exclude particular groups.

chairperson, and *humankind*. Along the same lines, many men may feel emasculated by practices such as referring to all nurses as women. When we allow both men and women to equally occupy a variety of roles in our language, we allow both men and women to feel more comfortable with a variety of roles in life.

NONVERBAL COMMUNICATION

As stated earlier, nonverbal communication encompasses all the ways we communicate without the use of words (Ivy & Wahl, 2014). Researchers have identified several different codes (categories) of nonverbal communication that encompass the following: environment, proxemics, touch, physical appearance, kinesics, and face and eyes. While many of the codes we examine relate to nonverbal communication in Western culture, it is critical to understand that interpretation of nonverbal cues is not universal. Different cultures, whether based on race, gender, socioeconomic background, or ethnicity, all carry their own unique nonverbal cues that set them apart and create a cultural identity for the group. **Cultural identity** can be defined as a dynamic production in and through intercultural contact and interaction with a cultural other (Chen, 2011). This position holds that individuals create their cultural identities through their interactions with others, both within their culture and outside it. After defining the following nonverbal codes, try to use a reflexive thought process to analyze how you create your own cultural identity as compared with others.

Cultural identity
a dynamic production in and through intercultural contact and interaction with a cultural other.

Inclusive language is a useful tool for fostering equality within roles that used to be associated with a particular gender.

© Dirk Ercken/Shutterstock.com

ENVIRONMENT

The **environment** refers to our surroundings that shape the communication context. People are influenced by environmental factors such as architecture, design, doors, windows, color, lighting, smell, seating arrangements, temperature, and cleanliness (Harris & Sachau, 2005; Jackson, 2005). The environment is a critical code when studying intercultural nonverbal communication because it influences the way we act and interact within our own culture and can also offer insight into how cultural others may perceive us.

Reflect on what types of decorations you use in your personal living space. What do they say about you? Do you have any decorations on your car? We shape our environments to express our own feelings and beliefs. Consider other things in the environment that can serve as nonverbal cues about who you are. These environmental factors you create and control serve as nonverbal messages to others who enter the space. Keep in mind that many of you have only recently begun to have in-depth interactions with people from different cultures. The personal environments you create for yourself can have significant effects on how others perceive you. As two intercultural scholars note, "Students in a multicultural environment speak somewhat differently from each other. All of these differences relate to their different language styles and different behaviors which are related to their different cultural backgrounds, beliefs and other factors" (Singh & Rampersad, 2010, p. 4).

Nonverbal actions can be meaningfully interpreted only when context is taken into account. The environment is important to the study of nonverbal behavior in two ways: (1) The decisions we make about the environment in which we live and work reveal a good deal about who we are, and (2) our nonverbal behavior changes according to the environments we communicate in. The first assertion can become problematic because the way one culture might perceive our personal environments can be quite different from your own. Research has indicated that cultural groups may view the processes and outcomes of intercultural interaction in different ways specific to their culture (Halualani, 2010). As you interact with individuals from a different culture, try to inventory their interpretations concerning the way you create your environment.

It's natural for us to structure the settings in which we work, study, and live to make them more unique and to make us feel more comfortable. The environments we create for ourselves often speak volumes about those relationships we consider most important (Lohmann, Arriaga, & Goodfriend, 2003). We alter our behavior and perceptions according to the physical environments in which we find ourselves. For example, we are more likely to wear formal clothes and whisper in church than at a sporting event, where we would probably wear comfortable clothes and scream wildly for our favorite team.

Environment
our physical, social, and contextual surroundings that shape the communication context.

IN YOUR *life*

Think about the environment you create for yourself in your dorm, house, or apartment. What message about yourself do you want to convey to people who see your environment?

What about environments we don't personally create? Do they influence us? And if so, do they influence people across all cultures equally? Think about the White House or the Statue of Liberty, for example. Does the statue evoke the sentiment of liberty and freedom across different nations? The Statue of Liberty has been used in other national dialogues and as a form of protest. In two photographs of the Goddess of Democracy (which bears similarities to the Statue of Liberty) created by Chinese student protestors before the Tiananmen Square Massacre of June 4, 1989, we see a contemporary example of the statue's transnational influence (Wong, 2004). Our verbal and nonverbal communication is impacted by these structures because those buildings have the ability to communicate a rhetoric that goes beyond cultural boundaries.

Just as there are environments we can own and operate, there are also environments we can't maintain. Imagine showing up for an international business meeting in another country and seeing a dirty office with disorganized papers everywhere and leftover food at the conference tables. What does an office like that tell you about the owner's professionalism, credibility, and organizational skills? An environment like that is all about *impression management*—the formation of an impression, perception, or view of others (Goffman, 1971). At this point, it is important to note that not all cultures value an orderly office as much as many Western cultures do; what seems comfortable to business professionals in the United States might not be considered comfortable in other cultures. This is why it is important to stay open-minded and respectful of other cultural norms. People want to communicate in comfortable environments, whether they have thought consciously about other cultural standards or not. The point is this: The environments created in offices, classrooms, and the like establish certain communication contexts, comfortable or uncomfortable, that have an influence on our perceptions of safety and comfort, as well as reflecting the attitude and character of the persons inhabiting the space (Ivy & Wahl, 2014).

PERCEPTIONS OF ENVIRONMENT

As you've noticed so far, the way we perceive our environment and the environments of others is an important factor in how we respond. Overall, we perceive the environment in six distinguishable ways (Knapp & Hall, 2006). First, there is *formality*, which is an understanding people have of environment that relates to how comfortably we can behave, in light of our expectations. Sometimes it is more about the atmosphere of a certain place than the place itself, especially when interacting in a different cultural environment. Have you ever gone to an ethnic restaurant and been surprised at the different atmosphere compared with your local restaurants? Some exotic restaurants discourage or do not even offer the use of eating utensils, instead preferring that patrons eat with their hands.

© Photographee.eu/Shutterstock.com

The way you choose to decorate your living spaces can speak volumes about you without your ever uttering a word.

The second way we can perceive the environment is *warmth*. This means that the environment can give off a certain sense of warmth—not necessarily meaning the temperature. Our sense of warmth describes how we see and desire a comfortable, welcoming context that is part of our past or current experience. Our perceptions of warmth are not universal, however. Cultural notions of warmth can vary greatly depending on the geographic location of a culture as well as population density. Residents in the southern United States might value open-air, rustic environments more than someone who lives in a high-population city, where space and open air are not readily available.

Privacy is the third way the environment can be perceived. Do you prefer a crowded and noisy restaurant or a peaceful and quiet one? We all have some sense of privacy, but privacy and issues of personal space can vary significantly across cultures. Some of us don't mind being around a lot of people, and some of us do. In many cultures, the high population density does not allow for what many people from the United States would consider adequate personal space and privacy.

The fourth perception of environment is *familiarity*, which means that we tend to react cautiously or anxiously when we meet new people or are confronted with an unfamiliar environment. Not knowing where we are and what to expect makes us feel less comfortable. That's why we tend to develop favorite hangouts or prefer certain restaurants over others. We like knowing what to expect and how to behave in the environment.

Fifth on the list is *constraint*. Many of you are living in apartments or college dorms. Do you feel you have enough personal living space in that environment? Whenever we feel as though our personal space is invaded, we feel constraint. Most of our perceptions of constraint are shaped by the amount of privacy and space available to us, which again is heavily influenced by living situation and cultural background.

The sixth perception of information is *distance*. Our perceptions of distance in an environment pertain to physical arrangements. We like to know how far away the closest door is or how many people can fit into an elevator. We create distance by avoiding eye contact or taking a longer route to avoid saying "hello" to a person we find annoying.

REACTIONS TO ENVIRONMENT

Now that you have some idea about how we perceive the environment, we can look at how people react to it. Remember that while environment serves as a form of nonverbal communication, it also impacts our interactions within it. The college classroom is one environment that can create many different responses depending on culture. A student from the United States going to Japan might find the classroom material more informal, as many Japanese universities are moving toward a more illustrated format for their reading materials, as opposed to the text-heavy books we see in the United States (Armour, 2011). Think of a course you're currently taking and the classroom where the course is delivered. What's the temperature in the classroom? How large are the tables or desks? What can you smell and hear? What's the lighting like? Are there windows? How does all this influence your perception of the learning environment? What type of interaction is encouraged by the arrangement of the environment? Our perceptions of classroom arrangement can vary greatly depending on what culture(s) we have been educated in throughout our lives.

CHRONEMICS

Chronemics
the study of the ways people use time to structure interactions.

We've established that the environment is communicative since people have perceptions of and reactions to environment. Let's now look at another element that influences the communicative environment—time. **Chronemics** is the study of the ways time is used to structure interactions. Have you ever been casually late to a party? In some situations, being late is a violation of important cultural norms. Yet, at many parties, the acceptable window of arrival is much larger. U.S. culture (and most of Western Europe) is monochronic. A *monochronic* time orientation stresses being on time and maintaining a schedule for events. In other cultures, such as South American and Mediterranean, you will find a *polychronic* time orientation. A polychronic time orientation places less emphasis on keeping a tight schedule and values greater flexibility. Time can also be used to denote power and role differences. Your boss might keep you waiting while she is talking on the phone. This might communicate a difference in power (as you must wait for her) or that her time is more valuable than yours. How has time influenced your life? Which perception of time can you best relate to?

PROXEMICS

Proxemics refers to the study of how we use space and distance to communicate. Making the connections between people, space, and distance is important for three reasons: (1) How we identify ourselves as a culture can be revealed by our preferred use of distance and space at home and at work, (2) our verbal and nonverbal communication is influenced by distance and space, and (3) we use metaphors of distance and space to talk about and explain our interpersonal and intercultural relationships.

Have you ever been on a crowded subway or elevator and been uncomfortable because it seemed as though people were invading your personal space? We are so used to our rules and norms about space that we don't think much about them until they are violated. Violations can be alarming, possibly even threatening, but it is

© Blend Images/Shutterstock.com

The time you dedicate to work compared with your social life can be a significant indicator about yourself to others.

important to note that our expectations for personal space vary significantly across cultures. Our relationships with others, power and status, and cultural backgrounds determine how physically close we get to others and how close we let others get to us (Burgoon & Jones, 1976).

What preferences do you have related to space and distance? In U.S. culture, we tend not to like people "in our bubble." Edward T. Hall (1963) identified four zones of space in middle-class U.S. culture. First, there is the *intimate zone* (0 to 18 inches). This is usually reserved for our significant others, family members, and closest friends. When a stranger occupies this space, it can lead to expectation violations. These interactions mostly occur in private and signify a high level of connection, trust, and affection. The *personal zone* (18 inches to 4 feet) is reserved for personal relationships with casual acquaintances and friends. The *social zone* (4 to 12 feet) is the distance at which we usually talk to strangers or conduct business. If you went to your boss's office to discuss your work, for example, you would most likely remain at a distance of 4 to 12 feet. The *public zone* (more than 12 feet) refers to the distance typical of large, formal, public events. In large lecture classrooms, campaign rallies, or public speeches, the distance between speaker and audience is usually more than 12 feet. Understanding these spatial zones is important to your everyday nonverbal communication competency, along with understanding that not all cultures place the same value or privacy expectations on spatial zones.

Like so many other things, spatial zones vary among cultures. Whereas we in the United States appreciate our personal space, other cultures have different ideas about the use of space. In Arab cultures, for example, it is common to have less personal space. Hall (1966) observed Arab cultures for their use of space and found significant differences between how Arabs and Westerners view public space and conversational distance. Arabs do not seek privacy in public space, preferring to converse intimately in public and viewing less-than-intimate conversations as rude behavior. What observations have you made concerning how space is managed across cultures?

New media also play a role in how we perceive issues of proximity. One recent study has even suggested that the way we use our mobile phones influences how we perceive spatial behavior (Qingchao, 2011). Do you ever use your smartphone as a buffer to distract yourself when someone invades your personal space? Have issues of distance between you and your loved ones decreased with the ability to Skype instantaneously via your mobile phone? Think about the different ways you use your personal devices to overcome issues of space and proxemics.

GENDER AND SEXUAL IDENTITY

Gender and sexual identity is another interesting factor that contributes to our discussion of proxemics and culture. Gender has an immense influence on our personal-space management, which leads to particular communication patterns. For example, it seems to be socially accepted and completely natural in U.S. culture for women to sit close together. Yet, looking at men, one can observe that some expectancy violation makes it inappropriate for them to sit right next to each other. Of course, men can and do sit close together, but it's likely to cause some uneasiness or lead them to feel that they need to joke to diffuse the awkward behavior. Have you ever seen a group of men at a movie theater, bar, or classroom who don't sit directly next to each other but instead insist on keeping one empty seat between them? One explanation we've heard for this behavior is that men simply need more space than women because they are larger in size. Does that sound reasonable to you, or could there be another reason? One possibility is that more space between males makes it clear to everyone that these men aren't gay. Homophobia is still prevalent in U.S. culture. And although homosexuality is perceived as more acceptable in our culture in recent years, the primary explanation we've heard for men's spatial behavior relates to homophobia—a fear of being perceived or labeled as gay. Most women don't have to deal with this perception, because acceptance for women's proxemics behavior tends to be wider than for men's. Do you think these actions and perceptions are standard across the globe? Again, perceptions of personal space can be very different across cultures, so it is important to be careful when making assessments about others' personal space in an intercultural setting.

Homophobia

a fear of being perceived or labeled as gay.

Self-Assessment: Nonverbal Communication

The following Scale-Observer Report will help you gain a better understanding of your own nonverbal immediacy. Complete each item thoughtfully, and then reflect on the results. How can this knowledge help you be a better communicator?

NONVERBAL IMMEDIACY SCALE-OBSERVER REPORT
This measure will allow you to assess your own nonverbal immediacy behaviors.
Directions: The following statements describe the ways some people behave while talking with or to others. Please indicate in the space to the left of each item the degree to which you believe the statement applies to you. Please use the following 5-point scale:

1 = Never; 2 = Rarely; 3 = Occasionally; 4 = Often; 5 = Very often

____ 1. I use my hands and arms to gesture while talking to people.
____ 2. I touch others on the shoulder or arm while talking to them.
____ 3. I use a monotone or dull voice while talking to people.
____ 4. I look over or away from others while talking to them.
____ 5. I move away from others when they touch me while we are talking.
____ 6. I have a relaxed body position when I talk to people.
____ 7. I frown while talking to people.
____ 8. I avoid eye contact while talking to people.
____ 9. I have a tense body position while talking to people.
____ 10. I sit close or stand close to people while talking with them.
____ 11. My voice is monotonous or dull when I talk to people.
____ 12. I use a variety of vocal expressions when I talk to people.
____ 13. I gesture when I talk to people.
____ 14. I am animated when I talk to people.
____ 15. I have a bland facial expression when I talk to people.
____ 16. I move closer to people when I talk to them
____ 17. I look directly at people while talking to them.
____ 18. I am stiff when I talk to people.
____ 19. I have a lot of vocal variety when I talk to people.
____ 20. I avoid gesturing while I am talking to people.
____ 21. I lean toward people when I talk to them.
____ 22. I maintain eye contact with people when I talk to them.
____ 23. I try not to sit or stand close to people when I talk with them.
____ 24. I lean away from people when I talk to them.
____ 25. I smile when I talk to people.
____ 26. I avoid touching people when I talk to them.

Scoring:
Step 1. Start with a score of 78. Add the scores from the following items: 1, 2, 6, 10, 12, 13, 14, 16, 17, 19, 21, 22, and 25.
Step 2. Add the scores from the following items: 3, 4, 5, 7, 8, 9, 11, 15, 18, 20, 23, 24, and 26.
Total Score = Step 1 minus Step 2

How did you score? What surprised you about your score? You can also try the measure on others. Simply fill out the measure with another person's behaviors in mind. For instance, you might find it interesting to fill out the survey for your least and most favorite professors to determine whether their nonverbal immediacy might play some role in the degree to which you like them. Do you notice differences in their use of nonverbal immediacy behaviors? Did you learn more in one class than the other? What class did you enjoy more?

Sources: "Development of the Nonverbal Immediacy Scale (NIS): Measures of Self- and Other-Perceived Nonverbal Immediacy" by Richmond, McCroskey, and Johnson. From *Communication Quarterly,* 51(4), September 2003, pp. 504–517. Copyright © 2003 Routledge. Reprinted with permission.

Sexual orientation and homophobia are still hot-button issues across the globe today.

© viewimage/Shutterstock.com

TERRITORIALITY

Another concept related to the study of proxemics is **territoriality**, which is the study of how people use space and objects to communicate occupancy or ownership of space (Ivy & Wahl, 2014). We determine our territory and want it to be safe from strangers; therefore, we will do our best to defend it from intrusion by using verbal and nonverbal means. Have you ever gone to a bar or dance club and used the environment around you to claim your "space"? The way you angle your chair, place your menu, or use body language in general can convey feelings of territoriality or ownership to those around you. Let's think about a less obvious example: How do you feel about people as territory? Have you ever noticed another person talking to someone for whom you have romantic feelings and felt that your territory was being threatened? It might be a little weird to look at people as territory in the first place, but we most likely all know people who view their boyfriend or girlfriend as their own private territory, and they can become seriously forceful when they feel that their territory is being invaded.

Territoriality
the study of how people use space and objects to communicate occupancy or ownership of space.

How do people violate our territories? Three types of intrusion are typically viewed as negative: violation, invasion, and contamination (Lyman & Scott, 1967). **Violation** is the use of or intrusion into primary territory without our permission.

Violation
the use of or intrusion into primary territory without permission.

Invasion

an intense and typically permanent intrusion that involves an intention to take over a given territory.

Contamination

a type of intrusion in which someone's territory is marked with noise or pollution.

Have you ever had a roommate or shared a dorm room with somebody? You might be able to relate to the experience of a roommate eating your favorite food or wearing your favorite sweater when you're not there and thus violating your personal territory. **Invasion** is an intense and typically permanent intrusion that involves an intention to take over a given territory. The original occupant of the territory is often forced out during or after the invasion. Perhaps you've experienced a situation in which you were enjoying some quiet time with a romantic partner at a beach or restaurant when someone or a group of people arrived and disrupted your solitude. Invasion can also include the way we use mobile devices. Have you ever wanted to throw your phone away simply so you could be left alone? Research has indicated that the problem of being reachable at all times is shared across cultures (Baron & Af Segerstad, 2010). People can invade your privacy simply by calling you at inopportune or socially unacceptable times. **Contamination** is a type of intrusion in which someone's territory is marked with noise or pollution. Contamination is about doing something to a territory to leave evidence that you were there, such as leaving the bathroom dirty or not cleaning up after a late-night get-together.

One territory that might be important to you is your classroom environment. Surprisingly, students can be very protective of their classrooms. Some students dislike it when people are in their classrooms who aren't supposed to be there. Especially in a college environment, you will be exposed more frequently to students from different countries and cultures. It is not uncommon for students to seek out others from the same or similar cultures and to occupy space near them. While this may seem comical or strange to you, be reflexive about the way you choose your initial seat in a new classroom. Do you try to pick a seat next to someone who dresses similarly to you? Imagine being in a class in another country where the language is unfamiliar to you. Would you want to sit next to someone who spoke your native language? The classroom can be a useful environment to observe the ways people choose and react to their territories.

HAPTICS

Haptics

the study of touch as non-verbal communication.

Haptics is the study of touch. Whether a handshake, a punch, or a hug, touch has the potential to communicate a powerful message. The lack of traditional touch in computer-mediated communication has led to the development of behaviors such as "poking" someone on Facebook to indicate a personal connection or using *lol* to refer to something we find humorous. Out of the five human senses, touch develops first (Montagu, 1978). Out of all the nonverbal codes, touch is the most powerful; however, it is also the most complicated and misunderstood, with a high risk of expectation violations in intercultural settings.

Whether communicating face to face or online, the use of touch and how to interpret it is always contextual. In the United States, we might shake a stranger's hand but hug a friend. It would be quite a violation of nonverbal norms to hug a stranger. This is especially prevalent among men in masculine cultures. While research generally shows that touching or holding someone by the arm while asking for something can be beneficial, a study conducted in Poland indicated that when a man requests something from another man, touch negatively affects chances of request fulfillment (Dolinski, 2010). In this sense, touch is influenced by relationship and culture. Touch is also influenced by the situation. You might see football players slap each other on the butt when on the field, but you are far less likely to see this touch off the field. Touch can also influence how others respond to our messages. A careful touch of the hand while delivering bad news can demonstrate concern and care. A high-five for a job well done communicates excitement and accomplishment. Touch can also show power and role differences between individuals. The president of the United States might approach you to shake your hand, but you would never be allowed to approach the president. A doctor might touch you in a physical examination, but you would not touch the doctor in return.

It's important to understand the **touch ethic**, or people's beliefs about and preferences for touch. It is also important to note that the touch ethic is not universal among all cultures. The touch ethic includes our rules about appropriate and inappropriate touch, our expectations for how people will receive touch and extend touch to us, whether we are a "touchy" person or not, and how we actually act regarding touch. Our touch ethic develops early in life and remains fairly constant; however, our relationships and experiences might influence touch preferences throughout our lives, as well as affecting our interactions within different cultures.

Touch ethic

people's beliefs about and preferences for touch.

© freya-photographer/Shutterstock.com

Touch is one of the most powerful forms of communication.

TYPES OF TOUCH

Several different systems for categorizing touch have been developed to help us better understand this complex code of nonverbal communication. One of the best means of classifying touch behavior was developed by Richard Heslin (1974). Let's explore his categories.

First, we have *functional/professional* touches, which serve a specific function. These touches normally take place within the context of a professional relationship and are relatively low in intimacy. An example would be a doctor giving a patient a physical exam. Second, there are *social/polite* touches. These touches are connected to cultural norms, such as handshakes or brief hugs and kisses as greeting. Once again, this signifies a relatively low intimacy within the relationship. Then there are *friendship/warmth* touches, which people use to show their platonic affection toward each other. Hugs and kisses on the cheek might be exchanged between two close friends, for example, but can vary greatly depending on both culture and gender. *Love/intimacy* touches, on the other hand, are highly personal and intimate. People communicate strong feelings of affection toward each other with these kinds of touches. In this case, hugs may last longer and kisses may be on the lips. The last category involves *sexual arousal*. These touches are extremely intimate.

APPROPRIATENESS OF TOUCH

The appropriateness of touch is a tricky topic because rules about appropriateness or inappropriateness of touch vary among individuals and cultures. When is touch appropriate? In the following section, we will focus on three aspects that can help answer this question.

Location
where on the body contact is made or the setting within which touch occurs.

The first aspect is **location**. Location can mean where on the body contact is made or the setting within which touch occurs. The first aspect has a significant impact on whether we believe a touch to be appropriate or inappropriate. You make your own rules about who can touch you, when, where on your body, and in what setting. Have you ever visited a distant relative or an acquaintance who gave you a kiss on the face as an initial greeting? Did you feel an expectancy violation because of the kiss? A light kiss on the cheek can be a socially acceptable greeting for acquaintances in some other countries and cultures. The second option determines the circumstances in which touch is made. For example, when you meet your boyfriend's or girlfriend's parents for the first time, should you shake hands with them or hug them? Location can be very important in other cultures as well; while people in the United States may not bat an eye at a couple kissing in public, in some cultures public displays of affection are frowned on.

Duration
how long a touch lasts.

Intensity
the degree to which one expresses their identity or the power, force, or concentration of bodily contact.

Duration is the next factor in appropriateness of touch. Duration means how long a touch lasts. A doctor's examination is never pleasant, so a good doctor will try to get the exam over with quickly and without using unnecessarily long touches.

Intensity is the last aspect. Intensity refers to the power, force, or concentration of bodily contact. The amount of intensity we put into a touch is influenced by our emotions. One interesting observation to note is that in some situations, even a low-intensity touch can have significant impact compared with no touch. One U.S. study had women approach men in a bar to ask for help, with some engaging in a light touch and others giving no touch at all. Results indicated that men who were touched expressed more interest in the female confederate than when no touch occurred (Guéguen, 2010). Do you think these results might be different in other cultures?

CULTURE AND TOUCH

Of course culture plays an important role when it comes to touch, which means we should interpret the meaning of a touch only within its appropriate cultural context. Hall (1966, 1981) distinguishes between **contact cultures**, which are frequent in touching, and **noncontact cultures**, which are infrequent in touching. Contact cultures include Latin America, India, France, and Arab countries, whereas noncontact cultures include Germany and Northern European nations, Canada and the U.S., and many Asian countries, such as China, Japan, Korea, Indonesia, and Malaysia. Greetings in different cultures are an excellent way to observe cultural distinctions in touch expectations. For example, typical greetings in the mainland United States involve a handshake for men and brief hugs for women, whereas Puerto Rican women often grasp each other's shoulders and kiss both cheeks in greeting. Saudi Arabian men shake right hands to greet each other and may also place their left hands on each other's shoulders while kissing both cheeks (Hickson, Stacks, & Moore, 2004).

> **Contact cultures**
> cultures that are characterized by frequent touching.

> **Noncontact cultures**
> cultures characterized by infrequent touching.

PHYSICAL APPEARANCE

Another nonverbal code is **physical appearance**, which refers to observable traits of the body and its accessories and extensions. Making the connection between physical appearance and intercultural communication is important for two reasons: (1) The way we represent ourselves and our physical appearance reveals to other people a lot about who we are, and (2) the physical appearance of other people influences our perception of them, how we talk to them, how approachable they are, how attractive or unattractive we find them, and so on. The level of physical attractiveness is an important dimension of physical appearance. Physical attractiveness is a perception of beauty derived from cultures, and each culture has a different idea about physical attractiveness. A given culture's concept of physical attractiveness is formed by features such as height, weight, size, shape, and so on. In other words, a certain standard of physical appearance dictates what *is* and is *not* attractive.

> **Physical appearance**
> observable traits of the body and its accessories and extensions.

A good example of the way culture impacts our standards of physical attractiveness can be seen in Renaissance art. Many Renaissance paintings depict women as pale and buxom. This standard of beauty was derived from the cultural insinuation that women who were pale and plump were richer and better cared for than other women. Their paleness indicated that they did not have to labor in the sun, and their plumpness signaled that they had enough money to eat well. Compared with the images of female beauty we see today, the differences are significant. Many depictions of women in the media tend to favor very skinny, tanned women. It has been argued that in today's culture, a tan indicates enough wealth for vacations and recreational time in the sun, and thinness suggests access to a healthy diet and workout facilities. These observations are open to interpretation, and by no means can they be applied to everyone. However, they do show that standards of beauty are marked by cultural implications and can change over time.

Even though we have limited power to dramatically alter our physical appearance, others treat our appearance as though it communicates important information. Teachers tend to judge attractive students as smarter and more social than less attractive students (Ritts, Patterson, & Tubbs, 1992), and attractive people often make more money in their jobs (Judge, Hurst, & Simon, 2009). Similarly, features of appearance such as height, weight, and skin color are interpreted as conveying important messages about who we are and our interests. However, people misjudge one another on the basis of physical appearance on such a regular basis that it's worth questioning whether you can make correct assumptions about another person based on aspects of appearance alone. Clothing and other **personal artifacts** (objects we use to represent our identities, interests, and backgrounds) are also a part of physical appearance. We may wear glasses or contact lenses, carry handbags or wallets, flaunt our smartphones, wear jewelry, or sport tattoos to express who we are or how we would like to be seen. What personal artifacts, if any, are important to your appearance? What messages do they convey in your culture?

Personal artifacts
objects we use to represent our identities, interests, and backgrounds.

© Taraskin/Shutterstock.com

Your physical appearance conveys to others a great deal of information about you.

BODY TYPE, SHAPE, AND SIZE

Have you ever avoided interaction with someone because of his or her body shape or size? Generally, the size and shape of our bodies communicate something nonverbally. Scholars have even developed a system called **somatotyping** that classifies people according to body type (Sheldon, Stevens, & Tucker, 1942).

Somatotyping
classifies people according to body type.

Let's talk about the different body types that have been classified over time. The first is the endomorph. **Endomorphs** typically have rounded, oval, or pear-shaped bodies. They tend to be heavy-set but not obese. The second body type is the mesomorph. People classified as **mesomorphs** have a triangular body shape. They have broad shoulders and are muscular, with a good balance between height and weight. They tend to look athletic. The third body type is the ectomorph. **Ectomorphs** are thin and tall. They typically have flat chests and not very much muscle, which makes them look fragile.

Endomorphs
individuals who typically have rounded, oval, or pear-shaped bodies.

Mesomorphs
a triangular body shape; broad shoulders and muscular, with a good balance between height and weight.

Shape and size also matter when it comes to judging physical appearance. The perception of **body weight** varies from culture to culture. American culture, especially, seems to have an obsession with body weight. In other cultures around the world, however, body weight isn't as much of an issue. We Americans feel as though we have to look as perfect as the models on TV, on billboards, and in magazines, and there seems to be a lot of pressure from the media, which are trying to make money off people's insecurities. It is also important to know that many of the images of "beauty" we see in media and advertising have been doctored with photo-manipulation software, almost to the point of unreachable perfection. In addition, obesity has grown to be a real problem in U.S. culture. The detrimental effects of obesity on health lead Americans to spend a lot of time listening to messages or reading books about weight loss.

Ectomorphs
thin and tall people, without much muscle, which makes them look fragile.

Body weight
perception varies from culture to culture.

Height and status play a huge role in the process of deciding who's attractive and who's not. Tall and wealthy men are generally favored by heterosexual women in U.S. culture. Since being tall is apparently more attractive than being short, it can add pressure especially to men, who can end up struggling with their self-confidence due to lack of height. In fact, many men's shoe companies advertise shoes that can discretely add several inches to a man's height. For women, the issue seems a little more complicated. Generally, people believe that, just as with guys, tall women are more attractive. Yet women who gain above-average height during puberty can feel as though they are at a disadvantage socially and professionally, especially after surpassing the height of the average male. They may appear intimidating to men due to their height. Do you think issues such as height, weight, and status are critical in physical attractiveness in other cultures? Can you think about any media images you have seen that differ from the traditional U.S. standards of "beauty"?

Height and status
both play a huge role in perceptions of wh is attractive and who is not.

KINESICS

Kinesics

the study of body movement, including both posture and gestures.

Kinesics is the study of body movement, including both posture and gestures. It's long been known that our kinesics can provide important information about ourselves to others. Every one of us has a certain walk, posture, and stance, which we make our own, we are recognized by, and can be impacted by our mood or emotions. A common saying in the United States makes reference to people's kinesics in the way they "carry themselves." We know we can't physically "carry ourselves," so this must mean our posture, stance, and movement. Have you noticed how some people seem to carry themselves in ways that make them unapproachable? Kinesics is another nonverbal code that has different meanings across cultures. In the United States, what is seen as a "confident" way of carrying oneself (shoulders forward, back straight, arms held stiffly to one's sides) can be considered belligerent in other cultures.

Have your teachers or parents ever chided you to "stand up straight"? As annoying as that command may be, posture displays important traits during our interactions. In many cultures, including the United States, an upright but relaxed body posture is associated with many attractive attributes, such as confidence, positivity, and high self-esteem (Guerrero & Floyd, 2006). We do judge others' personalities based on something as subjective as posture; so it's worth being aware of your own kinesics. Do you ever pay attention to your posture? Are you aware of the way you stand? How do mood and emotions affect your posture? Posture conveys much information about dominance and status throughout different cultures. Social psychologist David Johnson (2006) contends:

> Individuals with high status and power may engage in a dominance display by puffing themselves up to full size, stiffening their backs, tightening their brows, thrusting their chins forward, and leaning toward the challenger in an attempt to convince others of their power. (p. 199)

However, dominant nonverbal behaviors aren't always linked to high-status behaviors. Think about any time you have interviewed for a job. An interviewer is typically much more relaxed than a job applicant. Audrey Nelson and Susan Golant (2004) explain:

> The more restricted, tight, pulled in, and tense, the less power we have. This is evident during a job interview. The interviewer is in a power position, relaxed and at ease; the interviewee looks like a private in the military, sitting in a straight-backed, full-attention position. (p. 171)

Gestures are the movements we make with our hands and arms. Some people "talk with their hands" in an effort to complement what they're saying, whereas others might prefer using fewer gestures, perhaps viewing them as distracting. Cultural differences can be seen in preferences toward certain codes of kinesics. A study comparing nonverbal gestures between U.S. and Persian English speakers revealed that Persian speakers relied more on facial expressions to convey meaning than on gestures or postures (Sharifabad & Vali, 2011). The next time you have a conversation with someone, try to be reflexive about the types of kinesics you use, as well as the ones used by people from different cultures.

Ekman and Friesen (1969b) classified movement and gestures according to how they function in human interaction. The five categories of kinesics include emblems, illustrators, affect displays, regulators, and adapters. Let's take a look at each in more detail.

CATEGORIES OF KINESICS

Emblems are specific, widely understood meanings in a given culture that can actually substitute for a word or phrase. Flipping someone off is an emblem because it has a direct translation to a written word (you know which word we mean). As we said, emblems have widely understood meaning, but it's critical to note that they don't have *universally* understood meanings. Only a handful of gestures have practically the same meaning across cultures. Three gestures that have the widest meaning cross-culturally are the pointing gesture, the "come here" gesture, and its opposite, the "stay away" gesture. Emblematic gestures should be used with caution, because emblems with seemingly innocent meanings can be considered offensive within different cultures. Our nonverbal behaviors can easily offend whole groups of people without us even knowing it. Consider this example: During his second inaugural parade, President George W. Bush displayed the "Hook 'em Horns" gesture to salute the University of Texas's marching band as they passed by his stand. Unfortunately, this gesture is seen as an insult or sign of the devil in Norse cultures, so Norwegians expressed anger over it. In this example, an innocent hand gesture related to a collegiate sports team outraged an entire culture, which shows the connection between nonverbal communication and cultural sensitivity.

Illustrators are gestures that complement, enhance, or substitute for the verbal message. If you were describing the length of the biggest fish you ever caught, you might use your hands to illustrate the size. Or when you are giving directions, you might point to show which way to go. Sometimes verbal messages are inappropriate or can't be heard, making illustrators a convenient nonverbal option. For example, suppose you are at a concert and there's too much noise to convey to the concessions workers what you want; instead of shouting your order, you can point at the food and hold up some fingers to indicate how many you want. This is a substitution function of an illustrating gesture.

Affect displays

nonverbal gestures, postures, and facial expressions that communicate emotions.

Nonverbal gestures, postures, and facial expressions that communicate emotions are called **affect displays**. Typically, nonverbal cues can be detected before they accompany the verbal message. Therefore, if you're happy, you are more likely to convey the happiness you feel through your nonverbal cues before you express it verbally to someone. The kind of emotion we feel is usually expressed in our faces, while how much we feel the emotion is expressed in our bodies. If we're excited, for example, our face may show our excitement to others. The movement of our hands, the openness of our posture, and the speed of our movement tell others just how excited we are. Affect displays, like emblems, can be widely misinterpreted depending on culture. For example, in many Asian societies, a common response to tragic or upsetting news is to cover one's mouth and laugh or giggle. In the United States, this would seem uncaring or insulting, which serves to emphasize how important it is to be sensitive to the nonverbal communication of other cultures.

Regulators

gestures used to control the turn-taking in conversations.

Regulators are gestures used to control the turn-taking in conversations. For example, we might make a hand motion to encourage someone or raise our own hand to get a turn at speaking. When we're eager to answer a message, we normally use indicators such as making eye contact, raising our eyebrows, opening our mouths, taking in a breath, or leaning forward slightly. We do the opposite if we don't want to answer. The little head nods, vocal expressions (such as *um*), facial expressions, body postures, and eye contact can be seen as connectors that keep the conversation together and coherent. When these sorts of nonverbal cues are absent from a conversation, it might trigger a negative reaction, and we could come to believe that our conversational partner isn't listening at all. However, in some cultures it can be considered rude to convey a regulator that indicates you want your turn to speak. This could be catastrophic in the scenario of a business meeting with a foreign company. Your best bet is always to do some research about the company and culture of your business contemporaries.

Adapters

gestures we use to release tension or fulfill some other emotional need.

Adapters are gestures we use to release tension. Playing with our hands, poking, picking, fidgeting, scratching, and interacting nonverbally with our environment are all adapters that reveal our attempts to regulate situations and make ourselves feel more at ease and able to function effectively. Adapters can alert us that another person is uncomfortable in some way. In many cultures, using too many adapters can be seen as rude and insulting. Be cognizant of how you use adapters when speaking with a cultural other.

Playing with your hair is an example of a distracting adapter.

© Rob Byron/butterstock.com

FACE AND EYES

The next nonverbal code that is important to study is the face. This code encompasses the use of the face to communicate emotion and feeling states. The face can be considered a gallery for our emotional displays (Gosselin, Gilles, & Dore, 1995). The face is so important in communication that it has become, according to communication scholars Domenici and Littlejohn (2006), "a symbol of close personal interaction" (p. 10). They explain that we use "expressions such as 'face to face,' 'face time,' 'in your face,' and 'saving face.' In other words, the metaphor of face is powerful in bringing many aspects of personal communication to the fore" (p. 10). Your face and your public identity are connected; in fact, your face is the *you* presented to others in everyday encounters. Scholar Erving Goffman (1967) wrote about this presentation of self in everyday life, explaining how face can be "lost," "maintained," "protected," or "enhanced."

It's important not only to have a basic understanding of the emotions communicated by the face but also to be aware of how we manage our faces in daily interactions, both within and outside of our culture. Social norms and communication expectations in our culture set the rules for what kinds of emotional expressions are appropriate in certain situations. Facial management techniques are categories of behavior created by Paul Ekman and Wallace Friesen (1969a, 1969b, 1975) that determine the appropriate facial response for a given situation. The four most common techniques include neutralization, masking, intensification, and deintensification.

The process of using facial expression to erase or numb how we really feel is called **neutralization**. People who neutralize their facial expressions are often referred to as having a poker face. **Masking** means to hide an expression connected to a felt emotion and replace it with an expression more appropriate to the situation. If we use an expression that exaggerates how we feel about something, it is called **intensification.** On the other hand, if we reduce the intensity of our facial expression connected to a certain emotion, it is called **deintensification**. Be critical of how you use these facial expressions in relation to other people. What might be acceptable within the culture of your family may not be acceptable in the classroom or a different country.

EYE BEHAVIOR

A significant part of facial expressions involves use of the eyes. About 80% of the information in our everyday surroundings is taken in visually (Morris, 1985). The eyes are said to be the window to the soul—do you agree with that? How much information do you think people can obtain about you by looking into your eyes? Are you comfortable making eye contact with most people or only with people you know well? If you want to flirt with someone you find attractive, you might stare, get his or her attention, and then look away. If you are angry at someone, you might stare him or her down. The eyes have social and cultural importance for communication. In U.S. culture, as well as in many other cultures, eye contact is extremely important. People tend to make all kinds of judgments about others—particularly about their trustworthiness and sincerity—on the basis of whether they make or avoid eye contact. We tend to trust those who will look us in the eye and to believe what they are saying. This is not the case everywhere, however; some Asian cultures see consistent, direct eye contact as a belligerent behavior.

Think of eye behavior in terms of its influence on the social interactive process. Eye behavior is very powerful and can stimulate **arousal**, which can be a positive or negative reaction to another person. Seeing another person always triggers some degree of arousal, whether conscious or not. It can be positive if we haven't seen a person for a while and we're excited to see him or her; however, it can also be negative if we see someone whom we don't like. The second influence of eye behavior relates to **arousal**. This means that what we do with our eyes is more obvious than other actions of the face and body. Put simply, the eyes truly matter in social interaction and are significant to our study of nonverbal communication.

Neutralization

the process of using facial expression to erase or numb how we really feel.

Masking

to hide an expression connected to a felt emotion and replace it with an expression more appropriate to the situation.

Intensification

using an expression that exaggerates how we feel about something.

Deintensification

reducing the intensity of facial expression connected to a certain emotion.

Arousal

a positive or negative reaction to another person.

The third influence of eye behavior is **involvement**, or the need to interact with another person even if just with a simple visual acknowledgment or head nod. Have you ever smiled at a complete stranger while you were passing? Although you don't know the person, you tend to want to get involved with him or her, even if only through a slight smile or head nod promoted by brief eye contact.

Let us now take a brief look at a different area of study regarding facial and eye behavior: **deception cues**. What stereotypical behavior can you think of that is associated with lying? Behavior such as avoiding eye contact, looking down at the floor, fidgeting, clearing one's throat, and using lots of vocal fillers such as *um* and *er* commonly indicate that someone is lying. Breaking or being unable to sustain eye gaze is commonly believed to indicate deception. One recent study indicated that children pick up this gaze-breaking behavior of lying at a young age (McCarthy & Lee, 2009). Other studies, however, found an increase in eye gaze in connection with lying, possibly because some deceivers try to compensate for their deception by making more eye contact (DePaulo et al., 2003). As stated earlier, however, remember that in other cultures, strong eye contact is discouraged; so these findings may not relate to every culture equally. Always remember to be sensitive to the cultural environment you are in and to adapt accordingly.

© Helder Almeida/Shutterstock.com

Appropriate eye behavior can vary greatly depending on culture.

WHAT YOU'VE LEARNED

In this chapter, you learned how the codes of nonverbal communication have an intercultural dimension. You also learned how environment, proxemics (space), physical appearance, touch, face and eye behavior, and kinesics connect to your study of intercultural communication. Finally, you engaged in a self-assessment of nonverbal immediacy. In the next chapter, you will learn about the intercultural dimensions of interpersonal communication.

REVIEW

1. All of the ways we communicate without the use of words is known as _____.

2. _____ are signs that information the speaker wishes to conceal verbally is spilling out nonverbally.

3. Communication that vilifies a person or group on the basis of color, disability, ethnicity, gender, race, religion, or any other characteristic that sets people apart is called _____.

4. _____ is the process of being aware of and understanding the world around us.

5. Collections of attitudes, perceptions, and personal backgrounds are known as _____.

6. Explain the linguistic relativity hypothesis.

7. What stipulates how our messages and behavior are interpreted? For example, what says that texting while at the dinner table is considered rude?

8. Which theory asserts that our points of view arise from the social groups we belong to and influence how we socially construct the world?

9. What is the name of the study of physical touch?

10. What are affect displays?

Review answers are found on the accompanying website.

REFLECT

1. Marcus hears his roommate, Devon, walk into their apartment and slam the front door much louder than usual. When Marcus asks him if he is okay, Devon—without making eye contact—says he is fine and walks to his room, closing the door behind him. Use the vocabulary from your text about verbal and nonverbal communication to explain why Marcus doesn't believe Devon's response to be truthful.

2. When learning or interacting with another professional from a different culture, how would you attempt to learn more about that person's culture while still being respectful? How would you identify questions that could be inappropriate or insulting?

3. Max has been asked by his boss, Raquel, to help her write an acceptance speech for a reward she will be receiving from their company's executive board. Max suggests beginning the speech by thanking the company chairmen who are presenting the reward to her, and Raquel seems annoyed by the suggestion. Why do you think Raquel seems annoyed, and what advice would you have for Max?

4. Kyle goes to his professor's office during her office hours to ask her a question. The first thing he notices about her office are the awards and degrees lining the wall. As he sits in the chair in front of her desk, she asks him to wait while she finishes drafting an email on her computer. Kyle feels tense and awkward as he waits, while his professor appears relaxed and maintains an upright posture as she types her email. Using the concepts and terms discussed in this chapter, explain how the differences in power are nonverbally communicated between Kyle and his professor.

5. How does culture impact workplace etiquette on issues such as time, space, and territoriality? What steps can you take to ensure you respect the corporate culture of an international company?

KEY TERMS

verbal communication, 113
nonverbal communication, 113
digital code, 115
analogic code, 115
symbols, 115
leakage cues, 116
hate speech, 118
racial slurs, 118
perception, 119
cultural influences, 120
fields of experience, 120
language, 120
linguistic relativity hypothesis, 121
coordinated management of meaning, 122
content, 122
speech act, 122
episode, 122
relationship, 122
self, 122
coordination, 123
constitutive rules, 123
regulative rules, 123
standpoint theory, 123
inclusive language, 123
cultural identity, 124
environment, 125
chronemics, 128
proxemics, 129
homophobia, 131
territoriality, 133
violation, 133

invasion, 134
contamination, 134
haptics, 134
touch ethic, 135
location, 136
duration, 136
intensity, 136
contact cultures, 137
noncontact cultures, 137
physical appearance, 137
personal artifacts, 138
somatotyping, 139
endomorphs, 139
mesomorphs, 139
ectomorphs, 139
body weight, 139
height and status, 139
kinesics, 140
gestures, 141
emblems, 141
illustrators, 141
affect displays, 142
regulators, 142
adapters, 142
neutralization, 144
masking, 144
intensification, 144
deintensification, 144
arousal, 144
involvement, 145
deception cues, 145

CHAPTER SIX
Conversing and Relating in Intercultural Contexts

CHAPTER OUTLINE

WHAT YOU WILL LEARN

After studying this chapter, you should be able to

1. understand the coordination involved in conversations, as well as how turn-taking and turn repair occur;
2. explain how language reflects culture, and how language differences can influence the nature of conversations;
3. discuss the role of emotions and emotional expression in intercultural conversations, and what cultural variations exist; and
4. describe the challenges and benefits of intercultural relationships, as well as the influence of relational dialectics.

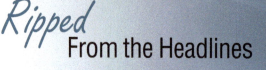

Ripped **From the Headlines**

© Jenny Anderson/WireImage/Getty Images

The film, *Get Out*, made a name for itself by becoming the second-biggest R-rated horror movie ever; while its budget was only $5 million, it ended up earning about $165 million (Mendelson, 2017). Jordan Peele, the writer and director of the film, has stated that his goal was to get audiences to see subtle racism that exists from the perspective of a black man. "It was very important to me to just get the entire audience in touch in some way with the fears inherent [in] being black in this country," Peele stated in an interview with NPR (Gross, 2017). This film has opened conversations about the experiences of people of color in the United States. While great progress has been made in the U.S., racism still exists and needs to be discussed, especially when discussing intercultural contexts. The importance of conversing in intercultural contexts cannot be overstated. It is through both professional and social interactions that individuals can truly immerse themselves in a new culture.

As you explore this chapter, you will learn the importance of conversation, which includes being not only a good speaker but also an excellent listener. You will learn that language rules and norms are not universal, and that the ways different cultures practice turn-taking can vary as well. Be cognizant of the emotional differences in conversational speaking among cultures, as well as other challenges and rewards of intercultural relationships. After finishing this chapter, you should be better prepared to practice cultural competency and have a good foundation for engaging in intercultural conversations.

Interpersonal communication is one of the most prevalent and productive means by which we accomplish many goals. Whether at work, at home, or out in the general public, our interpersonal conversations help us make sense of the world around us and enable us to derive meaning in our lives. Crucial to the success of a conversation between individuals who grapple with linguistic or cultural differences is the achievement of a common understanding or shared meaning between the two parties (Schegloff, 1992).

In this chapter, we will explore interpersonal communication, particularly the influences on our ability to engage in conversation with diverse others. This will be accomplished by exploring the nature of conversations and how we coordinate them, especially within intercultural settings. We will move on to discuss the role of language and its variations, as well as how norms vary in terms of emotional expression. In the latter part of the chapter, we will progress to relationship issues—particularly, the challenges and rewards of intercultural relationships, as well as matters associated with romantic relationships and friendships. Finally, we will discuss relational dialectics and their influence on intercultural interactions.

CONVERSATIONAL TURN-TAKING

Turn-taking and coordination of talk is the foundation of what happens during conversation. We usually think of conversations as ordered and linear, with conversational partners uttering phrases and sentences that feed off each other. In addition to most conversations being sequential, the fundamental nature of talk is the collaboration required by both partners (Lee, 2003). Naturally occurring talk involves taking turns and coordinating transitions from one conversational topic to the next, and this is usually true regardless of the context (Schegloff, Jefferson, & Sacks, 1977). In simple terms, one person says something that triggers a thought or memory in the other person, who then makes an utterance that follows up on that of the first person. This pattern can repeat back and forth for any amount of time. This skill seems to be inherent and natural in most adults to some extent, and we have been learning it since we were first held as newborn infants (Bloom, Russell, & Wassenberg, 1987; Snow, 1977).

Turn taking

one person says something that triggers a thought or memory in the other person, who then makes an utterance that follows up on that of the first person.

Not all conversational episodes run as smoothly as our description might indicate. In many cases, partners experience a lull, an abrupt topic shift, or a disruption in the turn-taking sequence. These disfluencies often require **turn repair** to get the conversation back on track. Turn repair is part of many turn-taking sequences. At some point during a conversation, there inevitably will be a disruption in the

Turn repair

the identification of a disruption or misunderstanding in conversation and the conversation is brought back on track with the turn-taking sequence restored.

Conversational turn-taking is learned before a child even learns to talk.

© pio3/Shutterstock.com

IN YOUR *life*

Have you ever engaged in an intercultural conversation where turn-taking and sequencing became problematic? How did you react and adapt to the situation?

turn-taking, which can result from one partner not hearing the utterance correctly, saying something that reflects a misunderstanding in the previous statement, or talking out of turn. For example, you could be telling your friend about having to take your car to the shop to get it repaired. You intend to explain that your car is leaking brake fluid, but instead of saying *brake*, you accidentally say *radio*:

You: "The mechanic said my car is leaking radio fluid."

Friend: "Hmm . . . I don't know . . . I think your mechanic is trying to cheat you."

You: "What do you mean? I've been being going to that shop for 2 years now."

Friend: "But you said your mechanic told you you're leaking *radio* fluid. That can't be right. Car radios don't use fluids or lubrication."

You: "What? . . . Oh, I meant to say brake fluid, not radio fluid."

Friend: "Oh, okay. Yeah, that would have been weird . . ."

As illustrated in this exchange, when the disruption or misunderstanding was identified, your friend initiated a turn repair by telling you of your mistaken utterance. Subsequently, the conversation was brought back on track and the turn-taking sequence was restored . . . and you and your friend had a good chuckle over the idea of radio fluid. Schegloff et al. (1977) explain that conversants engage in turn-taking repair by several methods. In general, the nature of the repair is based on such factors as who first utters the statement that causes the misunderstanding or disruption and who initiates the repair sequence.

Turn-taking and initiating turn repairs can be challenging enough when both people are speaking the same language. However, linguistic differences can make this process more complicated and can play a role in conversational difficulties and misunderstandings. Some Asian international students attest to how much easier it is to speak English with other nonnative speakers, regardless of the language system with which they are most familiar, compared with speaking to students whose first language is English (Lee, 2003). Lee looked at turn-taking and turn repairs in conversations with individuals conversing in a language that is not their primary one (e.g., a Chinese-speaking person conversing with another person in English). Lee found that nonnative speakers of English had fewer difficulties with turn repairs when they were speaking with other nonnative English speakers than they did speaking with individuals whose first language was English. To explain these findings, Lee concludes that when nonnative speakers are interacting, there is less of a likelihood that one will feel a face threat or embarrassment, and they might view turn repair as a friendly effort at helping the other rather than criticism or ridicule for having difficulty with the language being spoken (which was English in the study).

In general, the sequencing of conversations can be influenced by cultural differences but, more important, by how conversational partners can move past those differences and be perceptive of each other's verbal and nonverbal communication. Such attention to these cues can enable intercultural partners to smooth out the disruptions in conversations and thus avoid serious misunderstandings.

LANGUAGE AND CULTURE IN CONVERSATION

As obvious a claim as it is, language is inextricably linked to culture. McCornack (2013) explains that a language is a system of symbols that reflect how members of a group typically express their thoughts and feelings to others. Besides nonverbal cues, the words made available to us through our language serve as a valuable tool for conveying the kinds of meaning we wish to share with the other person. The nature of this meaning, and the way it is shared, is tied to the kind of conversation that develops between communication partners.

In addition, words and linguistic patterns enable a culture to develop a sense of its identity and to convey that identity to others (Sumaryono & Ortiz, 2004), both inside and outside the cultural group. Cultural differences can be made more obvious when conversational partners convey different concepts and worldviews through their language. Whorf (1950) points out that the Hopi Indians have a limited concept of time (if you apply traditional Western standards of time). As a reflection of this worldview, the Hopi language contains no words that could be translated as *time*, nor does it refer to things past, present, or future. This is an illustration of how a culture's language or linguistic patterns reflect what that culture thinks about, what is important to its members, and how they want to project their identity to out-group members. However, not all cultures value the same things, and this difference is often reflected in the presence or absence of certain concepts in one's language system. The Native American view of time (or lack thereof) might be incomprehensible to someone who treats time as a commodity and values punctuality. For example, if you ask your friend to be "on time" for a meeting, she might not understand what you mean by "on time" if that phrase is not a normal part of her culture or language. As a result, she might show up to your meeting 2 hours late and be confused as to why you are upset with her. Even when conversing with those we perceive to be part of our culture, there can still exist different conceptualizations of similar terms. The phrase "on time" can mean right at the scheduled time, 10 minutes early, or within 5 minutes of the start time.

This discussion of language in conversation might remind you of high- and low-context cultures. Recall that high-context cultures do not rely a great deal on explicit language in the communication of thoughts and feelings. This is partially

© Ammarik/Shutterstock.com

because members of such cultures expect their conversational partners to share their knowledge and perception of the world; therefore, it seems more appropriate to use nonverbal cues, to hint, or to rely on contextual signals to get their message across. On the other hand, low-context cultures do not necessarily assume that others share their understanding of the world. Because of this and other factors, low-context individuals rely more heavily on language use and are accustomed to stating explicitly what they think and mean to avoid misunderstandings. Unlike high-context individuals who are more accustomed to "talking around" a subject, low-context cultures place more value on being direct and informative (Hall & Hall, 1987), even if it seems extremely forward or makes the other person uncomfortable.

Asian cultures tend to be more high-context in their communication style than Western cultures. It's important to be mindful of these differences when engaging in intercultural communication.

EMOTIONAL EXPRESSION IN CONVERSATION

Emotional expression is what many people rely on when they do not want to say what they are feeling. In fact, we tend to express very few of our emotions verbally (Adler & Towne, 2002), which leaves us to convey them through nonverbal means (e.g., facial expressions, hand gestures, posturing). An **emotion** is a physiological and affective reaction to some circumstance or event that compels a person to interpret a meaning for it (Gross, Richards, & John, 2006). Emotions are reactive in that they are triggered by events, people, and circumstances often interpreted through a cultural filter. For instance, a 42-year-old woman going to the doctor might feel frustrated or patronized if her doctor says to her, "Okay, girl, you can get down from the exam table now." Her emotional reaction might be caused by an interpretation of "girl" as a label given to someone the doctor does not take seriously. Her emotional reaction might compel her to think or say, "I can't believe he talked to me that way! Heck, I'm older than he is!" Also, emotional expression is informed by societal, cultural, and situational norms of which we might be aware (Metts & Planalp, 2002). In her ongoing research on communication among families using hospice care, one of your authors has been told by several care providers that some cultures differ in the amount of sadness or grief they express, or in how much sympathy and consolation they want to receive from others. Therefore, if a father of a dying child wishes to keep to himself and not express sadness openly, he is likely not going to be receptive of a chaplain who approaches him, throws his arms out, and gives him an unsolicited hug. The chaplain's disregard for the father's emotional needs—and assumption that the father had the same emotional upbringing as the chaplain—might do more harm than good to the family, who might need social support in other ways, such as being allowed to grieve as they wish.

Emotion

a physiological and affective reaction to some circumstance or event that compels a person to interpret a meaning for it.

The process of grieving is different for each individual.

© ker_vii/Shutterstock.com

You might have learned about the six emotions that are considered basic and universal: happiness, sadness, anger, disgust, fear, and surprise (Gudykunst & Kim, 1995; Shaver, Wu, & Schwartz, 1992). A mix of any of these emotions might then be considered a hybrid or emotional blend (Ekman & Davidson, 1994). For example, at your anticipated university or college commencement ceremony, you might experience both happiness (at your accomplishment and newly acquired degree) and sadness (at leaving your college friends and the campus with which you have become familiar).

Despite the general acceptance of the six basic emotions, scholars still disagree on how many basic emotions there are, as well as which emotions are purely physiological as opposed to learned or acquired through socialization. Kemper (1987) identifies anger, depression, fear, and satisfaction as emotions that are mainly physiological. We also should not assume that all cultures categorize emotions in the same way. For example, emotional labels such as *anger*, *fear*, *love*, and *sadness* do not have equivalent translations in Machinguengan, the language spoken by indigenous people in the Amazon basin (Russell, 1991).

Emotions do have a perceptual component, and the same emotional expressions might be the result of different thoughts and experiences. Although emotions have a physiological component, conceptual and social factors influence how we feel in a given moment or context. For instance, cultures vary on what they believe is beautiful or ugly, pleasant or unpleasant, and so on. Cultures vary a great deal in their emotional responses to pleasant and unpleasant ideas, things, people, and experiences. That is probably why the thought of eating skewered scorpions might elicit a smile of delight in one culture and a scowl of disgust in another.

Diverse individuals also vary in the cognitive labels they might attach to the same emotion. For example, Miyuki and Lester are in the same class and get their exams back. They both happened to get a poor grade on the exam, and they both feel tense, sensing a knot in their stomachs. On the one hand, Miyuki is utterly ashamed by her exam results and sees the grade as a sign of her stupidity. Although Lester is also tense, he does not see his poor grade as evidence of his stupidity but, rather, as a momentary setback and a motivation to study harder for the next exam. Do you notice how both students feel the same physiological reaction but assign different meanings to their similar emotions?

DISPLAY RULES AND CULTURAL VARIATIONS

Not everyone agrees on what emotions are appropriate to express in certain contexts, or the extent to which those emotions should be expressed. When you are engaged in conversation and become angry with the other person, you probably have an opinion about what is appropriate in expressing your anger to your conversational partner. Perhaps you feel comfortable intensifying your facial expressions but do not think it right to raise your voice. The other person, however, might think it is normal and acceptable to raise one's voice in anger, which might cause misunderstandings and hurt feelings as you both try to resolve your dispute.

Anger can be shown in many ways, including through facial expressions and gestures.

This difference in perceptions of appropriateness can in part be linked to cultural background, particularly with the inculcation of display rules.

We all have been taught **display rules**, which are prescriptions for what kinds and amounts of emotional expression are appropriate (Naito & Seki, 2009). Cultures can vary a great deal on their attitudes toward emotions, particularly on which ones to express and conceal (Gullekson & Vancouver, 2010). Wu and Tseng (1985) point out that traditional Chinese culture emphasizes control and moderation of emotions, and some Chinese fear that intense emotions might bring harm to the body and spirit. These attitudes and beliefs take shape in the form of display rules individuals have been taught by their families and influential members of their culture. Therefore, if someone believes that intense emotional displays will result in tension in the body, that person is likely to temper his or her emotional expression. This might become a problem if this person has a friend or romantic partner who expects open displays of emotion. In this case, an emotionally expressive person might perceive such a partner to be unfeeling or uncaring in the relationship.

Display rules

prescriptions for what kinds and amounts of emotional expression are appropriate.

Hochschild (1979) summarizes the research on cultural influences on emotions in her explanation of framing rules, feeling rules, and emotion work. First, **framing rules** are the standards taught to us by society or culture that help us define what certain situations are supposed to mean to us emotionally. For instance, there are different framing rules regarding how one perceives the death of a loved one (Lofland, 1985). Some communities in Africa view death as a time to celebrate the life of the deceased, while many families in the United States see death as a more somber occasion. According to Lofland's research on emotions and grief, reactions to bereavement vary across groups and cultures according to the deceased person's significance to the grieving person's life, the circumstances of the death, the grieving person's character, and the context or setting in which the grieving takes place.

Framing rules

the standards taught to us by society or culture that help us define what certain situations are supposed to mean to us emotionally.

In Mexico, people celebrate the dead on a day called Día de los Muertos.

Feeling rules

refer to what people should feel or have the "right" to feel in a given situation.

Emotion work

the amount of effort we expend to engender feelings we think are appropriate for a situation.

Feeling rules refer to what people should feel or have the "right" to feel in a given situation (Hochschild, 1979). Wood (2013) points out that feeling rules imply a lot about a culture or society's values and the roles people are to play in these emotionally charged situations. For instance, Wood explains that because some Asian cultures are more collectivistic, one's feelings in these cultures are less about how one feels individually and more about how feelings reflect the needs or experiences of the larger group or society. Therefore, any feeling one has in response to a situation takes into consideration the situation's impact on the group as a whole.

Finally, Hochschild (1979) talks about **emotion work**, which is the amount of effort we expend to engender the feelings we think are appropriate for a situation. This could mean the ease with which we express an emotion, or the effort we put into suppressing a feeling that might be considered inappropriate. Hochschild points out that we usually do not think about our emotion work unless we think the feeling we want to show is deemed culturally unsuitable. In such cases, we feel a great deal of incongruity between what we actually feel and what we think we should be feeling. For example, suppose you come from a high-power-distance culture in which reverence and deep feelings of respect for a leader are expected. But what if you secretly harbor distrust for that leader? Your inward feelings, then, contradict the emotions you are expected to show in public, which can cause some internal conflict and emotional stress, especially within workplace environments (Zapf, Vogt, Seifert, Mertini, & Isic, 1999).

Some research has documented cross-cultural differences in how emotions are expressed, how much they are expressed, and the appropriateness of their expression. For instance, Hwang and Matsumoto (2012) found that the European American students in their study endorsed emotional expression more than did Asian American students and that the Asian Americans leaned more favorably toward modifying or subduing emotional expression. These findings do not necessarily suggest that Asian Americans are automatically less emotionally expressive; Hwang and Matsumoto acknowledge that such individuals might be expressive about certain things that are important to them, such as a very close relationship. In actuality, we might expect collectivistic individuals to be more wary of conveying negative emotions out of concern for keeping the peace and avoiding conflict. In addition, being selective about the context in which one is more emotionally expressive might be typical of a high-context person who pays careful attention to what he or she thinks is appropriate for the situation.

Sadfar et al. (2009) also documented cross-cultural comparisons of display rules among Canadians, Japanese, and Americans for the emotions of happiness, surprise, anger, contempt, disgust, sadness, and fear. They found that individuals from North America favored powerful expressions (anger, contempt, and disgust) more so than the Japanese respondents, who indicated that the positive emotions (happiness and surprise) should be expressed less often than did the Canadians. The researchers also found similar gender differences across the three cultures. Men expressed more powerful emotions, and women expressed more powerless emotions (happiness, sadness, fear), which suggests that some differences in masculine and feminine orientation might be slightly more universal across the cultures studied.

ETHICAL CONNECTION

Travis and Evan are graduate students at a small Southeastern university. One of their fellow students, Nora, is a foreign-exchange student from Germany. As Evan and Travis got to know Nora better, they began to engage in playful teasing with her about her accent and occasional grammar errors when speaking English. The teasing continued for several weeks, and Travis began to notice that Nora did not want to socialize with them anymore. After a couple of weeks, Travis approached Nora to see what the problem was. Nora informed him that their teasing had been hurtful to her and she was tired of dealing with the embarrassment in social situations. When Travis replied that the teasing was all in good fun and she should not take it seriously, Nora gave up and moved away from their social circle in the graduate department soon after.

Questions to consider:
1. What ethical consideration did Travis and Evan fail to take into account in their interactions with Nora?
2. Why is it important to be sensitive to another person's culture, accent, and grammar when communicating across language barriers
3. Do you agree with Nora that Travis and Evan were out of line during their communication, despite the fact that they said they were only teasing?
4. How could Travis and Evan have handled the situation differently without offending Nora and losing her friendship?

EMOTIONAL INTELLIGENCE

The appropriate type and amount of emotion in a given situation is believed by many to be a function of emotional intelligence. Referred to as EQ (sometimes EI), **emotional intelligence** was conceptualized by Daniel Goleman (1997, 2002) as the ability to understand and identify one's emotions, handle stress, empathize with others, and manage emotions in positive ways. EQ is often differentiated into two models: ability EQ and trait EQ. **Ability EQ** assumes that emotions can be useful tools in understanding the meaning of a situation. Under this assumption, one might tap into an emotion to make sense of the environment in which that emotion is experienced and to derive meaning from it. These emotions can be those you feel yourself or those you perceive in others. For example, if you walk into a room and sense that people are nervous or uptight, you might look to the contextual cues to determine if there is some danger or threat to you if you stick around. **Trait EQ** is a construct made distinct by psychologist Konstantin Vasily Petrides (cited in Petrides & Furnham, 2003), who claimed that emotions occupy a lower level of one's personality. In other words, trait EQ reflects our self-perceptions of our emotional abilities (based on our understanding of our own personality), rather than the abilities we actually demonstrate in real life. As an illustration of trait EQ, some people might believe that they are innately prone to emotions or that women are naturally more emotional than men.

While some might question whether EQ is a real form of intelligence, many scholars attest to the importance of being able to handle one's emotions in even the most stressful situations. Various skills are involved with maintaining a high level of EQ, such as understanding what others might be feeling and being able to sense others' emotions to some extent. High EQ also involves being more mindful of the emotions you find yourself experiencing, finding productive ways to reduce stress, dealing with conflict in positive ways (see Chapter 8), using humor to deal with difficulties, and having strong nonverbal skills. Even cutting down on your caffeine intake has been found to be helpful in this area (Bradberry, 2012). In terms of culture, high EQ might also empower a person to be mindful that different people hold different display rules and that one should not impose one's own standards of emotional display and appropriateness on members of other cultural groups.

Emotional intelligence
the ability to understand and identify the emotions one is experiencing, handle stress, empathize with others, and manage emotions in positive ways.

Ability EQ
assumes that emotions can be useful tools in understanding the meaning of a situation.

Trait EQ
a construct claiming that emotions occupy a lower level of one's personality.

IN YOUR *life*

How strong do you believe your EQ is? How do you practice and strengthen your understanding of and empathy for others?

Do you think that gender differences are learned or innate?

© paulista/Shutterstock.com

Some research has looked at variations in EQ, particularly between genders. Petrides and Furnham (2000, 2003) claim that gender is a significant predictor of self-estimated EQ (i.e., guessing or estimating how emotionally intelligent you are). They found that the males in their study reported having higher trait EQ scores than did the women. It should be noted that the estimated and actual scores of both men and women were positively correlated, meaning that the study's respondents could have had some insight into their own EQs. It is probably not enough simply to compare men and women on their reported levels of EQ. For instance, EQ comes into play both at home and at work, and there is some evidence that men and women differ in their abilities depending on the extent to which they act out traditional masculine and feminine gender roles. In keeping with this viewpoint, Rivera Cruz (2004) found that men displayed higher EQs at work and women higher EQs in the home environment when they exhibited behavior in line with their respective gender roles. One quick (and perhaps too hasty) explanation could be that women have a better handle on their emotions at home, as do men at work. But we might also argue that these differences are more learned and socialized than innate and that such a finding should be interpreted with caution. After all, it would be unfortunate for a woman to be discouraged from excelling in the workplace because of the belief that she will not be able to handle the pressures of management. In turn, plenty of men feel comfortable in more domestic roles of home management and child care, despite certain masculine stereotypes to the contrary.

There have been some cultural variations in EQ, particularly within the context of cultural adjustment, and the level of EQ does have an effect on one's ability to adjust to a new cultural environment. In such situations, EQ can also affect one's cultural intelligence (CQ), which is the ability to interact and communicate effectively across different cultural contexts (Lin, Chen, & Song, 2012). When comparing ethnic groups in their perceived EQ scores, it is more informative to focus on specific aspects of EQ, such as attention to, clarity of, and repair of emotions. For instance, Martines, Fernández-Berrocal, and Extremera (2006) studied ethnic differences in the United States and Mexico. Mexicans scored lower on attention and clarity than did African Americans, white Americans, and Latino Americans. In addition, women scored higher on attention and men higher on clarity. As with some of the gender findings, a word of caution is warranted. The authors warn against making blanket assumptions about which ethnic groups have more EQ. Rather, there might be common proclivities toward certain aspects of EQ based on culture.

BUILDING BRIDGES, BUILDING RELATIONSHIPS

Understanding how people manage conversations and emotions brings us to one of the fundamental reasons why communication scholars study interpersonal communication—building and maintaining relationships. Here we are talking about all kinds of relationships in which you interact on a daily basis, from the most intimate and personal to the professional and formal. Coordinating emotional expression, nonverbal cues, and conversational turn-taking is subordinate to the ultimate goal of building a connection with the other person, even if only for a brief moment. We establish and maintain relationships through our communication because we need these relationships to accomplish work-related tasks, we gain satisfaction from connecting with others, or we simply do not want to be alone. Regardless of the reason, learning to navigate our interpersonal communication—and working with the perceived differences between us and our communicative partners—can increase our relational satisfaction in virtually any context.

CHALLENGES AND REWARDS OF INTERCULTURAL RELATIONSHIPS

Most people can say quite easily that they belong to some kind of intercultural relationship, which carries the assumption that at least one perceived cultural difference separates relational partners. This does not have to mean a romantic relationship; relationships are also found within families, among good friends, in our places of worship, at work, and in many other contexts in which we engage in interpersonal communication. Intercultural relationships can offer us many benefits, such as learning unique things from someone who comes from a different background or has different experiences. In many cases, our diverse friends and loved ones can teach us much about the world we have yet to explore, as well as help us rethink stereotypes we might hold about members of certain ethnic groups or cultures. According to Martin and Nakayama (2007), these benefits represent aspects of **relational learning**, which includes the insights and new ways of thinking that result from the people with whom we are in relationships, especially when we have interesting dissimilarities with our relational partners.

Relational learning
the insights and new ways of thinking that result from the people with whom we are in relationships, especially when we have interesting dissimilarities with our relational partners.

Each intercultural relationship comes with its own unique set of challenges. Martin and Nakayama (2007) point out that the differences we perceive with our partners tend to be more noticeable in the early stages of the relationship. Sometimes these differences can remind us of stereotypes we hold or have learned, which can make finding common ground difficult. However, as the relationship progresses, both partners are more likely to discover their similarities, which can have more impact than the original dissimilarities. Martin and Nakayama (1999) go on to say that there is interplay between similarities and differences in intercultural relationships. Because the differences seem obvious—and perhaps overwhelming—at first, the challenge is to discover the things both partners have in common and to build on those similarities to strengthen the relationship.

Ultimately, the similarities can outweigh the differences as well as the negative stereotypes that might emerge in earlier stages of the relationship. For example, Saira and Sheila met in their public speaking class and started studying together in the evenings. Saira is a Muslim, and both her parents are from Afghanistan. Sheila is from Lincoln, Nebraska, and although she identifies as Methodist, she goes to church only when she goes home to see her parents on holidays. When the two young women first started spending time together, they did not know a lot about each other. In fact, Sheila grew up with stereotypes of Muslims as terrorists and was not accustomed to seeing women in hijab before coming to college. On the other hand, Saira has always lived in a large metropolitan city and does not know anyone from Nebraska; in fact, she assumes that most people from Nebraska are farmers and do not live with modern comforts such as cable television and the Internet. However, as the two spend more time together and disclose more personal information to each other, they realize that they both like their public speaking instructor and have the same major. They also discover that they both like Indian food and bike riding on the weekends. They even share a habit of gesturing a lot when they talk, about which they jokingly tease each other. The discovery of these similarities helps Saira and Sheila realize how limited their stereotypes of the other were, and they eventually build a strong relationship that lasts throughout college and beyond. Although differences and conflict will still occur in the strongest of friendships, Martin and Nakayama (2007) would likely say that Saira and Sheila are now better able to handle differences when they do occur and probably will feel more comfortable establishing and maintaining intercultural relationships with other people as well.

ROMANTIC RELATIONSHIPS

Romantic relationships can bring many of us enjoyment and fulfillment, as well as conflict and heartbreak. In many ways, cultures approach romantic relationships differently. Gao (1991) compared U.S. and Chinese students in their perceptions of romantic love; U.S. students tended to stress passion and physical attraction, while Chinese students placed more value on connectedness, particularly with regard to families. Some cultures also differ in the open display of intense emotion. For instance, Chinese American couples typically have fewer periods of openly expressed positive emotions toward each other than do European American couples (Tsai & Levenson, 1997), who have fewer of these periods than do

IN YOUR *life*

Have you ever engaged in an intercultural romantic relationship? In your experience, was the cultural gap a major obstacle to having a healthy relationship?

Mexican American couples (Soto, Levenson, & Ebling, 2005). These and other such findings might make sense considering that Chinese culture tends to be collectivistic, often emphasizing harmony and community. The other groups in the study might come from more individualistic cultures, which often embrace more outward expressions of emotion.

So far, you might assume that we have been talking only about heterosexual relationships, which typically get most of the attention from communication and relationship researchers. However, a growing amount of scholarship has been focusing attention on gay and lesbian romantic relationships. **LGBTQIA+** individuals (i.e., lesbian, gay, bisexual, transgender, queer, intersex, asexual, and other individuals questioning their gender) are being taken more seriously as a cultural community. Individuals who belong to such groups typically face additional challenges, such as being misunderstood or feared by some members of mainstream society, as well as suffering blatant discrimination, especially regarding access to civil rights and health care (Ross, Scholl, & Castle Bell, in press). As this book is being written, 17 U.S. states (California, Connecticut, Delaware, Illinois, Iowa, Maine, Maryland, Massachusetts, Minnesota, New Hampshire, New Jersey, New Mexico, New York, Rhode Island, Utah, Vermont, and Washington) and the District of Columbia have statutes that legalize same-sex marriage, and many other states recognize out-of-state same-sex unions (Human Rights Campaign, 2014). Due to the growing awareness and acceptance of same-sex couples, scholarship is increasingly seeing these types of romantic relationships as worthy of study. While it is not our intent to draw undue attention to such individuals or "exoticize" them, we do argue that talking more about nonheterosexual romantic relationships will reduce the fear, stigmatization, and misunderstanding still directed toward them.

The concept of an intercultural romantic relationship does not have to seem as unusual or exotic as some might believe. In fact, people generally list the same reasons for dating within as well as outside of their culture, reasons that often include physical or sexual attraction (Lampe, 1982). Nonetheless, intercultural

LGBTQIA+

lesbian, gay, bisexual, transgender, queer, and other individuals questioning their gender or sexual orientation.

© albund/Shutterstock.com

romantic relationships can present additional difficulties. Finding your one true love might be the easy part; staying with that person through the tough times and negotiating conflict is another thing entirely. Intercultural romantic relationships can pose unique challenges, whether these challenges are attributed to religious differences or not understanding the beliefs or reasons behind a partner's routine behavior.

Intercultural couples often have their own strategies for working out disagreements. Romano (2008) found four distinct styles that reflect the way couples handle power imbalances. The **submission style** is the most common and involves one partner abdicating power to the other partner's culture or cultural preferences. For example, a Jewish husband and a Christian wife might come to a point of conflict when discussing the religion in which to raise their children. It might be the case that, to preserve harmony in the family, the Christian wife agrees to help raise the children in the Jewish faith. This might cause distress and conflict down the road if the practicing Christian laments not being able to pass along some of her faith traditions to her children. Because submission often involves denying certain aspects of one's own culture, this style rarely works in spite of the fact that it is the most common, according to Romano.

> **Submission style**
> most common way couples handle power imbalance; one partner abdicates power to the other partner's culture or cultural preferences.

With the **compromise style**, each partner gives and takes to bring power in the relationship back to equilibrium. In this case, the Jewish–Christian couple might agree to retain certain faith-based aspects of both parents' cultures, such as putting up a Christmas tree in the house but decorating it with blue garlands and trimmings (instead of the standard red and green) and Star of David ornaments. The result of the compromise is not as important as the conversation and negotiation in which the couple engages as a family, which can help them discover similarities and bring them even closer together.

> **Compromise style**
> to handle power imbalances, each partner gives and takes to bring power in the relationship back to equilibrium.

Some couples employ the **obliteration style**. In this case, the couple might abandon their own traditions and norms and come together to form a new "culture." This can be difficult, because cutting oneself off from one's culture of origin can be extremely hard and might create problems with other family members or members of the couple's respective cultures. Nonetheless, our Jewish–Christian couple might decide to settle for celebrating a general, secular holiday (e.g., the winter solstice) instead of trying to balance Christmas and Chanukah. While difficult, it can be done if the couple can look to the process of forming a third culture as transformative and beneficial to their emotional intimacy.

> **Obliteration style**
> a couple might abandon their own traditions and norms and come together to form a new "culture" to resolve power issues.

The **consensus style** is the ideal, according to Romano (2008), and is based on negotiation and mutual agreement. Both parties assume that they do not have to

> **Consensus style**
> to resolve power issues by negotiation and mutual agreement.

abandon their own cultures but might at times suspend them to adapt to certain situations. For example, the Christian spouse might not adhere to Jewish dietary restrictions, such as refraining from consuming meat and dairy products in the same meal; however, if the husband's Jewish family is coming to dinner, she could take measures to keep the milk and meat dishes separate out of respect for her in-laws.

Regardless of the style or styles a couple chooses, Romano (2008) strongly recommends that people considering an intercultural romantic relationship prepare for the cultural aspects of the relationship and make sure they are truly committed to the endeavor. Interfaith couples, because of their unique challenges, are at greater risk for divorce than are couples that share the same faith (Lehrer & Chiswick, 1993). Hughes (2004) and Hughes and Dickson (2005) have studied communication within interfaith couples. Instead of studying the influence of spouses' religious affiliation, they have focused more on religious orientation, which is conceptualized as intrinsic or extrinsic. **Intrinsic religious orientation** is characterized by a strong commitment to one's faith. For an intrinsically oriented person, his or her religion and the doctrines and practices associated with it are inherently important. A person who has an **extrinsic religious orientation** does not necessarily put importance on the faith tradition itself but sees it as a means to an end. More specifically, the extrinsically oriented person might adhere to a religion or attend worship services to meet new people or gain some other personal benefit. Intrinsics are more regular and committed to consistent worship attendance than are extrinsics. Religious orientation has been found to be strongly linked with the conflict tactics in which interfaith partners engage. Specifically, intrinsics might resort to more mutually constructive communication during conflicted conversations and be more satisfied with their marriages. Examining religious orientation in relation to marital conflict and satisfaction can shed light on how interfaith couples argue, resolve conflict, and negotiate cultural differences. Figuring out ways to navigate potentially difficult conversations can enable couples to withstand most difficulties that stem from cultural differences.

Intrinsic religious orientation

characterized by a strong commitment to one's faith.

Extrinsic religious orientation

a person who does not necessarily put importance on the faith tradition itself but sees it as a means to an end.

INTERCULTURAL FRIENDSHIPS

When discussing "relationships," it can be easy for some people to slip into exclusive talk about romantic relationships or marriage. However, we also have to acknowledge the nonromantic relationships and friendships that enhance our lives and help us learn more about who we are as humans. When we think about intercultural friendships, we not only acknowledge the actual and perceived differences between friends but also that friendship is a construct that means different things across cultures (Martin & Nakayama, 2007). These different notions about friendship are a function of variations in values as well as the identities avowed by individuals.

For example, people who tend to be individualistic often view friendship as a voluntary endeavor that is more spontaneous and focused on individual goals (i.e., what individual benefits might be received by befriending a particular person). Collectivists, on the other hand, have more obligatory views of friendship, seeing it as a long-term situation that involves mutual support.

Collier (1996) reports differences among racial groups in the United States, particularly in perceptions of how long it takes to form a strong friendship. The European Americans in her study reported that it takes only a few months, but other ethnic groups perceived that it takes closer to a year. Ethnic groups might also differ in what is considered important in close friendships. Latino Americans value relational or social support, while Asian Americans emphasize showing caring and exchanging ideas in a positive manner. African Americans identified respect as an important consideration, while Anglo Americans placed emphasis on the fulfillment of individuals' needs.

This is not to say that different cultures cannot have similar views on friendship. Various cultures can value the same things, such as honesty and trustworthiness, but simply prioritize them differently. To illustrate, Barnlund (1989) compared U.S. and Japanese perceptions and found that both groups tend to identify similar characteristics of friendship, such as understanding, trust, respect, and sincerity. However, the U.S. and Japanese individuals in the study prioritized these characteristics differently. People from the United States tended to place more importance on honesty and individuality, whereas the Japanese valued harmony more.

© MikeDotta/Shutterstock.com

Different cultures have different views about friendship.

Even straight and gay individuals differ in the way they approach friendships, especially when it comes to same-sex versus cross-sex friendships (Martin & Nakayama, 2007). Close relationships and friendships are especially important for gays and lesbians, who often rely on these ties in the face of societal stigma, family ostracism, and discrimination. When examining differences, straight males look to females for emotional and social support, whereas gay males will turn to other males to fulfill these needs. Women—both straight and lesbian—typically do not cross gender lines for emotional support, which might not surprise you if you see women as the usual sources of emotional intimacy. Gay and straight people might also view the role of sex differently when it comes to friendships. Many heterosexuals see sex as typically not playing a role in nonromantic friendships. On the contrary, some gays' and lesbians' friendships might start with sexual involvement, but the friendships are likely to continue long after the physical aspect of the relationship ceases.

RELATIONAL DIALECTICS

Have you noticed that when communicating in relationships, you often feel a tug-of-war between two competing emotional tendencies? For instance, most of the time, you cherish the closeness and connection you share with a best friend or romantic partner. At other times, however, you just want time to yourself and not to have to talk to that person. These contradictory feelings are okay; in fact, they are quite normal. This tension between opposing feelings is referred to as dialectics, a group of philosophical theories written about by such prominent scholars as Hegel, Marx, Engels, Bakhtin, and Kant. The general theory of dialectics suggests that there are coexisting, yet opposing, tensions in many aspects of our lives. For example, you might feel close to your best friend such that you spend a lot of time together; at other times, you might crave alone time and find it difficult to express this need to your friend. A common mistake is to view the dialectic as a pendulum, with a swing in one direction toward one tendency, then in the other direction toward the polar opposite of that tendency. In other words, you do not crave only closeness with your friend, then completely switch gears and prefer only solitude. Rather, it is helpful to think of a dialectic as a tug-of-war, meaning that as you are enjoying the closeness that comes with watching a favorite TV show with your friend, you might also be thinking of relaxing at home in your room with a good book. Remember, these tensions *coexist*.

Relational dialectics
describe how relationships are fraught with coexisting, yet opposing tensions.

More specific to intercultural conversations, the dialectics we are discussing here are referred to as **relational dialectics**, which address the contradiction or interplay between opposing tensions within a personal relationship (Baxter & Montgomery, 1992). Baxter (1988) explains that these tensions coexist and are interdependent but often act as though they refute each other. For instance, you love the way your best friend makes you laugh and always seems to lighten your mood; yet your friend also has an annoying way of nagging you about your smoking habit. So you find yourself grappling with the tension of enjoying your friend's company and wanting to avoid that person when your smoking habit is mentioned.

Baxter and Montgomery's (1992) research on relational dialectics has revealed tensions common in most relationships, the first of which we have already alluded to—the **integration–separation dialectic**. This tension acknowledges the dual needs of being connected to people and at the same time enjoying a certain level of autonomy or independence. Despite the amount of satisfaction we might be experiencing in a relationship, we will likely crave solitude at times. The tricky part is expressing this need in a way that does not hurt our relational partner. Saying, "Just leave me alone, okay?!" could have a negative effect on the person from whom we want temporary independence. Therefore, finding a more nurturing way to express this need deserves some consideration (e.g., "Hey, I really enjoy hanging out with you, but I just need some alone time, okay?").

> **Integration-separation dialectic**
>
> a tension that acknowledges the dual needs of being connected to people and at the same time enjoying a certain level of autonomy and independence.

Another tension discovered by Baxter and Montgomery (1992) is the one between certainty and uncertainty. We might view this **certainty–uncertainty dialectic** as the balance between predictability and spontaneity. On the one hand, we want to be able to count on our partner, to know how he or she will respond in certain situations and that we can trust him or her. On the other hand, too much certainty or predictability can make things seem uninteresting or boring. For example, suppose your partner typically schedules dates with you in advance; it might be a pleasant surprise for that person to show up at your door unannounced with two tickets to a movie you've been dying to see. This is the kind of uncertainty that might spice up a romantic relationship.

> **Certainty-uncertainty dialectic**
>
> the balance between predictability and spontaneity.

A third dialectic is the **openness–closedness dialectic**, also described as expression–nonexpression. Baxter and Montgomery (1992) explain that this tension refers to the extent to which we disclose our feelings, intentions, or desires to the other person in a relationship. According to **social penetration theory** (Altman, Vinsel, & Brown, 1981), increased self-disclosure can signal increased desire for closeness, but most relationships do not move in a straight line toward intimacy. Rather, couples can communicate in ways that bring them closer, such as sharing more intimate details and expressing feelings (e.g., "I think I love you"), but then might take a step back to preserve a sense of privacy (e.g., "I just said the 'L word.' Not sure how she took it, so I think I'll zip it before she really freaks out"). Griffin (2006) describes the movement within all three tensions as being similar to the phases of the moon, in that relational communication waxes and wanes in terms of being close and being apart, being predictable and being spontaneous, and staying connected and being autonomous.

> **Openness-closedness dialectic**
>
> the extent to which we disclose our feelings, intentions, or desires to the other person in the relationship.

> **Social penetration theory**
>
> proposes that as relationships progress, non-intimate communication decreases and deeper, more intimate communication increases.

Martin, Nakayama, and Flores (1998) extend Baxter and Montgomery's (1992) three relational dialectics to the study of intercultural relationships. These researchers argue that employing a dialectical way of thinking about relationships can help us overcome cultural differences and even help us avoid destructive and counterproductive stereotypes. Their dialectics include differences–similarities, cultural–individual, privilege–disadvantage, personal–contextual, static–dynamic, and history/past–present/future. First, the **differences–similarities dialectic** acknowledges that relational partners share both similarities and differences but that the key is not to let the differences overshadow the similarities. As we saw with the example of Saira and Sheila, both women recognized the interests, characteristics, and mannerisms they had in common, and because these appeared to outweigh their differences, they were able to establish and maintain a strong friendship. This is not to say, however, that differences should be ignored or disregarded. In Saira and Sheila's case, they can learn a great deal about each other's region of origin and religion, and perhaps learn about and develop more appreciation and acceptance of each other's traditions.

Another dialectic put forth by Martin et al. (1998) is the **cultural–individual dialectic**. In many circumstances, someone might feel compelled to communicate in ways that stand in opposition to her or his culture, especially if that person's wishes are different from what her or his culture might prescribe. For example, a Jewish woman might choose to go to Christmas Eve Mass and sing Christmas carols with her Catholic husband's family. The cultural–individual dialectic might also come into play when we feel the need to make a distinction between attributing someone's communication behavior to cultural background or to that person's individual characteristics. The tension between these two might come into play if you have a close friend who chews loudly and smacks his or her lips while eating. This might be a behavior or habit you do not yet understand or appreciate. If you decide to attribute this behavior to your friend's culture, you might be more tolerant of it. On the other hand, if you think this behavior is idiosyncratic, you might find it more annoying and decide to express your displeasure.

The **privilege–disadvantage dialectic** can be especially prevalent between individuals who come from cultures that do not enjoy the same level of privilege or power in the larger society. This could be true, for example, with two friends named Mike (a white, straight male) and Tony (a gay male of color). Suppose Mike, having no negative intent, says, "I'm going to throw out this shirt. It looks so gay on me." Tony will likely be offended by Mike's remark because he guesses Mike means "silly," "stupid," or some similarly negative descriptor. When Tony expresses his displeasure, Mike might respond with, "Hey, don't get upset. You know I have no problem with your being gay. It was just a harmless remark." Unfortunately, Mike may be forgetting that he, unlike Tony, does not have to

Differences–similarities dialectic

acknowledges that relational partners share both similarities and differences but that the key is not to let the differences overshadow the similarities.

Cultural–individual dialectic

the extent to which one communicates in ways that stand in opposition to a person's culture, especially if that person's wishes are different from what her or his culture might prescribe.

Privilege–disadvantage dialectic

especially prevalent between individuals who come from cultures that do not enjoy the same level of privilege or power in the larger society.

worry about hearing anti-gay slurs as he goes about his normal day. Martin et al. (1998) might point out that Mike enjoys relative privilege because his sexual orientation is rarely or never criticized in public. Because Mike cannot completely understand what Tony goes through as a gay male, he might not be aware of his own privilege and might neglect to treat Tony with more sensitivity and respect.

The **personal–contextual dialectic** acknowledges that we do not communicate the same way with all people. Rather, we switch styles and codes when in different contexts. In addition, the role someone takes in his or her primary culture or society might vary when that person is in another culture. For example, a woman might enjoy an egalitarian role in her marriage with her husband. In her home culture, it is not unusual for her to make joint decisions with her husband about money or raising the children. However, if she visits her husband's family who reside in a different country, she might be expected to adjust her role as a wife and could possibly receive disapproval if she does not adopt a more subservient role when in the presence of her in-laws.

> **Personal-contextual dialectic**
> acknowledges that we do not communicate the same way with all people.

The **static–dynamic dialectic** recognizes that some aspects of a person are trait-like, meaning they are solid and will not likely change over time. Other characteristics (i.e., states), however, are more adaptable and might change according to circumstances, age, experience, or the people with whom one associates. For example, you will read in Chapter 11 about the discrimination that doctors and medical researchers perpetuated against African Americans and other ethnic minorities in the recent past. Because of this long history of ill treatment, many ethnic minorities still harbor a mistrust of the medical field and might even have a hard time envisioning a doctor who will treat them with respect and dignity. Nonetheless, such patterned behaviors are not static but merely need to be unlearned. Not all medical providers discriminate based on race, and patients of typically marginalized groups can realize that conditions are increasingly changing and can perhaps begin to feel more comfortable about seeking medical care.

> **Static-dynamic dialectic**
> recognizes that some aspects of a person are trait-like, but other characteristics are more adaptable and might change according to circumstances, age, experience, or the people with whom one associates.

The final dialectic is the **history/past–present/future dialectic**. A culture might feel compelled to change or alter its values, beliefs, or traditions if its overall goals change or it wants to adapt to the changing times. For example, years ago it was scandalous within Catholic communities for a woman to become pregnant out of wedlock. However, for some Catholics in contemporary society, out-of-wedlock parenthood might not be seen negatively. Such a transformation does not always take generations or an extended time period to occur. A lesbian who comes out of the closet to her parents might first experience tension or even ostracism because her family does not accept her sexual orientation. After some time, however, the family might decide to alter their views to maintain a close relationship with their daughter, and they might even change their stance on gay and lesbian rights.

> **History/past-present future dialectic**
> the extent to which one feels compelled to change or alter its values, beliefs, or traditions if its overall goals change or it wants to adapt to the changing times.

Some dialectics might be unique to intercultural romantic relationships. Cools's (2006) research found several issues couples appeared to tackle when negotiating their dialectical tensions. Some of these issues involved being an adapting spouse, resolving conflicts while raising children, and understanding and enacting male and female roles. Cools's study also uncovered the dialectical tension of privilege–disadvantage. This was especially prevalent when there were language difficulties between partners. In particular, the partner who found himself or herself speaking the "other" language—or the partner's language that was not his or her own—was often at a disadvantage, especially when arguing.

WHAT YOU'VE LEARNED

In this chapter, you learned about the significance of turn-taking and turn repair in interpersonal contexts. You then overviewed how language reflects culture in conversation and how language differences can influence the nature of conversations. Next, you learned that emotional expression in conversation can vary based on the cultural context people find themselves in. Finally, you were given various benefits of engaging in intercultural relationships, and you learned how relational dialectics influence your interpersonal communication. As you move forward in your studies of interpersonal communication, be mindful of the concepts you learned from this chapter and how they might influence your future interactions.

REVIEW

1. To get a conversation back on track and clarify things, a person might engage in a _____.

2. _____ is a system of symbols used to convey a message and the meaning behind it.

3. An _____ is a physiological and affective reaction to some circumstance or event that compels a person to interpret a meaning for it.

4. Prescriptions for what kinds and amounts of emotional expression are appropriate are referred to as _____.

5. _____ refers to the amount of effort we expend to engender the feelings we think are appropriate for a situation.

6. Discuss the difference between *ability EQ* and *trait EQ*.

7. Which style of managing power imbalances in romantic relationships does your text say is ideal?

8. Explain the difference between *intrinsic religious orientation* and *extrinsic religious orientation*.

9. Define *relational dialectics*.

10. Explain the *certainty–uncertainty dialectic*.

Review answers are found on the accompanying website.

REFLECT

1. Kimberlie is talking about her day with her boyfriend, Andy, and she mentions how she had to take Phoebe to a clinic after she discovered that Phoebe had eaten a bar of chocolate. Andy, forgetting that Kimberlie had been dog-sitting that week, mistakenly thought Kimberlie was talking about a human. He then asks if Phoebe has medical insurance, and Kimberlie looks confused. Discuss how either Andy or Kimberlie could then use a *turn repair* to clarify the conversation.

2. Create an example of when practicing *emotion work* might cause stress to a person while at work, and explain why it would be stressful for that person.

3. Think of a time when you engaged in *relational learning* while conversing with someone who comes from a different culture. Did you have any preconceived stereotypes about that person? If so, were they debunked as you learned more about them?

4. Samantha recently moved in with her girlfriend, Harmony. Harmony maintains a strictly vegan diet, and now that Samantha lives with her, she feels pressured to also practice having a plant-based diet. Samantha has been vegan for a month, and although she is not happy with it, she continues to eat only vegan-friendly foods to make Harmony happy. What type of power imbalance style is the couple currently practicing, and what are some ways they might practice a more *consensus style*?

5. Amira and Natalie are eating together during their lunch break at work. Natalie begins to tell Amira about the "crazy" day she had at work the previous day and concludes her story by describing a customer as being "retarded." Amira, who has an intellectual disability, is offended by the descriptors Natalie uses during her story. Which type of dialectical tension is at play in this scenario, and what types of words could Natalie have used in place of the descriptors that offended Amira?

KEY TERMS

turn-taking, 151
turn repair, 151
emotion, 155
display rules, 157
framing rules, 157
feeling rules, 158
emotion work, 158
emotional intelligence, 160
ability EQ (emotional intelligence), 160
trait EQ (emotional intelligence), 160
relational learning, 162
LGBTQIA+, 164
submission style, 165
compromise style, 165
obliteration style, 165

consensus style, 165
intrinsic religious orientation, 166
extrinsic religious orientation, 166
relational dialectics, 168
integration–separation dialectic, 169
certainty–uncertainty dialectic, 169
openness–closedness dialectic., 169
social penetration theory, 169
differences–similarities dialectic, 170
cultural–individual dialectic, 170
privilege–disadvantage dialectic, 170
personal–contextual dialectic, 171
static–dynamic dialectic, 171
history/past–present/future
  dialectic, 171

CHAPTER SEVEN

Intercultural Issues in Group Communication

CHAPTER OUTLINE

WHAT YOU WILL LEARN

After studying this chapter, you should be able to

1. understand the nature of groups and differentiate groups from teams;
2. explain the functional perspective of groups and identify the task and maintenance functions;
3. identify the psychological and personality characteristics that contribute to diversity in groups and teams;
4. discuss the influence of the dimensions of cultural variability on groups and teams;
5. explain in-group and out-group distinctions and their influence on the group process; and
6. apply the principles of group and team diversity toward overcoming and managing diversity.

Ripped From the Headlines

© Dmytro Zinkevych/Shutterstock.com

As Millennials—people born between 1982 and 1999—continue to enter the workforce, researchers have focused on the ways in which this generation interacts with older generations in the workplace. Although we may not always think about it, age plays a large role in our interactions with others, and these differences become more prominent when people from different generations are communicating with one another. These differences, discussed below, are beneficial to keep in mind when interacting with groups that are diverse in age.

Because Millennials have never experienced life without technology, they tend to experience the world as being highly connected and prefer speed and instant responses when communicating. In the workforce, they tend to enjoy watching and learning from others; however, Baby Boomers—individuals born between 1946 and 1964—who tend to be more independent, may perceive this desire to be mentored as a lack of initiative. In contrast to the collaborative nature of Millennials, Generation X individuals—people born between 1965 and 1981—are often perceived as poor team players and prefer to approach projects by themselves (Patterson, 2007; Schullery, 2013).

In this chapter, you will learn what the group dynamic is, as well as how groups can be affected by intercultural interactions such as age. As you move forward, try to think of times you have had to work in an intercultural group and how both you and the quality of your work were affected (both positively and negatively) by the interaction.

Group work already is and will become an even more important part of your academic and work life.

Whether for a class assignment or a new product idea at work, participating in a small group or team is not something most of us look forward to. The process can be time-consuming and frustrating and can leave individual members disliking each other. Making matters worse is the fact that group members don't always see eye to eye. They come to the table with different values, points of view, cultural backgrounds, and experiences, and it is understandable that group members often find themselves fighting over the "right" way to do things. While diversity in small groups can be an enriching thing, it might lead to havoc if not handled effectively.

© Rawpixel.com/Shutterstock.com

We constantly find ourselves in situations that require **small-group communication**, and our reliance on groups will only increase in the future (LaFasto & Larson, 2001; Rothwell, 2004). In light of the hard work necessary to make the group process a success, it can end up being a rewarding experience. After all, it pays to build your

Small-group communication
?

intercultural group communication skills. In fact, proven success with small-group work can make you more upwardly mobile in your profession, as well as in social and civic situations where you communicate with diverse others.

© Rawpixel.com/Shutterstock.com

In what ways can decisions be enhanced when they are made by a group rather than an individual?

More specifically, think about the problems plaguing many communities that require great ideas from their citizens. Being a member of the parent–teacher association or your neighborhood watch program can give you opportunities to work in groups that make a real difference in your community. In addition, applying your intercultural competence to the group context will provide you with expanded opportunities to show your leadership and effect positive changes through your group's efforts, as well as to navigate the differences often perceived as barriers to decision making.

The purpose of this chapter is to review briefly the basics of small-group communication, discuss how cultural variability affects the group dynamic, and equip you with skills to negotiate all kinds of differences in groups. This chapter opens with a review of small-group communication and the difference between groups and teams. The functional perspective of group communication is also discussed by highlighting the importance of task and relationship functions. Next, the chapter discusses different types of diversity characteristics, particularly those that are psychological in nature (e.g., motives for joining groups, learning styles, personality types). Other types of diversity include dimensions of cultural variation (e.g., individualism and collectivism), as well as ethnicity, gender, and generation or age group. The final section presents theoretical and practical implications for appreciating and overcoming differences in the group communication context.

GROUP COMMUNICATION IN CONTEXT

The small group is perhaps the most significant social context of which we can be a part (Frey, 1994; Keyton, 2006). Furthermore, group memberships help us define our identity, or who we think we are:

> This is obvious when we consider groups such as fraternities or sororities, spiritually based groups . . . , gangs, book clubs, and poker clubs. . . . Each of [the groups to which we belong], though not expressly formed as an identity-supporting group, will affect how you see yourself in relation to other people. (Adams & Galanes, 2009, p. 5)

The opportunities you take now to engage in small-group communication will prepare you for the professional and personal life ahead of you. Virtually every job requires people to work together (Devine, Clayton, Phillips, Dunford, & Melner, 1999). Plus, the higher you progress up the career ladder, the more time you will spend in groups and the more groups to which you will belong (Adler & Elmhorst,

IN YOUR *life*

Have you ever had a bad experience working on a group project in school or at work? In your opinion, what is the best way to rectify problems in small-group communication?

2010). Prospective employers rank communication skills as one of the most valued qualities in a job candidate, and the ability to work in small groups with diverse members is a big part of those desired skills.

The most effective groups incorporate a variety of knowledge, experiences, and skills. Small groups are tasked with solving all kinds of complex problems, and members need to know how to pool and coordinate their diverse resources. To process all kinds of information and resources, group members must be able to acknowledge and coordinate their differences. What follows is a discussion of what makes up a small group, how groups are different from teams, and how groups and teams have to balance their tasks and relational functions.

THE NATURE OF GROUPS AND TEAMS

A **small group** is a collection of 3 to 20 people who are focused on a goal and are interpersonally aware of each other during interaction (Keyton, 2006; Wilson, 2002). To some extent, a group can develop an identity, which is achieved when members behave as though they're in a group, feel as though they belong, and have positive feelings toward one another and the group tasks (Henry, Arrow, & Carini, 1999). Groups are also characterized by their norms, which are patterns, rituals, and beliefs that become standards for acceptable behavior in a group (Keyton, 2006). Group norms reflect and perpetuate the group's culture—the kinds of things most valuable to the group. For instance, if your group culture stipulates that members arrive 5 minutes early for meetings, that norm might reflect a group culture that values punctuality and formality.

Small group
a collection of 3-20 individuals who share mutual influence, have one or more common goals, and are interpersonally aware of one another.

© arka38/Shutterstock.com

Team members have more expectations than group members, and they tend to be more accountable to one another.

Compared with groups, a **team** tends to be more demanding and requires a higher standard of performance and commitment from its members (Harris & Sherblom, 1999; Katzenbach & Smith, 1993; Kinlaw, 1991). Teams have responsibilities that tend to be more structured and coordinated than those of small groups. In addition, teams' goals are clear and specific to the overall objective, as well as to each member's role (Beebe & Masterson, 2003). Teams also tend to interact regularly on an ongoing basis (Wilson, 2002). Perhaps the most important characteristic of teams is that they are able to empower themselves. Instead of being accountable to an outside person (e.g., a manager), team members can be accountable to one another. Members accomplish this by setting their own goals, developing their own work schedules and deadlines, and dividing the work relatively equally; they are also willing to remove ineffective and irresponsible members (Rothwell, 2004; Wellins, Byham, & Wilson, 1991).

Regardless of the level of responsibility, goal achievement, and shared leadership, group work is not always the cure-all for personal and professional problems. In other words, there are times when a group is required, but at other times, work is best left to the individual. It is best to leave work to the individual when the problem has only one correct solution, the task is simple enough to be done by one person, one skilled person can do the job, it is too difficult or inconvenient to coordinate work schedules or meeting times, a crisis occurs and there is little or no time to deliberate, group members have personality or procedural conflicts that cannot be resolved, or members are not highly motivated to work on the task (Adams & Galanes, 2009; Hare, 2003; Rothwell, 2004; Wilson, 2002).

When group or team members represent different backgrounds, perspectives, and levels of experience, tension inevitably arises when these diverse members try to coordinate their efforts. An understanding of how small-group communication works will help members know the causes of those tensions and how to manage them. With knowledge of the diversity-related influences on the group process, "the members gain from the group, and the organization that gave birth to the group is improved by the group's work" (Adams & Galanes, 2009, p. 8).

FUNCTIONAL PERSPECTIVE OF SMALL GROUPS

Ideally, groups serve several different functions. The **functional perspective** (Gouran & Hirokawa, 1983, 1996) stipulates that the group dynamic must emphasize both the tasks and the relationships among members to be successful (Ellis, 1979; Fisher, 1979). **Task concerns** contribute to the group's productivity and might include whether or not to have a meeting, what kind of decision must be made, the leadership style used for running the meeting, and how much members are expected to participate (Wilson, 2002). But to ensure commitment to the task, group members also must grapple with **relational issues**, such as how people use or abuse power, give one another encouragement, relieve tension, and manage conflict. These are examples of a group's relational—or maintenance—concerns.

Relational issues
the group's maintenance concerns, such as how people use or abuse power, give one another encouragement, relieve tension, and manage conflict.

Group members can take on roles that facilitate the task and maintenance dimensions (Mudrack & Farrell, 1995). The roles or parts members play during group discussion can be utilized—intentionally or unintentionally—to bring about goal attainment (task) and group cohesiveness (maintenance). Members often play more than one role, and they might play both task and maintenance roles (Table 7.1 lists the different kinds of task and maintenance roles that often emerge in the group context). Moreover, the diverse preferences of members can influence how roles are played or designated, as well as how certain members respond to the task and maintenance functions of others in the group. For example, when a member of a newly formed group begins brainstorming to develop the best way to achieve the group's goal, that member is engaging in a task-oriented activity; he or she is working on the issue at hand. However, when a disagreement about a certain idea arises, someone who attempts to play "devil's advocate" or to make sure that all ideas and opinions are heard is engaging in a maintenance-oriented activity; he or she wants to make sure the group remains happy and cohesive without any conflict. Both of these roles are important, as groups must complete tasks and typically need ideas and support from all members to achieve those tasks.

TABLE 7.1

Task Roles	Maintenance Roles
Initiator/contributor—Provides ideas/solutions to achieve tasks **Information seeker**—Gets ideas and support for those ideas from members; seeks clarification to ensure successful implementation of ideas **Opinion seeker**—Solicits agreement/disagreement and opinions from other group members **Information giver**—Provides information to group springing from prior experience or existing knowledge **Clarifier/elaborator**—Makes ideas clear by offering explanations or examples **Coordinator**—Brings facts and ideas together and promotes collaboration **Secretary/recorder**—Records the group's history via note taking and record retention **Director**—Maintains attention to group goal by keeping discussions/activities on track **Devil's advocate**—Offers alternate points of view, not to stir conflict but to explore all possible scenarios for viability	**Supporter/encourager**—Encourages ideas from all members and keeps group focused on positive outcomes **Harmonizer/tension reliever**—Keeps the peace by reducing stress and acting as conflict negotiator **Gatekeeper/expediter**—Decides how communication is shared internally and externally and promotes equal input from all group members **Feeling expresser**—Surveys group mood to determine if intervention is necessary to avoid conflict or exchange of hurtful dialogue Sample of task and maintenance roles in small groups (adapted from Rothwell, 2004)

DIVERSITY CHARACTERISTICS

Groups usually can benefit from having diverse members, and the research strongly supports this assertion. In this section, we talk about the ways diversity can manifest in groups. Specifically, group members can represent different motives for joining. They also reflect other psychological dimensions such as learning styles and personalities. Group members can also be diverse in terms of their demographics (e.g., ethnicity, age, gender) and cultural variation (e.g., individualism/collectivism, power distance).

PSYCHOLOGICAL AND PERSONALITY DIFFERENCES

Motives for Joining a Group

Differences among group members are often reflected in their motives or reasons for joining the group. The group dynamic can indeed be interesting when members of the same group have different—sometimes clashing—reasons for being there. For instance, some members might be there to satisfy needs for inclusion and validation. According to Bales (1970), a pioneer in small-group behavior, people who join to feel included or to achieve a sense of belonging will focus more on the relationship dimensions of the group (e.g., keeping harmony, providing encouragement). People who have a need for control or personal achievement will be more interested in task dimensions (e.g., offering opinions, directing the discussion). Oetzel and Bolton-Oetzel (1997) note that task and relational dimensions are not mutually exclusive, meaning that a task-oriented person doesn't necessarily ignore or disregard the relational needs of the group, and vice versa.

Sometimes we join groups to receive validation and affirmation from people we consider our peers.

© wavebreakmedia/Shutterstock.com

Group members can also be characterized as having functional diversity, which is the range in which members vary in their predominant skill sets and professional backgrounds (Bunderson & Sutcliffe, 2002). There are many ways to conceptualize functional diversity, and one way is to focus on the functional areas in which members have spent their careers (i.e., dominant function diversity). For instance, some members have dealt with math and statistics, while others have more experience in operations. Bunderson and Sutcliffe reviewed the research on functional diversity in groups and teams and found that this kind of diversity can be a double-edged sword. More specifically, while diversity can enhance creativity and the introduction of a variety of ideas, it can sometimes hinder information sharing and group performance.

Learning Styles

Aside from motivations to join a group, members likely differ in the way they learn and process information, or in **learning style**. We all have different ways of learning, and we take in and understand new information according to our strengths and preferences. For instance, one person might be comfortable learning about a new process if it is conveyed in an illustration or video. Another person might be better at learning that same process if it is spelled out in a series of steps using clear, concrete language. According to Adams and Galanes (2009), "our learning preferences affect how and what we talk about, whether we understand one another, and what aspects of a group's task we feel most comfortable taking on" (p. 143). The key is to see through our learning styles what each of us brings to the table in group discussions. Diversity in learning can ensure that multiple perspectives enter the process and that creativity is enhanced. However, "our learning style differences can set us up for misunderstandings if we aren't careful" (p. 144).

Learning style
the way people learn and process information.

Kolb's (1984) learning styles model includes four types that fall on a "cycle of learning." First, the **concrete experience** (CE) learning style exhibits a preference for doing and participating. These individuals learn best when they engage in activities and are given opportunities to be in touch with concrete experiences or objects. In opposition to CE is **abstract conceptualization**, which reveals a preference for solitary investigation and working alone rather than in groups. Whereas CEs tend to rely on how they feel about their experiences, ACs prefer to think logically about their experiences. Although ACs might not want to start a project, they enjoy synthesizing information and pulling together research for the group. The continuum between CE and AC implies that individuals have a stronger tendency toward either thinking or feeling.

Concrete experience
(CE) learning style that exhibits a preference for doing and participating.

Abstract conceptualization
learning style that reveals a preference for solitary investigation and working alone rather than in groups.

Moving forward in the model, people who prefer **reflective observation** (RO) gain perspective about an experience by reflecting on it; they feel more comfortable watching how others do things or observing how something works. ROs prefer to stand back and gain psychological distance from the experience, as well as to learn through others by example or observation. Finally, individuals who exhibit **active experimentation** (AE) like to try different solutions to see which one works best. AEs prefer to learn by doing rather than by observing, even to the point of trial and error. In addition, AEs can easily apply information in a variety of ways and are able to think on their feet. As opposed to ROs, who prefer to watch and observe, AEs thrive more when they are allowed to do it themselves. This represents a continuum between watching (ROs) and doing (AEs).

Many people exhibit elements of all four of these styles, but most likely exhibit a blend of two. Based on Kolb's (1984) model, these learning types are part of a larger model of four learning styles—accommodating, diverging, assimilating, and converging. **Accommodating** represents the combination of AE and CE, which implies preferences for doing and feeling. Accommodators might rely on others' information to help carry out solutions instead of engaging in their own analyses. However, other group members can rely on these accommodators to take initiative and carry out actions, and accommodators are adept at working in teams and facing challenges head-on. Next, a combination of CE and RO can be found in the **divergent** learning style. Divergents can look at one issue from multiple perspectives, are sensitive, and are willing to gather outside information for the group. Divergents are good at brainstorming and like to work in groups, as well as to receive feedback. The **assimilating** learning style is the combination of RO and AC, and promotes a logical approach to problem solving. To the assimilator, ideas are more important than people and relationships. Because these individuals are good at working with abstract concepts, assimilators can help the group organize and present information in a clear format. These group members favor theoretical explanations over practical approaches and prefer lectures, readings, and being able to think things through. Finally, the **convergent** learning style combines AC and AE. Convergents solve problems, gravitate toward technical tasks, and are less concerned with relationships. Convergent learners can convert ideas and theories into practical solutions. Like the assimilating learners, convergent learners like to experiment with new ideas.

One can see how conflict might erupt when group members exhibit different learning styles. For example, some members who exhibit convergent styles might want to jump right into tackling the problem and not spend any time getting to know the other members. Such an individual, who might be individualistic, could be more interested in the task and individual achievement and disregard the need of some of the other members to share in the sense of accomplishment. Also, when a divergent member presents reasons for adopting a particular solution and provides statistical data to support that conclusion, an accommodator might reject that recommendation because it goes against his or her instinct for what is the right solution, and he or she might want to spend more time asking how other members feel about the proposed solution.

Different learning styles can serve as diverse roles that can elevate group collaboration (Kanisin-Overton, McCalister, Kelly, & MacVicar, 2009). Saleh, Lazonder, and Tong (2007) found that students of average ability are more motivated to participate in groups when they interact with members who have advanced abilities. The complementary strengths students bring to the group often manifest as learning styles, which reflect how students learn and integrate new information (Kolb, 1984).

Personality Differences

Personalities are going to clash; what matters is how members handle those clashes and learn to understand and accommodate one another. Given the important balance between task and maintenance needs, the group will be unsuccessful in accomplishing its objectives if the relationships among members, and inevitable personality differences, are ignored. The inability to move past personality differences can have negative impacts on the group's productivity.

© Danielle Balderas/Shutterstock.com

Think of the last time personality differences made an impact on your group's productivity.

One of the most used inventories of personality characteristics is the **Myers–Briggs Type Indicator** (MBTI) (Myers, 1987). The MBTI outlines four dimensions, and according to the inventory, we all fall on some point of each dimension or continuum. These dimensions represent preferences for how we tend to interact with our world and the people in it. For instance, one dimension is extraversion/introversion, which indicates the extent to which you are outgoing and tuned in to the world (i.e., extravert) versus independent and likely to work alone (i.e., introvert). Next is the sensing/intuiting dimension. People closer to the sensing end of the continuum tend to rely on facts and evidence to make their decisions, and they prefer to be concrete rather than abstract. Intuiting individuals are more creative and don't mind going with their "gut" when making decisions. They don't like detail and would rather look at the big picture. The third dimension is thinking/feeling, which involves the extent to which one prefers to evaluate critically versus use empathy to make decisions. Finally, there is the perceiving/judging dimension, which involves how people organize the world around them. Perceivers typically are more flexible and can adapt quickly to changes in plans. Judgers, on the other hand, work best with tightly set plans, and they like to stick to them.

If you have never taken the inventory, it might be worthwhile to look into it to see what dimensions of your personality appear to stand out in interpersonal and group situations. The results will likely give you insight into why you get along better with some group members than others. For example, if you happen to be a flexible perceiver, you might be challenged by a member who advocates for strict adherence to an agenda. For the two of you to move past your personality differences, you can acknowledge the clash between your flexibility and the other's rigidity and perhaps find a way to accommodate each other's styles. To learn more about the dimensions of your own personality, you might want to check with your campus's career services center or student counseling center; these departments might administer the MBTI and many other inventories for free.

DIMENSIONS OF CULTURAL VARIATION

Individualism and Collectivism

Individuals and their cultures tend to vary in terms of their search for individual autonomy and independence (i.e., **individualism**) versus their desire for connection and conformity with others (i.e., **collectivism**). In general, individualistic cultures value individual needs and goals as well as a sense of competition, whereas collectivistic cultures place more emphasis on the needs and goals of the group (Hofstede, 1983). Although most of us have a stronger leaning in one direction (Gudykunst, 1991), we all exhibit a combination of both (Rothwell, 2004). Hui and Triandis (1986) argue that the individualism/collectivism dimension is perhaps the most important value that distinguishes cultures.

Within the group context, individualistic members might talk about privacy, independence, and the self, while collectivistic members' talk might reflect the ideas of loyalty, community, and responsibility (Samovar & Porter, 2001). Because individualists can be focused on the self:

> it is easy for group members who value collectivism to become frustrated with a highly individualistic member, whom they will perceive as selfish and uncaring. However, it is also easy for individualistic members to perceive collectivistic ones as caring too much about what others think. (Adams & Galanes, 2009, p. 151)

These distinctions can also find their way into the language choices group members make. A study by Kim and Sharkey (1995) suggests that group members who are individualistic tend to be direct and unambiguous in their verbal communication with others. Collectivistic group members might use more ambiguity in their talk to gloss over differences and clashes; their talk also illustrates desires to be more harmonious and tentative. While both orientations can have their strengths and limitations, it might be advantageous for groups to place slightly more emphasis on collectivistic thinking. Individual goals, while valid and important, need to take a backseat to the group's goals (LaFasto & Larson, 2001) for the group to be effective.

Power Distance

In addition to preference for individual versus group goals, group members also differ in how they want to see power and leadership distributed. Perceptions of how much power differences are acknowledged also differ. These variations are concerned with **power distance**, which has to do with maximizing or minimizing status and power differences among people (Hofstede, 1983). Group members from low–power-distance cultures (e.g., United States, Australia, Canada) will likely believe that everyone should have a say in the discussion and decision making, regardless of role or status in the group. People from high–power-distance cultures (e.g., Japan, Saudi Arabia, India) tend to believe in the value of hierarchies and status differences; such individuals might communicate in ways that show deference to a designated leader while discouraging low-ranking members from participating much or getting to know their superiors on a more personal level. Adams and Galanes (2009) point out that high–power-distance members expect the leader to exert a great deal of control over the discussion, and they might not welcome

IN YOUR *life*

Do you consider yourself to be more individualistic or collectivistic in your group interactions? Do you think one approach is superior to the other, or should they be used interchangeably?

Power distance

the extent to which a culture maximizes or minimizes status and power differences among people.

© Monkey Business Images/Shutterstock.com

leadership that invites input from all members. On the other hand, low-power-distance members likely expect a more democratic style of leadership, enjoy a more informal relationship with superiors, and might get upset if their input is discouraged, sanctioned, or ignored.

High- and Low-Context Cultures

Cultural differences also manifest in the level of concreteness or abstraction in group members' talk, as well as in communication that conveys assertiveness versus harmony. Hall (1959) describes this distinction as a difference between high- and low-context cultures. In **low-context cultures** (e.g., United States, Canada, German-speaking countries), being direct and concrete is highly valued, and the words spoken convey more meaning than does the context or situation in which they occur. Members of **high-context cultures** (e.g., Japan, Arab countries, Italy, Brazil) might rely on features of the context or situation to get their ideas across. To illustrate, suppose a group member thinks the group is spending too much time on an agenda item. If she were low context, she might simply blurt out, "Look, we're spending too much time on this. We should table this until later." On the contrary, if she were high context, she might not say anything at all but try to make eye contact with other members to suggest her frustration or fidget and look at her watch.

Have you ever felt uncomfortable in a low-power-distance, discussion-based class?

Low-context cultures

being direct and concrete is highly valued, and the words spoken convey more meaning than does the context or situation in which they occur.

High-context cultures

members rely on features of the context or situation to get their ideas across.

You are probably picking up on the similarity between collectivistic and high-context individuals. Both tendencies reflect the importance of group harmony, and relying on the situation more than on direct language preserves harmony by allowing disagreements to happen gradually, rather than causing an abrupt upset in the group (Adams & Galanes, 2009). Such group members might view individualistic and low-context members—who tend to be direct and unambiguous in their language—as rude and aggressive. Because relational harmony is important in high-context cultures, high-context members have a hard time saying no and might not openly express needs and opinions (Wilson, 2002). In the low-context culture, expressing opinions is important, and the low-context group member might attempt direct persuasion of other members to achieve consent or acceptance.

High and low context also concerns how people utilize silence and language formality. First, the use of silence in some cultures (e.g., Native American,

Asian) often represents careful use of words and consideration of what has been communicated (Gudykunst & Ting-Toomey, 1988). Therefore, individuals who are used to talking a great deal might get frustrated with silent group members, assuming that they don't care about participating or don't agree with what has been said. Gudykunst and Ting-Toomey also point to differences in language formality across cultures. People from the United States and Canada, for example, are usually comfortable with informal ways of relating to other group members (e.g., calling people by their first names or nicknames). On the other hand, individuals with African or Asian backgrounds might take offense to such informality, often assuming that informality communicates disrespect for status differences among group members.

Feminine and Masculine Orientation

Within the small-group context, conveying a **masculine orientation** or **feminine orientation** often reflects the extent to which one is task oriented or relationally oriented—something we already alluded to in our discussion of the functional perspective. In general, coming from a more feminine culture might mean that you prefer that male (masculine) and female (feminine) roles overlap or that the group foster a sense of community and relationship maintenance. Group members who are more masculine in orientation might instead like to see masculine and feminine roles clearly defined, with very little or no overlap. Moreover, masculine members might be expected to take on leadership roles and to be more task oriented, whereas feminine members might be expected to be more modest and less confrontational. As with any discussion on sex and gender differences, keep in mind that we use *male* and *female* to refer specifically to biological sex, while *feminine* and *masculine* refer to ways of being or performing a particular gender role.

Masculine orientation reflects the extent to which one is task oriented or relationally oriented. In general, coming from a more masculine culture might like to see masculine and feminine roles clearly defined, with very little or no overlap.

Feminine orientation reflects the extent to which one is task oriented or relationally oriented; generally, coming from a more feminine culture might mean that you prefer that masculine and feminine roles overlap or that the group foster a sense of community and relationship maintenance.

While men and women share many similarities, Reich and Wood (2003) found four types of communication-related differences between men and women that might emerge in small groups. The first is the difference between expressive and instrumental behaviors, which involves women's tendencies to focus on relationships and feelings versus men's inclination to use direct and task-oriented language (think low context). The second type is the task–relationship difference. The general tendency is for men to place more emphasis on the task at hand, whereas women invest effort in building and maintaining relationships within the group. Third, men and women differ in forcefulness, which involves how much someone talks, draws personal attention, asserts oneself, and interrupts or takes the floor in discussion. According to Reich and Wood's findings, men tend to be more forceful in group discussion. While a male member might simply say, "Okay, here's what we're going to do," a woman might offer, "Well, this seems like a good idea, but what do the rest of you think?" In terms of interruptions, men tend to do this more in mixed-sex conversations than do women (Borisoff & Merrill, 1992). When women interrupt, they tend to do it to communicate agreement or to expand on another member's idea or contribution (Stewart & Stewart, 1985; Stewart, Stewart, Friedley, & Cooper, 1990). The fourth difference is between individual and group orientation. In the spirit of the individualism/collectivism dimension, men tend to exhibit more individualistic behaviors in the way they assert themselves and emphasize their personal status in relation to other group members. Women, on the other hand, are more collectivistic in the way they call attention to the needs and accomplishments of the entire group.

Are men and women as different as our society seems to make them out to be? Dindia (1997) argues that men and women are like residents of North Dakota and South Dakota, two neighboring states that are distinct but seem to have much in common. In fact, Canary and Hause's (1993) review of studies found that men and women were 99% similar in their communication behaviors. Overgeneralizing men and women's differences can be misleading and even harmful to the group process. Other factors besides sex and gender affect group members' communication: for example, nature of the task, roles of members, leadership style, and situational constraints. Perhaps the differences are more in how we're socialized and the kinds of expectations we have for the way women and men communicate. Adams and Galanes (2009) give this advice:

> As with any cultural variable, we should stay away from either–or thinking—that is, thinking that men are only *this* way and women are only *that* way, and one way is better. . . . When men and women are treated as being socialized in two different cultures, we tend to stereotype men as instrumental/powerful and women as affiliative/powerless. (pp. 160–161)

We're certainly not saying or requiring that men and women communicate and act in identical ways. Furthermore, we don't argue that one style (masculine or feminine) should dominate. Tannen (1990) asserts that applying one standard can make resentment and misunderstandings worse. As with other contexts, we can allow for and even celebrate the differences. In fact, both masculine and feminine styles add something valuable to group discussion, and both should be allowed to flourish. Group members can adapt to each other's styles, which in the end reflects flexibility and a wider set of communication skills. Specifically, feminine-oriented members can learn to be more assertive in their opinions and contributions. In turn, masculine-oriented individuals might curb their interruptions, ask more questions, and engage in more active listening.

Racial and Ethnic Differences

Research has documented differences along ethnic and racial lines when it comes to group participation. Many communication studies instructors try to find ways to encourage class participation from all their students and often worry about the lack of involvement from ethnic minority students, especially during small-group discussions (Kirchmeyer, 1993; Kirchmeyer & Cohen, 1992). This might not always be due to mistreatment or marginalization from the instructor or majority students. Rather, some cultures simply place more value on silence, which is often viewed negatively in U.S. culture (Rothwell, 2004; Samovar & Porter, 2001). Ethnic Asians, who typically come from collectivistic cultures, often view excessive talking as arrogant and conceited rather than respectful and connoting of trustworthiness (Inagaki, 1985; McDaniel, 1993). Another factor in reduced participation is some minorities' unfamiliarity with the host language, as well as being uncomfortable in an environment that seems to condone or reward aggressive communication and dominant behavior by majority group members (Kirchmeyer, 1993).

Generational Differences

Never before in our history have we witnessed the coexistence of so many generations and age groups in the workforce and in higher education. Just as differences in gender, background, and ethnicity can impact communication in groups, so can differences in age. Older members of a group, for instance, might have a hard time trusting younger members to participate or contribute their fair share of work; at the same time, younger members might view older members as interfering with their chances to show off leadership skills. Generational differences are important to consider, first, because our early influences from family, friends, and the media affect the way we perceive the world around us and the way we communicate, which in turn affects our behavior in groups. Second, understanding something about members of generations different from ours—their hopes and fears, the pressures that operate on them, the formative events in their lives—will help us find common ground, be understood, and reach a mutually agreeable solution.

Age by itself might not necessarily influence your values and beliefs, but each age group is influenced by a series of major events and people that are prominent during that group's formative years. It's true that at 10 years old, forces outside the family—friends, teachers, the media—begin to assume increased and lasting importance in our lives. For example, individuals who remember when President John F. Kennedy was shot might have a different worldview or set of values than those who lived through the Great Depression or those who saw an African American elected president of the United States. Adams and Galanes (2009) explain that "our early influences from family, friends, and institutions such as the media affect the way we

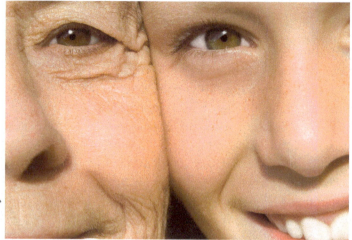

© Mandy Godbehear/Shutterstock.com

What are some challenges that you've faced when it comes to generational differences?

perceive the world around us and the way we communicate, which in turn affects our behavior in small groups" (p. 166).

Differences among age groups often boil down to potential clashes in values. Hicks and Hicks (1999) have written about these value differences and how they emerge out of each generational group. A summary of each of the generations, along with their major influences, values, and tendencies, can be found in Table 7.2. When people from different generations—and different value systems—come together in a group, what often develops are misunderstandings and negative interpretations of how decisions are discussed and made. For example, suppose you work in the purchasing department of an auto-manufacturing company and your department is hiring an additional member. A meeting is called for the current members to decide on a standard list of questions to ask during the interview phase of the job search. One of the members, a baby boomer, insists on using Robert's Rules of Order to conduct the meeting and is mostly interested in what the older, more experienced members of the group have to say. Furthermore, suppose you are one of the younger members (e.g., a Millennial), and you're anxious to share your ideas about some interview questions and how some of the interviews could be conducted over Skype. You want to be heard, but you feel bored with the use of Robert's Rules. Plus, you fear that you are being ignored by the rest of the group, who appear to be hesitant to incorporate new technology.

As this example illustrates, the formality and seniority valued by the older members is in conflict with the younger member's eagerness to show his or her leadership and incorporate more innovative and technological methods. While this conflict might seem difficult to overcome at first, members can be more mindful of the values that guide their own and others' thoughts and decisions. Subsequently, members can figure out what values they share and work on mutually agreeable solutions.

TABLE 7.2 Generational differences in characteristics and influences (Hicks & Hicks, 1999)

	Builders	Boomers	Generation X	Millennials
Born	Before 1946	1946–1964	1965–1976	1977–1997
Formative Events	Great Depression WWII	Post-WWII affluence Sexual revolution Vietnam War Civil rights	Struggling economy Divorce/single-parent households MTV	Internet Technology AIDS
Values	Financial security Sacrifice Value government Extended families Teamwork Delayed gratification Careful with resources Plan ahead Disciplined	Disillusionment with institutions Civil rights Individualism Material wealth Personal fulfillment Work as fulfilling Education Challenge old ways	Skepticism of big organizations Divided loyalties Cautious Distrust institutions Endure education Sensitive/tolerant Computer literate Pessimistic/negative	Access of to information Family/parent Consumerism Networking Tolerance Innovation Collaboration

Implications of Diversity Characteristics

Appreciating diversity in small groups is not just a nice idea; diversity can actually enhance the experience of group members and lead to productive outcomes. There is some compelling research on how group diversity can help members achieve their goals, but this often depends on other factors affecting the group. For instance, Polzer, Milton, and Swann (2002) examined the effect of interpersonal congruence, which is the extent to which members see others in the group as they see themselves. They found that groups with higher interpersonal congruence received more benefit from group diversity, particularly in better task performance. On the other hand, diversity hindered the effectiveness of groups when interpersonal congruence was lower.

Leadership style also can affect the influence of diversity within the group. While there is some inconsistency in the effects of diversity in small groups, Greer, Homan, De Hoogh, and Den Hartog (2012) contend that studying leader behavior, particularly leader categorization, can give us a clearer picture of diversity's impact. Greer et al. studied leaders with visionary behaviors and found that those who tended to categorize their team members into in-groups (those who belong) and out-groups (those who don't belong) appeared to see a negative effect from ethnic diversity, particularly on communication and financial performance. On the other hand, diverse teams with visionary leaders who did not categorize their members tended to see more positive outcomes from ethnic diversity. Additionally, a study of several research and development teams (Kearney & Gebert, 2009) looked at the impact of **transformational leadership**, which is leadership that taps into the higher-order needs of followers (e.g., achievement, self-actualization), motivates followers to perform beyond their expectations, and seeks to create change in a person for the better (Bass, 1985). Kearney and Gebert examined transformational leadership as it affected the relationships among three diversity variables: age, nationality, and educational background. They found that high levels of transformational leadership did affect the relationships of the three diversity variables, thus positively affecting team performance.

No single dimension of cultural variation is presented here to serve as the totality of a group member's identity. Also, we might not always act in accordance with our expressed cultural identity (e.g., individualistic and low context). Rather, the combination of our cultural and individual tendencies influences how we talk to and respond to one another in groups (Oetzel, 1998a, 1998b). In other words, to understand how a person behaves or talks in a group is to acknowledge the complexity of that individual—not just how he or she enacts a low–power-distance tendency, for example. This is the main premise of **effective decision-making theory** (EDMT), which focuses on self-construals as a way to explain cultural differences. According to EDMT, there are two types of self-construal, or one's image of oneself. The **independent self-construal** reflects group members who see their thoughts and beliefs as uniquely their own. Such individuals are goal driven and thrive on concreteness and low uncertainty. People who have an **interdependent self-construal** see themselves as connected or related to others and the world around them. They like fitting in and acknowledge the role that others play in goal achievement. Adams and Galanes (2009) point out that these two self-construals are related to individualistic cultures and collectivistic cultures, respectively, and are found in virtually every individual, regardless of cultural identification. The point we make with self-construals is that, while it is important to explore each dimension of variation within the group context, it is also important to acknowledge that people are multifaceted. Their communication is influenced by a variety of factors that reflect the diversity often found in groups.

Transformational leadership

leadership that taps into the higher-order needs of followers, motivates followers to perform beyond their expectations, and seeks to create change in a person for the better.

Effective decision-making theory

focuses on self-construals as a way to explain cultural differences.

Independent self-construal

reflects group members who see their thoughts and beliefs as uniquely their own; they are goal driven and thrive on concreteness and low uncertainty.

Interdependent self-construal

people who see themselves as they are connected or related to others and the world around them; they like fitting in and acknowledge the role that others play in goal achievement.

Sometimes the combinations of diversity characteristics can influence the group to split into subgroups, called **group faultlines**. Within the group context, faultlines refer to situations in which members—intentionally or unintentionally—align themselves according to their diversity dimensions (Trezzini, 2006). For example, one group might split into a subgroup of three young, white males and another subgroup of four older, Latina women. Such a split can create subgroups that are even more homogenous than the original group; at the same time, these subgroups can end up being more different from each other. Such a faultline can place even more emphasis on the diversity that already exists within the original group.

Group faultlines
subgroups; situations in which group members—intentionally or unintentionally—align themselves according to their diversity dimensions.

ETHICAL CONNECTION

Drew's marketing group has been instructed to find a way to market the company's product to the 18-to-25 age demographic. Drew is a recent college graduate, but many of the other members of his group have been out of college for years or decades. While brainstorming advertising ideas, Drew grows increasingly frustrated with some of the opinions offered by his older group members. Drew favors a racy, sensational campaign, while the older members of his group object to his "obscene" ideas. He frequently shoots down many of their ideas as "old-fashioned" or "out of touch." When asked for his insight, Drew is condescending and points to their generational differences for the reason none of their ideas have any marketable value. Drew's group fails to reach a consensus on an effective strategy, and their project is passed on to another group.

Questions to consider:
1. What strategies might Drew have used to enable his older group members to participate more effectively in the discussion?
2. What conflicts did Drew not consider when communicating with his other group members?
3. With so many different age groups in the workforce at the same time, how can companies integrate the diverse workforce without losing effective communication?
4. To what extent did generational values affect Drew's group communication?

IN-GROUP AND OUT-GROUP DISTINCTIONS

© Cienpies Design/Shutterstock.com

Over time, a group will develop its own patterns and norms for behaving.

We might argue that a group's existence is tied to the strength of its members' common identity (Abrams, Hogg, Hinkle, & Otten, 2005). After a certain amount of time, a small group typically develops its own culture, which includes "the values or ideals of the group, as agreed upon over time by its members" (Wilson, 2002, p. 12). Perhaps you've been a member of or seen groups that seem to exhibit a common identity, such as "the young ones," "the guys," or "the generous folks."

Behaviors, rituals, and ways of doing things can impact and reflect the group's communication patterns. Wilson (2002) explains:

Social concerns are evident in repeated behaviors that build and reveal the group's identification with its members and its task. . . . The group develops its values and customs for dealing with social and task concerns through its interaction and the communication rules it establishes. (p. 12)

As with any culture, a group with a strong identity might develop common patterns or customs of communicating. Such customs might include using humor every time conflict emerges or shutting out dissent when a decision seems likely. These patterns might reflect the combination of member characteristics and personalities (Frey & Sunwolf, 2005). For instance, the tendencies to discourage dissent might come from some members' leanings toward assertiveness or dogmatism.

Social identity

a group's social identity is based on common attributes held by its members and serves as a way to categorize people as well as provide an identity common to everyone in the group.

These repeated communication patterns become defining characteristics of a group's culture, which we can also call a **social identity** (Tajfel & Turner, 1979). A group's social identity is based on common attributes held by its members and serves as a way to categorize people as well as provide an identity common to everyone in the group (Abrams et al., 2005). Members of a group with a strong social identity will tend to share the goal of strengthening that group's identity and image to outsiders, as well as enhancing the group's power and status.

Groups can develop such strong cultural identities that they start to make **in-group** and **out-group distinctions**. Put simply, an in-group is a group with which one identifies as a member. Out-groups are those groups to which one does not feel one belongs (Tajfel, 1970, 1974; Tajfel, Billig, Bundy, & Flament, 1971). When we perceive someone to be a member of our group or similar to us, we might refer to that person as an in-group member. An out-group member is someone with whom we are dissimilar or whom we see as a member of another group. Sometimes these in-group and out-group distinctions are not made in the context of small groups but simply in terms of seeing others as like or unlike ourselves. Furthermore, out-group distinctions can occur within a single group. For example, if a member of a group is perceived to be different from the others (e.g., the only one of a particular age group or ethnicity), he or she might be viewed as an out-group member despite membership in the group. This can happen when the perceived outsider has not conformed to in-group norms. When out-group distinctions are made, in-group members will often interact with one another in more positive ways than they do with outsiders (Abrams et al., 2005).

A social identity perspective explains how members develop a sense of belonging within their groups and how they see distinctions between themselves and out-group members (Tajfel & Turner, 1979). Group members usually want to maintain a positive group identity, and they often accomplish this by differentiating their

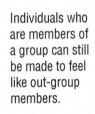

In-group distinction
a group with which one identifies as a member.

Out-group distinction
those groups to which one does not feel one belongs.

© lightwavemedia/Shutterstock.com

Individuals who are members of a group can still be made to feel like out-group members.

group from others. For example, the members of a sales department at a paper company might see themselves as extremely motivated and might set themselves apart from the accounting department, whose members they view as introverted and unmotivated. This perceived sense of being motivated and outgoing might compel those in the sales department to see their department as unique and special compared with other departments in the company.

Some evidence suggests that a strong group identity might hinder a group's willingness to help other groups. A study by van Leeuwen and Mashuri (2012) shows that when groups help other groups merely to show off their group identity in a strategic way, their willingness to help other groups tends to decrease. Taken to extremes, tightly knit group members sometimes develop an "us versus them" mentality concerning other groups or even members within their own group, often stereotyping outsiders as negative, threatening, or bad. This outcome can be unfortunate when groups are often required to work with those outside of their close-knit circle on an important project, especially when two departments of employees (e.g., sales and accounting) are working on a problem that affects that entire organization (e.g., incorporating a new software system that keeps track of expense accounts).

Inclusion and exclusion, intergroup conflict, and stereotyping are prevalent notions within the social identity perspective (Poole, Hollingshead, McGrath, Moreland, & Rohrbaugh, 2005). These patterns are quite normal but can be destructive if the result is unwarranted negative views of out-group members, unwillingness to cooperate with other groups and teams, or marginalization of members within the group. While developing a strong group identity is something we recommend later in this chapter, this objective should never get in the way of establishing productive relationships and collaborations with members of other groups.

MINDING THE GAP: OVERCOMING DIFFERENCES IN GROUPS

As we discussed earlier, individuals come to the group discussion from different backgrounds, perspectives, and cultures, which might lead to disagreements. While we tout the advantages of diversity throughout this book, it's not enough simply to have diversity. In the group context, if members can't appreciate their differences and learn how to negotiate them, the outcomes of the group will be unproductive and detrimental to the process and the group members. In fact, some group members might create a backlash against any perceived dissent in the group. More specifically, if an obvious minority is present in the group, the majority members might do a number of things either to get the minority person/

people back in line or exclude the minority altogether (Larkey, 1996; Thomas, 1995). One tactic is to exclude the minority member(s), which can happen when majority members communicate with and acknowledge—through verbal and nonverbal means—only the other majority members. Another response is to assert one's communication style when other styles are being used. This communicates unwillingness to accommodate others' communication needs, such as ignoring the need to appreciate silence or flaunting one's own achievements when others want to recognize the group as a whole. A third tactic is to disregard ideas that minority group members bring to the table. Unfortunately, such a tactic curtails productivity because it limits the creativity that comes from diverse ideas.

Differences among group members are inevitable. The goal doesn't have to be complete agreement or absolute homogeneity of opinions, backgrounds, traditions, and beliefs; that would be neither realistic nor ideal for group development and productivity. On the contrary, a group can retain its diversity and at the same time learn unique ways of finding common ground, which can transcend the seemingly difficult differences members perceive. As members of a group meet together, they gradually share common concerns based on their experiences with the group. These concerns might be perceived pressures from the entire organization or common frustrations with a difficult problem (Bales, 1970). Once group members realize the concerns and frustrations they share, they can communicate in ways that form a common "language" through which to talk to one another.

IN YOUR *life*

How would you respond to being shut out of a group project by majority members? What are some tactics you would use to try to reconcile your opinions with the majority group members?

Seeking commonalities can help groups resolve differences and reach mutually agreeable solutions.

© Photographee.eu/Shutterstock.com

Symbolic convergence theory

provides a framework for group members to use communication to achieve common ground or commonly shared experiences.

Convergence

refers to the way people use symbols to come together, overlap on ideas, or express common ground.

Our small-group communication skills can help us create a "meeting of the minds," and **symbolic convergence theory** (SCT) can give us a framework for how that is done. SCT (Bormann, 1982, 1996; Bormann, Bormann, & Harty, 1993) proposes a group dynamic that enables members to achieve unity and empathy. Through the words and actions they communicate, group members can converge and create common themes that unify the group despite the differences among members. According to Bormann (1996), **convergence** refers to the way people use symbols to come together or overlap on ideas. The use of overlapping symbols can help group members unite and strengthen their group consciousness. The exchange of symbols might be the telling of a joke, an anecdote of a shared experience, or "portraying some persona in action at some place and time other than the here-and-now meeting of the group" (p. 93). Here's an example of an instance of convergence: One person might start a joke, and another person might contribute some dialogue and add content to the joke. An additional member laughs and uses the joke to make reference to another group member. The other members then have a good laugh, and the joke serves as a "trigger" the next time the group needs some comic relief.

Fantasy chains

a series of symbolic cues that represent an exchange, conversation, or a series of connected thoughts or themes.

Fantasy theme

the content of the dramatizing message that sparks the fantasy chain.; an observable record of the nature and content of the shared imagination.

Group fantasy

a collection of accounts and experiences that form a general social reality in the group.

The exchanges and conversations that help create the running joke are called **fantasy chains**. Bormann (1996) explains that "the content of the dramatizing message that sparks the fantasy chain is a **fantasy theme**. The fantasy theme is an observable record of the nature and content of the shared imagination" (p. 93). This fantasy theme is a product of the group that represents a small aspect of that group's culture. The creation of fantasy themes results in a **group fantasy**, which is a collection of accounts and experiences that make up a general social reality of the group. For instance, imagine that a group is working on a demanding project over an extended period of time. To alleviate pressure and even anticipate the finishing line of the project, one group member begins talking about the vacation he or she will take when the project is complete (fantasy). That vacation sounds appealing to another member, at which point that member chimes in with details about his or her own plans once the project is done. Eventually, everyone might agree that a vacation is the best way to bounce back from such a grueling project, and a "group vacation" to various exotic destinations (fantasy theme) becomes a group fantasy. This fantasy chain is maintained throughout future dialogues to help perpetuate cohesiveness and reinforce group productivity.

The notions of convergence and fantasy chains will give you and other group members a framework on which to create a common bond and transcend any differences that emerge during the discussion. We present some additional guidelines to make the most of the diversity within your group. First, make it a priority to appreciate and work through differences among group members (Adams & Galanes, 2009; Wilson, 2002). Instead of ignoring those differences or pretending conflict doesn't exist, gently point out any issues and actively find ways to accommodate one another. Second, don't spend all your time working; take some time to socialize and get to know one another, which can yield common experiences and activities that everyone can enjoy (Oetzel, 1995; Triandis, 1995; Wilson, 2002). Third, question the notion that "it's always been done this way." Keep an open mind; don't cling to a procedure just because it's been used in the past (Adams & Galanes, 2009). Group discussion and deliberation can lead us to better solutions. Kelley and Littman (2001) suggest creating a **solidarity symbol**, which is a name or logo that gives the group a unifying image or theme. If you are in a class that assigns group work, you might want to suggest to your instructor that each group create a name; this could make the assignment more interesting and help your group come together under a unifying identity. Finally, stay focused on the goal. While members have different ideas about policy and procedure, what still unifies them is the ultimate outcome they're trying to achieve (Triandis, 1995; Wong, Tjosvold, & Lee, 1992).

Solidarity symbol
a name or logo that gives the group a unifying image or theme.

WHAT YOU'VE LEARNED

Being able to recognize and manage diversity in the group context can help you become a more effective communicator and can lead to some positive experiences and fruitful outcomes. In the first section of the chapter, we explained what actually makes up a small group and described the nature of small-group communication. Groups are different from teams, which require more shared leadership, greater accountability, and higher standards of performance. In addition, according to the functional perspective, groups need to maintain a balance between task and relational roles to be effective.

Next, the chapter discussed the characteristics on which group members might differ, particularly their motives for joining groups, preferred learning styles, and personality types. Group members can also represent diversity in terms of individualism and collectivism, power distance, high- and low-context cultures, and feminine and masculine orientation. This section also discussed how groups can be affected by differences in ethnicity, gender, and generation. It would not be informative to understand diversity in groups in terms of just one diversity characteristic. According to effective decision-making theory, an individual's independent or interdependent self-construal represents multiple cultural identities that reflect how much one communicates with others in the group setting. When group members align themselves along group faultlines, the resulting subgroups can become even more different from one another.

Diversity does not occur just within the group; we also have to consider differences between groups as they pertain to intergroup communication. Over time, a small group can develop its own culture with a unique set of behaviors, values, and common experiences. Social identity theory explains how group members develop a sense of belonging based on common characteristics, often distinguishing themselves from out-group members.

In the final section, the chapter presented theoretical and practical implications for appreciating and overcoming differences in the group communication context. Symbolic convergence theory illustrates how groups can develop a meeting of the minds through their use of fantasy chains and fantasy themes. Additionally, group members can take certain steps to help work through differences and improve their performance.

REVIEW

1. One of the most prevalent communication contexts in which we find ourselves is called a _____.

2. A _____ is different from a small group in that it requires a higher standard of performance and commitment from its members, tends to be more structured and coordinated, and serves to empower its members.

3. _____ posits that in order to understand how a person behaves or talks in a group is to acknowledge the complexity of that individual.

4. One of the most used inventories of personality characteristics is called the _____. This assessment outlines four dimensions that represent preferences for how we tend to interact with the world and the people in it.

5. The existence of several dimensions of variation in the group can result in the formation of _____; this is when members align themselves according to their diversity dimensions.

6. Explain what comprises a group's social identity.

7. Discuss some factors that might contribute to an out-group distinction.

8. Which theory provides a framework for group members to use communication to achieve common ground?

9. What is a group fantasy?

10. Identify some of the guidelines the chapter provides for overcoming group differences.

Review answers are found on the accompanying website.

REFLECT

1. List the various groups to which you belong. How does belonging to these groups help to shape you and your identity?
2. Paris is the editor of her school newspaper. When submission deadlines are approaching, Paris has been known to make her staff miss important events, such as practices or religious holidays, in order to work through the night. Her staff members have begun to resent Paris and her focus on productivity.

Using the vocabulary from the *functional perspective*, discuss what is wrong with this group dynamic and offer suggestions for improvement.

3. Angela is an American who works for an international company. She has recently been assigned to work on a project with employees who work for company branches in China and Japan. While Skyping with her Chinese and Japanese coworkers, they seem uncomfortable and unhappy when Angela openly offers constructive critiques of their work. Use the content on cultural variation to discuss why Angela's coworkers might be made uncomfortable by her comments. Then, offer suggestions for how Angela might adjust her communication for the better when working with her coworkers in the future.

4. What are some examples of in-group and out-group dynamics that you have noticed either in your personal or public life? How possible is it for you to see these dynamics switch roles?

5. Drake has been assigned to work on a group project with two other people— Colby and Marsha—for a class. He feels anxious about working with them because he doesn't feel as though he will have much in common with them; Colby is a school athlete, and Marsha is a nontraditional student who appears to be in her 50s. The first group meeting feels awkward for everyone, but Drake notices Colby has his favorite novel in his bag and knows Marsha is a creative writing major. Use the terms from *symbolic convergence theory* to discuss how Drake might attempt to unify his group and alleviate some of the awkwardness everyone feels.

KEY TERMS

small-group communication, 177
small group, 179
team, 180
functional perspective, 180
task concerns, 180
relational issues, 181
learning style, 183
concrete experience, 183
abstract conceptualization, 183
reflective observation, 184
active experimentation, 184
accommodating, 184
divergent, 184
assimilating, 184
convergent, 184
Myers-Briggs Type Indicator, 186
individualism, 186
collectivism, 186
power distance, 187

low-context cultures, 188
high-context cultures, 188
masculine orientation, 189
feminine orientation, 189
transformational leadership, 194
effective decision-making theory, 194
independent self-construal, 194
interdependent self-construal, 194
group faultlines, 195
social identity, 196
in-group distinctions, 197
out-group distinctions, 197
symbolic convergence theory, 200
convergence, 200
fantasy chains, 200
fantasy theme, 200
group fantasy, 200
solidarity symbol, 201

CHAPTER EIGHT
Intercultural Communication and Conflict

CHAPTER OUTLINE

WHAT YOU WILL LEARN

After studying this chapter, you should be able to

1. define conflict and explain its five characteristics;
2. explain various cultural attitudes toward conflict;
3. describe the types of conflict and how they vary across cultures;
4. explain the five styles of conflict and two dimensions along which they vary;
5. discuss cultural differences with regard to conflict styles;
6. understand how one can introduce conflict to engage in it; and
7. apply the steps of principled negotiation.

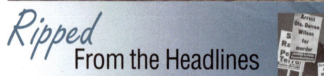

Ripped From the Headlines

In August of 2014, protests and riots erupted in and around Ferguson, Missouri after the shooting death of Michael Brown, an unarmed black teenager, by a Ferguson police officer. These protests and riots were the result of community accusations of racism on the part of the officer and the local police department. This conflict had a rippling effect that spread to other parts of the country in the form of protests and riots, and this event led to the formation of the Black Lives Matter movement that continues to advocate against police brutality and institutional racism (Lowery, 2017).

Conflict happens to everyone, but it is especially difficult when social categories, such as race, are at the heart of a dispute. It is important to be mindful of the role these social categories play in conflict because the notion of privilege is still prevalent in our own culture; for example, researchers have found that police officers stop racial minorities, immigrants, the impoverished, and the homeless at disproportionately high rates (Hayle, Wortley, & Tanner, 2016). It makes sense that when a person or group feels attacked, they are more likely to be defensive as opposed to being receptive to the perspective of the other party. Learning to navigate conflict in various cultural contexts will help you in being a more cultured and ethical communicator.

In this chapter, you will learn about the different types of conflict, as well as cultural influences on conflict styles and negotiation strategies. After reading this chapter, you should be well versed in managing conflict and practicing effective negotiation skills. Above all, you should recognize the critical importance of cultural competency and its role in proper conflict resolution.

For many people, increasing productivity and effectiveness means avoiding conflict. On the contrary, no successful team, group, organization, or family has experienced a lack of conflict, or at least survived without knowing how to overcome such struggles. It makes intuitive sense that when you have a disagreement with someone else, such as a fellow team member on a class project, what is likely underneath that conflict is an issue that needs resolution (e.g., how to organize the presentation, what theory to use, how to distribute the workload). Instead of trying to avoid a conflict, or the person with whom you have conflict, you might decide to address the disagreement head-on and work toward a mutually agreeable solution. This type of engagement, when carried out in the spirit of collaboration (and some compromise), can bring the conflicting parties and the rest of the group closer together, and can even result in a better product in the end.

As if conflicts weren't difficult enough, cultural backgrounds and differences can add to the difficulty of managing conflict. Culture and conflict are inseparably related. However, that does not mean that cultural differences always lead to conflict. Our cultural upbringing and influences can shed light on how we view conflict (e.g., harmful, beneficial, embarrassing), which in turn can affect how we engage others when conflict does arise. Moreover, when parties are engaged in conflict, their perceived or actual cultural differences might lead to misunderstandings or misperceptions about the other party. By addressing conflict in this chapter, we can learn how to navigate the difficulties that sometimes come with managing conflict when cultural factors are at play. More important, we can learn to appreciate the differences and even use them to come to a conflict resolution.

Here is the bottom line: We all *need* conflict. If this notion seems counterintuitive to you, that's okay. How you engage in conflict depends partly on your perspective or worldview. But consider that the Chinese character for *conflict* comprises two symbols: one that embodies danger and another that represents opportunity (Hocker & Wilmot, 1995). As we explore conflict in this chapter, we can decide whether to respond to conflict with trepidation or to see conflict as an opportunity for transformation. In this chapter, we will talk about what conflict truly is and how it can contribute to productivity and effectiveness. Also, we will discuss conflict styles and the cultural factors that affect differences in the choice of style. Finally, this chapter reveals positive ways to introduce and engage in conflict, with special emphasis on principled negotiation.

WHAT IS CONFLICT?

Before we define conflict, we need to acknowledge that some of the roots of conflict might lie in our need to project as well as protect our identity (Folger, Poole, & Stutman, 2009). Our identity comes from two sources. One source is **social identity**, which includes those identity aspects we get from membership in larger social groups (Tajfel & Turner, 1979). For example, if you identify as a member of a certain ethnic group, you might seek and get confirmation of that identity in your interactions with others of that same ethnic group. You might even take extra measures to be part of social groups to which those individuals belong, which is the process of **social categorization**. Throughout life, our identity is continually shaped by the perception of the social groups with which we identify and to which we belong. Your identity is also shaped by awareness of the groups to which you do *not* belong (Rothbart, 2003).

Individuals with a strong sense of identity can come in conflict with others who do not hold the same perceptions, values, and norms. This struggle has the potential to occur virtually every time we work, play, and relate with others. For instance, when friends and coworkers get together to work on problems or make a decision, they bring a variety of ideas and perspectives to the table, some of which are deeply rooted in identity. When diverse identities converge, complete agreement will not always be possible. Thus, within each group discussion, meeting, or informal gathering, conflict will sometimes occur. The conflict can even center on a disagreement over whether conflict is a good or bad thing (Gudykunst, 2004). Conflict does not have to hinder the group's process. In fact, when managed effectively, conflict can help uncover the real issues affecting a group and can enable group members to make real progress toward their goal. Unfortunately, the word **conflict** often has a negative undertone, and this negative view of conflict can differ across cultures. According to Collier (1991, 1996), Whites might see conflict as having a positive, long-term impact on personal and workplace relationships, while Latinos see both negative and positive long-term impacts.

Before we can appreciate how conflict can be managed effectively, we need to understand what it really entails. The notion of conflict might refer to countries at war or rival organizations. While the topic of intergroup conflict will be addressed later in this chapter, we primarily place the focus on **dyadic conflict**, which is conflict that occurs between two people (Gudykunst, 2004). In some cases, we can also be referring to small factions of people within a group that clash with each

Social identity

a group's social identity is based on common attributes held by its members and serves as a way to categorize people as well as provide an identity common to everyone in the group.

Social categorization

taking extra measures to be part of social groups to which individuals from your ethnic group belong.

Conflict

an expressed struggle that occurs when diverse identities converge and complete agreement is not always possible. Characteristics of conflict include perceived incompatible goals and scarce resources.

Dyadic conflict

conflict that occurs between two people.

Interaction with others from the same ethnic group builds one's identity.

other. To get a sense of what conflict might look like, we will consider Hocker and Wilmot's (1995) definition. They claim that conflict is an expressed struggle between interdependent parties who perceive incompatible goals, scarce resources, and interference from others.

Dyadic conflict can occur not only in personal life but in professional life as well.

Let's break down Hocker and Wilmot's (1995) definition. First, a conflict has to be an *expressed struggle*, meaning that the struggle needs to be expressed or communicated to the other party. One can choose to express the struggle in a range of ways, from leaving a sarcastic note to approaching the other person directly and explaining the conflict in objective terms. It makes sense that the manner in which the conflict is initially expressed can set the tone for emerging struggle, for better or for worse. Expression of conflict means that when two

people are in conflict, they both know it. To illustrate, if you are having a true conflict with your roommate, you will have somehow expressed your conflicted feelings and thoughts to your roommate. On the contrary, if you're angry with your roommate for leaving meat on your side of the refrigerator (because you're vegan) but have not expressed this anger clearly, then you are just engaged in **intrapersonal conflict**, which is internal strain that can create feelings of resentment and ambivalence, and

Intrapersonal conflict
internal strain that can create feelings of resentment and ambivalence, and can often prevent resolution from occurring.

can often prevent resolution from occurring (Hocker & Wilmot, 1995). However, being upset with that roommate for long enough might compel you to go ahead and say something anyway. So if you're peeved at your roommate for not being more careful about keeping his meat products out of your way, he might not realize what he's doing. If you tell him directly, he might genuinely be sorry and pledge to be more careful about how he uses the fridge space in the future. In this case, intrapersonal conflict can serve as a precursor to actual conflict engagement.

Another characteristic of conflict is that it occurs between interdependent parties. **Interdependence** means that the actions of one party will affect the other and vice versa. For example, Joseph is assigned to a student group that has to write a research paper. He is asked by the group to submit a first draft to another group member, Marta, by 10:00 a.m. on Wednesday so she can add the reference pages in time to turn in the paper by noon on Thursday. However, Joseph is held up on the paper because he remembers it is Lent, and as a Catholic he's made a personal commitment to attend Mass every morning at 9:00 during Lent. This prevents him from finishing the paper by 10:00, and he doesn't send Marta the draft until 5:00 p.m. Wednesday. Joseph's lateness impacts Marta, who needs the final draft so she can add the references. Despite the reason, Joseph's inability to send his draft on time impedes Marta's ability to complete her task before the paper is due. Marta could be upset enough with Joseph to perceive a conflict with him. In turn, despite Joseph's lateness and the reason for it, his grade is partially dependent on Marta's ability to finish the paper and turn it in on time. As this case illustrates, Joseph's and Marta's actions have dual influence, and when that influence is negative, conflict can erupt. However, if Marta does not express her displeasure with Joseph, who at the same time doesn't mention his Mass obligation, Marta might feel tempted to hold onto resentment and even complain to the other group members instead of to him. In the end, there is no more understanding of the circumstances, and the conflict is neither expressed nor resolved.

Another characteristic of conflict is the perception of scarce resources. We should emphasize that this is about perception. Even if there is enough time, money, and materials to go around, the mere perception of scarcity is enough to fuel conflict. In the case of Joseph and Marta, Joseph might rationalize taking until 5:00 p.m. because he thinks Marta still has plenty of time to finish the paper. On the contrary, Marta believes she needs more time to accomplish her task, so she perceives the scarcity of time to be Joseph's fault.

The perception of incompatible goals is another feature of conflict and can be a major point over which conflicting parties butt heads. The incompatibility could be that both parties want different things. For example, members of a fundraising group might disagree on what kind of project they will develop to bring in money.

Some members might advocate partnering with an elementary school for a car wash. Other group members might argue that they should seek sponsorship from a local church to organize. In this case, members who disagree might see these fundraising ideas as very different from each other, especially if some of the nonreligious members take offense at the idea of partnering with a place of worship. Also regarding incompatibility, both parties actually might want the same thing but in different amounts, ways, or degrees. Back to Joseph and Marta: Both want to turn in a well-written paper, but they might have different ideas of what "well written" means. Joseph could be satisfied with a grade of C, while Marta would not be happy with anything less than an A. Having this difference in grade expectations, Joseph and Marta might not work with the same rigor, which might lead to conflict. Again, we should emphasize that the incompatibility of goals might not be actual but only perceived. To address this, members in conflict might take the time to discuss what their goals are, identify the actual discrepancies, and see if some collaboration or compromise might be reached.

The final characteristic of conflict is perceived interference from others. **Interference** might appear to come from the person with whom you have conflict; it also might appear to come from a third party. In Joseph and Marta's situation, Marta might perceive Joseph's lateness on his part of the paper as interfering with her chances of getting an A on the final paper grade. In terms of a third party or outside influence, Marta might believe that Joseph's Mass obligation was an interference that kept him away from his work. If Joseph had the chance to explain the importance of daily Mass during Lent, then Marta might be more understanding of his situation and, if told ahead of time, could have given him more time to work on the draft.

Notwithstanding Hocker and Wilmot's (1995) conflict characteristics, people might disagree on whether or not a conflict is actually occurring, and this interpretation might be linked with cultural background. For instance, Gudykunst (2004) explains that white culture in the United States recognizes conflict as a situation in which people raise their voices. On the other hand, raised voices among Blacks are usually not seen as a sign of conflict but, rather, as indicative of "discussion." It is possible, then, that two people who are part of the same conversation might walk away with one person thinking they were arguing while the other person does not have that impression. Another difference between Whites and Blacks, according to Gudykunst, is the perception of when a conflict ends. For Whites, it is typically bound to time, meaning that a conflict is seen to end when the conversation ends, whereas Blacks typically perceive conflict to end when both parties reach a resolution. Collier's (1991, 1996) research on interethnic friendship reveals some discrepancies as well. She found that African Americans see conflict as a difference in understanding, whereas Whites see conflict as a product of differences in both parties' goals.

IN YOUR
life

Have you ever been involved in a conflict where you were unable to reach a resolution? What were the major barriers to reaching an agreement?

CULTURAL VARIATIONS IN ATTITUDES TOWARD CONFLICT

Our attitudes, expectations, and past experiences have a significant impact on how we approach conflict, or whether we decide to approach it at all. Folger et al. (2009) point out that our feelings about conflict are not innate; we are told various messages throughout life that shape our current conflict-related beliefs. For instance, Roloff and Miller (2006) and Hocker and Wilmot (1995) summarize several common beliefs about conflict: *Conflict is not helpful. Men and women act differently during conflict. We can avoid conflict if we just talk more. Conflict is not normal. Conflicts and disagreements are the same thing.* In addition, there are commonly held standards about how conflict should be handled: *Never go to bed angry. Arguments only make people more firm in their positions* (Roloff & Miller, 2006). Standards are value-laden statements intended to guide our behavior.

Cultural background can have a profound impact on the beliefs and standards we come to hold about conflict. In fact, Hofstede and Bond (1984) assert that culture is a primary influence on our belief systems. Kozan (1997) identifies three distinct models that reflect how different cultures view conflict. The **harmony model** is often seen in cultures that see the importance of maintaining relationships, avoid open communication of conflict, rely on third parties to help resolve conflict, and strive to maintain honor and pride. Given these characteristics, the harmony model might find favor among collectivistic cultures. The **confrontational model** values forceful pursuit of individual goals, open engagement in conflict, and expression of emotions during conflict. These features can conceivably be found in more individualistic societies. As with the harmony model, the confrontational model values the use of third parties during negotiations. Finally, the **regulative model** emphasizes reliance on rules and codes of conduct, procedural justice during negotiation, and downplaying the personal issues involved. This model also promotes the involvement of third parties during conflict resolution.

Harmony model

often seen in cultures that see the importance of maintaining relationships, avoid open communication of conflict, rely on third parties to help resolve conflict, and strive to maintain honor and pride.

Confrontational model

values forceful pursuit of individual goals, open engagement in conflict, and expression of emotions during conflict.

Regulative model

emphasizes reliance on rules and codes of conduct, procedural justice during negotiation, and downplaying the personal issues involved; also promotes the involvement of third parties during conflict resolution.

© Photographee.eu/Shutterstock.com

A third party can be especially useful under the harmony and regulative models of conflict.

TYPES OF CONFLICT

Besides characteristics, there are various types of conflict. These types represent the reasons or situations over which people clash. Hall (2005) discusses three types of conflict, one of which is **object conflict**, which is typically a misunderstanding or disagreement about something or about whether something is true or false, such as a fact or what some people hold as common knowledge. For example, people who hold different political views might have conflicts over the original intent of the Second Amendment to the Constitution (the one dealing with the right to bear arms). Keep in mind that object conflicts concern whether something is factual, not moral or proper (e.g., right or wrong). A **relational conflict** is about rights, responsibilities, and roles people hold or are expected to hold in a given situation (e.g., a relationship, the workplace). Relational conflicts often involve disagreements in power distribution and expression. For instance, cultures vary in their idea of what a superior–subordinate relationship at work should look like. Some prefer more formal, hierarchical distinctions between boss and employee, while others enjoy an informal relationship in which boss and subordinate can exchange thoughts and opinions freely. Finally, a **priority conflict** is about issues of morality, right versus wrong, or what is more or less important. Cultures differ widely on the morality of certain issues or behaviors, such as access to health care, rights of women, how we punish those convicted of crimes, and countless other matters. For instance, people from different cultures who sit on the same decision-making board or governing body can experience a significant clash on how laws that influence the lives of community members can and should be written.

Gudykunst (2004) points out that conflict is often a result of misinterpretation of another person's behavior. For instance, while many European Americans value direct eye contact when speaking to others, many Asians see eye contact as rude and disrespectful under certain circumstances. So if an Asian person—especially an older adult—is given eye contact by a younger person, he or she might feel slighted and perceive malicious intent in the other person's message. Such divisive misunderstandings can occur between cultural groups as well; this pertains to cross-cultural conflict. According to Shenkar and Ronen (1987), differences exist in how Chinese individuals and U.S. citizens approach negotiation. For one thing, the Chinese prefer restraint and avoidance of forceful communication, which suggests a more relational orientation. On the other hand, Americans tend to be more task oriented and view themselves as forthcoming, even if it means being less tactful. An honest confrontation is viewed by Americans as directly dealing with the conflict, whereas the Chinese see it as disrespectful. In fact, the Chinese way of addressing conflict involves decision making that occurs behind the scenes, which can be disconcerting to many American negotiators, who might feel uncertain about the progress of the negotiation.

Object conflict
typically a misunderstanding or disagreement about something or about whether something is true or false, such as a fact or what some people hold as common knowledge. Concerns whether something is factual, not moral or proper (e.g., right or wrong).

Relational conflict
rights, responsibilities, and roles people hold or are expected to hold in a given situation (e.g., a relationship, the workplace). Often involve disagreements in power distribution and expression.

Priority conflict
issues of morality, right versus wrong, or what is more or less important.

A misunderstanding might manifest as one of two types of conflict: **expressive** (differences in how people think feelings and emotions should be expressed and released) and **instrumental** (differences in how people articulate goals and understand how tasks should be completed) (Gudykunst, 2004). Expressive conflicts, for example, can happen when there are cultural differences in how people express grief over the death of a loved one. One of the authors does qualitative research in hospice and palliative care settings, and she has been told several times that white nurses who see subdued crying as "normal" might be shocked by Latino families who wail loudly and pray openly during times of death and loss (Scholl & Hughes, 2011). Being unfamiliar and uncomfortable with these displays of grief might make it difficult for the nurse to provide the compassionate care she or he might otherwise give. As previously stated, instrumental conflicts are disagreements over how tasks are completed, how goals are articulated and achieved, and how resources are utilized. An instrumental conflict can occur when an individualistic person prefers to work alone on a task but more collectivistic members in the group want to engage in brainstorming with the whole group. This can be frustrating for the individualistic member, who believes that initial brainstorming on one's own is more productive.

To move beyond our fear of or discomfort with conflict, and the threats to identity it might imply, we can do what Quintanilla and Wahl (2014) suggest, which is to replace the word *conflict* with a term such as *idea sharing* or *discussion*. The resulting connotations are more positive, but we're still dealing with a conflict or disagreement. Tackling conflict is hard; it's a struggle that most of us don't enjoy, but it is a necessary one if we are to resolve differences. To take the sting out of the struggle, injecting more positivity and ideas about discussion might help conflicting parties deal with the issue while still maintaining their relationship. Moreover, while other definitions about struggle and scarcity might imply a change in the actions of one or more parties, the more positive connotations suggest that transforming conflict means a change in people's perceptions of the conflict or the circumstances leading to it.

DIFFERENCES AND THEIR INFLUENCE ON CONFLICT INTERACTION

CONFLICT STYLES

People differ in their approach to or style of conflict. You might have some friends or family members who don't appear to like conflict and avoid it at all costs. Others might be more aggressive and even seem to enjoy a good argument. Not only do people differ in conflict style according to the situation, but they might also vary based on their cultural background.

Before we get into cultural differences, however, we will explore conflict styles in general. First, consider that most people have one or more *styles* with which they approach conflict. We do not present what is known about conflict styles with the assumption that people have one and only one style. Rather, assuming that most people reflect some combination of styles, we present these styles separately only so we can understand them better.

IN YOUR *life*

In your experience, does cultural background play a significant role in conflict management and resolution? How does your cultural background affect your conflict management style?

ETHICAL CONNECTION

Krista was a hospitality manager for a large hotel in the Dallas/Fort Worth area. Many of her patrons were international travelers with a great variety of cultural backgrounds. Recently, the hotel hosted a large group of Muslim investors in town for business meetings. Krista had complaints from other patrons about the daily prayer rituals practiced by the investors; some patrons cited the prayers as "offensive" or "creepy." Krista decided to approach the investors and ask them not to practice their prayer rituals outside of their rooms. When the investors pointed out that other patrons were allowed to pray in the hotel restaurant before meals, Krista dismissed their objections as overly dramatic and insisted they keep their prayer rituals inside their rooms. The group of investors immediately terminated their stay at the hotel, and Krista was demoted by the hotel ownership for failing to meet the hospitality needs of her patrons.

Questions to consider:
1. How did Krista fail to take cultural implications into consideration before making her decision?
2. What steps could Krista have taken to avoid a confrontation with her Muslim patrons?
3. Was it fair for Krista to ask the Muslim patrons to practice their religion in private but not to require other patrons to do the same?
4. How would you have handled the conflict in Krista's situation? Would you have ignored the other patrons' complaints?

Much has been written about conflict styles (c.f., Blake & Mouton, 1964; Kilmann & Thomas, 1975), and research suggests that there are five styles that vary on two dimensions: concern for self and concern for the other. One might view these two dimensions as factors that influence how one acts when engaged in conflict with another person or party (Ruble & Thomas, 1976). In terms of this behavior, one can show a certain level of concern for one's goals or desired outcomes (i.e., **concern for self**). This concern for self can come out as assertiveness or even competitiveness. At the same time, one can have a certain level of consideration for what the other person wants from the conflict (i.e., **concern for other**). When one shows a certain level of consideration for the other party, he or she might be acting more cooperatively than assertively. To put it all together, concern for the self means the extent to which one wants to promote his or her own goals, while concern for the other considers what the other person will lose or gain during the conflict. To visualize this, think of these two dimensions as the vertical (concern for self) and horizontal (concern for other) axes on a grid that represents the various conflict styles (see Figure 8.1).

Concern for self
showing a level of concern for one's own goals and desired outcomes.

Concern for other
having a certain level of consideration for what the other person wants from the conflict.

FIGURE 8.1 Conflict Styles

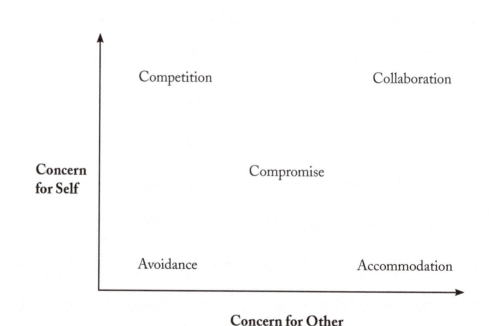

One's style of conflict, then, is based on one's placement along the two dimensions of self-concern and other concern. The style of **avoidance**, also called withdrawal,

Avoidance
also called withdrawal; a conflict style that reflects a low concern for both the self and the other person's goals.

reflects a low concern for both the self and the other person's goals. As suggested by its position on the grid, avoidance means that a person will not assert his or her position in the conflict and at the same does not show concern for the other person's goals. This is why avoidance is on the low end of both dimensions. On the low end of concern for self but on the high end of concern for other is **accommodation**, which implies that one shows little or no assertiveness but, rather, gives in to the other party. Some might view this style as self-sacrificing, while others see it as conciliatory (Folger et al., 2009). The opposite of accommodation is **competition**, or assertiveness, which reflects a high level of concern for the self's goals while ignoring the goals of the other. Individuals who use this style likely want to "defeat" the other person or force him or her to acquiesce. **Compromise** assumes that both parties give and take a little in reaching their goals, which represents a moderate level of concern both for self and the other. Generally, both parties come away with some of what they want, but they have to give up something as well. Finally, on the high end of concern for both self and other is **collaboration**. This style is often viewed as the most desirable but is difficult to enact because it requires both parties to reach a mutually agreeable solution that satisfies both sides completely. Furthermore, organizations that adopt a more collaborative management style tend to foster more job satisfaction than cultures that embrace more dominant or competitive styles (Choi, 2013).

INTERCULTURAL INFLUENCES ON CONFLICT STYLES

What would make one person competitive and another more accommodating and yielding during a conflict? Personality characteristics might play a part, and so might the actual reason for the conflict. We can also look to cultural variation as a factor. Although much research has yet to be done on cultural influences on conflict style (Folger et al., 2009), some available evidence suggests that there is a connection. Culturally specific values, attitudes, or behavioral norms can have an impact on the conflict style you employ in a given situation. We certainly are not saying that all members of an ethnic or cultural group will adopt the same style. Rather, as Ting-Toomey (2002) would assert, there are cultural inclinations toward certain styles.

Admittedly, much of what we know from the culture and conflict research is based on data collected in the United States and other Western countries, so we might see findings that tend to favor more collaborative and assertive methods of conflict engagement (Folger et al., 2009). In support of such findings, Croucher and colleagues (2012) report that low-context cultures, such as the United States and Ireland, prefer more dominating or competitive styles. On the other hand, cultures and societies (e.g., Asian countries) that favor harmony and collectivism

Accommodation

a conflict style that is on the low end of concern for self but on the high end of concern for other; accommodation implies that one shows little or no assertiveness, but, rather, gives in to the other party.

Competition

a conflict style that reflects a high level of concern for the self's goals while ignoring the goals of the other; individuals who use this style likely want to "defeat" the other person or force him or her to acquiesce.

Compromise

a conflict style that assumes that both parties give and take a little in reaching their goals, which represents a moderate level of concern both for self and the other.

Collaboration

the conflict style that is on the high end of concern both for self and the other; both parties reach a mutually agreeable solution that satisfies both sides completely; most desirable but difficult to enact.

might prefer more accommodation, avoidance, and compromise (Croucher et al., 2012; Kozan, 1997). In particular, Japanese study participants have been shown to prefer accommodation and avoidance (Krauss, Rohlen, & Steinhoff, 1984). Also, collaboration and cooperation are often preferred to competition in some parts of the Middle East (Kozan, 1997).

SEX DIFFERENCES IN CONFLICT

Communication differences tradition

presents separate and distinct conflict behaviors attributed to men and women.

Self-in-relationship movement

this body of theories focused on mutual interdependence of parties (rather than one having power over the other), constructive conflict rather than use of authority, and achieving understanding through reciprocal empathy.

Partnership perspective

suggests that gendered communication during conflict can be about equal collaboration; neither gender is limited to a certain group of behaviors.

Report talk

task oriented and focuses on direct expression of ideas; typically attributed to men's style of communication.

Rapport talk

attributed to women's style, which is more feminine, collaborative, and empathetic, and focuses on maintaining the relationship between conversational partners.

Conflict style preferences can also vary according to gender, but the research is not quite conclusive on the exact variations. In fact, studies overall suggest that the differences between women and men are not as drastic as we might imagine (Folger et al., 2009). In making sense of the findings, we should distinguish gender (masculine, feminine, androgynous) and biological sex (female, male), and point out that biological sex alone does not typically drive differences in conflict style (Nicotera & Dorsey, 2006). In their summary of gender research in conflict, Hocker and Wilmot (1995) claim that there have been three general approaches to studying gender influences. One of these approaches is the **communication differences tradition**, which presents separate and distinct conflict behaviors attributed to men and women. This research was done in the 1970s and 1980s, and some of it has been shown to be inaccurate. The second tradition is the **self-in-relationship movement**, and this body of theories tended to focus on mutual interdependence of parties (rather than one having power over the other), constructive conflict rather than use of authority, and achieving understanding through reciprocal empathy. The self-in-relationship movement placed more emphasis on conflict being constructive and sensitive to the parties' relationship with each other. Development of this research eventually led to the **partnership perspective**, which suggests that gendered communication during conflict can be about equal collaboration. Although the genders might display different communication patterns, the assumption is that neither gender is limited to a certain group of behaviors. In other words, women and men have their unique styles but are not necessarily limited to those styles. Included in this group of theories is Tannen's (1990) report/rapport talk, which can help distinguish the gendered styles. More specifically, men are said to engage in **report talk**, which is task oriented and focuses on direct expression of ideas. **Rapport talk** is attributed to women's style, which is more collaborative and empathetic, and focuses on maintaining the relationship between conversational partners.

The research that explores gender differences most often reveals differences in the expectations we tend to have for how men and women approach and act during conflict. For instance, Ivy and Backlund (1994) found that women are expected to be more supportive and nice, and when they act forcefully, they are judged more

© Sidarta/Shutterstock.com

While gender plays a role in conflict style, the individual person may not fit the norm for his or her gender.

harshly by both women and men. On the contrary, men are expected to act more assertively. Men and women might also differ in the styles they recall or report from past conflict. Rogan (2006) found that women tend to frame their past conflicts in terms of reaching mutually agreeable solutions, while men tend to view their conflicts as struggles to determine a winner and loser. Gender differences can also be seen among adolescents. Black (2000) conducted a study of adolescent conflict resolution among best friends. She found that when given a conflict resolution task, females engaged in less withdrawal and demonstrated more supportive communication skills than did their male counterparts. In addition, the males in her study rated their friendships as having more conflict than did the females.

Perhaps the best way to understand gender differences in conflict is to place them in context. In terms of personal relationships, research has found some common patterns with regard to gender differences in heterosexual marital conflict. Christensen and Heavey (1993) acknowledge a demand–withdraw pattern widely documented in many couples in which the wife demands attention from and criticizes the husband, who in turn engages in withdrawal and retreats to avoid a conflict. This withdrawal subsequently solicits more demand and criticism from the wife, which leads to more withdrawal from the husband. Christensen and Heavey further point out that the presence of this downward spiral is strongly associated with dissatisfaction in the marriage, whereas reversal of this pattern can signal more constructive changes in the relationship.

IN YOUR *life*

Have you ever noticed gender differences in conflict styles and resolution strategies? How might gender affect the ways people argue and negotiate?

FACE-NEGOTIATION THEORY

One way to explain cultural preferences is to explore Ting-Toomey's face-negotiation theory of conflict (Ting-Toomey, 1988, 2005; Ting-Toomey & Kurogi, 1998; Ting-Toomey & Oetzel, 2003). According to this theory, conflict style is a reflection of how one might enter into a conflict negotiation, which requires a certain amount of facework. **Face** is the public image we want to convey to others, and **facework** is supporting another person's face or projected self-image "while at the same time not bringing shame on one's own self-face" (Ting-Toomey, 1988, p. 216). The use of facework in a conflict negotiation involves the coordinated effort to maintain one's face or image (which also implies one's goals) and to be delicate with how one treats the other person's face. In this case, maintaining one's own face is akin to concern for self, while helping maintain the other person's face is the concern one has for the other. However, when someone is using a competitive style in a conflict situation, that person might engage in **face-threatening acts**, which could include insults, attempts to embarrass, or questioning of the other's argument or position (see photo). Conflict itself might be viewed as a face-threatening act given that issues of incompatible goals, interference, and other disagreements are likely to be raised. Simply raising the issue of conflict with another person can threaten or challenge that person's face.

Keeping in mind the significance of face during conflict and how one's face can be threatened or challenged, let us return to our discussion of conflict styles. As we stated earlier, Ting-Toomey's research suggests that particular cultures prefer

Face

the image of self that we project to others.

Facework

the portrayal of one's face is an inherently communicative act that is an extension of one's identity.

Face-threatening acts

behaviors that insults, embarrasses, or question another person's face.

One way children engage in face-threating acts is through bullying.

certain conflict styles. Face-negotiation theory can help explain how certain cultural variables, such as individualism and collectivism, are linked with preferences for certain conflict styles. Recall that individualistic people tend to be more direct and honest with others, and they typically prefer to address conflict in more direct ways. That said, individualists prefer more competitive and collaborative strategies. While these types might seem opposed to each other, keep in mind that while they differ in their concern for the other, they both require one to approach the other person in the conflict directly. Such a direct approach is what some cultures do not favor. For instance, collectivistic cultures prefer to be indirect during conflict, partly because of the concern for saving and maintaining face. This requires being subtle and not challenging the other person. Therefore, collectivistic cultures tend to prefer avoidance, accommodation, and compromise.

Face-negotiation theory also attempts to explain conflict style preferences with power distance, which is the extent to which one accepts differences in status and hierarchy among individuals and in society. More specifically, Ting-Toomey (1998) predicts that low-status individuals might get defensive during conflict if they live in a low–power-distance culture but will be more modest when in a high–power-distance culture. High-status people in low–power-distance cultures will tend to be more competitive, whereas in high–power-distance cultures they will use strategies that shame the other person.

Ting-Toomey (2005) provides more specific predictions regarding power distance. Within low–power-distance cultures, parties in conflict will show little respect or deference for the other. Also, high-status individuals in these cultures will do things such as criticize and threaten the other person to get him or her to acquiesce, as well as acting more dominating. Ting-Toomey has a set of predictions for individuals living in high–power-distance cultures; one is that facework is typically done in an up–down fashion, with respect and deference given to those with higher status. In addition, low-status members will use strategies such as accommodation and avoidance to resist complying with the other person in conflict.

Self-construal is another dimension of cultural variability to which face-negotiation theory has been applied. Oetzel (1998) has written about self-construals, which is a concept that explains the extent to which people see themselves as independent from others (i.e., independent self-construal) or connected to others (i.e., dependent self-construal) in particular situations. Oetzel claims that there is a strong connection between one's self-construal and one's behavioral tendencies toward conflict. For instance, an independent self-construal is associated with the use of competitive strategies during conflict, whereas dependent self-construal tends to predict the preference for avoiding or accommodating (Ting-Toomey, 2005).

INTRODUCING CONFLICT

The thought of introducing conflict might not excite you; it might even cause you a great deal of discomfort. We all have had negative experiences with conflict, and at times it might seem easier just to avoid it. Unfortunately, in most cases, simply avoiding the conflict will not make the underlying issue disappear. As we have discussed, groups and teams will likely remain stagnant and be unable to grow and transform if they do not first deal with and manage conflict. Also, introducing conflict does not have to be drastic; it can be subtle and can be spread over several steps. You don't have to see conflict as a battle but, rather, can view it as a meeting of minds to reach a mutually agreeable solution.

It is even possible to develop skill or expertise in introducing and managing conflict. In fact, having a proven track record of engaging in and overcoming conflict will work in your favor. Quintanilla and Wahl (2014) advise that professional excellence implies viewing positive conflict as a valuable tool. Before thinking about how to manage a conflict that has already erupted, first consider introducing it or getting more comfortable with the idea of engaging in conflict when it might arise. Learning to view conflict as a natural, even necessary, part of your personal and professional life can help you become more comfortable with the prospect of conflict.

Groupthink

the tendency for a group to strive for harmony and agreement at the expense of productivity and growth.

In many cases, introducing conflict means rocking the boat, so to speak, or temporarily disrupting the harmony of the group setting. When raising a controversial issue seems too undesirable, there is a tendency toward **groupthink**, which is much more than the inclination to avoid conflict. More specifically, people caught up in groupthink feel compelled to preserve harmony at the cost of productivity and growth. Groupthink, according to Irving Janis (1972, 1982, 1989), is the tendency for a group to strive for harmony and agreement at the expense of productivity and growth. In practical terms, groups suffering from groupthink discourage dissent and disagreement, even if this means failing to detect a serious problem or confront an important issue. Groups suffering from groupthink tend to be highly cohesive, even to the point where group members feel pressured to confirm and agree, and dissenting members hesitate to express divergent opinions. This can also be the case when a dissenting member is perceived to be different from the others (e.g., in age, ethnicity, gender). The signs of groupthink include members' feelings of invulnerability, tendency to rationalize a decision or idea collectively without question or debate, belief that the group is morally right in its cause, negative attitudes and perceptions of those outside the group, stifling of dissenting viewpoints, and informal appointment of "mind guards" who protect the group from information or insights that could threaten perceptions of cohesion.

Unfortunately, when dissenting opinions are not allowed, the group or team can put itself on the path toward failure or stagnation. In all, operating under the cloak of groupthink and, thus, avoiding conflict can prevent a group from receiving valuable feedback from within and outside. In the end, although everyone appears to agree, the group can end up making bad decisions and not experience growth and development as a whole.

Addressing groupthink or avoiding it altogether means introducing conflict. Quintanilla and Wahl (2014) recommend establishing normative behaviors that make it easy to introduce conflict, whether in small groups, your family, or your personal relationships. When you need to engage the conflict, you can do so by seeking additional information, as well as by testing or challenging assumptions in tactful ways. Keep in mind that such behaviors, no matter how gently executed, can be seen as face threatening, especially when cultural variation is at play. So, for example, if you know you are engaging with a person who is collectivistic and high context in orientation, you might consider using methods that are indirect; do not attack the person, but focus on the issue at hand. It might also be good to start from some common ground, rather than immediately pointing out the disagreement. On the other hand, if the other person is more direct and individualistic, then he or she will likely appreciate a more honest, upfront approach and might feel frustrated if you waffle or are hesitant in raising the subject.

MANAGING CONFLICT

An individual's conflict style reveals a great deal about how he or she attempts to manage the conflict situation. But what we are focusing on with management is the attempt to reach some resolution. The idea of "managing" conflict essentially means how one deals with it once it becomes apparent to all involved parties. Individuals have a choice when reacting to an emerging conflict. They can flee the situation, stay and fight, or engage in some form of principled negotiation (Quintanilla & Wahl, 2014). In some cases, fleeing the situation might be the most appropriate response. This means you simply choose not to engage the other person in conflict because the conflict is not worth your time or a mutually agreeable solution just is not possible. However, even when a resolution is only remotely possible, it is usually not best to avoid the conflict. In other cases, fighting or competing might be necessary, especially when your stance or position is something you believe in strongly. The fight approach does require confrontation, a reality some people find too uncomfortable. In addition, fighting means that both parties face off as adversaries, which results in a winner and a loser.

Resolving conflict is easier said than done in most cases.

© marekuliasz/Shutterstock.com

In many cases, however, both parties can work to gain something when engaging in conflict. When fighting and avoiding are not feasible or ideal, both parties can try principled negotiation (Fisher & Ury, 1981; Fisher, Ury, & Patton, 1991). This approach is interest based, meaning that the process encourages both parties to focus on the topic or interest at hand, rather than on personal differences or motives. Such an approach is germane to our discussion of intercultural conflict because, while differences can lead to the introduction of more perspectives and better decisions, sometimes they can be the source of conflict and one of the factors that exacerbate difficulties. Therefore, keeping conflict resolution focused on interests, both parties can work past their perceived and actual differences and toward a solution.

PRINCIPLED NEGOTIATION

Negotiation

involves a conversation or discussion between people or parties in conflict who wish to reach an agreement.

A more specific discussion of conflict management leads us to talk about negotiation strategies. **Negotiation** involves a conversation or discussion between people or parties in conflict who wish to reach an agreement. Both parties enter the conflict with their own interests, which they try to maximize. There is no doubt that much has been written in the popular press about negotiation, and much of it focuses on getting the upper hand and treating negotiation as if it were a debate that results in a win–lose outcome. You might also have the idea that negotiation is just about making compromises and giving up something to get something else. However, we propose that negotiation is about engaging in a productive conflict that ends with a mutually agreeable resolution. Seasoned negotiators tend to understand this and approach such conflicts in a spirit of "discussion" and "dialogue" (Hocker & Wilmot, 1995). Fisher and Ury (1981), in *Getting to Yes: Negotiating Disagreement Without Giving In,* advocate **principled negotiation**, which puts forth four principles: (1) Separate the problem from the people involved in the negotiation, (2) focus not on positions but interests, (3) create options for mutual gain, and (4) insist on objective criteria.

First, separating the problem and the people means that both parties do their best to stick to the issue at hand and to put aside their relationship or personal difficulties. In other words, the issue underlying the conflict is the substantive matter, whereas emotions, perceptions, and bad feelings toward the other should be dealt with another time. Suppose Roger, a 45-year-old man, and Jacqueline, a 28-year-old woman, both work in the same purchasing department and have been assigned to work together. Both Roger and Jacqueline are charged with working on a project. When the two coworkers stumble on a disagreement, Roger might assume that Jacqueline is being too emotional and immature, while Jacqueline might believe that Roger is being old-fashioned and antagonistic toward her because she is a woman. In this case, both individuals need to recognize their personal feelings toward each other and do their best to put them aside if they are to approach their disagreement in the spirit of resolution.

A particular problem might emerge when people neglect to separate the problem from the people: One or both parties might become overly concerned with facework. Based on our discussion of face-negotiation theory, the act of maintaining face can override the discussion about the actual conflict issue (Folger et al., 2009). As a result, the interaction can be drawn away from the problem at hand and focused instead on preserving or attacking the other person's face, which is a secondary issue. Face-saving issues are tied to the substantive issue of the conflict, but they should not dominate.

The second principle, which is to focus on interests and not positions, is important because it forces both parties to figure out exactly what the problem is. Unlike an interest, a position already puts both individuals in adversarial roles, pushing each to adopt his or her stance and stick to it *no matter what.* When people adopt positions, they are slow to change them, even if it is best to do so. Furthermore, people sometimes adopt the extreme version of their positions to contradict their opponent, which can only make finding common ground more difficult.

Have you ever had an argument that ended up being about winning instead of what triggered the actual argument?

© Roman Kosolapov/Shutterstock.com

On the other hand, an interest can be changed or adapted. Fisher and Ury (1981) explain that interests are about what people really want and need, not what they say they want and need. In this case, an interest could reflect a want or need shared by both parties. Not all wants and needs are mutually exclusive; it might turn out that the interests of both parties are compatible. Returning to Jacqueline and Roger, suppose they were asked to plan their department's annual awards ceremony. Jacqueline wants a large gala affair with formal dress and an elaborate buffet, while Roger wants to cut costs and organize a simple but professional event. Instead of taking separate positions on the issue—formal and fancy versus simple and professional—Jacqueline and Roger might remind each other that their common interest is to create a memorable evening to honor the best of their department (the common interest). Focusing on the common interest, rather than advocating opposing positions, could help Roger and Jacqueline work together to plan a great awards ceremony that everyone in their department will talk about for months afterward. To get this kind of conversation started, Roger and Jacqueline can use such phrases as, "What would be the perfect situation?" "What concerns you the most?" or "What if we tried . . . ?" to start moving the conversation toward common interests (Yarbrough & Wilmot, 1995).

Principled negotiation also involves creating options for mutual gain. This means that Roger and Jacqueline should do their best to create a win–win solution, something with which they (and the rest of the department!) can be happy. After some interest-based discussion, Jacqueline and Roger might discover that they would both like to see a buffet table at the event, as well as some kind of musical performance before the awards are distributed. Decisions about the kind of music and number of musicians, as well as the food on the buffet, will need to be worked out, but at least they both can see what options they have to reach mutual gain. Again, we emphasize that the options should lead to a win–win solution, rather than encouraging both parties to fight it out until there is a winner and a loser.

Finally, the negotiating parties need to generate criteria with which they will make their decision. These criteria represent the conditions that must be met to resolve the conflict, and these criteria must be objective and agreed on by both parties. Fisher and Ury (1981) suggest that the negotiators look outside to find objective criteria, which in Roger and Jacqueline's case might be a finite budget for the awards ceremony set for them by their supervisor. They might also consult with employees in other departments to find out what they did for similar events and use those ideas to establish a set of objective criteria.

We have said that cultural differences and the resulting difficulties are often a product of perceptions. Fisher et al. (1991) suggest that when handling negotiations, both parties need to get a handle on the perceptions at play. They offer several strategies, which include trying to see the situation from your opponent's perspective, not assuming that your fears about the other's intentions will materialize, avoiding blaming the other person for the problem, discussing each other's perspectives, and making sure you and your opponent have a stake in the final outcome of the negotiation process.

Fisher et al. (1991) claim that very few disputes are inherently win–lose, meaning that virtually every conflict can be resolved with principled negotiation. In fact, they argue that bargaining in this manner is almost always superior to less cooperative approaches. Nonetheless, this approach, by its very nature, might be more amenable to Western cultures that embrace rationality as opposed to emotions when dealing with conflict. Additionally, individuals who are more accepting of power distance might not be accustomed to the idea of reaching a mutually agreeable solution, especially when the conflict is between individuals of unequal status.

When the individuals involved in the conflict are unwilling or unable to engage in the negotiation process objectively, then it is a good idea to enlist an impartial mediator. Such a person can sometimes help resolve the dispute productively (Lewicki, Barry, Saunders, & Barry, 2011), mainly because he or she is not emotionally involved and has no personal interest in the outcome of the negotiation. The mediator serves a number of functions, one of which is to set the stage; this involves choosing the setting, stating the purpose of the negotiation, identifying each participant, and even arranging seating. Once this is done, the mediator can obtain a commitment from each party to maintain professionalism and to approach the negotiation with decorum. The mediator might decide who speaks first, how long each person gets to speak, and other procedural issues that might otherwise arouse contention. The mediator should also take notes and restate important points that have been made during the negotiation. Another function of the mediator is to help set priorities, which can help resolve disagreements and keep participants focused on the main issues, rather than on their own positions. Another important function of the mediator is to restate any agreement that is reached and to make sure all parties understand it. It is important to emphasize that the agreement is one the conflicting parties—not the mediator—generate and own.

WHAT YOU'VE LEARNED

From reading this chapter, you learned the definition of conflict and its five characteristics—there needs to be an expressed struggle, interdependence, a perception of scarce resources, a perception of incompatible goals, and a perceived interference from others. Once this foundational information was discussed, you overviewed various cultural attitudes towards conflict, and you were given the different types of conflict. The text then outlined the five styles of conflict—avoidance, accommodation, competition, compromise, and collaboration—which then led to a description of cultural differences with regard to these aforementioned conflict styles. Finally, you learned how one can introduce conflict to engage in it, and you overviewed the steps of principled negotiation.

This chapter's focus on conflict is important in your daily life, but it is especially important to keep in mind when engaging in intercultural contexts. Having an understanding of cultural attitudes and perceptions of conflict will help you navigate your communication between varying cultural contexts.

REVIEW

1. _____ happens when a person takes extra steps to be part of social groups to which certain individuals belong.

2. Conflict between two people is called _____.

3. _____ is when the actions of one party will affect the other and vice versa.

4. When a conflict is about rights, responsibilities, and roles people hold, it is a _____ conflict.

5. _____ is a type of conflict that is about differences in how people articulate goals and understand how tasks should be completed.

6. Explain the difference between *concern for self* and *concern for other*.

7. What type of conflict style has a low concern for self and a high concern for other?

8. Why is a *collaboration* conflict style difficult to enact?

9. Explain the difference between *report talk* and *rapport talk*.

10. What are the four principles of *principled negotiation*?

Review answers are found on the accompanying website.

REFLECT

1. Kayley prepares most of her meals for the week on Sunday night because her vegan diet makes it difficult to eat lunch while she is on campus during the week. She approaches her roommate, Dan, because she ran out of her prepared food before the week was over and suspects him of having eaten some of it. Kayley is especially frustrated because Dan is not vegan, so she feels as though he has more food options than she does. Describe Kayley and Dan's conflict using the characteristics of conflict discussed in this chapter.

2. Do you tend to have more *concern for self* or *concern for other*? What are some pros and cons of the type of concern you tend to have?

3. Sasha is from Egypt and lives with her boyfriend, Tom. Tom is frustrated because she has not yet paid her share of the utilities, and he has been trying to approach her about the issue. Sasha, who is not accustomed to directly approaching conflict, has been actively avoiding Tom and his phone calls. Which conflict style would be beneficial for Tom to adopt in this situation?

4. Drake is a manager at a local paper company and oversees multiple employees. One day during a company meeting, one of Drake's employees, Logan, suggests changing a major vendor for the purposes of saving the company money. His comment does not seem to be received well by Drake, and the remainder of the meeting feels uncomfortable for everyone. Using the concept of face-negotiation theory, discuss why Logan's comment was not well received.

5. Think of a conflict you have recently experienced. Discuss how implementing the concept of *principled negotiation* might have changed the outcome.

KEY TERMS

social identity, 208
social categorization, 208
conflict, 208
dyadic conflict, 208
intrapersonal conflict, 209
interdependence, 210
interference, 211
harmony model, 212
confrontational model, 212
regulative model, 212
object conflict, 213
relational conflict, 213
priority conflict, 213
expressive, 214
instrumental, 214
concern for self, 216
concern for other, 216

avoidance, 216
accommodation, 217
competition, 217
compromise, 217
collaboration, 217
communication differences tradition, 218
self-in-relationship movement, 218
partnership perspective, 218
report talk, 218
rapport talk, 218
face, 220
facework, 220
face-threatening acts, 220
groupthink, 222
negotiation, 224
principled negotiation, 225

CHAPTER NINE

Communicating Social Class and Understanding the Culture of Poverty

CHAPTER OUTLINE

WHAT YOU WILL LEARN

After studying this chapter, you should be able to
1. define social class;
2. identify examples of social class across communication contexts;
3. understand social class from a communication perspective;
4. define poverty; and
5. understand the culture of poverty.

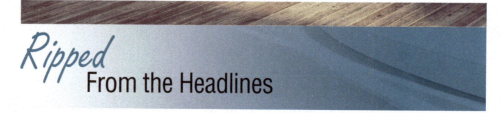

Ripped
From the Headlines

The water crisis in Flint, Michigan began when city officials were looking to save money on the city's water and sewage costs. In April of 2014, the city cut off its original water source from the Detroit Water and Sewerage Department and switched to receiving water from the Flint River. Shortly after the switch, residents of Flint started complaining about the quality of their water; city and state officials denied that any problem was occurring with the new water source. The poor water quality was causing major corrosion in the pipes, and lead was leaching into their water (Kennedy, 2016). The World Health Organization explains that high levels of lead in the blood can cause a variety of health concerns, especially in children; it can cause irreversible effects including learning disabilities, behavioral problems, and mental retardation (World Health Organization, 2001).

Many have argued that the water crisis in Flint is a form of racial and social class discrimination. Several advocates assert that the issues in Flint are a form of "environmental racism." The NAACP, for example, has said, "Would more have been done, and at a much faster pace, if nearly 40 percent of Flint residents were not living below the poverty line? The answer is unequivocally yes" (Martinez, 2016). The United Nations has also weighed in on this issue by saying that racism and class discrimination possibly played a key role in the scandal (Sands, 2016). Do you agree that racism and/or class discrimination may have played a role in the poor handling of this crisis?

As you read this chapter, remember to think about the expectations or stereotypes you might have about people outside your social class. Use the Flint example as a point of reference for how you expect people with (or without) wealth to use their money. Remember that social class involves more than monetary income; our economic backgrounds, ethnicity, and culture all play major roles in how we frame our personal standing in society.

Your study of communication and culture would be incomplete without an awareness of social class and an understanding of poverty as a culture. The way we communicate about social class and poverty is clearly related to cultural sensitivity. This chapter explores social class and poverty to get you to think more critically about these issues from a communication perspective. The first section in this chapter defines social class, as well as what influences your own view and communication about social class. You will also learn why social class is important to your study of communication and culture. Next, you will read about the presence of social class across communication contexts, such as in the workplace, education, media, and more. Third, you will engage the definition of poverty and understand it from a cultural perspective. Finally, you will be encouraged to think about the issues and implications of communication about social class and the culture of poverty. Let's begin by focusing on the definition of social class in the section that follows.

DEFINING SOCIAL CLASS

What is your definition of social class? If you had to place your family in a particular category, in what social class would you place yourself? In the United States, the majority of people affiliate themselves with the middle class, which has a relatively broad definition. The criteria for belonging to a particular class can be unclear, but most people equate social class with household income or economic status. However,

What does drinking bottled water, or the particular brand of bottled water, communicate about social class?

© Art Allianz/Shutterstock.com

the foundation of social class consists of much more than economics; culture plays a significant role in perceptions of social class, and social class itself forms the basis for many cultural identities as well. Social class is based on **social stratification**, which involves the ranking of groups according to various criteria, with higher positions given more value, respect, status, and privilege than lower positions (Allen, 2010). It is important to note that not all cultures place the same value on

Social stratification

the ranking of groups according to various criteria, with higher positions given more value, respect, status, and privilege than lower positions.

certain criteria; what is considered a valuable group in one culture or country may not carry the same worth in a different culture.

Most research on ideas about social classcan be attributed to Karl Marx and Max Weber, both of whom based their work on an economic foundation. Marx identified two major social classes related to economy and production: the **bourgeoisie**, who own the means of production, and the **proletariat**, who form the working class and instruments of production (Artz & Murphy, 2000). Weber believed that social class involved more than just economics, insisting that property, power, and prestige also play a significant role in social stratification. Think about how you perceive class structure in the United States. Do you believe that most perceptions about social class relate to the positions people hold from an economic standpoint? In many capitalist-based economies, social classes are greatly defined by their impact and position within a given economy, but it is important to remember that many cultures do not place as much importance on income and economic power in regard to social standing.

While culture does play a significant role in the concept of social class, most perceptions of social standing are based on an economic perspective. In the United States, many leaders and politicians construct their discussions on social class based on income and economic value, which frame most of the discussions on issues relating to social problems. Many debates involving social class involve the idea of upward mobility, or the ability to improve your class standing within a society.

Bourgeoisie

one of the two major social classes related to economy and production; these owned the means of production.

Proletariat

one of the two major social classes related to economy and production; these formed the working class and instruments of production.

Senator Bernie Sanders became popular with many voters during the 2016 presidential campaign because of his policy positions related to social class.

© Gino Santa Maria/Shutterstock.com

The placement of many people regarding social class involves three major factors: ascription, achievement, and capital.

ASCRIPTION

Now that you have an understanding of social class as a concept, let's take a look at the factors that frame your perceived social standing. A major factor in social class standing involves ascription. **Ascription** refers to conditions at birth, such as family background, race, sex, and place of birth. People are born into certain situations that can either hurt or benefit their social standing. Think about your own situation as it relates to ascription. Were you born into a wealthy family? Was cost a significant barrier to entering college? Besides your family's income, be critical of other factors that might help or impede your ability to move up the social ladder. For many years in the United States, people were regularly denied beneficial opportunities based on their ethnic or cultural background. Certain universities were closed to non-Whites, and religious affiliation could bar someone from access to social opportunities. Even the geographic area where you were born can significantly impact your social class. Certain parts of the United States have lower access to higher education, health care, and high-paying jobs. Think about it: In your experience, have you ever lived in a city or region that did not have the tools and opportunities available in other areas of the country? The particular section of a city where you live can also positively or negatively affect your chances of gaining upward mobility; low-income neighborhoods commonly have high crime rates, higher rates of substance abuse, and low-paying jobs, which create a series of barriers to raising social standing.

From a cultural standpoint, ethnocentrism is a major obstacle for many out-groups looking to gain higher social standing within a society. **Ethnocentrism** is defined as "the view of things in which one's own group is the center of everything, and all others are scaled and rated with reference to it" (Sumner, 1906). In relation to ascription, being born into a cultural group that is in the minority can lead to intercultural conflicts stemming from ethnocentrism. Since communication from an ethnocentric perspective ultimately functions to maintain the integrity and dignity of the in-group, ethnocentrism is a major barrier to effective intercultural communication, which has serious consequences for in-group favoritism and out-group discrimination (Lwin, Stanaland, & Williams, 2010).

ACHIEVEMENT

Another major factor in social class standing involves achievement. **Achievement** is defined as the result of individual effort or merit; examples include running

Ascription
conditions at birth, such as family background, race, sex, and place of birth.

Can you think of examples in popular culture and marketing that make particular statements about social class (e.g., products, brands, clothing, food choices)?

Ethnocentrism
placing your own cultural beliefs in a superior position, which leads to a negative judgment of other cultures.

Achievement
the result of individual effort or merit; examples include running a financially successful business, earning a college degree, and receiving a promotion in any professional environment.

The "American Dream" and achievement in U.S. culture are often reflected in owning a home and driving a nice car.

a financially successful business, earning a college degree, and receiving a promotion in any professional environment. Achievement is considered a major milestone in U.S. culture and embodies the concept of the "American Dream," wherein everyone can become successful and improve their standing as long as they put forth the effort to achieve their goals. While many individuals have succeeded in improving their social standing through personal achievement, some cultural out-groups and economically disadvantaged people face greater obstacles to achievement than do others. Achievement is linked to ascription; the initial tools and opportunities you have greatly increase your chances of success. People born into a culture of poverty face more significant challenges than do those people born into an economically strong environment.

It is important to remember that different cultures carry different interpretations of achievement and success. One specific example involves the cultural differences between the United States and China. The United States is typically defined as having an individualistic culture, while China has a more collectivistic culture. Individualists stress human independence and the importance of self-reliance and autonomy; collectivists care more about human interdependence and the success of the collective group over the success of a single individual. Recent studies have supported this link from culture to the attribution and motivations of gaining success (Feeny & Qi, 2010). Do you have a more individualistic or collectivistic view when gauging achievement? Do you believe there are certain strengths in either of these cultural approaches? As you continue to move through this chapter and learn more about cultural differences in social class, try to look at the situations and examples through both an individualistic and a collectivistic lens. Also, be sure to reflect on the perspective of people who live in poverty; whether you have personally experienced or interacted within a culture of poverty or not, always be cognizant of the specific obstacles disadvantaged people face that others do not.

CAPITAL

Capital
a person's, family's, or business's accumulated goods and their overall value.

A third attribute that greatly affects perceptions of social class is an individual's or family's combined capital. **Capital** is a person's, family's, or business's accumulated goods and their overall value. In the United States and other capitalist economies, capital can be the greatest factor in determining a person's perceived social class and standing. It is important to note that people can possess different types of capital. French sociologist Pierre Bourdieu elaborated on the concept of capital to emphasize certain ideological conditions, as well as the different ways people can use capital to compete for position and improve their social standing. Bourdieu identified three specific types of capital: economic capital, cultural capital, and social capital.

Economic Capital

Economic capital encompasses a person's total financial assets. When most people think of capital, economic is the first type that comes to mind. While it would be unfair to say that economic capital is the most important with regard to social standing, it cannot be denied that most people consider financial standing to be the overall indicator of social standing. When someone is referred to as being from the upper class, what image comes to mind for you? Typically, people from the upper class are considered to be financially rich, with easy access to even more potential economic capital. Similarly, members of the lower class are considered to be financially poor, sometimes even living below the poverty line.

> **Economic capital**
> a person's total financial assets.

Another interesting question regarding economic capital and social class is, How do you define the middle class? While many people associate themselves with the middle class and most politicians preach about protecting the middle class, there is no concrete definition for that category. Of all the different social classes, the middle class has the most variety and encompasses the greatest amount of people. Terms such as *upper middle class* and *lower middle class* are used generally; one person's definition of *upper middle class* can be quite different from another's, and many cultures also have distinctive ideas about what constitutes being middle or upper class.

Cultural Capital

A second type of capital is cultural capital. **Cultural capital** encompasses specialized skills and knowledge, including linguistic and cultural competencies passed down through family or personal experiences in social institutions (Bourdieu, 1987). Another type of capital closely tied to ascription, cultural capital involves your cultural worldviews and the experiences you have framed within your cultural context. While cultural capital cannot be objectively measured, it is nonetheless a critical component for success in maintaining or improving your social class. Cultural capital also involves linguistic, social, and communication processes that can help foster interclass membership and cultural competency.

> **Cultural capital**
> specialized skills and knowledge, including linguistic and cultural competencies passed down through family or personal experiences in social institutions.

Certain social institutions are beneficial for increasing cultural capital and competency. For example, in the United States the emphasis on higher-education degrees and certifications reflects the importance of cultural capital in U.S. society. Numerous other institutions reflect and cultivate the cultural capital of the United States, which has led to a worldwide market for U.S. cultural products such as cinema, music, and writing. Obviously, most other countries also create practices and institutions to increase cultural capital. Think about certain cultural institutions or landmarks from other countries that are easily recognizable. The Royal Society for Arts in Britain is one such institution, and even a structure such as the Eiffel Tower in France can reflect and impress cultural capital on many different people and cultures.

In one particular study, scholar Zhongwei Song (2012) discussed Sun Tzu's seminal work, *The Art of War*, as well as its place in Chinese society among important cultural works. Tzu's work has been translated into more than 30 different languages, reflecting its cultural impact on a worldwide scale. However, Song noticed that the translations widely varied depending on the cultural background of the translator. After researching this discrepancy, Song asserted that despite translating a different culture's piece of work, the translators still exhibited an underlying desire to place their own cultural identity in that work. Essentially, we all have a desire to increase our cultural capital, even in conjunction with another cultural work or object. Think about the ways you leave your cultural mark on your work, and reflect on its impact on the project as a whole.

Social Capital

Social capital

networks or connections among people who can help one another.

Networking

the ability to use one's personal social connections to achieve goals.

The third type of capital Bourdieu identified is social capital. **Social capital** consists of the networks or connections among people who can help one another. A major aspect of social capital is **networking**, or the ability to use one's personal social connections to achieve a goal. Fraternities and sororities are great examples of sources of social capital. Through the social relationships people build when they join a fraternity or sorority, they create potential connections they can use later in life to advance in professional careers and social institutions.

A major premise of social capital can be accurately summarized in the old saying, "It's not what you know; it's who you know." While some people may balk at the idea of relying on others for social advancement as opposed to relying on personal achievement alone, the importance of social capital and networking cannot be denied. Have you ever used your social capital or networking to get a job you wanted, or to get into an exclusive school or club? Humans are social creatures, and whom we choose to interact with and how we interact with others help foster people's perceptions of us. As with the other forms of capital, your initial ascription also plays a major role in the accessibility of social capital (Allen, 2010). Many elite educational institutions still honor the practice of "legacy admissions," or giving preferential treatment to the children of alumni. Again, this reasserts the obstacles facing those in the lower class or in poverty, who do not have social capital to give them an advantage in moving upward on the social ladder. Even at the high school level, research has consistently revealed a pattern of preferential (or differential) academic counseling based on the student's social class (Dworkin & Dworkin, 1999).

To understand the importance and impact of social capital, let's look at the communication choices of Shawn and Jake. Shawn and Jake are close friends who attend the same university. Jake has always been socially outgoing and made it a point to join a fraternity and several clubs related to his major. Shawn, on the other hand, chose to keep to himself, to focus only on his classes and grades, and to hang out with a group of friends outside of his academic field. As Jake and Shawn approached graduation, Jake began using his fraternity and club connections to get recommendations and leads on potential job opportunities. Shawn relied only on newspaper, bulletin board, and Internet listings in his job search. By networking with an older fraternity graduate, Jake was able to land an excellent entry-level job right after graduation with a company related to his academic degree. Shawn, however, suffered through numerous interviews without ever getting a callback and, 6 months after graduation, is still working at the same restaurant where he worked while in school.

From a communication perspective, how does this example reinforce the importance of cultivating social capital throughout your interactions in school? What communication dialogues did Jake take advantage of that could have helped Shawn find a professional job after graduation? As you move forward with your education and professional career, remember the significance of using your communication skills to create avenues of social capital.

From looking at these examples, it is easy to see why social capital can be so conflicting; in one sense, it is useful for gaining access to groups or institutions that might otherwise be inaccessible. However, it is also apparent that this type of networking clearly favors individuals who already have a high social standing. Recent studies on social capital in the United States continue to reveal its importance and attraction to most people, especially scholars and political policymakers (Ameli & Motahari, 2010). How do you feel about using social capital and networking? Have either of these benefited or hindered you in your life? As you continue to move forward in your educational and professional career, remember to be aware of the presence of social capital and the ways it can be used to benefit you and your family.

What connections can you make between networking opportunities and social class?

WHY IS SOCIAL CLASS IMPORTANT?

As you can see from the previous section, social class plays a vital role not only in your standing within a particular society or culture but also in your ability to gain upward mobility in an economic, cultural, and social perspective. Class difference and class struggle have been significant themes throughout U.S. history. Whether in accessibility to resources, potential for success and advancement, or self-esteem, the positioning of particular social classes has been in a constant state of flux, advancement, and learning. Perhaps the most visible instance of class warfare and struggle in recent memory is the civil rights movement of the 1960s. This is not to discount the numerous other instances of struggle in U.S. history, but in the modern era there are few (if any) examples more relevant to the discussion of social class and its effect on society and culture. One of the major cultural ideals in the United States is the belief that all people, regardless of race, creed, ethnicity, religion, or culture, should have the ability to pursue a better life and advance beyond their initial means. As time moves on and perceptions and worldviews change, it is critical for society to adapt and evolve. Think about your personal beliefs regarding social class and social mobility. Do you believe U.S. society has adapted to allow everyone equal access to life, liberty, and the pursuit of happiness? Although significant advances have been made in social equality, we must still be cognizant of particular discrepancies between classes as related to their ability to maintain or improve their standard of living.

Self-Assessment: Social Class

Put a check by each item you know how to do.

_____ 1. I know how to keep my clothes from being stolen at the laundromat.
_____ 2. I know which rummage sales have "bag sales" and when.
_____ 3. I know how to live without electricity or a phone.
_____ 4. I can get by without a car.
_____ 5. I know where the free medical clinics are.
_____ 6. I know what to do when I don't have money to pay the bills.
_____ 7. I know how to live without a checking account.
_____ 8. I know how to get and use food stamps or an electronic card for benefits.
_____ 9. I know which stores are most likely to carry the clothing brands my family wears.
_____ 10. I talk to my children about going to college.
_____ 11. I know how to get one of the best interest rates on my new-car loan.
_____ 12. I repair items in my house almost immediately when they break—or know a repair service and call it.
_____ 13. I know how to get a library card.
_____ 14. My children know the best name brands in clothing.
_____ 15. I understand the difference among the principal, interest, and escrow statements on my house payment.
_____ 16. I know how to get my children into Little League, piano lessons, soccer, etc.
_____ 17. I can read a menu in several different languages.
_____ 18. I know how to read a corporate financial statement and analyze my own financial statements.
_____ 19. I have at least two or three "screens" that keep people whom I do not wish to see away from me.
_____ 20. I know who my preferred financial adviser, legal service, designer, domestic-employment service, and hairdresser are.
_____ 21. I know how to ensure confidentiality and loyalty from my domestic staff.
_____ 22. I have several favorite restaurants in different countries.
_____ 23. I know how to host the parties that "key" people attend.

What is your view of social class in your life? How, if at all, does social class influence your communication choices?

Even today, social class can still make a significant difference in all aspects of a person's life. Research indicates that most working- and lower-class mothers see a doctor for the first time during the last month of pregnancy, while middle- and upper-class women receive top-quality prenatal care throughout their pregnancy. As a result, lower-class families see higher rates of infant mortality, birth defects, maternal mortality, and illnesses than do families in the upper class. Social class has also been linked to academic success (Spade, 2001). Students from a higher social class typically have more success in school than do students from a lower-class family. It is not uncommon for schools in wealthy suburban neighborhoods to have 2 or 3 times the total budget per student than urban or rural schools. As you can see, while significant strides have been made in increasing access to social mobility, the playing field is by no means level for all social groups.

Although money and resources remain the most critical factors in defining social class, culture is increasingly playing a significant role in the everyday reproduction of class consciousness, privilege, and power (Paul, 2012). Culture affects our personal tastes and serves as a mark of distinction among social classes. Think about your personal interactions with other people. We judge others by their accents and clothing, as well as by their taste in books, television, and movies. Consciously or unconsciously, we judge and classify people based on their appreciation (or lack thereof) of common cultural and social institutions. Even this causes an unfair discrepancy for lower-class individuals and families; middle- and upper-class people have the "proper" accents and know how to behave in "polite society." The idea of a proper culture or social interaction creates a self-fulfilling prophecy in which those who are elite remain so and those who come from lower-class or poverty backgrounds remain disengaged from accepted cultural and social interactions (Wilkinson & Pickett, 2010).

Socioeconomic Status

Now that you understand why perceptions of social class are so important, let's take a look at the standard measurements that define social class in the United States. As we have already pointed out, social class includes several different factors that constitute our overall perception of social class and standing. To perceive these different factors as they relate to the whole, it is important to transcend the idea of social class and examine socioeconomic status. **Socioeconomic status** (SES) is determined by the combination of income, education, and occupation. It is critical to examine these factors together because they impact one another greatly. For example, having a low education level limits the occupation opportunities available. Since higher-paying jobs generally require certain educational prerequisites, the few low-education jobs that can potentially pay well can also be dangerous. This opens up the potential for injuries,

Socioeconomic status determined by the combination of income, education, and occupation.

or even career-ending accidents. With no education or income to fall back on, many workers who find themselves injured have no safety net to keep them or their families from falling into poverty. SES generally pertains to one of three categories: high SES, middle SES, or low SES. Research has indicated that individuals or families with low income and little education have a greater potential to suffer from a variety of physical and mental health problems. These problems can be attributed to a variety of factors, such as environmental conditions in the workplace, lack of access to basic health care, and stress stemming from living environments. People who come from high-SES groups generally are strong in education, income, and occupation, and are better equipped to handle the problems facing low-SES individuals. As you can see, the culture of poverty can be a difficult cycle to break. Be aware of these discrepancies during your intercultural interactions as you try to increase your cultural competency.

ETHICAL CONNECTION

Andrea and Jeff are a recently engaged couple planning their wedding reception. Andrea comes from an extremely wealthy upper-class family. Jeff, however, grew up in poverty, and his family continues to struggle financially. While working on wedding plans, Andrea made it clear that she wants a destination wedding in the Caribbean with their family and friends. Jeff balked at this idea, stating that many of his family and friends cannot afford such an expensive trip. Andrea pointed out that both of them want an intimate wedding anyway, so having fewer guests might not be such a bad thing. However, Jeff grew increasingly uncomfortable with the idea of not having many of the people he grew up with at his wedding. Jeff's family and community are close-knit, and he knew it would hurt many of their feelings if they could not spend this special day with him and his bride. As the argument grew increasingly heated, Andrea and Jeff decided to postpone the wedding until they could agree on a setting for their nuptials.

Questions to consider:
1. What are some of the social and cultural class differences between Andrea and Jeff?
2. What are some other possible barriers to dating or marrying someone from outside your social class?
3. Do you think it is possible for a person to maintain a system for automatic detection of alarm sounds that uses the knowledge about their frequency and time structure.
4. How does this story exemplify the need for greater understanding of social class between groups?

William H. Macy and Emmy Rossum star in *Shameless*, a television series about a family with low SES living in the South Side of Chicago.

SES also affects our ability to handle emergencies and sudden disasters. Hurricane Katrina, one of the deadliest hurricanes in U.S. history, hit the coast of Louisiana in the summer of 2005. Research indicated that SES played a major role during Katrina, with a considerable "knowledge gap" of crisis information leading to many people being stranded or killed during the storm (Lachlan & Spence, 2007). While many of those stranded or killed during the storm did come from low socioeconomic backgrounds, the biggest contributing factor in the catastrophe was linked to inadequate crisis education and low crisis awareness. Hurricanes such as Ike and Sandy were followed by a significant drop in individuals stranded or killed during a severe storm, which has been attributed to an increase in crisis awareness education after the catastrophe in Louisiana. As you move forward in your study of social class and the culture of poverty, remember this study and the implications it carries when discussing educational discrepancies among different social classes.

SOCIAL CONSTRUCTION OF SOCIAL CLASS

Now that we have examined the importance of social class and its measurement through SES, it is time to analyze how social class is constructed. Throughout the history of the United States, power dynamics have played a major role in the social construction of social class. The initial colonies practiced an almost feudal society, with wealthy white male landowners forming the top crust of society and the majority of labor performed by women, indentured servants, and slaves. From this period until the outbreak of World War I, class was primarily ascriptive. The majority of wealthy people were born into money, and there was very little movement up the social ladder for everyone else. When the economy became more prosperous after the war, political figures invoked the ideals of individualism and materialism, leading to the emergence of a massive consumerist society. Still, political and social constructions favored the interests of the extremely wealthy. It was not until after World War II that the United States began to invest heavily in social and economic programs for the middle and lower classes. The Great Depression had exposed the lack of social safety for many citizens when the stock and job markets crashed.

In an effort to improve the SES of the country, significant bills such as the Social Security Act (which provided retirement income to workers) and the GI Bill of 1944 (which provided educational opportunities to veterans of all races from poor backgrounds) allowed a large portion of the population to improve their social positions.

With this historical backdrop in mind, how do you think we construct social class in the United States today? Do you have the same opportunities your parents had, or are you better or worse off than they were at your age? Currently in the United States, there has been an ongoing discussion of class separation as well as the increasing divergence of social well-being among classes. Perhaps you have heard someone referred to as "the 99%" or "the 1%." In current times, a lengthy recession has severely impacted the lower and middle classes, leading to major debates as to what role the high upper class should have in solving this problem. While there are numerous viewpoints and philosophies, two major schools of thought address how to deal with this problem. The first position affirms that the upper class should not be heavily taxed since they are the major job creators; taxing high earners impedes their ability to invest their capital, thus preventing the creation of jobs that would enable the middle and lower classes to improve their standing. A second position asserts that the upper class should pay more in taxes since they have the means to do so; the money in taxes could then be reinvested into social and work programs that would give the lower and middle classes the tools they need to increase their social mobility.

In discussing social class and its relationship with capitalism, several scholars disagree with traditional academic approaches to studying the culture of poverty. Communication studies have been criticized from a sociological perspective for serving capitalist interests at the expense of the working class. According to these critics, sociology is not simply the scientific practice of collecting universal social facts but, rather, of collecting specific facts for specific capital interests (Snedeker, 2012). The information collected from social communicative studies serves the capitalist interest of control in labor and the workforce; the information collected does not do enough to help explain or benefit the plight of the working class. As you read more about poverty and social class, be critical of the information given and whether the information is relevant to the very rich or the very poor.

As stated earlier, this by no means encompasses the entire argument or gives voice to every viewpoint on this subject. However, the preceding schools of thought do allow us to discuss the fundamental roles that social classes play in both their creation and advancement. As we continue our discussion of the construction and culture of social class, we must examine four main aspects: labor, news, education, and workplace.

Social Class and Labor

Social class is closely tied to issues of labor. The industrialization of the United States relied heavily on its labor force; the demand for railroads and urban expansion helped catapult the United States into an industrialized, capitalist economy. Currently, the United States still leads the world in gross domestic product (GDP), which measures the overall market value of all goods and services within a given period of time. The principle of labor is also heavily ingrained in U.S. culture; the "working man" is a celebrated icon, and many working-class people are proud to associate themselves with this image.

In the discussion of social construction of social class, the impact of labor has particular value. All capital, whether economic, cultural, or social, can be based on the construction of the labor class itself. In many capitalist countries, labor is associated with the working and/or lower class. The term *blue-collar worker* refers to working-class people who make up the labor force, typically in manufacturing, construction, maintenance, and several other areas. Throughout any country's evolution into an industrial nation, there is always a massive influx of labor force to meet the ever-increasing demands of a manufactured-goods market. So while considered "lower class," blue-collar workers are an indispensable component in the formation of a middle and upper class.

IN YOUR *life*

Can you think of examples of communication about social class and labor in your life? Do particular job titles communicate something to you about social class?

Fight for 15 protests, calling for an increase in minimum wage, are an example of class tensions resulting in societal conflict.

© arindambanerjee/Shutterstock.com

Labor and the working class have a unique relationship with social structure in the United States. The paradoxical relationship labor shares with social structure can be summed up by comparing the "Working-Class Promise" with the "American Dream." The Working-Class Promise socially constructs the working class as a constellation of highly regarded values such as work ethic, dignity of all workers, and humility. The promise helps the working class form group solidarity and pride in their roles in society. The American Dream, on the other hand, is a philosophy that embraces the idea of social mobility and encourages individuals to rise out of the ranks of the lower class. This creates an almost contradictory relationship with the perceptions of social class. Whereas the goal of the American Dream is to rise out of the ranks of the lower class, the goal of the Working-Class Promise is to maintain membership in the class by upholding a shared, work-related value system (Lucas, 2011). As you create your personal understanding of social class and its construction, remember the dual nature of the working class—namely, pride in position versus desire to move beyond this class standing.

Social Class in the News

There is a significant imbalance in the amount of time major news media devote to the working and lower classes compared with the middle and upper classes. The news media report significantly less on working- or lower-class people and their concerns. This problem stems from an issue of class divide; the market for most news media tends to focus on middle- and upper-class viewers. Advertising also plays a critical role in how the news is formed and marketed to the viewers. Many news organizations rely on advertising to keep running, and advertisers generally want to reach specific demographics. The lower class's lack of purchasing power therefore negatively affects the coverage of many problems facing the lower class. This situation has implications beyond basic news coverage, however. Exposure to news media forms a core foundation for the formation of public opinion; what we see on the news plays a major role in our perceptions of how society works and how we think government should administrate public policy. By limiting the exposure of working-class conditions and dilemmas, the working class and its needs are increasingly excluded from the national conversation.

To better understand the relationship between social class and the news media, let's look at the following communication between Katy and Susan. Katy is a recent college graduate who landed a job as a television reporter for a local news outlet. Part of her job involves finding leads on new stories and submitting television segment ideas to her superiors. After interviewing the sponsor of a local soup kitchen, Katy found out that the soup kitchen was serving twice as many people as it had the previous year; a local economy crash had led to many people losing their jobs and relying more on social welfare programs. After her interview, Katy submitted a news story that focused on the economic crash and its consequences. Her boss, Susan, immediately rejected the news segment, stating that the story was not relevant to the station's viewers. After pressing her boss for more information, Katy discovered that the majority of the station's viewership was middle and upper class; most of their viewers were unaffected by the economic downturn and therefore paid little attention to it. While Katy insisted the story had relevance to the community, Susan pointed out that the station's income relied heavily on advertising, and catering to the unemployed members of the community would lead to the station losing money and possibly shutting down.

From a communication perspective, what does this interaction indicate concerning the relationship between media and social class? Obviously, a conflict of interest exists between the needs of the community and the financial obligations of the television station. As you continue to hone your communication skills, reflect on this problem and think about some innovative ways for lower-class and poverty-stricken people to make their voices heard.

Researchers Peter Funke, Chris Robe, and Todd Wolfson (2012) studied the media's role in creating and reinforcing class-based identities. They asserted that class consciousness emerges out of a dialectical relationship between objective and subjective conditions. Specifically, although social class emerges from the context of objective socioeconomic and political structures, it is through the subjective idea of class struggle that a class unites and stands for itself. The researchers indicated that there has been a fragmenting of the working class; with many blue-collar manufacturing jobs moving overseas to developing nations, many lower-class or blue-collar workers find themselves in a culture of poverty, with no job or Working-Class Promise to live by. This has created an identity crisis within the lower class. Further compounding this problem is the lack of exposure in the news media for the plight of the working class; with no visibility or voice given to their struggles, it has become increasingly difficult for working-class people to form an identity for themselves. As you move beyond your academic experience and into your professional life be critical about the types of stories you see in the news media. Reflect on what classes are represented, and see if you can observe any discrepancies in the amount of coverage the different classes receive.

Social Class in Education

Education systems typically reflect class structure and corporate environments in capitalist societies. If you think about it, most academic settings are still based on a factory-line mentality. You have the ringing bells to indicate a change in shift or class, separate facilities, and subjects separated into specializations. Even the way children move through the education system is based on factory practices. They are still separated by age, as if their "date of manufacture" is the most important defining feature regarding the type and difficulty of subject matter they study. We graduate students in batches, after they have gone through some semblance of quality assurance to ensure their effectiveness.

The working class in the United States is currently struggling to find and maintain a group identity.

This factory-line mentality also exists in higher education, but perhaps not to such a severe degree. Rather, one of the major problems with higher education involves the elitist and exclusive traditions held by the middle and upper classes. An important factor when picking a university is the "prestige" of the school. When people think about prestigious universities in the United States, typically they think of Yale, Harvard, Stanford, Princeton, etc. What do these universities have in common? They are private, expensive, and exclusive. The "legacy admission" problems are pronounced in these schools, and the exorbitant cost of tuition frequently locks out lower-class students. However, these schools look good on a job résumé, and a degree from a prestigious university gives a significant advantage to graduates competing in a limited job market. This is not to say that all schools and universities are soulless entities that do not try to develop you as a human being, but it is critical that you be aware of the relationship between education and class structure and corporate philosophy.

IN YOUR *life*

Have you been influenced by social class in your educational experience? Can you think of communication examples connected to social class and education?

Social class has also been shown to be a predictor of academic success. A recent study provided analyses of particular variables (social capital, cultural capital, and parental education level) and indicated that they have significant and important effects on achievement (Pishghadam & Zabihi, 2011). These findings reinforce the idea that while social mobility is possible, its difficulty increases the further down the ladder you find yourself. Many school counselors urge students to enroll in either college preparatory or trade technical courses based on students' social class or their parents' perceived ability to pay for their higher education (Dworkin & Dworkin, 1999). The middle and upper classes have always had an unfair advantage when it comes to educational systems and their content, which leads to further crisis for the lower class in upholding its value system. For educators, it is critical to be sensitive to the values and beliefs of all students, regardless of social class.

Social Class in the Workplace

Social class presents itself in many different forms in the workplace. Lower-level workers are typically held more accountable for how they spend their time at work (Allen, 2010). They must fill out time sheets, take specified breaks, and receive permission to call in sick or take vacation time. Higher-level workers are usually not held to such close scrutiny; their ability to be flexible with their time is greatly increased. Think about a personal example: Have you ever been part of a workplace culture that gave certain people benefits that others did not enjoy? Organizational hierarchies are based on necessity, in that some type of chain of command is needed to ensure that the workload is delegated properly and there is a unified focus on the task at hand. However, this class structure inevitably leads to class bias. Employee recruitment often occurs through social networks; this means that networking often takes place within a particular social class, thus restricting out-groups from job opportunities. One popular networking tool in new media, LinkedIn, plays off this social class structure by allowing members to add connections similar to the way one adds friends on Facebook. By not belonging to a particular social group, many workers are left without a viable means of finding well-paying and secure employment.

Social class and poverty play a significant role in determining the quality of school, teaching, and higher-education opportunities available to people.

© De Visu/Shutterstock.com

Social class and culture influence the way we communicate at work. From an intercultural standpoint, divergence in effective communication can develop because of clashes relating to cultural values and norms. For instance, in the United States, the motivation and drive to succeed at work is closely related to the philosophy of the American Dream; you work hard, succeed at work, advance in the workplace, and increase your social standing. However, this is not a universal value; many cultures do not place such importance on property ownership and financial capital. One study examined Caribbean immigrants' stories and experiences relating to their place in U.S. work culture and how they have adapted to a new cultural environment. Researchers found an interesting balance in the way the immigrants positioned themselves within the idealistic images of the American Dream as opposed to the realistic aspects of working in the United States (Bridgewater & Buzzanell, 2010). The immigrants conformed to their workplace culture by constructing professional identities while simultaneously resisting the urge toward cultural conformation by creating solidarity and co-cultural dialogues with one another in the workplace. This study serves as a reminder of the importance of having more than simple work–life balance; you must also create a balance between the persona you are expected to portray at work and your cultural and social identity.

UNDERSTANDING THE CULTURE OF POVERTY

Now that we have covered social classes and class construction, it is important to familiarize yourself with the culture of poverty. Poverty is more than simply a lifestyle and economic situation. It encompasses entire social classes and has a unique culture of its own. As noted earlier in the chapter, poverty is defined by more than a shortage of economic resources; it also includes a shortage of cultural and social resources. Therefore, it is important to agree on a definition of poverty that is cognizant of these different factors. For the purposes of this chapter, **poverty** is defined as the extent to which an individual does without resources (Payne, 2005).

Poverty
the extent to which an individual does without resources.

Think about situations you might have encountered where money, social standing, or your personal culture became a barrier to accomplishing a goal. Most of us can think of countless money examples: not being able to go to the school of your choice because tuition is too high, not buying a house you love because of its price, or not being able to purchase a car that either costs too much or has a high insurance rate. As significant as economic barriers are, social and cultural barriers can be just as daunting when trying to improve your social class standing. There are many social barriers facing lower-class individuals that middle- and upper-class people take for granted; something as simple as knowing how to apply for

The people you work, live, and go to school with help create solidarity within your social class.

© Syda Productions/Shutterstock.com

a student loan or grants and scholarships can be a daunting task. Knowing the strategies and steps necessary to maintain or improve social class are not inherent in all people. Hidden rules within different classes influence our values, priorities, and beliefs; these can include biases against certain institutions and ideals, such as government assistance and higher education. From a cultural standpoint, an ideal of maintaining solidarity within our social groups can sometimes inhibit our motivation or ability to move out of our social classes. The cultural relationships we develop are generally formed within our social groups, which heavily influence our ability to network into more positive social groups and careers. As you continue through this chapter and learn to better understand and define poverty, reflect on other social and cultural barriers that can positively or negatively affect a person's ability to gain social mobility.

DEFINING POVERTY

Generational poverty
poverty that spans two or more generations.

It is important to distinguish between two major types of poverty: generational poverty and situational poverty. **Generational poverty** is defined as poverty that spans two or more generations. More often than situational poverty, generational poverty has deeply ingrained themes of culture, hidden rules, and belief systems. These sets of values can be damaging because they can cultivate scenarios that allow little outside influence to the family group; middle-class goals and values such as education and social networking are never introduced, leading to an even greater lack of resources that could improve the family's situation. Many individuals stay in generational poverty because they don't know they have a choice. Even when lower-class individuals do have a drive to improve their social standing, they have no one to teach them the hidden rules of higher classes or to provide them with the resources necessary to gain social mobility. It is important to note that this situation is not unique to a particular area, region, or even country. As scholar Oscar Lewis (1971) pointed out, certain universal characteristics concerning the culture of poverty transcend regional, rural–urban, and national boundaries. Themes such as family structure, interpersonal relations, time orientations, spending patterns, and the sense of community solidarity share common ground whether a person lives in Harlem, London, Paris, or Mexico City.

Now that you have an understanding of poverty as an important concept, let's take a look at situational poverty. **Situational poverty** involves a shorter amount of time than generational poverty and is generally caused by circumstances (death, illness, divorce, etc.). Typically, families struggling with situational poverty bring better relationships and resources with them. Their knowledge about the "hidden rules" of higher social classes, as well as their networking connections, gives situational families better access to improve their situation compared with families immersed in generational poverty. As stated earlier, an unexpected event (such as death of the primary family earner) is usually what causes situational poverty. Even in such cases, victims of situational poverty generally have helpful support systems—whether family, friends, or coworkers—that create a better chance of gaining upward mobility. Reflect on a time when either you or another family member experienced an event that led to situational poverty. When I was a young child, my house was destroyed in a flood, which led to a year-long period of situational poverty. However, since I came from a middle-class family with many social connections, we were able to move out of that poverty situation within a year. We had relatives who offered financial and constructional aid, support from our local church, and a network of family friends who took care of day-to-day chores to give us time to repair our house. Remember, though, this is not a situation that all people share; many people do not have such support systems to lean on in times of need. The cycle of hardship is much greater for those who are perpetually stuck in a culture of poverty.

The culture of poverty is often underrepresented in mainstream U.S. culture. Research has indicated a tradition of U.S. media outlets framing large societal problems into "episodes," which focus on individual problems and solutions instead of framing them in larger social conditions (Sei-Hill, Carvalho, & Davis, 2010). Basically, news media tend to communicate larger social problems as personal instances and experiences, which leads many people to think of poverty as an individual choice instead of a larger societal issue. Think about your own media-consuming experiences: How many times has a story about social welfare

IN YOUR
life

What connections do you make between poverty and communication? What types of communication behaviors and choices exemplify insensitive treatment of people living in poverty?

Situational poverty
a shorter amount of time than generational poverty and is generally caused by circumstances (death, illness, divorce, etc.).

focused on a single person's need for or abuse of the system? As you engage in news media communication in the future, reflect on this phenomenon and consider what aspects of the larger problem are being neglected.

As we move forward in this chapter, remember to create a mental checklist for the types of resources people use as they navigate their way through social class and culture. The amount of resources, as well as the ways people use them, have critical impacts on the construction of social class. The next sections follow many of the significant resources available to most individuals: financial, emotional, mental, spiritual, and physical resources, as well as the types of support systems and relationships available to most people. Last, we will discuss the knowledge of hidden rules within different social classes and their effect on social mobility.

FINANCIAL RESOURCES

Now that you have a definition of poverty and its different stages, let's look at the resources available to combat poverty. **Financial resources** are defined as the money to purchase goods and services. When people talk about poverty, they typically discuss it in terms of financial resources only. However, while financial resources are extremely important, they do not explain the varying success with which individuals leave poverty or the reasons many stay in poverty. Rather, many other resources have a critical impact on an individual's success. The ability to gain financial resources, like most others, also depends on your initial social class standing. The ability to pay for training, attain higher education, and travel to job interviews hinges on the ability to pay for it all. Many middle- and upper-class individuals already have these resources available within their families, but the barrier to entry is much higher for lower-class people. This fact, coupled with the lack of learning opportunities about potential avenues for gaining financial resources, can make it difficult, if not impossible, for many lower-class people to attain financial security.

Another aspect of financial resources involves managing money once you have it. Many middle- and upper-class individuals can treat money as a commodity to be saved and invested to ensure a foundation of positive resource growth. However, many people living in poverty do not have the luxury of saving money; as soon as it is received, it must be spent on utilities, groceries, and rent. Money management tools are ineffective when there is almost no financial capital to work with. This is also a reason why many lower-class people who do receive a financial windfall spend the money almost immediately; such behavior relates back to the culture of poverty, because there is an ingrained belief that money must be spent before it disappears. This spells out an important point as to why financial resources alone do not dictate success: Many people in poverty know how to handle the stress of being poor from a lifetime of experience but have no tools to handle the new and alien stresses of wealth.

EMOTIONAL RESOURCES

Emotional resources provide the endurance to withstand difficult and uncomfortable emotional situations or feelings. Emotional resources are considered one of the most (if not *the* most) important resources an individual has at his or her disposal. When present, they keep individuals from returning to old habit patterns that hinder their ability to move upward socially. To move from poverty to middle class, or from middle class to upper class, a person must suspend his or her emotional memories tied to previous social standing (Payne, 2005). This is necessary because the situations and hidden rules in a new social class are incredibly different from what the person has previously experienced. This goes back to the previous point concerning financial resources: Emotional resources are necessary to prepare for the new stresses of financial security and/or wealth. This facilitates the need for persistence and ability to stay with a new situation until it becomes a learned and natural thing. Having the tenacity to change your social situation, or any situation that has become routine and stagnant, is proof that emotional resources are present. Emotional resources also tie into the need for support systems and role models, which is where many of our emotional resources are generated. We will further discuss those aspects later in this chapter.

> **Emotional resources**
> the endurance to withstand difficult and uncomfortable emotional situations or feelings.

When discussing emotional resources in relation to poverty, it is important to identify the inherent sex and gender differences in perceptions of emotional resources. Men are often depicted as having to "pull themselves up by the bootstraps," while women are perceived as playing a more helpless role. In popular culture, women are often depicted as needing outside resources (often a man) to help improve their situation. Not only is this untrue, but it points to a cultural and academic need to communicate the plight of poor women in a more accurate light. As scholar bell hooks (2000) asserts in *Feminist Theory*, "Many poor and exploited women, especially non-white women, would have been unable to develop positive self-concepts if they had not exercised their power to reject the powerful's definition of their reality" (p. 92). As we communicate issues of poverty, it is critical that we do not develop preconceived notions of what the plight of poverty looks like for men and women.

To better understand the impact of emotional resources in relation to poverty, let's take a look at the following communication between Tom and Clint. Tom and Clint were friends who opened a business together. The business experienced relatively quick success; both Clint and Tom found themselves making 3 times their previous yearly incomes. As their fortunes continued to increase and they found themselves moving up the social ladder, Tom began experiencing some new problems. Tom found the social functions of the business to be too stuffy and perceived many of their new acquaintances as "stuck up" and "arrogant." Tom often found himself alienating their business contacts by being rude and impolite. He also continued to spend his money as soon as he earned it, much as he used to do before he had money to spare on luxuries. Clint, however, worked hard to understand the social expectations of their new business associates and also began taking advice on how to invest and save his newfound wealth. Tom began to resent his partner's continued success and accused him of selling out and losing touch with his roots. After several big conflicts, Tom agreed to sell his share of the company to Clint, who continued to be a successful businessman and foster new contacts for the company.

From a communication perspective, how did Tom's lack of emotional resources affect his communication with his partner and new business associates? Without the proper emotional resources to handle the stress of his recent success, Tom continued to act as he did when he was in a lower class, which caused him to alienate himself from his new social group. As you move forward and develop a professional career, remember the importance of creating emotional resources for yourself; they will prove invaluable when trying to move upward on the social ladder.

Emotional resources give people the ability to handle significant events with more ease.

A positive trend in generating emotional support has recently come from an unexpected source: news media. Recent analysis of television and newspaper coverage concerning poverty indicates that coverage has transitioned from individual cases of poverty to a societal-level discussion of the problem (Sei-Hill, Shanahan, & Boo-Hun, 2012). There are two opposing schools of thought concerning the responsibility of handling poverty. One view asserts that social problems are largely caused by deficiencies in the individuals affected by the issue of poverty. The other view holds that many issues regarding

© Ravupixel.com/Shutterstock.com

CHAPTER 9: Communicating Social Class and Understanding the Culture of Poverty

poverty are the result of flaws in the social and environmental conditions in which poverty-stricken people often find themselves. The study found that many news media outlets are embracing the idea of attacking poverty on a society-wide scale as opposed to an individual one. Having the solidarity of one's own society can create a valuable deposit of emotional resources for poverty-stricken individuals.

MENTAL RESOURCES

Mental resources involve the mental abilities and acquired skills (reading, writing, computing) needed to deal with everyday life. While the United States does enjoy a high literacy rate, individuals with access to better schools and higher education have a decided advantage over others. Individuals living in the lower class or poverty are oftentimes not afforded the opportunity to attend good schools and to receive the same standard of education as people from the middle and upper classes. This can be a major obstacle, since many decent-paying jobs require at least a high school or college degree. Besides academic credentials, mental resources involve being able to analyze a problem effectively and see many different solutions. Also, having effective mental resources allows a person to access information from many different sources, enabling him or her to gain more self-sufficiency in solving a problem. Have you ever been in a situation where you were confronted with an issue you knew nothing about but were able to address by accessing different sources of information? Maybe you watched an instructional video on YouTube or did some research at your local library; whatever your method, this would be an instance of displaying effective mental resources.

> **Mental resources**
> the mental abilities and acquired skills (e.g., reading, writing, computing) needed to deal with everyday life.

A tragic aspect of living in the culture of poverty involves lack of proper mental health care for those who cannot afford it. Old, culturally dominant ideas about severe mental illness regarded it as a sign of personal weakness, or something shameful; this led to major instances of social isolation and disenfranchisement (Young, 2009). Not having effective mental resources is not always a product of poor educational opportunities; there are many cases of people not being diagnosed or treated for legitimate mental disorders. The effects that social class and culture have on health care are too numerous to be covered in a single chapter, but be aware that having mental resources is tied not only to educational opportunities but to health care opportunities as well.

SPIRITUAL RESOURCES

Spiritual resources involve the belief that help can be obtained from a higher power and that one has a purpose for living. People tap into many different types of spiritual guidance, and while we can have conflicting views as to what is truly

> **Spiritual resources**
> the belief that help can be obtained from a higher power and that one has a purpose for living.

right, we all carry the ability to cultivate spiritual resources. Such resources can be powerful, because spiritual individuals do not see themselves as hopeless or useless but as having worth and value. While some people choose not to participate in this type of resource, its value among poverty-stricken communities is significant. Many poor communities rally around their shared faith as a means of coping with poverty-related problems. The sense of solidarity fostered can create a social support system that would otherwise be unavailable to poor communities. As such, developing spiritual resources within a social group can pay positive dividends toward increasing social mobility by creating a role model and support system.

As the United States increasingly becomes a more diverse nation, the diversity of faith communities increases as well. Changes to immigration law, increased ease of transportation, and social media's impact on ever-expanding globalization have transformed U.S. society into a culture that must be sensitive to different spiritual beliefs. Researcher Donn James Tilson (2011) studied this trend and asserted that the increase in spiritual diversity has led to an increase in interfaith initiatives aimed at addressing social problems. The study also indicated that socially responsible behavior often has a foundation in faith that is common across many spiritual communities, further emphasizing the importance of spiritual resources. Regardless of how you view spirituality or practice it in your life, be aware of its usefulness as a social resource and its place in developing communities and fostering social support systems.

PHYSICAL RESOURCES

Physical resources

having a body that works and is capable and mobile.

Physical resources involve having a body that works and is capable and mobile. Having proper physical resources helps ensure self-sufficiency, which is critical for poverty-stricken individuals who may not have a strong support system. As with mental resources, many lower-class individuals do not have access to proper health care, which can lead to debilitating physical health problems (Payne, 2005). As stated earlier, when there is not a strong support system in place, lacking physical resources such as mobility can have drastic consequences on social well-being. While the government provides access to disability benefits and social security, these provisions are typically not enough to foster upward social mobility; many individuals living off disability or social security benefits have a tightly fixed income that does not offer the financial resources to sustain or improve social class standing.

Another problem recognized in poverty and health care relates to the ways different social classes consume information. Researchers Brian Southwell, James Hamilton, and Jonathan Slater (2011) assert that a significant barrier inhibits informing people in poverty about possible free health care opportunities: The "digital divide" will exclude individuals who do not have access to cable television or Internet. Access to satellite, cable television, and high-speed Internet is something many middle- and upper-class people take for granted, but a large segment of the lower class does not have access to these services. Public information campaigns about health and other issues affecting lower income people need to recognize this divide and work to overcome it by utilizing new media channels such as Twitter, text messaging, and geographic messaging that are mobile-phone based and thus more likely to reach the economically underprivileged. As you learn more about issues regarding physical and mental health care, try to think of some other potential barriers that may keep underprivileged people from receiving important health care information.

SUPPORT SYSTEMS

Support systems are safety nets that help people take care of themselves in situations where they would otherwise be unable. Individuals who are available and will help are the resources that form support systems. When people think about support systems, they generally think about meeting financial or emotional needs. Examples include borrowing money from your parents to fix your car, having family and friends present after the death of a loved one, or asking someone to pick up your children from school when you are sick or stuck at work. While these are all important aspects of support systems, it is important to know that support systems can be knowledge bases as well. A parent, friend, or tutor helping you with algebra homework and someone helping you pick out a college and apply for scholarships are both instances of using knowledge bases. Many people in poverty or lower-class households do not have knowledge bases as rich as those in other classes. Being able to hire a tutor or pay for a tax preparation class enables individuals to cultivate their mental resources and interact more competitively in social situations. Have you ever experienced an issue that was beyond your means and your support system? Such situations are mercifully few for people living in the middle or upper class, but too many lower-class individuals simply do not have the knowledge bases or support systems to properly address these problems as they relate to social class. As college students, you will find a rich support system in your fellow students and university faculty. A recent study indicated that many college students view fellow students as their primary source of academic support (Mazer & Thompson, 2011). The study assessed informational, esteem, motivational, and venting support. The results showed a positive correlation between student academic support and beneficial increases in the variables examined. As you continue on with your college career and eventually move into professional fields, remember that your support systems are always evolving; be cognizant of the tools available to you, as well as how to utilize them to their full extent.

Support systems
safety nets that help people take care of themselves in situations where they would otherwise be unable.

RELATIONSHIPS/ROLE MODELS

Role models are a critical contributor to the development of emotional resources. Most of you can think of at least one role model you have had in your life (if not several). Whether a parent, teacher, coach, or any other leader, role models help form the foundations of your belief system and supply you with emotional resources. To better understand the importance of role models and relationships, it is important to know how functional and dysfunctional systems impact the effectiveness of the relationship. A **system** is a group in which individuals have rules, roles, and relationships. A sports team is a good example of a system built around relationships and role models. You have a coach who plays the role of mentor and leader of the team and players who have a subordinate role and look to the coach for guidance. In a healthy system, the coach can help the players develop effective emotional resources and can serve as a knowledge base. It is important to remember, however, that all systems are dysfunctional to a certain extent. A system is **dysfunctional** to the extent that an individual's needs are not met within that system. For example, continuing with the sports team example, suppose the coach is giving extra attention and care to the star players and ignoring other players on the team. The other players' emotional needs will not be met, which will result in a dysfunctional relationship within the system. Reflect on your own experiences within a system, whether family, sports, academic, etc. Have you ever been in a relationship where your needs were not being met? How did you react when the relationship took on a more dysfunctional aspect? As you move forward in life, there will be instances where you will become a role model yourself. Always try to be aware and accommodating of everyone's individual needs as you take a leadership role in your systems.

Recently in the United States, there has been much discussion about the role of teachers in public education, as well as heated debates about the financial value of educators. While many of the arguments have revolved around test scores or standardized education benchmarks, many people have overlooked the other critical role teachers play in the classroom—namely, serving as role models for students. Research has indicated that teachers play a vital role in almost every development that takes place in the school environment (Ramzan, Perveen, & Gujjar, 2011). Since primary education is generally an individual's first social interaction outside the home, many of the resources we discussed earlier can be generated from having effective role models in the classroom. As the debate continues in the United States, remember to be aware of the many roles teachers play outside of academic learning in relation to students' social development.

System

a set of interdependent parts that relate to each other at various levels.

Dysfunctional system

a system in which an individual's needs are not met.

KNOWLEDGE OF HIDDEN RULES

Regardless of your initial social class, knowing the hidden rules of your social group is a crucial aspect of social development. When attempting to move upward on the social ladder, learning the hidden rules of the class you wish to join can be one of the most difficult obstacles. Hidden rules exist in poverty, the middle class, the upper class, and different ethnic groups or other units of people. These rules tend to be unspoken understandings that can cue whether a person belongs within a particular social class or not. Think about a time when you might have felt out of place because the environment you were in was either "too classy" or "too trashy." As stated earlier, dealing with and adapting to these hidden rules requires a high level of emotional resources. You can experience significant internal conflict when moving upward in a social class, feeling as though you might be "losing your roots" or "selling out." Although many people still manage to respect and honor their class culture after they have moved upward, adapting to the lifestyle and hidden rules of a new social class is critical if you wish to remain in it. Generally, when you move from one class to the next, it is beneficial to have a spouse or mentor from the class you wish to join; he or she will already have a built-in ability to teach you the hidden rules of the class and how to adapt to them as well.

To understand the hidden rules of poverty, let's take a look at the following communication between Monique and Jai. Monique comes from a wealthy family, and she sometimes makes insensitive remarks about things being "trashy." Her

© Fotokostic/Shutterstock.com

Athletic coaches, among others, can serve as foundational role models for many people.

boyfriend, Jai, comes from a lower-class family and is very proud of what he has accomplished. After his college graduation, Jai's family threw a party for him to celebrate. As with many other major celebrations, Jai's family organized a barbecue at the local park and invited their friends from the community to join them. When Monique and her family arrived at the barbecue, Jai overheard Monique and her mother referring to the other guests as "ghetto" and "wild." When Jai confronted her about this, Monique claimed that she was only telling the truth and Jai should separate himself from his family and old friends. Jai broke up with Monique shortly thereafter.

From a communication perspective, how could Monique have practiced better communication with Jai about his friends and family? Should Monique have tried to communicate with Jai's family and friends before asserting her opinion about them? As you continue to practice more effective communication, remember the mistakes Monique made and reflect on how you would improve on her communication.

When analyzing hidden rules of social class, it is important to be critical of the hidden rules in your own social group. What are some of the hidden rules in your social class? If you come from a class of poverty, you might have unspoken rules about shopping: You know where the best thrift store sales are, when the discount store gets a new shipment in, or what generic brands work the best and last the longest. Deviating from these unspoken rules can lead to feelings of resentment, which can isolate an individual from his or her own social group. While this is only one example, there are numerous other rules within each separate social class. As you go about your daily routine, be critical of your actions and reflect on whether they could constitute hidden rules of your particular social class.

KEY POINTS AND STATISTICS ABOUT POVERTY

As we conclude this chapter about the culture of poverty and social class, there are some critical points to remember as you move forward in this book. It is important to realize that poverty occurs in all races and all countries; while statistics can show what countries might be handling poverty better than others, some aspect of poverty will always be present in any nation or culture. With that in mind, remember that *poverty* can be a relative term; if most people around you are in similar circumstances, the ideas of poverty and wealth can become vague. Think about what your idea of "wealthy" might be. If you believe, for example, that someone making $200,000 a year is wealthy, that conclusion is relevant only in your particular social group. Someone who makes millions of dollars per year might consider $200,000 a year to be poor, and someone from a developing country who

Fostering positive communication about how to combat poverty is critical to helping those in need.

© wjarek/Shutterstock.com

makes one tenth of your income might consider you wealthy. Our ideas about wealth fluctuate depending on our social class, culture, and the circumstances of those around us.

As of 2006, the poverty rate for all individuals in the United States was 12.3%. For children under the age of 18, the poverty rate was 17.4%, and for children under the age of 5, the rate jumped to 20.4% (U.S. Census Bureau, 2007). Think about these numbers for a minute. One in every five children (under the age of 5) is born into poverty in the United States. Since poverty has been shown to correlate with poor health care, this statistic helps explain why the United States currently has such a high infant mortality rate in comparison with other developed countries. The United States' child poverty rate is higher (often 2 to 3 times higher) than that of every other major Western industrialized nation. While culture does play a significant role in the particular ways people approach the problem of poverty, these are sobering numbers for a democracy as wealthy as the United States. This is not to say that there is a particular "right" or "wrong" way to attack the problem of poverty, but these are numbers you should be aware of. As you take your place as a voter and member of the professional world, pay special attention to the methods and rhetoric used to describe and act on the issue of poverty in this country.

WHAT YOU'VE LEARNED

From reading this chapter, you learned what social class is ascribed to us depending on the class we were born in, and while achievement and personal gain of capital can aid in social mobility, our initial starting point forms a foundation for how we view the world around us. You were then given examples of social class across communication contexts, and you learned to understand social class from a communication perspective. Finally, you were given the definition of poverty—the extent to which an individual does without resources—and you learned of the culture of poverty.

As you reflect on what you've learned from this chapter, keep in mind that social class is a complex piece of a person's identity that comprises many different components. Reflect on your own social class status and try and observe some of the hidden rules of social class that change the way you communicate with others.

REVIEW

1. The ranking of groups according to various criteria is called _____.

2. _____ refers to conditions at birth, such as family background, race, sex, and place of birth.

3. _____ encompasses a person's financial assets; _____ consists of the networks or connections among people who can help one another; and _____ encompasses specialized skills and knowledge.

4. _____ is determined by the combination of income, education, and occupation.

5. Poverty that spans two or more generations is referred to as _____.

6. Why are *emotional resources* considered one of the most important resources an individual has at their disposal?

7. What are some examples of *mental resources*?

8. Define *support systems*.

9. Explain why a *dysfunctional* system is problematic.

10. Discuss why deviating from unspoken rules of social class can be problematic for an individual.

Review answers are found on the accompanying website.

REFLECT

1. Alex and Mark are on a blind date together, and Mark mentions he recently took a job at a fast food restaurant to help meet his financial needs while he is enrolled at a local community college. Alex, who has a four-year degree and comes from an upper-middle class family, asks Mark why he would ever want to work at a fast food restaurant. Use the concept of *ethnocentrism* to discuss what is problematic with Alex's point-of-view and question.

2. How important is having access to effective education in ensuring social and economic success? Are there any other factors you feel are more important?

3. Meredith has recently made her 500th connection on LinkedIn. What type of capital is Meredith experiencing, and how might that type of capital benefit her in her future?

4. Kyle's wife, Grace, recently passed away. Grace worked outside of the home to support her family, while Kyle stayed at home during the day to take care of their three children. Without Grace's income, Kyle knows he will temporarily be unable to meet his family's financial needs. What type of poverty is Kyle and his family currently experiencing, and what types of resources do you think Kyle will need during this difficult time?

5. How are hidden rules used in your classroom? Do you feel that a particular social class is represented above all others at your college or university?

KEY TERMS

social stratification, 233
bourgeoisie, 234
proletariat, 234
ascription, 235
ethnocentrism, 235
achievement, 235
capital, 236
economic capital, 237
cultural capital, 237
social capital, 238
networking, 238
socioeconomic status, 242

poverty, 251
generational poverty, 252
situational poverty, 253
financial resources, 254
emotional resources, 255
mental resources, 257
spiritual resources, 257
physical resources, 258
support systems, 259
system, 260
dysfunctional, 260

CHAPTER TEN

Intercultural Issues in Health, Wellness, and Medicine

CHAPTER OUTLINE

WHAT YOU WILL LEARN

After studying this chapter, you should be able to

1. explain what it means to be healthy and describe what is studied in the field of health communication;
2. differentiate the biomedical and biopsychosocial models of health care;
3. discuss Western and Eastern perspectives and their influence on health care and health-related decisions;
4. understand the importance of cultural differences that exist in health care interactions and be able to manage them;
5. recognize instances of diversity within the health care or medical organization; and
6. explain how some cultures experience marginalization within health care and how this can impact health care outcomes and health literacy.

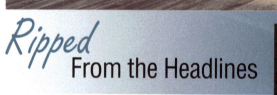

Ripped From the Headlines

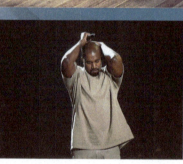

© Kevork Djansezian/Getty Images Entertainment/Getty Images

Between his outspoken personality and in-your-face antics, Kanye West is no stranger to headlines. In November of 2016, he was again in the spotlight when he was placed on psychiatric hold. He was hospitalized at UCLA Medical Center for exhaustion and stress after many chaotic days on tour. Leading up to his hospitalization, there were many instances of incoherent political statements at his concerts. There was one occasion where he compared himself to then President-elect Donald Trump, which was confusing to his audience members because it was in the middle of a concert. He then went on to speak for 17 minutes about a wide array of topics, including award show politics, radio programmers, MTV, Hillary Clinton, and many other random topics (Coscarelli, 2016).

On November 21, 2016, West was hospitalized after an ambulance responded to a call from his home in West Hollywood. While few details are known about his condition, friends and family close to West attribute the episodes to stress and exhaustion (Andrews & Bever, 2016). His condition and hospitalization bring to light the importance of self-care and the necessity to not stigmatize the need for rest. What are some of the ways your own culture contributes to the ways in which you view health and wellness? Do you think the fast-paced and work-oriented nature of American culture contributes to cases of extreme exhaustion such as the instance with Kanye West?

When discussing health, wellness, and medicine in an intercultural sense, it is important to be aware of and sensitive to the social and cultural barriers many people face. As with any other area, health care and medicine can vary greatly depending on cultural tendencies. As you move forward in this chapter, think about the previous story and how it could relate not only to your view of health but to your perception of cultural others as well.

Culture is inherent in many aspects of health, particularly in the interpersonal encounters that occur within the health care system, whether between doctors and patients or among different professionals in a health care organization. Our cultural background flavors the way we make sense of our health experiences (Kreps & Thornton, 1992). Du Pré (2010) explains it well:

> The way you talk about health, how you describe your aches and pains, the reasons you seek medical care or encourage others to— all these go beyond physical manifestations of illness . . . [W]e base our current understanding on what we know from personal history, culture, and knowledge. (p. 194)

Meanings about an illness or disease often derive from one's own experiences and feelings about it.

The idea of culture within health care also alerts us to similarities and differences we have with others. When we walk into an examination room and wait for the doctor to come in, we are already thrust into an encounter defined by difference. We, the patients, are not medically trained as the physicians are. Also, some of us might not enjoy the same kind of income or lifestyle or may not speak English as well. As Cline and McKenzie (1998) point out, "the greater the cultural distance, the greater likelihood for interaction based on an 'us' and 'them' relationship" (p. 68).

The population of the United States is projected to become older and more diverse in future decades. According to the U.S. Census Bureau (2012), the non-white Hispanic population will become the largest single group by 2060, but no group will be in the strong majority. Additionally, the number of people aged 65 and older will increase from 43.1 million in 2012 to 92 million in 2060, bringing the ratio for this age group from 1 in 7 people in the United States to 1 in 5. People who identify as multiple races or ethnicities will triple in number, from 7.5 million to 26.7 million. By 2043, it is projected that the United States will become a majority–minority nation for the first time in its history, with minorities increasing from 37% to 57% of the total population by 2060.

What this means, among other things, is that within the health care context we are more likely to interact with someone from a different culture or background, which will have significant implications for how we seek medical care and get answers to our health questions. Furthermore, the dramatic changes in minority populations present major challenges to health care professionals who still don't know how to communicate effectively with diverse patients (Beck, 1997; Ndiwane et al., 2004). As more underserved individuals enter the health care system, they will face greater challenges talking to their providers about their concerns, describing their symptoms, and asking for what they need and want (Andrulis, 2003; Chiu, 2004; Wenger, 2003; Witte & Morrison, 1995). To meet these challenges, patients and providers must learn about their communication styles and how they might conflict within medical encounters.

In this chapter, you will be exposed to a variety of health care issues that are affected by cultural differences. First, it will be important for you to understand how health can be defined, as well as what health communication is and how it is studied. Once these terms are addressed, you will learn different perspectives from which health and health care are approached, particularly the biomedical and biopsychosocial models of health care. You will also understand Eastern and Western approaches to medicine and how they complement each other. Next, you will explore interpersonal issues of health, especially how cultural differences influence how we talk to our doctors and important others about our health. In addition to issues of access to care and marginalization, this chapter will expose you to health literacy and the problems associated with low health literacy.

DEFINING HEALTH AND HEALTH COMMUNICATION

IN YOUR
life

Have you ever visited a health care professional from a different cultural background than yours? How did the intercultural dynamic affect your communication?

What does it mean to be healthy? Does it mean just not being sick or injured? Is it enough to feel good physically, or must one also experience emotional well-being? Until recently, most experts have focused on illness and illness behaviors (Mechanic, 1999). The World Health Organization (WHO, 2003) defines **health** as "a state of complete physical, mental and social well-being and not merely the absence of disease

Health

a state of physical, mental, spiritual, and social well-being, as well as the absence of illness.

© Gts/Shutterstock.com

Being healthy can mean many things: eating right, exercising, maintaining proper weight, and other factors.

or infirmity" (p. 100). WHO later expanded this definition to include spiritual, intellectual, and environmental health.

Good health is something for which many people are thankful but often take for granted. Our state of health influences many aspects of our lives—how well we perform our jobs, activities in which we engage, how we relate to family and loved ones, our general attitude on life, and how we typically feel day-to-day. More specifically, the cultural influences in our lives play a part in how we view our health and how we talk about it. "Many cultures attribute illness to spiritual forces, and this is in direct conflict with the western biomedical model that attributes disease to microorganisms . . . or to lifestyle influences" (Wright, Sparks, & O'Hair, 2013, p. 104). For example, many Mexican Americans hold a sense of fatalism about illness and health, believing that God or a higher power has control over their destiny (Heuman, Scholl, & Wilkinson, 2013). For instance, although they acknowledge free will, devout Muslims believe that Allah has ultimate control over our destiny.

Some researchers in communication and related fields explore how these cultural influences correlate with our health. Many of these researchers are in the field of **health communication**, which can be defined as (1) the construction and sharing of meanings about the provision of health care delivery and (2) the promotion of public health through mediated channels (Scholl, 2013). Communication competence and sensitivity training have become increasingly important in health care organizations, especially given that patients are becoming more diverse. The increased use of translators and intercultural communication training programs is commonplace within most health care organizations today (Wright et al., 2013).

> **Health communication**
> the construction and sharing of meanings about the provision of health care delivery and the promotion of public health through mediated channels.

WORLDVIEWS AND PERSPECTIVES

BIOMEDICAL AND BIOPSYCHOSOCIAL MODELS OF HEALTH CARE

Our attitudes about health and illness often reflect what we think is the cause of ill health. Is getting sick something that just happens to us? Did I get sick because I've been eating the wrong kinds of food? For some, ill health is primarily a physical occurrence, which is discovered by seeking information about its source and treating it through physical means. This notion represents the **biomedical model**, which is common in a culture such as the United States that is accustomed to machines, computers, and engines (du Pré, 2010). According to the biomedical model, doctors are like mechanics and scientists who look for physical signs of what is wrong. Once the symptom is identified, physical means (e.g., drugs) are

> **Biomedical model**
> states that doctors operate much like mechanics and scientists, looking for physical signs and symptoms of what is wrong. Once the problem is identified, physical means are used to heal the illness or injury or address the medical issue.

used to get rid of the problem. Providers who operate from a biomedical model might communicate in ways that focus on efficiency and logic. They might ask questions that elicit a short response or a yes/no answer (e.g., "How long have you had that rash?" "Does it hurt?" "When did it first occur?"). This approach consumes very little time, which is especially useful when doctors are pressured to see several patients in a day. However, it leaves little room for patients to express their feelings or describe their experiences in more detail. Plus, some patients might not like being treated like machines and would rather be acknowledged as human beings who are more than just their symptoms.

Biopsychosocial model

a holistic approach that states that ill health is caused by many physical, social, and environmental factors. Also, the health of the entire person is considered, not just the physical body.

The **biopsychosocial model** acknowledges that illness is not always just a physical thing. Disease and illness are often influenced by environmental and social factors, which include routine activities and everyday patterns (e.g., sitting at the office computer for long periods of time, smoking two packs of cigarettes a day). Other factors include one's socioeconomic status (SES), the nature and number of social networks, and life events (Mechanic, 1999). The biopsychosocial approach also considers patients' emotions and lived experiences, which are tied to their health just as much as the physical symptoms are. Most of us agree that stress can be harmful to our physical bodies, but excessive stress has also been shown to diminish the immune system, which can account for our getting sick more often (Gouin, Hantsoo, & Kiecolt-Glaser, 2008). Understanding how anxious patients might be feeling, finding out what's going on in their lives, or getting a sense of their emotional well-being can give clues as to what might be ailing them.

Communication exhibiting the biopsychosocial approach tends to elicit more open-ended responses from the patient (e.g., "This knee pain is really frustrating at times"; "I'm not sure if I'll remember to take my pill at the times you suggested"). Patients also can weigh in more on how they like or dislike their treatment or how they are feeling emotionally. While they might not have much to complain about regarding the medical treatment they receive, many patients care deeply about the communication that takes place and whether the doctor shows care and concern for them (Greene, Adelman, Friedmann, & Charon, 1994).

WESTERN AND EASTERN PERSPECTIVES

Much like the biomedical and biopsychosocial approaches, Western and Eastern medicine represent different but often coexisting worldviews. **Western medicine** relies on the scientific method and the principle of verification to understand what causes ill health. Warfare seems to be a strong theme in Western medicine. Treating disease is often portrayed as "waging war" or "eradicating the enemy" (Todd, 1999). As with the biomedical model, the Western or traditional approach to medicine

Western medicine

relies on the scientific method and the principle of verification to understand what causes ill health.

focuses on the physical, evidence-based causes of illness and injury. Continuing the machine metaphor, the organs are components that serve specific functions, and when they don't work properly, we seek to restore them as much as we can to get them functioning again. You might think of it as taking your car to the shop for a repair. If you know your head gasket is shot, you expect your mechanic to focus on replacing the head gasket and not to get distracted by the tires, air conditioning, or radiator.

Of course, we don't mean to say that sick people are nothing more than broken-down cars. On the contrary, the Western approach has led to the discovery and testing of many wonderful medicines and treatments that have saved countless lives and enhanced our overall quality of life. While medicine is certainly not an exact science, using science and principles of verification can prevent costly mistakes in diagnosis or determining what drugs are the best to use. But all approaches have their limitations. Western medicine does not take into consideration nonphysical causes of illness, such as attitude, environment, and social factors (e.g., relationships). An approach that treats the body as a machine doesn't leave much room for inquiring about other influences on illness, such as an abusive relationship in which one feels stuck or the amount of stress one is enduring at work.

Eastern approaches to medicine have been around for thousands of years and focus on the whole person, not just the disease. Eastern thought teaches that the body doesn't simply exist; it coexists and shares mutual influence with its environment.

Eastern medical treatments use natural plants and substances and work with the natural processes of the body.

The way to achieve health is not just to fix the illness or injury but to maintain harmony among the body, the mind, and the natural environment. While Western medicine views disease as an invasive element to be destroyed, **Eastern medicine** describes disease as a signal that the body is out of balance. Instead of seeing illness as something to eradicate, Eastern thought might encourage some of us to view it as a reminder to slow down and take better care of ourselves.

Eastern medical treatments take many forms, such as acupuncture, guided imagery, and yoga. (See Figure 10.1 for a list of common Eastern medical practices.) Although widely practiced for thousands of years, Eastern medicine has not been commonly accepted among Western-minded practitioners, perhaps because of the lack of scientific evidence to support its effectiveness. However, less conventional and traditional methods of treatment are becoming more commonplace (Todd, 1999). Moreover, some practitioners advocate for integrative medicine, which is a combination of Western and Eastern approaches. For example, many cancer patients undergoing scientifically verified treatments such as radiation therapy and chemotherapy might complement those treatments with other methods such as yoga and medication to achieve harmony of mind, body, and spirit.

Beliefs about the nature and causes of illness are varied. For instance, Pacific Islanders and Asians do not embrace the dual mind/body separation that Westerners do. Instead, they see the mind and body as an interconnected whole. Despite this approach, some Eastern cultures tend to be sensitive when it comes to mental health and often consider mental illness dishonorable, a source of shame. In such cases, individuals who are told by a doctor that they are clinically depressed might deny they are ill or refuse treatment (du Pré, 2010). Many Latinos hold the belief of *susto*, which is the idea that a sudden, shocking, or frightening experience can actually bring about illness (Willies-Jacobo, 2007). Latin culture can also embrace a sense of fatalism about sickness. Sometimes ill health is attributed to powerful spiritual or external forces that are beyond one's control (Colón, 2005). Such a force might be God or fate. If one believes that one's health is mainly in God's hands, this view might motivate one to skip treatment of a serious or life-threatening condition, especially if death is viewed as a natural part of life and thus something to be celebrated (Talamantes, Gomez, & Braun, 2000).

Causes of illness are often due to the lived experiences shared by certain populations. Many Arabs have emigrated because of war and violent conflict, and they often face few professional opportunities in their new country. As a result, some suffer depression and anxiety, even suicidal tendencies (Douki, Zineb, Nacef, & Halbreich, 2007). As with many other immigrants to the United States,

FIGURE 10.1 Common Eastern Medical Practices

Acupressure—Combines acupuncture and pressure; used to apply pressure with the hand or elbow to various points on the body to enhance flexibility and circulation

Acupuncture—A technique involving inserting needles in certain points on the body to relieve pain and pressure

Aromatherapy—Uses essential oils from plants to alter a person's state of health or mind, as well as to improve cognitive function

Ayurveda—An ancient Hindu system of medicine that utilizes the body's humors to eliminate toxins, achieve balance, and diagnose serious ailments

Biofeedback—Used to increase health and performance; teaches a person to become more aware of physiological changes in the body to control them

Cupping—Creating a vacuum in a glass cup placed upside down on the skin to create suction, which manipulates blood flow to promote healing

Gua sha—Used to treat pain; involves creating pressurized marks on the skin, called "sha," with a rounded instrument

Herbalism—The use of plants as medicine, which is taken in the form of tea, incense, or another method

Homeopathy—A diluted form of a harmful substance, such as a virus, taken to cure the disease associated with that substance

Hypnotherapy—Also called hypnosis; alters the consciousness of the person to reduce pain, anxiety, or discomfort

Meditation—Used as either a healing tool or a spiritual practice to train the mind to promote relaxation and a self-regulated state of consciousness

Reiki—A Japanese technique that involves the laying of hands to promote energy flow throughout the body

Yoga—The practice of holding various body positions to reduce stress, align the spine, and lessen health problems

Types of alternative and complementary medicine originating from China, India, and other parts of the world

many Arab Americans come from countries with universal health care and are unaccustomed to copayments and insurance deductibles (du Pré, 2010).

When the cause or nature of an illness cannot be explained, sometimes the illness is attributed to some fault on the part of the afflicted. People who become disabled or ill often experience shame, guilt, and loss of self (Charmaz, 1999; Murphy, 1999), especially when it comes to conditions that, to some, appear preventable, such as HIV or AIDS. Although Western medicine appears to couch such conditions in scientific terms, unfortunately, Western society often attributes getting sick to being lazy or immoral (du Pré, 2010). Disease is often treated as **stigma**, which is a social rejection in which the stigmatized people are ignored and/or dishonored (Goffman, 1963). As a result, many people suffer discrimination and prejudice based on their illness. Many AIDS and HIV patients, for instance, have suffered ill treatment and prejudice in the health care system. More education about the causes of such conditions, as well as more sensitivity and compassion, can ease the patient's anxiety and avoid making him or her feel less than human.

Despite the differences between Eastern and Western approaches, which are summarized in Figure 10.2, both share some similarities. For one thing, both embrace the idea of the opposition and integration of parts. On the one hand, the Eastern perspective is represented by the dual concepts of yin and yang, which represent conflicting forces (e.g., masculine/feminine, light/dark) that can coexist in harmony and balance. On the other hand, Western thinking also embraces this dualistic way of thinking in terms of opposition and integration of parts (Todd, 1999). The mind and body are often treated as separate entities, yet many people recognize the mind/body connection as it influences all aspects of health.

FIGURE 10.2 Differences Between Eastern and Western Medicine

Western Medicine	Eastern Medicine
Illness has a single cause	Illness has multiple causes
Treatment	Prevention
Hierarchically held knowledge	Both doctor and patient are "knowers"
Battling disease	Achieving harmony and balance
Validity from controlled studies	Knowledge passed down for thousands of years
Zero in on the sick part of the body	Look at both mind and entire body
Be strong and brave when treating disease	Be flexible and follow the body's natural rhythms when treating disease
Take action at the first sign of illness	Strive for good health all the time
Seek a cure from without	Seek health from within

BRIDGING CULTURAL DIFFERENCES IN THE CONVERSATION

Notwithstanding the elements of race, ethnicity, sex/gender, sexual orientation, and other differences, the patient–provider interaction itself is an intercultural encounter. The notion of **patient role** could help emphasize the dissimilarity between physician and patient. The nature of the patient–provider relationship is one of unbalanced power. Even when the doctor is attempting to encourage more patient participation, the patient enters the encounter from a subordinate position, assuming that the patient takes a more passive role while the doctor remains in charge (Cline & McKenzie, 1998).

The status differences between patient and provider, as well as the anxiety and depression patients often experience, can only be exacerbated when both parties perceive themselves to be culturally different from each other (Mechanic, 1999). The word *perception* is crucial here, because similarity to another individual might be in the eye of the beholder. One of your authors describes herself as a white female in her early 40s. She might go to the doctor's office for a checkup and realize that her doctor is at least 15 years older than she is. However, as the patient, she might pay more attention to the fact that, like herself, her doctor is also female and appears to be white, and she therefore might perceive a great deal of similarity with the doctor in spite of their apparent age difference. It goes without saying that we often feel more comfortable with people who share one or more significant similarities with us, which might compel us to trust these individuals more. In

IN YOUR *life*

How would you respond to a doctor visit in which the doctor was rude or dismissive of your opinions? How important do you think it is for a doctor to listen to your opinions and worries about an illness?

Patient role

helps emphasize the dissimilarity between patient and provider; it often places the patient in a lower-status role relative to the healthcare provider.

© Rocketclips, Inc./Shutterstock.com

The cultural differences that exist between doctor and patient might be real or based only on our perceptions.

short, we tend to like people who are like us. To look at this in a more practical way, if a doctor perceives a patient to be like him or her, then that patient might get preferential treatment (Cline & McKenzie, 1998).

Perceived and tangible differences between patient and doctor can play a huge role in the direction of the medical conversation, as well as in the actual medical outcomes. According to Cline and McKenzie (1998), "Participants must contend not only with professional role differences . . . but also with the full array of linguistic and value differences . . . that, in turn, shape the meanings of discourse in health care" (p. 68). Brown and Scholl (2006) analyzed statements by doctors and physicians about their intercultural encounters during the doctor visit, and both parties often described language differences as barriers or hurdles one must overcome before understanding and rapport can be achieved. Some of their respondents even expected to get better medical care once these so-called barriers were broken.

Cultural differences between doctor and patient, when seen as too difficult or frustrating, can contribute to a patient's inability to understand his or her doctor's directions for taking medication. To illustrate, most English speakers understand the phrase "take one pill once daily" to mean take the pill one time and one time only per day. However, the word *once* in Spanish means "eleven." If a Latino patient whose first language is not English confuses the Spanish and English meanings of *once*, then the patient might take the medication 11 times per day, which would likely result in a serious overdose.

Overcoming linguistic, ethnic, and cultural hurdles requires sensitivity. Recognizing and working through cultural differences is not only an admirable trait; it is essential to effective and efficient health care (Wright et al., 2013). Patients' cultural conceptions of health and illness influence their medical decisions and how they talk about their health. For example, Heuman et al. (2013) interviewed Hispanic parents and children who talked about the prevalence of diabetes in their families, often claiming that despite how well they ate and exercised, they were likely to get diabetes because it "ran in their family." Such cultural conceptions about illness (e.g., perception that one's culture is vulnerable) might discourage a person from taking more preventive measures against a condition such as diabetes. In turn, health care providers can be influenced by culture in how they treat their patients and the kinds of treatments they prescribe. Most people—including doctors—harbor some stereotypes. A doctor might draw a conclusion about a minority patient, such as her inability to pay for health care, and thus might offer her fewer advanced treatment options than would be offered a white patient (Agency for Healthcare Research & Quality, 2000). Some health disparities are well documented. LaVeist, Nickerson, and Bowie (2000) compared patient satisfaction between African American and white cardiac patients, and although patients did not point to racism as a cause, the African American patients reported more distrust and less satisfaction and did tend to cite more racism in the overall health care system.

As our population becomes increasingly diverse, we continually need to learn the culturally varied ways people view disease, illness, and health. Without an understanding of how other cultures view and talk about their health, such differences inevitably lead to misunderstandings, which could have serious health-related consequences. For instance, an oncologist might assume that her Hispanic patient has a large extended family. Because of this assumption, the oncologist might not think it important to refer this patient to some community resources for social support or might not ask if she needs the assistance of a home health care nurse. Without such important services, the patient's ability to overcome the illness could be impaired.

To proceed with our discussion of cultural differences in the medical context, it might not necessarily be effective for us to create lists of different cultures and then describe how each one approaches health and medicine. Providers, educators, and other professionals "can no longer approach healthcare from a single cultural perspective and be effective in treating patients from other cultures in a competent manner" (Wright et al., 2013, p. 101). Instead of viewing culture as a function of language, nationality, gender, and so on, we introduce this section by uncovering the underlying sources of cultural difference in the health care context. What follows are the different forms of cultural variation with which patients and providers often contend, as well as ideas for how patients and providers can accommodate each other and overcome their cultural hurdles.

ETHNIC DIFFERENCES

As human beings, we give off cues about who we are, what is important to us, how we want to be treated, and even how we want others to see us. In the medical context, it is important for both patients and providers to be aware of the assumptions they make about the other; such assumptions might be wrong and could lead to misunderstandings. Misunderstandings due to ethnic differences in medical interactions often arise from several factors, including different cultural values, language differences, failures of physicians to recommend or provide information on screenings and preventive care based on ethnic or racial characteristics, and different views regarding how much information the health care professional discloses to the patient (Cline & McKenzie, 1998).

Communication theory of identity, or CTI (Hecht, 1978, 1993; Hecht, Collier, & Ribeau, 1993; Hecht, Jackson, & Pitts, 2005; Hecht, Jackson, & Ribeau,

Communication theory of identity illustrates how individuals make assumptions about each other based on their backgrounds, and helps explain how misunderstandings occur in the medical context. Identity is often communicated through *identity salience* and *identity intensity*

2003; Hecht, Ribeau, & Alberts, 1989), explains that people make assumptions about each other based on their backgrounds, and this can help explain how misunderstandings occur in the medical context (Scholl, Wilson, & Hughes, 2011). As you recall from Chapter 3, CTI posits that our identities vary in **identity salience** (the importance of one aspect of a person's identity in relation to other aspects) and **identity intensity** (the degree to which we express or communicate our identity). Salience and intensity influence how we identify with our ethnic groups, how we project those identities to others, and how others respond.

Identity salience
the importance of one aspect of a person's identity in relation to other aspects..

Identity intensity
the degree to which we express or communicate our identity.

CTI can help explain intercultural misunderstandings and difficulties in medical interactions. When people from different cultures intermingle, they interact according to their expectations of how people of certain ethnic and cultural groups communicate. For example, a Spanish-speaking patient who speaks broken English seeks care in the emergency room. She decides to request an interpreter because she's worried about not understanding the doctor. The English-speaking doctor, upon seeing the interpreter in the room, assumes the patient has no English proficiency whatsoever and ends up making eye contact with the interpreter instead of the patient when speaking. The doctor might even assume that the patient is not very intelligent and is incapable of understanding the simplest of suggestions. In this case, the language barrier is the most salient part of the patient's identity for the doctor. Unknown to the doctor, however, the patient could also have been a nurse in her home country—another aspect of her identity that isn't as salient to the other individuals in the room but could still help the doctor understand the reason for the patient's emergency room visit, as well as help establish some common ground to build rapport.

Patients are not the only ones who might be concerned about their expressed identity. Providers often express their identities in ways intended to enhance their credibility. A doctor might choose to wear a white lab coat and avoid markers that signal other aspects of his or her identity (e.g., ethnic, religious) to fit in with the mainstream culture. With regard to identity intensity, a doctor might embrace a particular religion but avoid wearing clothing or other markers of that religion to keep from alienating a patient who might not have similar religious beliefs.

Just as cultures differ on the projection of identity in the medical encounter, perspectives vary on how best to treat illness and communicate with health care professionals. For instance, some cultures' respect for authority might manifest as a patient's unquestioning deference to the suggestions of the health care provider. Asian culture allows for very little questioning of authority (i.e., doctors), not to mention considering practices or ideas that go against one's own wishes (Purnell, 2008). Some Asian patients are more willing to let the doctor make the medical decision for them than to make the decision themselves (Management Sciences for Health, 2005).

Some cultures have a distrust of Western or "modern" medicine and prefer the help of their local community. For example, many Latinos seek the help of the local *curandero*, a neighborhood healer who utilizes what some might call "folk medicine," often relying on religious tradition and natural remedies (e.g., herbs) to provide care. While community members believe they can be healed by such an individual, more technically trained practitioners believe these practices might be harmful and may even be intolerant of a patient's reliance on such care (Scholl & Hughes, 2011). While some traditional caregivers see themselves at odds with a "folk healer," it is possible to cooperate with such a person to gain the patient's trust and to find ways to combine efforts of both modern and traditional healing methods, especially if it helps win the patient's confidence (Mull & Mull, 1983).

© Horst Petzold/Shutterstock.com

Eastern medicine can complement Western approaches.

Curandero

a neighborhood healer who utilizes what some might call "folk medicine," often relying on religious tradition and natural remedies.

Distrust of the health care system is shared by other ethnic groups, particularly African Americans, who have suffered physical and emotional harm in the name of medical experimentation and scientific advancement. Between 1932 and 1972, the U.S. Department of Public Health conducted an experiment on almost 400 African American men from some of the poorest counties in Alabama. These men already had syphilis but were never informed of their actual diagnosis or treated for it. Instead, they were told they were being studied and treated for their "bad blood" (Brunner, 2009). The doctors conducting the experiments had no intention of treating these men; they only wanted to conduct autopsies on them after they died. For negligent treatment of the men and for the far-reaching effects of the untreated disease on their families, President Clinton offered a formal apology in 1997.

A controversy receiving more recent attention has its beginnings in 1951, when Henrietta Lacks, an African American woman living in Baltimore, was being treated for cervical cancer at Johns Hopkins University. During her treatment, doctors extracted some of her cancer cells without her knowledge or consent; these cells have since been referred to as HeLa cells, taking the first two letters of her first and last name. This first batch of cells reproduced, and this immortal line has been used extensively in medical research and has been crucial in cancer research to this day. The controversy, however, is that these cells have been used, duplicated, and sold for profit to research labs all over the world without the Lacks family's knowledge or benefit from the sales of those cells (Skloot, 2010). Given this extensive history of mistreatment and misinformation, a long-standing distrust of medicine among African Americans and other ethnic minorities exists to this day and has led many individuals to avoid doctors. Health care providers who want to be more culturally sensitive need to be mindful of this distrust, acknowledge it with the patient, and communicate in ways that are open, honest, and sincere. They might also give the patient opportunities to be more participative in health care decisions.

Not all ethnic groups are equal in their distrust of physicians or the health care system. In other cultures, a more informal patient–provider relationship is desired. For example, Arabs tend to be emotionally expressive and welcome the opportunity to converse with their providers, often getting to know them on a personal level. Such patients generally want opportunities to be open about their feelings and to contribute to their own health care. This usually requires a relaxed and informal tone from the provider, and some Arabs might be offended by health care professionals who come across as unfriendly or assert their authority for the sake of formality (Ahmad, 2004).

Health care providers should also acknowledge the role a patient's religion plays. Religious variations involve such elements as fasting, the need for cleanliness and purifying the body, and the importance of modesty in attire and in dealing with

Cultures differ in the level of formality and openness they desire with their doctors.

© Andresr, 2014. Shutterstock, Inc.

members of the opposite sex. Ahmad (2004) points to several considerations for Arabs and Muslims seeking medical care in the U.S. health care system. For example, most devout Muslims prefer to be seen by a physician of the same sex; this is especially true of women. It is also often the case that nurses and nursing assistants are seen as helpers, not as health care professionals, and so their suggestions or directions might not be taken seriously. Also, many Muslims prefer treatments in the form of pills or injections and might not consider medical counseling real treatment.

Patients' religious preferences might appear to clash with providers' recommendations, and the resulting conflict might create a health care dilemma. For instance, Orr (1996) documented a case in which a woman being treated for a critical condition wanted to leave the hospital against her doctor's strong recommendation. She insisted on leaving because she believed that her soul would remain where she died. A religious dilemma might also emerge when a physician prescribes medication. Suppose a doctor prescribes medication for a Muslim man, recommending that the patient take one pill three times a day with food. The Muslim man would likely have a problem with this recommendation if he were observing Ramadan, which is the holy month of abstaining from all food and drink during daylight hours. Taking the pill with food three times a day would be problematic under these circumstances. But a doctor who is sensitive to such religious requirements might work with the patient to determine a satisfactory solution to this dilemma.

As we will discuss later, many minorities underutilize health care services, partly because they harbor distrust for the medical field, which we have already discussed. There are other prohibitive factors, especially among Latino and Hispanic populations, such as language differences, lack of familiarity with available services, and limited financial means (Colón, 2005; Cristancho, Garces, Peters, & Mueller, 2008; Heuman et al., 2013). Nonetheless, more members of minority and disenfranchised populations are entering the health care system, making it more likely that patients and providers will interact with someone of a different culture. It is becoming increasingly important for health care providers of all professions and backgrounds to learn how to communicate with such a wide diversity of people.

GENDER AND SEX DIFFERENCES

While men and women share many similarities, they do exhibit real medical and health-related differences. In terms of physical distinctions, women have a longer life expectancy than men; however, women report more acute illnesses and visit the doctor more often (Lillie-Blanton, Martinez, Taylor, & Robinson, 1999). Called the "weaker sex" only a century ago, women now live longer and appear sturdier than in the past, but they do have higher rates of illness and disease than men (Verbrugge, 1999). These illnesses include nonfatal conditions such as digestive disorders, thyroid diseases, urinary conditions, and anemias.

Sex differences in health and mortality are influenced by more than just the physical. Women and men have different risks associated with gendered activities (e.g., football is more often played by men), and in general, women take fewer risks than men in recreational activities and in their health and safety (Harris, Jenkins,

& Glaser, 2006). Given that women are often sexualized in our popular culture and viewed in the medical world in terms of their reproductive function, aging women who have passed their childbearing years are often stigmatized. Menopause—when a woman's ovaries stop producing eggs—is sometimes referred to as a *disease* in the medical literature (Martin, 1999), which might be suggestive of an older woman's lowered value in the view of medicine and society at large.

Research has also found some differences between the sexes with regard to medical conversations. Gendered socialization has compelled women in general to take the traditional roles of nurturer, comforter, and supporter, which might contribute to the tendency of women to use more verbal fillers and indirect talk than do males (Beck, 1997). It would make intuitive sense, then, that men and women don't necessarily talk about their health, report their health problems, or remember things in the same way (Verbrugge, 1999). Despite most women's desire to be more involved in the medical interaction, they have not been as encouraged to take a partnership role in their health care, and they tend to use more restraint when asserting themselves as cohorts in the medical context (Beck, 1997). This could be linked to the level of encouragement or discouragement they experience from their doctors. For instance, physicians have been known to interrupt their female patients more often than their male patients, even when the physician is female (Irish & Hall, 1995). Fisher and Groce (1990) report how men and women account for their unhealthy or risky behavior to their physicians. Although the men in their study offered more accounts and justifications for their behavior, the physicians were more likely to reject the accounts and justifications offered by the women.

To combat such dismissive tendencies, many female patients go to female physicians thinking they will get more equal treatment, but female providers often adopt the same patriarchal tone as their male counterparts (Beck, 1997). This tendency goes along with a whole range of symptoms of a larger disparity affecting women who seek health care, particularly in terms of higher health insurance costs for women (Pear, 2012), limited access to reproductive health care such as contraception and testing for sexually transmitted infections (Teliska, 2005), misdiagnoses, and unnecessary medical procedures (Smith, 1992; West, 1994). Beck also tells of "women who complain of classic symptoms of a heart attack but are sent home unexamined for heart problems from hospital emergency rooms, and women who do not obtain preventative screenings for cancers that are treatable if discerned early" (p. 1). Many people—doctors included—still do not realize that women can suffer heart disease and have heart attacks (WomenHeart, 2012), and because of this lack of knowledge, too many women's symptoms go undetected.

DISABILITY

People with disabilities face many challenges in their daily interactions, as well as in their health care encounters. Du Pré (2010) points to an interesting dichotomy, which is that people either focus on the disability as the most important aspect about the person or avoid the issue entirely. Such a dichotomy can create uncertainties for both the disabled and the able-bodied in

Many misconceptions exist regarding people with disabilities.

how to communicate with each other. Health professionals have not received much training in communicating with people with disabilities and will sometimes focus on the disability rather than the medical issue on the patient's mind. Other people might consider it taboo to discuss or acknowledge disability and will avoid it as an issue altogether (Braithwaite & Thompson, 2000).

Many people with disabilities share common experiences, viewpoints, and even beliefs. One common result of becoming disabled is a loss of self-esteem and an altered sense of one's place in the world. Kundrat and Nussbaum (2000) found that people with heart disease tend to consider themselves older than others their same age; such perceptions might be due to diminished physical activities and being forced to confront mortality. The individual dealing with the disability also might experience social isolation, whether complete separation from others or diminished interactions during social gatherings. Murphy (1999), a university professor diagnosed with a tumor that led to the loss of his legs, describes his confinement to a wheelchair:

> My social isolation became acute during stand-up gatherings, such as receptions and cocktail parties. I discovered that I was now three-and-a-half feet tall, and most social interaction was taking place two feet above me. . . . My low stature and relative immobility thus made me the defenseless recipient of overtures, rather than [a conversation] instigator. This is a common plaint of the motor-disabled: They must wait for the others to come to them. As a consequence, I now attend only small, sit-down gatherings. (p. 64)

This diminished self-esteem and increased isolation can lead to feelings of altered identity, an identity often based more on one's disability or what one is no longer able to do. Many patients with disabilities also experience an altered sense of personhood in the health care arena. While many providers view such patients with care and concern, they often harbor negative perceptions of living with a disability, which include isolation, depression, and frustration; these assumptions might compel providers to treat patients with excessive sympathy (Iezzoni, Ramanan, & Drews, 2005) or inappropriately cast them as heroes (Nemeth, 2000). In the medical interaction, such misunderstandings and misguided perceptions can result in poor health care (Iezzoni et al., 2005). One should keep certain things in mind to communicate with sensitivity and understanding. First, it would be a good idea to avoid using the term *disabled*, as in "disabled people." Such a term might imply that the disability is the one and only noteworthy aspect of the individual. Rather, phrases such as "person who is blind" or "person who uses a wheelchair" acknowledge that the disability is just one aspect of that person in light of all the other things that make him or her unique.

Also important is addressing people with disabilities directly, rather than focusing the conversation on interpreters or companions. Such individuals wish to be treated like adults, and unless otherwise indicated, you should not assume that the individual's cognitive capacity is too diminished to understand normal conversation. In terms of offering assistance, it is best to wait for someone to ask before you step in to help. It is okay to offer the same courtesies you would extend to anyone; however, the assistance you offer might be respectfully declined. The most important thing to remember is that being treated as "other" or "less than human" because of limited sensory or physical ability is something none of us would appreciate.

AGEISM AND OLDER ADULTS

Older adults possess knowledge and experience that differentiate them from other age groups. Many of them have lived through the Great Depression, several wars, social changes, and many ups and downs in our economy. Most of us have been taught to "respect our elders," but Cline and McKenzie (1998) observe that "older persons are seen as more likely to 'take' from society. Specifically, they require greater health resources than other groups in society . . . , making them less valued than other age groups" (p. 65). Additionally, adults who are both old and ill carry a double stigma, which might magnify the differences in patient–provider interactions (Kreps, 1990).

Elderly persons are relatively optimistic about their health, perhaps because they tend to lower their expectations for what is considered optimal health as they age. To be realistic, most people do not expect their eyesight at age 65 to be as sharp as it was at age 25. Additionally, there is no reason for most older adults to stop enjoying popular activities such as swimming, biking, and walking. But the body does lose speed, endurance, and strength with age. While these changes are normal, lowered expectations about one's physical abilities might compel one to dismiss a lingering pain as a sign of slowing down rather than a symptom that should be checked out by a doctor (Mechanic, 1999).

In many ways, older adults are individuals with unique health-related needs and characteristics (Verbrugge, 1999). For example, the elderly are more likely to require combinations of prescription medications, present with a complex set of symptoms and complications, and be accompanied by a third party to a doctor visit. Older adults do have specific health issues that make them vulnerable to stereotypes and less-than-ideal treatment by medical professionals. These stereotypes might also influence how older adults are treated by others in their everyday lives, especially with regard to their physical and mental well-being. For example, a doctor with preconceived notions about aging and older adults might be dismissive when an older patient complains of knee pain. Instead of aggressively finding the cause of the pain and treating it, the doctor might just prescribe a pain medication and encourage the patient to "slow down" and accept knee pain as a part of growing old.

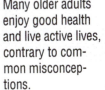

Many older adults enjoy good health and live active lives, contrary to common misconceptions.

Preconceived notions about older adults can have serious implications for the kinds of health care they receive, as well as how they are treated when they seek medical care. Stereotyping older adults as weak, sick, and feeble-minded might compel a provider to avoid contact with them altogether (Giles, Ballard, & McCann, 2002). When providers do communicate with older adults, some might speak slower and louder and even use simple words and phrases, as though speaking to a child (Hummert & Shaner, 1994).

Such communication patterns can be seen as a way to accommodate the older adult when communicating. According to communication accommodation theory (Coupland, Coupland, & Giles, 1991; Giles & Wiemann, 1987; Street

& Giles, 1982), certain variables such as nature of the relationship, likeability, and impression-management needs influence the extent to which a person in conversation converges with or diverges from the other person's verbal and nonverbal behavior. **Convergence** occurs when people mirror each other, such as using the same gestures, posture, and tone of voice. Convergence often indicates affinity for or feelings of similarity with the other person. **Divergence**, on the other hand, occurs when a person acts differently from the other, such as facing one's body away when the other person is trying to face forward. Divergence hints at attempts to remain socially distant from the other person. Such convergence and divergence patterns help maintain the desired psychological distance between conversational partners. In a doctor–patient interaction, a doctor might show convergence by leaning forward, meeting the patient's gaze, and mirroring the patient's facial expressions to show empathy and make a connection. On the contrary, a doctor who diverges might avoid the patient's gaze or sit facing a different direction to keep the conversation short or discourage questions.

Communication accommodation theory can be used to explain some provider behaviors that reflect stereotypes of older adult patients. For instance, when providers hear the quivery, breathy voice of an older patient, they might assume the patient has diminished intelligence and so start to speak loudly and slowly to that patient. The patient, in an attempt to show liking, might respond in a similar way and also speak even louder and more slowly. Such communication patterns suggest an overaccommodation on the part of the provider, which is an exaggerated response to the patient's perceived cognitive abilities (du Pré, 2010).

BRIDGING THE CULTURAL GAP

Communication problems resulting from conflicting identities and perceptions can be overcome with sensitivity and accommodation. Brown and Scholl (2006) and Scholl et al. (2011) studied patients' and providers' accounts of intercultural medical conversations. While most of their respondents denied real problems associated with cultural differences, patients and providers did display language that differentiated "we" or "us" from "them." Respondents also pinpointed similarities in how they expressed the need for competence from the other person. Patients talked about how doctors needed to show a desire to speak and learn the patients' language better; such a show of effort might help doctors convey as part of their identity a commonality with the patient. Providers desired more expressions of competence from patients as well, especially when it came to asking questions or showing they understood what was being said.

Convergence

refers to the way people use symbols to come together, overlap on ideas, or express common ground.

Divergence

occurs when a person acts differently from the other, such as facing one's body away when the other person is trying to face forward.

Although each culture might have its own patterns of communication, there are general guidelines for communicating more effectively with patients. If providers are working in a community with a predominant cultural group, such as Mexican Americans, it would be beneficial to try to learn some Spanish—not necessarily to achieve complete fluency but to make a connection and to show respect. If the language difference requires the assistance of an interpreter, the provider should remember to maintain eye contact with the patient, even when listening to the interpreter. Also, providers can greet patients in a warm and friendly way, and show respect by using desired titles, such as Mr./Mrs. or Señor/Señora/Señorita. In addition to attending to the patient, they might try to acknowledge and include family members as much as possible. Many ethnic groups place a great deal of importance on family and their input. Also, providers are well advised to be open to religious influences on patient and family attitudes and on their medical decisions (Scholl & Hughes, 2011; Zoucha & Broome, 2008). When conflicts arise between the patient's preferences and the doctor's orders, a compromise or some form of accommodation might be possible. Even if a compromise can't be reached, any effort to work with the patient's preferences will be appreciated.

Patients also have a responsibility in communicating effectively with their providers, even when there is a perceived cultural or ethnic difference. If a patient is anticipating a doctor visit sometime in the future, he or she might consider the possibility that the doctor will not understand or be aware of patient cultural preferences. Patients need to communicate their wishes openly and be honest about any behaviors or concerns. Also, if a patient has trouble reading or understanding something, she or he should ask for help and not be shy about it. As with any doctor visit, patients can prepare their questions in advance and bring them to the appointment and should make sure those questions are answered before leaving the doctor's office. If patients can't get all the answers they need from the doctor, they might try asking one of the other providers (e.g., nurse, technician). It might help to bring to the appointment a trusted friend, spouse, or family member who can provide some advocacy.

The existence of cultural differences and the misunderstandings that might result should not discourage individuals from asking questions, accommodating each other, and working to narrow the cultural gap. Willies-Jacobo (2007) provides several recommendations for practitioners who want to become more culturally sensitive. Because both provider and patient are responsible for the success of the medical interaction, we present these recommendations as something for both parties to keep in mind and put into practice. First, providers and patients should conduct a cultural awareness assessment of each other. This sounds more complicated than it needs to be. An assessment simply means learning as much as one can about the other person's culture and considering that insight when discussing diagnoses and recommendations. Patients can help with the assessment by providing as much detailed information as possible, such as dietary restrictions because of religion. The provider, in turn, can reveal certain personal information, which could make the interaction more informal and help the provider come across as friendly. For example, a provider might disclose a desire to learn more of the patient's primary language or that he or she came from the same country or region as the patient.

Second, the provider should consider individual family preferences. As we stated earlier, not all members of a particular culture are the same; each individual or family has its own unique set of values, traditions, and beliefs. For instance, one family might have a grandmother who is always consulted when medical decisions need to be made. This tradition might reflect a matriarchal family structure or the family's need to include the older and wiser members in medical decisions.

Third, one should anticipate the possibility of cultural conflict and find ways to manage and negotiate it. In other words, Willies-Jacobo (2007) suggests that both parties need to balance the preferences of the patient and family while staying within the bounds of what is medically appropriate and prudent. Instead of focusing entirely on the cultural clash, both patient and provider might talk more about the ultimate goal they both desire. Otherwise, merely highlighting the cultural difference without working through it might exacerbate the conflict (Wachtler, Brorsson, & Troein, 2005).

Another strategy is for the provider to give patients the chance to tell their story on their own terms. The dominant medical paradigm describes a medical interview in which the doctor tries, among other things, to reveal the patient's "hidden agenda"—the "real" but hidden reason for the doctor visit. Under this model, doctors might interrupt or cut off patients in their stories to encourage them to get to the point. "An alternative approach," suggests Mechanic (1999), "is to give patients greater latitude to tell their stories and to explain what they expect and hope for from the encounter" (p. 10). While many providers might argue that there is simply not enough time to allow a patient to divulge a complete story, simple questions such as, "Is there something else you'd like to discuss with the doctor today?" can encourage the patient to be more open and less likely to hide important information, such as religious or dietary restrictions.

ETHICAL CONNECTION

Audrey is a medical student interning at a hospital in her city. Her job consists of entering the patients' personal information and their reported symptoms into the database. Because the city has such a diverse population, many of the patients Audrey comes into contact with do not speak fluent English and come from many different cultural backgrounds. Oftentimes, Audrey becomes frustrated in her interactions with patients and files their forms as quickly as possible, sometimes not entirely understanding their complaints or patient history. One particular patient she entered into the database suffered a severe allergic reaction to a particular medicine because Audrey did not note the allergy on her entry form. Audrey was reprimanded and placed under close supervision for the rest of her internship.

Questions to consider:
1. How does the above situation apply to the bigger argument of more diversity in health care institutions?
2. What steps should Audrey have taken to better understand the patients' needs and concerns?
3. How might a cultural awareness assessment have helped avoid this situation?
4. Does Audrey's situation point to a need for health communication studies to play a larger role in health-provider training?

DIVERSITY WITHIN THE HEALTH CARE ORGANIZATION

Health care professionals working under the roof of one health care organization (e.g., hospital, clinic, rehabilitation facility) come from different educational and professional backgrounds. For example, after earning a bachelor's degree, aspiring physicians attend 4 years of medical school and complete up to 7 years of residency; other professionals (e.g., nursing assistants, radiology technicians) require fewer years in school and receive more specialized medical training. Health care professionals also take different career paths. Many physicians are self-employed, while other professionals are employed by a health care organization. Language differences abound in the medical field, with the various professionals using their own jargon and terminology. Also, there are class and SES differences among professionals,

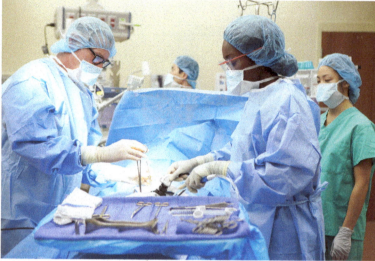

© Monkey Business Images/Shutterstock.com

Health care teams encompass a great deal of diversity, which can be appreciated and used to the team's advantage.

with some earning more income and acquiring higher status than others. In addition, there are gender and racial differences, along with differences in values.

Conflict is inevitable when professionals of different backgrounds and disciplines get together. While achieving the best medical goal is the ultimate outcome, some members might use the group discussion to "flex their muscles" or establish their status and rank within the group (van Servellen, 2009). It might seem as though the path of least resistance is to hire people who are like-minded and likely to conform to the dominant beliefs of an organization. However, as we discussed in the section on groupthink in Chapter 8, this extreme similarity across the organization can cause it to become stagnant and prevent it from growing and improving. "Diversity is valuable because it enhances the potential for creative problem solving . . . innovative thinking is enhanced when diverse people bring different viewpoints to bear on a problem" (du Pré, 2010, p. 231). In addition, diverse staff can better attend to the varied needs of their clients and patients.

HEALTH CARE ACCESS AND MARGINALIZATION

MARGINALIZED POPULATIONS

Not all individuals have equal access to health care. U.S. citizens and residents who have limited access to health care tend to be racially or culturally marginalized (Colón, 2005; Olson & Anders, 2000; Safeer & Keenan, 2005; van Servellen, 2009; Ward, Clark, & Heidrich, 2009). Also, poor health in inner-city urban areas might be due to such factors as poor living conditions, diminished municipal services (e.g., closing of libraries, rerouting of bus lines), and stress due to community violence (Williams & Collins, 1999). Another factor is the increasing income inequality in the United States. As part of this income inequality, the gains in economic status of African Americans relative to Whites have stagnated. This economic downturn, as well as rising unemployment, is associated with declining health among African Americans who are disproportionately affected (Perron, 2010).

Racism is a significant determining factor of the health status of oppressed minority populations. Williams and Collins (1999) explain:

> Racism can restrict access to the quantity and quality of health-related desirable services such as public education, health care, housing, and recreational facilities. . . . [T]he experience of racial discrimination and other forms of racism may induce psychological distress that may adversely affect physical and mental health status, as well as the likelihood of engaging in violence and addiction. . . . In color conscious American society, skin color may be an important determinant of the degree of exposure to racial discrimination, access to valued resources and the intensity of the effort necessary to obtain them. (p. 361)

These resources include preventive care, immunizations, and mental health services, as well as others. There has been steady improvement in access despite how slow it might seem to marginalized populations. The civil rights movement has had positive impacts on access to health care. For instance, reducing educational and occupational segregation has improved the socioeconomic conditions of many African Americans (Williams & Collins, 1999). Racism and the resulting health disparities often affect people who immigrate to the United States. Immigrant populations who don't speak the language and are unfamiliar with the health care system have a difficult time finding needed medical care and are often unfamiliar with the services available to them.

A great deal of health disparity is influenced by variations in SES, such as income, amount of debt, education, occupation, and property. The existence of a positive association between SES and health is generally accepted (Gallo & Matthews, 2003; Williams & Collins, 1999). Much of the gap between the high- and low-SES groups in terms of health has a lot to do with the increased gains in health for high-SES groups relative to low-SES groups, but the gap can also be explained by the low-SES groups' worsening health condition. In their review of the literature, Gallo and Matthews (2003) found that lower SES relates to more negative emotions and thoughts, which in turn relate to poorer health. Such negative emotions might be the result of the racial **marginalization**. Also, Williams and Collins (1999) point out that persons in low-SES groups are more likely to experience risky occupational circumstances, such as increased exposure to toxic chemicals and poor working conditions.

Serving individuals of low-SES groups and other marginalized populations is often a challenge because they are at a higher risk for health problems such as

IN YOUR *life*

Have you ever had to visit a hospital in a country where you did not know the language? How important is the intercultural and language gap when trying to obtain adequate health care?

Marginalization

health disparity influenced by variations in SES, such as income, amount of debt, education, occupation, and property; lower SES relates to more negative emotions and thoughts, which in turn relate to poorer health.

mental illness (Belle, 1990), respiratory problems (Evans & Kantrowitz, 2002), and cardiovascular disease (Mensah, Mokdad, Ford, Greenlund, & Croft, 2005). Health educators and message designers work hard to generate and disseminate messages targeted specifically to these at-risk groups. Yet these campaigns remain largely ineffective, even contributing to a wider gap between the affluent and economically disadvantaged in terms of health behaviors and knowledge (Freimuth, 1990).

Despite educators' efforts to reach vulnerable and disenfranchised populations with crucial health information, the results have been disappointing overall. The knowledge gap hypothesis (Tichenor, Donohue, & Olien, 1970, 1980) might explain the lack of effectiveness in improving the health of some minority populations. This hypothesis claims that as media (e.g., TV, radio, Internet) disseminate new information into society, groups with more education and means will receive that information faster than will groups who have less education. As a result, the gap in knowledge will increase rather than decrease (Tichenor et al., 1970). This knowledge gap depends on three factors: "level of mass media publicity in a particular setting, level of individuals' education, and level of individuals' knowledge about a specific subject" (Freimuth, 1990, p. 174). In other words, (1) if a health issue is not widely publicized or talked about in a community, (2) if targeted audiences aren't educated enough to attend to and understand the message, and (3) if audiences have little knowledge about that issue, that community will suffer even more from the lack of this information on all three counts than will more knowledgeable audiences.

While easier said than done, there are ways to reach an at-risk audience and help them stay informed about important health issues. One way is to frame the issue in more local terms instead of national or international ones. While topics such as breast cancer, smoking, and HIV have national and international implications, perhaps information on such issues can better reach less-educated individuals if it carries a local spin. For instance, audiences might be informed about a local fundraising event and told that proceeds will benefit the local hospitals. Audiences could also be informed about local statistics for HIV infection. Another tactic for circumventing the knowledge gap might be to know what issues are of interest to those with low SES, as well as discussing issues in more conversational terms (Gaziano, 1983).

HEALTH LITERACY

Literacy
refers to the ability to read or write at a functional level or calculate basic math.

Literacy generally refers to the ability to read or write at a functional level or calculate basic math. Literacy—or illiteracy—means several different things, but from a practical standpoint, most literate people can read and follow traffic signs while driving, understand instructions in written form, interpret and fill out a job

Low health literacy can have negative effects on one's health and the ability to make appropriate health care decisions.

© Diego Cervo/Shutterstock.com

application, review a household utility bill, and understand the directions on a medical prescription bottle. While the United States is a highly literate society, many children and adults slip through the educational cracks. About 22% of U.S. adults have minimal literacy skills (National Institute for Literacy, 2008).

Health literacy has to do with understanding medical and health information (van Servellen, 2009). The Centers for Disease Control and Prevention (2011) define health literacy as the ability to seek, obtain, and understand health information and services, as well as to make informed health care decisions. More specifically, being health literate means being able to read and understand health information, comprehend the language in which health information is conveyed, gain access to reliable and relevant health information, follow prescription instructions, discuss health matters with others, and apply relevant information to solve health problems. Health illiteracy and low levels of functional health literacy are national problems (Young, 2004). The National Patient Safety Foundation (2011) reports that the health of about 90 million people in the United States is at risk due to low health literacy. Most health care materials are written at the 10th-grade level or above, yet most Americans read at the 8th-grade level, with one in five reading at 5th-grade level or below. Many immigrants and minority groups also exhibit lower literacy levels, partly due to limited English competency (Shaw, Huebner, Armin, Orzech, & Vivian, 2008). It is also documented that older adults, even though they

Health literacy
understanding and being able to act on medical and health information.

have the greatest burden of illness, are known to be low in health literacy (Safeer & Keenan, 2005). Diminished health literacy can have tremendous impacts on the health care system as well as the individual. Such impacts include greater health care costs, lower levels of patient compliance, increased risk of hospitalization and longer hospital stays, more treatment and medical errors (Institute of Medicine, 2004; National Patient Safety Foundation, 2011), and poorer self-management of disease (van Servellen, 2009).

Certain factors contribute to our country's low health literacy, one of which is SES. Besides being stereotyped as individuals who are lazy or don't care about maintaining their health (van Ryn & Fu, 2003), individuals of low SES might not benefit from a doctor visit as much as their more affluent counterparts would. For instance, low-SES people tend to reveal fewer concerns about their health and ask fewer questions of the doctor (van Servellen, 2009). Also, research suggests that they do not receive as much information or as high quality care from their doctors as more educated patients do (Agency for Healthcare Research & Quality, 2004). Their limited educational levels might make it difficult for them to understand and benefit from written materials such as pamphlets and promotional health posters. Finally, because of limited means, they might not be offered as many treatment options—often because doctors make assumptions about their ability to afford certain medical treatments.

Another influence on low health literacy is language difference (van Servellen, 2009). Language is perhaps the most important determining quality of an ethnic group, and when a person is unfamiliar with the language of the dominant culture, he or she can feel lost. This is also true when one is unfamiliar with crucial medical terminology. Some patients do not know that a myocardial infarction is a heart attack. Also, earlier in this chapter, we mentioned the word *once* and its different English and Spanish meanings.

While getting more educated and becoming more literate might be ultimate goals for seekers of health care, there are things both patients and providers can do in the short term to overcome the barriers associated with low health literacy. Patients should look for opportunities to speak up when they have questions or don't understand words their providers use (du Pré, 2010). In turn, providers need to remind themselves that not all patients read and write at the same level or have the same proficiency in English. As mentioned earlier, most of the health education literature is written at a relatively high reading level, and providers can work with patients to help them understand the content of such information. Providers should also remember that simply asking patients whether they understand is not enough.

Many patients will nod or say "yes" even if they don't completely understand; they might be too shy to ask for clarification. If the provider can find ways to have patients repeat instructions back, this will help the provider determine patients' level of understanding and get them more involved in the conversation. In the case of a significant language barrier, an interpreter might be helpful, although not all words are easily translated from one language to another.

Some health-based organizations and agencies have come up with innovative and successful ways to promote patient comprehension, as well as ways to overcome health literacy barriers. If language difference is a problem, medical clinics can provide medical pamphlets and brochures in both English and Spanish. Some resources also exist to help patients with low reading comprehension and educational levels. The "Ask Me 3" program (National Patient Safety Foundation, 2007, 2011) teaches patients what kinds of questions they should ask their doctors. These questions are as follows:

- What is my main problem?
- What do I need to do?
- Why is it important for me to do this?

Anyone anticipating an upcoming doctor appointment can bring these questions along and be prepared to ask them. Related to the "Ask Me 3" campaign, some other strategies can assist providers in helping patients with low health literacy (see Figure 10.3).

FIGURE 10.3 How to Help Patients with Low Health Literacy

- Use statements that include small words, brief statements, and simply worded phrases.
- Talk at a pace that is comfortable for the patient.
- Repeat important material and ask the patient to repeat it back.
- Use visuals for support, such as illustrations, photos, videos, or cartoons.
- When using a medical term, pair it with a term with which the patient is more familiar (e.g., *myocardial infarction* paired with *heart attack*).
- Tell stories of hypothetical cases similar to the patient's, leaving out confidential information.
- If describing a series of steps to take, ask the patient to act out or repeat the steps back to test his or her understanding. Write those steps down for the patient to take home.

Strategies to help patients with low health literacy (van Servellen, 2009)

WHAT YOU'VE LEARNED

In this chapter, you learned what it means to be healthy, and you overviewed what is studied in the field of health communication. You then learned about two different models of health care and which perspectives the East and West align themselves with; the biomedical model looks for physical signs of what is wrong, while the biopsychosocial model acknowledges that illness is not always just a physical thing. The importance of cultural differences in medical contexts were then discussed, and you learned about diversity within health care and medical organizations. Finally, you overviewed how some cultures experience marginalization within health care and how that can impact health care outcomes and health literacy. As you continue in your study of intercultural communication, reflect on how cultural differences can impact the quality of care a person receives. Have you ever experienced marginalization within a health care context because of your culture?

REVIEW

1. _____ is the construction and sharing of meanings about the provision of health care delivery and the promotion of public health through mediated channels.

2. According to the _____, ill health is caused by many physical, social, and environmental factors.

3. _____ medicine teaches that the body coexists and shares mutual influence with its environment, whereas _____ medicine relies on the scientific method and the principle of verification to understand what causes ill health.

4. The _____ could help emphasize the dissimilarity between physician and patient.

5. _____ illustrates how patients and providers can make assumptions about each other based on their backgrounds, and helps explain how misunderstandings occur in the medical context.

6. Explain the difference between *convergence* and *divergence*.

7. Why is a lack of diversity a problem within health care organizations?

8. _____ has compelled women in general to take the traditional roles of nurturer, comforter, and supporter, which might contribute to the tendency of women to use more verbal fillers and indirect talk than do males.

9. Explain the ways in which ageist language is often used when speaking to older adults.

10. Define *health literacy*.

Review answers are found on the accompanying website.

REFLECT

1. According to the biopsychosocial approach, what other processes besides medicine affect our overall health?

2. What are some ways in which hospitals and health providers in the United States might benefit by taking an *Eastern medicine* perspective?

3. Harmony has been having issues catching her breath throughout the day, and she decides to visit her doctor to discuss the problem. Harmony immediately notices her doctor doesn't seem to be taking her seriously, and he continually interrupts her while she is answering his questions. Explain the role gender and sex is playing in this interaction, and discuss what is problematic about the doctor's behavior.

4. Abbey is applying for an editing job she is very qualified for. When she walks into the room where her interview will be conducted, she is greeted by the interviewer, who is hearing-impaired, and a translator who is there to sign what Abbey says to the interviewer. The atmosphere of the room feels awkward when Abbey references the interviewer's disability by saying, "Oh, I wasn't expecting this!" Then, throughout the interview, Abbey looks at the translator while speaking instead of looking at the person interviewing her. Abbey doesn't get the job. Discuss what may have gone wrong during her interview.

5. Why is diversity within a health care organization critical to effective treatment for people from many different cultures?

KEY TERMS

health, 270
health communication, 271
biomedical model, 271
biopsychosocial model, 272
Western medicine, 272
Eastern medicine, 274
susto, 274
stigma, 276
patient role, 277

communication theory of identity, 279
identity salience, 280
identity intensity, 280
curandero, 281
convergence, 288
divergence, 288
marginalization, 293
literacy, 294
health literacy, 295

CHAPTER ELEVEN

Intercultural Communication in Business and Professional Contexts

CHAPTER OUTLINE

WHAT YOU WILL LEARN

After studying this chapter, you should be able to

1. define the term *diversity*;
2. identify the importance of cultural competence in the workplace;
3. discuss discrimination in the workplace and how it can be related to your study of intercultural communication;
4. apply cultural competence to the requirements of professional excellence in the workplace; and
5. explain the dynamic of power in the workplace and how the different aspects of workplace power are good or bad.

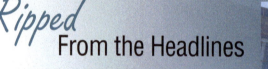

© Benny Marty/Shutterstock.com

As the world becomes more interdependent, companies are looking to better represent diverse populations in their own workforces. For instance, large tech companies such as Google have traditionally not been diverse in their hiring practices; Google and other Silicon Valley companies have long had a workforce consisting of white and Asian men. However, Google has recently taken steps towards diversifying its workforce by focusing on hiring, inclusion, education, and communities; these are the areas in which the company believes it can have the greatest impact. Google first began tracking and publishing its workforce demographics in 2014. That year, only 17% of its employees were women; by 2017, that number nearly doubled to 31% (Donnelly, 2017). While men are still over-represented in the company, their initiative is clearly making an impact.

Google's new diversity practices go beyond the basic goals of simply hiring more women and people of color. Rather, they are aimed at including a wider variety of voices and experiences, which means employees and recruiters are being trained differently. Current employees are participating in anti-bias training and recruiters are willing to look beyond a small handful of majors from elite universities when interviewing candidates (McGirt, 2017). What are some of the possible strengths and weaknesses of diversity initiatives such as these? Do you think other industries could benefit from these initiatives?

As you think about Google's diversity initiatives, what are some of the voices and experiences that still need greater representation? How can Google and other companies more effectively include those voices? As you move forward in the chapter, reflect on the benefits a diverse workforce can offer a company, as well as some of the unique challenges that may arise.

A s the business marketplace increasingly becomes more global, it is important to understand the impact of culture in your professional life. With new friendships and colleagues, intercultural communication plays a major role in how relationships form and prosper in the workplace. From our own personal vision of a successful worker to how we function within an organization, effective intercultural communication can help support a healthy work environment. Understanding culture in the workplace is one of the most critical skills you must learn. This chapter is designed to set you up for a leadership role in your career by developing your cultural competence and discovering how you function in relationship with different cultures. In this day and age, it has become critical for organizations to reduce the harm caused by discrimination by any means possible (Triana, Garcia, & Colella, 2010). Being a valuable team player and marketable employee means you must be a leader who works to help reduce cultural clashes.

In this chapter, we will explore the importance of cultural recognition and inclusion across business and professional contexts. Applying communication and cultural competence across business and professional contexts is important because discrimination produces unproductive work environments. Also, diversity is a positive aspect of the workplace and can even improve productivity. By adhering to the cultural competence practices learned throughout this text, you can make yourself a more valuable employee in the modern workplace. Besides diversity, we will also discuss discrimination laws and how power and corporate colonization affect both the workplace and the employee. Think about how culture plays a role in the following example:

© Darren Brode/Shutterstock.com

The Chrysler/Fiat merger introduced a major intercultural shift to the traditionally American (Chrysler) company.

Sarah has just graduated from college and been hired for a management job at BP. She has been assigned to the Mexico office. During the first few weeks, she decides to meet with all her employees in the Mexico division. She schedules the meeting for 11:00 a.m. on a Wednesday. She arrives early to prepare for the meeting. 11:20

a.m. rolls around, and only two members of her team have arrived. Most of the team is in attendance by 11:30 a.m., but by this time she is frustrated and angry at the tardiness of her team members.

In the above situation, do you feel that Sarah responded appropriately? Should she have reprimanded her whole staff for tardiness or taken cultural norms into account? Many Latin American cultures (including Mexico) have a more relaxed and informal corporate environment, where hard deadlines and meeting times are not strictly enforced. When conducting business in another country, a leader is responsible for learning the social expectations and cultural construction of that country. In most workplaces, some cultural groups will stand out more than others; so it is important to remain sensitive to all your coworkers' and employees' cultural backgrounds.

Along with learned cultural practices, the workplace is a breeding ground for internal cultural creations. Take an athletic team, for example, which has a culture all its own. Team members communicate with one another about and through sports, and they engage in team-specific rituals and share a sense of community. Communication may include slang, gestures, and phrases that people outside of the athletic team don't recognize or understand, including some interesting nonverbal rituals such as butt slaps, body bumps, and high-fives. These types of nonverbal behaviors are ways for athletic teams to celebrate or convey a strong effort. In a setting different from the team environment, others may view butt slaps and body bumps as odd or even inappropriate. Outsiders working with such a group must learn or immerse themselves in this distinct culture. This dynamic is also true in the workplace. In terms of the communicative patterns appropriate to their specific workplace environment, individuals construct their day-to-day identities as employees through language, use of verbal and nonverbal symbols, and ongoing interactions with colleagues (Holmes & Marra, 2005).

Assimilating into the organization's culture becomes a way for the employee to become more successful in the workplace and gives him or her a chance to develop and benefit from intercultural relationships. "Organization assimilation is generally considered the process of learning how to function in an organization environment" (Jablin, 2001). Culture, both inside and outside of the organization, is powerful and ever changing. It's imperative that you understand how you represent your culture and how to be sensitive and accommodating to other cultures as well.

Assimilating into a workplace culture can easily be paralleled with assimilating into a fraternity or sorority; becoming a member means reinventing identity through affiliation. How can someone's fraternity or sorority affiliation, for example, be viewed as positive or negative in the workplace? Experience with a high-caliber organization adds a positive highlight to a résumé, but if the organization has a poor reputation or one linked to discrimination, this could work against the individual. Does affiliation dictate identity? Obviously not, but isn't it true that each member of an organization is an individual and that we still categorize everyone by the organizations to which they belong? With these questions in mind, why is it important for you to know how to pinpoint identities within culture? Looking deeper than the label placed on particular cultures and finding the value of future employees, coworkers, and customers is the focus of the following sections.

FOSTERING CULTURE AND DIVERSITY IN THE WORKPLACE

Culture can be effectively promoted in the workplace by fostering a diversity-friendly environment. To be effective in this endeavor means to cut at the heart of racism, sexism, and classism. Promoting diversity in organizations requires active changes in overtly racist, sexist, and homophobic behaviors among members of the organization; however, it is also important to be cognizant of subtle and passive behaviors that may be even more destructive than overt acts (Ragins, 1995, pp. 93–94). Communicative respect and inclusion are the keys to ensuring your company

© Volodymyr Kyrylyuk/Shutterstock.com

Global companies, such as Google and Microsoft, are increasingly relying on a culturally diverse workforce.

is fostering culture and diversity in the workplace. Fostering diversity has numerous positive benefits to a business organization. Studies have shown that the presence of many divergent perspectives can be helpful when groups are trying to come up with creative ideas or solve complex problems (Prieto, Phipps, & Osiri, 2009). Think about how beneficial several different perspectives would be in tackling a common problem. What are some initial benefits you can think of? Reflect on your own real-life examples of problem solving in a diverse group.

Diversity

a term used to describe the unique differences among people. These differences are based on a variety of factors such as ethnicity, race, heritage, religion, gender, sexual identity, age, social class, and the like.

IN YOUR *life*

Have you ever been discriminated against at school or work? In your experience, what is the best way to work past workplace discrimination?

Diversity in nature is the representation of various differences in a shared space. Understanding diversity requires analyzing a set of conscious practices that involve understanding and appreciating the interconnectivity of humanity, cultures, and the natural environment (Patrick & Kumar, 2012). One of the greatest barriers to a diverse business environment is the presence of discrimination. Therefore, the important question to answer is, How does one work toward eradicating discrimination? The big idea is to allow each culture the opportunity to represent itself without imposing stereotypes or privileges. The construct of diversity includes a shared acceptance of and mutual respect for one another (Patrick & Kumar, 2012). Fostering diversity in the workplace requires business professionals to allow cultures the space to fully manifest without attempting to oppress or change their core identity.

In the workplace, it is important to remember that everyone fulfills a role in the organization. Company policies are created, and employees working within the organization are expected to adhere to these policies regardless of their cultural background. Every organization has a hierarchy that all employees must respect and follow; however, look back at Sarah's story regarding her meeting in Mexico. Employers in the United States would show grave concern for employees arriving 45 minutes late. Yet the laid-back atmosphere in many Latin cultures simply does not adhere to a strict, time-oriented regimen. Therefore, a supervisor who is informed about various cultures and how they value time and space differently will have a better outlook and attitude toward communicating across cultural lines. By improving cultural awareness among employees, organizations can avoid offending employees, customers, business partners, and the public. By minimizing the possibility of offending or violating cultural norms, organizations will improve their communication (Kienzle & Husar, 2007). Now that we have reviewed the importance of diversity in the workplace, the next section emphasizes how diversity initiatives will only continue to advance in the future. Having knowledge about the diversity in your workplace will help you be a competent communicator in your professional life.

DIVERSITY INITIATIVES IN THE WORKPLACE

Diversity initiatives seek to raise organizational members' awareness and sensitivity to differences between minority and majority groups (Soni, 2001). With the power hierarchy present in all workplaces, the issues of power and oppression should be handled with extreme care and sensitivity. When you enter the workforce, you will more than likely work with people from a variety of cultural backgrounds. Intelligent managers and organizations look at diversity and see how it can help the future of the organization. In 2012, the U.S. Census Bureau asserted that the country's minority population is consistently increasing. With this overall growth in population diversity, the makeup of the professional workforce will likely follow suit. It is important to note that diversity does not include only racial minorities; it also includes sex and gender, people with disabilities, sexual orientation, and many other traits that make up who we are as human beings. Many organizations in the United States acknowledge the challenge of fostering diversity in the workplace and try to define communication as they seek competency in this area (Brach & Fraser, 2000). Equal Employment Opportunity (EEO) and Affirmative Action (AA) legal mandates have made organizations participate in more ethical and effective communication in the workplace.

The Equal Employment Act of 1972 protects the rights of applicants and employees by monitoring to make sure that promotions, benefits, classifications, and referrals, to name a few, are not withheld due to discrimination associated with color, race, religion, sex, or national origin. **Affirmative Action**, more specifically, is a set of public policies and initiatives designed to help reverse and eliminate past and present discrimination based on race, color, region, sex, or national origin. These mandates are necessary because of the increasing diversity in the workplace. Managers cannot afford to supervise and communicate with workers using outdated techniques that were acceptable in the past (Wanguri, 1996). It is important to adopt a leadership style that incorporates cultural inclusion beyond the legal mandates. Doing so will avoid potentially negative consequences for organizations and their employees.

> **The Equal Employment Act**
> protects the rights of applicants and employees by monitoring to make sure that promotions, benefits, classifications, and referrals are not withheld due to discrimination associated with color, race, religion, sex, or national origin.

> **Affirmative Action**
> a set of public policies and initiatives designed to help reverse and eliminate past and present discrimination based on race, color, region, sex, or national origin.

While complying with the EEO/AA mandates provides boundaries in the workplace, practicing diversity is highly complex and subject to a variety of interpretations (Point & Singh, 2003). It has become necessary to understand the mandates and develop appropriate intercultural communication skills and techniques that uphold and expand on them. In one sense, workplace diversity is based on identity, including race/ethnicity, gender, age, socioeconomic status, religion, sexual orientation, country of origin, etc. (Allen, 1995). Still, the meaning of diversity in an organization at any given time largely depends on the organizational actors in power and their perspectives on diversity (Witherspoon & Wohlert, 1996). Who holds the power? How does power affect the operation of an organization? How does power reinforce cultural norms? To understand different cultural perspectives, take into account the different ways people identify with a particular country, as well as the ways their culture has traditionally interacted in that setting. Take the time to explore how culture and its connection to the workplace have been influenced by power.

Today, a generation of well-educated and diverse individuals is graduating and entering the workplace, continuing to make modern businesses a crossroads for cultural interactions. It is healthy for an organization to hire and retain employees of diverse cultural backgrounds and worldviews. A **worldview** is a culture's orientation toward supernatural, human, and natural entities in the cosmological universe, and other philosophical issues influencing how its members see the world (Samovar, Porter, & McDaniel, 2009). Our worldview shapes how we understand and react to what is happening around us. How would you describe your worldview? Understanding how you personally function in the world and within organizations leads to better understanding of other people's worldviews, which can help prevent culture shock. Remember from Chapter 4 that **culture shock** is a state of confusion, anxiety, stress, or loss felt when one encounters a culture that has little in common with one's own. Have you ever experienced culture shock? Think about how you reacted to your initial shock and what steps you took to relieve your anxiety and integrate into the new environment.

As you develop as a student and potential leader in the workplace, it's critical to strive for **cultural diversity awareness**—being aware of the diversity present in any working or social environment (Fine, 1996; Quintanilla & Wahl, 2014). This awareness can help prevent an uncontrolled response to feelings of culture shock. Awareness is not an easy task, because we all share different worldviews, but it is necessary because it is the key to effective intercultural communication. Redfield (1953) created a way to define personal worldview using the following elements: self, other, gender differences, "us versus them," religious differences, various ways people manage time (e.g., fast-paced, relaxed), and spirituality. How does someone's worldview affect his or her work ethic, concept of time and space, and workplace relationships? Can you describe your own worldview? How does religion affect how you feel about children born out of wedlock? Did you grow up in a household that taught time management? How can such views affect a relationship with someone who does not share your same worldview on these subjects?

A good way to learn more about a variety of worldviews is to foster openness in your professional relationships. Allowing open communication with others creates

Worldview

a culture's orientation toward supernatural, human, and natural entities in the cosmological universe, and other philosophical issues influencing how its members see the world.

Culture shock

a state of confusion, anxiety, stress, or loss felt when one encounters a culture that has little in common with one's own.

Cultural diversity awareness

being aware of the diversity present in any working or social environment.

© Rawpixel.com/Shutterstock.com

It is critical to the business/client relationship that a business professional practice effective cultural competence.

opportunities to bring other people's worldviews into consideration along with your own. How do you define yourself? Have your interactions with other people helped define and expand your personal worldview? Now that you are more familiar with the notion of cultural diversity awareness, let's consider the importance of communicating competently with customers and clients.

DIVERSITY AND CUSTOMER RELATIONS

One of the most important applications of cultural diversity awareness focuses on customers and clients. Diversity competence at the organizational level is critical to remaining competitive in an increasingly global marketplace and in fostering diverse employee labor markets (De Anca & Vega, 2007). The concept of globalization requires businesses to connect customers and employees from opposite ends of the globe. **Globalization** is an integration of economy and technology that creates a worldwide and interconnected work environment. The idea of a "global marketplace" is a worldwide phenomenon that influences how businesses interact with other cultures both inside and outside the organization. If fostered correctly, embracing globalization can increase workplace performance and service for customers and clients. With this in mind, why would the absence of cultural diversity awareness hurt a business? What role do you play in your career or education when it comes to the application of cultural diversity? Try to be inclusive of other cultures during your interactions at school or work.

Globalization
an integration of economy and technology that creates a worldwide and interconnected work environment..

More often than not, your job will require you to deal with coworkers and customers who represent different cultures. This creates the need to be cognizant of the major complications that can arise when discrimination is allowed in the workplace. Have you ever worked with someone who used racial slurs or openly discriminated against others while at work? As more businesses adapt to a global marketplace, many old and preconceived notions of identity must be set aside. Stereotypes related to a person's race, gender, age, or sexual orientation have no place in the professional environment. It is important for you, as a business professional, to represent the organization in a positive manner; tolerating discrimination can have severe consequences for the company and for your job as well.

The tendency to stereotype is inherent in all of us, since we use stereotypes to help define and categorize groups of people. This is a natural process, and not necessarily a poor one; it is important to be able to recognize group traits and behaviors. However, it is also important to frame your interactions with other individuals without letting preconceived stereotypes influence your communication. When stereotypes manifest into discrimination in the workplace, problems arise. Stereotypes need to be shed to foster mutual cultural respect. Cultural awareness improves communication in the global workplace by avoiding offensive situations and eliminating confusion between personnel and clients (Archer, 1997; Hamilton, Parker, & Smith, 1982; Kirby, 2005; Ling, 1997; Thomas & Inkson, 2005). An organization must maintain a positive public image to stay successful in any industry. Understanding and eliminating discriminatory acts toward both coworkers and clients is essential for positive public relations.

Let's consider several examples of how organizations foster cultural awareness in the workplace and how this has evolved over the past 10 years. In Figure 11.1, look at the five companies listed among *Fortune* magazine's "50 Best Companies for Minorities" in 2002 and how their diversity statements have evolved. In the list, you can see a trend: Each company advocates the rhetoric of inclusion. This trend represents a shift from what was once simply tolerance to the more beneficial practice of acceptance. When thinking about your current or future career, how do you (or how does your company) practice inclusion in the workplace? Try to invite others who have different cultural backgrounds to join in your cultural rituals, and join in theirs when an invitation is extended.

FIGURE 11.1 Excerpts from diversity statements posted on the public websites of select companies listed in *Fortune* magazine's "50 Best Companies for Minorities"

Company	Diversity Statement (2002)
McDonald's	Diversity at McDonald's is understanding, recognizing, and valuing the differences that make each person unique. McDonald's is committed to recognizing the talents and job performance of all employees and values the contributions that come from people with different backgrounds and perspectives.
Fannie Mae	Our corporate philosophy on diversity is based on respect for one another and recognition that each person brings his or her unique attributes to the corporation. Fanny Mae will be most successful in meeting its public mission and our corporate goals when we fully capitalize on skills, talents, and potential of all our employees.
Sempra Energy	When we talk about diversity at Sempra energy, we mean more than race, age, sexual orientation, and gender. We believe that diversity includes: Human diversity, characterized by our employees' physical differences, personal preferences, or life experiences, Cultural diversity, characterized by different beliefs, values, and personal characteristics, Systems diversity, characterized by the organizational structure and management systems in the workplace.
PepsiCo	We respect individual differences in culture, ethnicity, and color. PepsiCo is committed to equal opportunity for all employees and applicants. We are committed to providing a workplace free from all forms of discrimination. We respect the right of individuals to achieve professional and personal balance in their lives.
Freddie Mac	To ensure the achievement of Freddie Mac's mission, vision, and strategic objectives, we must foster an increasingly diverse work culture, where all employees have the opportunity to be included, add value, and contribute to their fullest potential.

Sources: Hickman (2002) and company websites.

FOSTERING CULTURAL COMPETENCE IN THE WORKPLACE

Cultural competence

the ability to interact effectively with people of different cultural or ethnic backgrounds.

Cultural competence can be defined as the ability to interact effectively with people of different cultural or ethnic backgrounds. Doing so takes an important set of skills that not only creates a positive work environment but also fosters personal growth in cultural competence. In today's workplace, displaying accurate cultural competence is key to the success of an organization. Higher levels of cultural competence and group performance are related to the development of more trust between individuals (Myers & McPhee, 2006). A higher level of trust makes working with people much easier.

Once you have recognized your standpoint, you must define your own attitude toward cultural differences. To become an asset in your organization, it is important to gain more understanding of other cultural values and norms. The easiest way to change your personal attitude toward cultural differences is to become knowledgeable about different cultural practices and respect those who practice them. Respect is necessary to truly display cultural competence.

Organizational culture

underlying, shared values that provide organization members with behavioral norms in the workplace.

As you grow closer to those you work with, your company and its employees will start to develop and cultivate their own culture specific to how the organization functions. **Organizational culture** refers to underlying, shared values that provide employees with behavioral norms in the workplace (Baird, Harrison, & Reeve, 2007; Chatman & Jehn, 1994; Deshpandé & Farley, 1998; Narver & Slater, 1998; Webster & White, 2010). As a leader in the professional world, it is important for you to help foster an environment that not only is sensitive to the individual culture but also allows for new cultures to flourish.

The questions in Figure 11.2 test your basic knowledge of culture. Culture is a socially learned practice and one of the most important aspects of any business. Intercultural communication behaviors are influenced by almost every communication interaction and manifest in all forms of communication in the workplace. Consider this example: Tom is a young clerk at a local bank and has worked for the company for 5 months. In the break room, he overheard Sarah and Katy, two coworkers, making fun of a lesbian couple who also work for the bank. After listening to Sarah and Katy insult their coworkers' attire, makeup, and personal relationship for several minutes, Tom had finally had enough and approached them. "As someone whose sister is a lesbian, I can't say I have ever worked with more close-minded people than you two," Tom said. "Please keep your insults out of the break room from now on, or I'll take this to Human Resources." Sarah and Katy were mortified about the confrontation and refrained from disparaging their coworkers from that point on.

How does this sort of confrontation affect workplace communication and relationships? Since communication is how we bridge the gap between cultures, it is important to respect whomever we are talking to at all times. Once you understand your workplace culture and how it operates with others, it will become easier for you to understand other standpoints. *Standpoint* has to do with one's point of view; we all have a standpoint, and each culture values things differently through the lens of its worldview.

Another important practice in proper intercultural communication is avoiding ethnocentrism. Remember that **ethnocentrism** is a belief in the inherent

Ethnocentrism

placing your own cultural beliefs in a superior position, which leads to a negative judgment of other cultures.

FIGURE 11.2 Putting Your Intercultural Communication Skills in Context

Choose the letter that best represents your answer. You can choose only one answer.

1. Which of the following communication behaviors are influenced by one's culture?
   a. How one communicates with coworkers
   b. How one communicates with direct reports
   c. How one communicates with a supervisor
   d. All the above

2. Which of the following scenarios does NOT involve intercultural communication?
   a. Coworkers of different ages communicating
   b. Coworkers with different religions communicating
   c. Coworkers with different sexual orientations communicating
   d. None of the above

3. It is accurate to say that culture . . .
   a. is socially learned versus innate.
   b. has to do more with race than gender.
   c. rarely influences people's communication patterns.
   d. is relevant only if you belong to a minority group.

4. Which of these is not a form of prejudice?
   a. Ageism
   b. Claustrophobia
   c. Sexism
   d. Homophobia

5. What is a characteristic of effective intercultural communication?
   a. Understanding cross-cultural norms
   b. Ethnocentrism
   c. Close-minded remarks
   d. Speaking only to people you understand

superiority of one's own ethnic group or culture. An ethnocentric organization typically hires from a singular culture or ethnic group and shows favoritism to this group in the interview and promotion processes. In a global workplace, this can have negative repercussions; diversity helps your organization more effectively represent those whom you are serving, and deviating from a diverse market only hinders growth. It is important to curb ethnocentric practices before they can take root in an organization.

Consider this example: Joy has been working in the management training program at a large rental car company for the past few months. An Asian American woman, Joy often experiences disappointment as coworkers, usually white males, are promoted over her. Joy has worked hard to stand out in the training program so that she might be promoted to manager status, and she has received the highest scores on the written test. Still, Joy is routinely passed over for the manager position. When she finally asked her supervisor why she had not been selected, he informed her that he felt that customers would feel more comfortable with an authority they could identify with. He explained, "Your lack of experience with our return client base would make it difficult for you to handle a supervisor position."

Can you understand how this story relates to ethnocentrism and discrimination? How would you react if you were in Joy's position? Always try placing yourself in the cultural other's position when debating whether a situation is discriminatory or not.

Now that you have applied cultural competence and ethnocentrism to the workplace context, let's take a look at the importance of culture in the process of getting the job.

INTERVIEWING THROUGH THE CULTURAL LINES

Interviewing

conversation between two parties that provides a platform for cultural inclusion; provides an opportunity for intimate conversation with individuals who may be from different cultural backgrounds.

Interviewing provides an opportunity for intimate conversation with individuals who may be from different cultural backgrounds. This conversation between two parties provides a platform for cultural inclusion. It is critical to hone your interviewing skills in conjunction with your cultural competence. Remember to ask yourself how another cultural worldview can aid your business in the global economy.

The initial interaction with someone entering the workplace is in many ways the most important. A handshake or warm hello may seem normal to you, but someone with different cultural rituals may not feel comfortable with such extensions of hospitality; certain cultural norms can seem strange or even offensive to people

When interviewing, it is important to be sensitive to other cultures and to know what questions are appropriate or inappropriate to ask.

© AshTproductions/Shutterstock.com

Self-Assessment: Assessing Your Tendency for Ethnocentrism

4	**3**	**2**	**1**
strongly agree	moderately agree	moderately disagree	strongly disagree

	4	3	2	1
1. I believe my culture has the best lifestyles.	4	3	2	1
2. My culture is advanced in comparison with other cultures.	4	3	2	1
3. My culture provides the best opportunity for its members to achieve their goals.	4	3	2	1
4. My cultural group has the most colorful language and vocabulary.	4	3	2	1
5. My culture has a rich history and traditions.	4	3	2	1
6. My culture's language is the easiest to understand.	4	3	2	1
7. People who come to my country should learn our language.	4	3	2	1

Scoring: Add up your scores. The higher the score, the more ethnocentric you are.

Source: Ting-Toomey and Chung (2005).

outside that culture. Have you ever analyzed your handshake? Think about handshake experiences where you felt as though your hand was being crushed or the other person was being too delicate or timid. Handshakes are the tip of the iceberg when it comes to understanding how a greeting can affect cultural norms. When interacting in an intercultural environment, how could a handshake be viewed differently by those with an Eastern background? After you recognize cultural differences between you and the interviewee, it is important to form a network of similarities that help you connect relationally. Alongside the cultural norms, there are many questions you should avoid in the interview process. See Figure 11.3 for a list of such questions. Why is it important to avoid these questions? As you review the list, reflect on how some of them could be offensive to people based on their backgrounds.

FIGURE 11.3 Illegal Job Interview Questions and Legal Alternatives

Nationality

What you can't ask: Are you a U.S. citizen?
What to ask instead: Are you authorized to work in the United States?

What you can't ask: What is your native tongue?
What to ask instead: What languages do you read, speak, or write fluently?

What you can't ask: How long have you lived here?
What to ask instead: What is your current address and phone number? Do you have any alternative locations where you can be reached?

Religion

What you can't ask: What religion do you practice?
What to ask instead: What days are you available to work?

What you can't ask: Which religious holidays do you observe?
What to ask instead: Are you able to work with our required schedule?

What you can't ask: Do you belong to a club or social organization?
What to ask instead: Are you a member of a professional or trade group that is relevant to our industry?

Marital and Family Status

What you can't ask: Is this your maiden name?
What to ask instead: Have you worked or earned a degree under another name?

What you can't ask: Is this your maiden name?
What to ask instead: Have you worked or earned a degree under another name?

What you can't ask: Do you have or plan to have children?
What to ask instead: Are you available to work overtime on occasion? Can you travel?

What you can't ask: Can you get a babysitter on short notice for overtime or travel?
What to ask instead: You'll be required to travel and work overtime on short notice. Is this a problem for you?

What you can't ask: Do you have kids?
What to ask instead: What is your experience with "x" age group?

What you can't ask: Who is your closest relative to notify in case of an emergency?
What to ask instead: In case of emergency, who should we notify?

What you can't ask: What do your parents do for a living?
What to ask instead: Tell me how you became interested in the "x" industry.

Age *What you can't ask:* How old are you? *What to ask instead:* Are you over the age of 18? *What you can't ask:* How much longer do you plan to work before you retire? *What to ask instead:* What are your long-term career goals? **Gender** *What you can't ask:* We've always had a man/woman do this job. How do you think you will stack up? *What to ask instead:* What do you have to offer our company? *What you can't ask:* How do you feel about supervising men/women? *What to ask instead:* Tell me about your previous experience managing teams. *What you can't ask:* What do you think of interoffice dating? *What to ask instead:* Have you ever been disciplined for your behavior at work? **Health and Physical Abilities** *What you can't ask:* Do you smoke or drink? *What to ask instead:* In the past, have you been disciplined for violating company policies forbidding the use of alcohol or tobacco products? *What you can't ask:* Do you take drugs? *What to ask instead:* Do you use illegal drugs?	**Marital and Family Status (continued)** *What you can't ask:* If you get pregnant, will you continue to work, and will you come back after maternity leave? *What to ask instead:* What are your long-term career goals? *What you can't ask:* How tall are you? *What to ask instead:* Are you able to reach items on a shelf that's 5 feet tall? *What you can't ask:* How much do you weigh? *What to ask instead:* Are you able to lift boxes weighing up to 50 pounds? *What you can't ask:* How many sick days did you take last year? *What to ask instead:* How many days of work did you miss last year? *What you can't ask:* Do you have any disabilities? *What to ask instead:* Are you able to perform the specific duties of this position? *What you can't ask:* Have you had any recent or past illnesses or operations? *What to ask instead:* Are you able to perform the essential functions of this job with or without reasonable accommodations?

DISCRIMINATION IN THE WORKPLACE

Discrimination is prejudicial treatment of an individual based on his or her actual or perceived membership in a certain group, based on age, ethnicity, gender/sex, national origin, sexual orientation, religion, or other characteristics. Discrimination can divide or even destroy a workplace. Since organizations cannot control all the individual interactions that may be perceived as discriminatory, it is important for them to put in place practices to mitigate the harmful effects of discriminatory

> **Discrimination**
> the verbal and nonverbal communication behaviors that foster prejudiced attitudes, including the act of excluding people from or denying them access to products, rights, and services based on race, gender, religion, age, sexual identity, or disability.

encounters (Triana et al., 2010). The individual-to-individual interactions that occur in the workplace form the foundation for how an organization functions. It is important for you, as a leader and coworker in the workplace, to focus on understanding and avoiding instances of discrimination. Although employment discrimination is illegal, it still happens in the United States. Discriminatory behaviors are painful, prejudicial attitudes that can create pain and strife in the workplace. These conflicts can lead to high turnover and low productivity (King, 1995). Have you ever felt left out or held back because of your differences? The workplace can be a political battlefield that either burns with discrimination or advocates acceptance. It is important to realize these pitfalls and avoid them.

Because we are all products of our own belief systems, regulations have been put into place to curtail instances of discrimination. But even with these regulations, many women are still limited by a glass ceiling, minorities are still judged by skin tone and facial features, and individuals with disabilities are still overlooked for positions because certain companies are unwilling to accommodate them. As a future member and leader of the business world, it falls to you to encourage diversity in the workplace. As you will find out, increasing diversity benefits not only you but also the overall health of most companies.

Up until the implementation of EEO/AA regulations, little to no effort was made to correct these discriminatory problems. In the current workforce, however, many guidelines are in place to combat workplace discrimination, and the initial interview has a significant role in curtailing discriminatory practices. In the interviewing process, it is important to avoid questions that refer to someone being inferior or inadequate for a job due to nationality/race, gender, sexuality, disability, or family status. Additionally, with coworkers, it is important to continue to be sensitive to cultural differences and avoid playing power games that lead to practices such as workplace bullying. Emphasizing someone's differences or disadvantages in the workplace can be considered bullying, which will be discussed later in this chapter. Comments you find humorous may cut the person on the receiving end. As a leader in your organization, it is important to lead by example. Knowing the EEO/AA laws associated with nationality/race, gender, age, disabilities, family status, and sexual orientation will lead to cultural competence. The next five sections discuss some discrimination pitfalls to avoid.

Nationality/Race

Dealing with differences in race and nationality is both critical and delicate. It is important to be aware of any history of discrimination in the dominant culture and the workplace; this means all nationalities should be treated with respect and dignity.

© alejandro dans neergaard/Shutterstock.com

It is vital that you, as a business professional, know the EEO/AA laws associated with potential workplace discrimination.

Race is a generalized categorization of people based on physical characteristics such as skin color, dimensions of the face, and hair texture and color. **Nationality** deals specifically with a person's place of origin or national affiliation through birth or naturalization. Discrimination concerning nationality and race is illegal under Title VI of the Civil Rights Act of 1964. An employer who discriminates against a job applicant or employee because of race, color, or national origin will bring serious consequences on the organization. Title VI also applies to a person treated poorly because of his or her relationship—by marriage or association with a person, organization, or group—to a person of a certain race, color, or national origin.

Consider Lydia's story: Lydia is a Caucasian female working for a Fortune 500 company. At the company's fundraising gala, Lydia introduced her husband to everyone. Her husband, an African American, greeted everyone pleasantly and held conversations with many people, including the partners of the company. The next Monday, Lydia's boss asked her to join him in his office. He told her that she had been removed from a special project involving a presentation to major company stockholders. When she asked why, her boss replied, "The partners of the corporation need to protect the image of the company." Lydia was unsure how this was relevant, because she was a hard worker who had been successful with all her assignments. Her boss replied, "We have conservative partners who do not agree with your alternative lifestyle." When Lydia asked what was alternative about

Race

a generalized categorization of people based on physical characteristics such as skin color, dimensions of the face, and hair texture and color.

Nationality

a person's place of origin or national affiliation through birth or naturalization.

her lifestyle, her boss asked her, "Do you have children with him?" Lydia left the company shortly thereafter and filed a legal suit against the company.

Racism has no place in a professional environment and can have drastic legal and financial consequences for businesses and individuals who engage in racial prejudice.

ETHICAL CONNECTION

Daniel recently began interviewing candidates for an opening in the accounting department at his company. As part of his interviewing process, Daniel made sure to ask every candidate about his or her marriage status and family life, citing extended travel requirements that might interfere with a traditional family setting. In addition to the extended travel, Daniel also inquired about age and health disabilities that might keep the candidates from performing their expected functions. After finally picking a candidate that met all his requirements, Daniel was surprised to learn that his boss had overruled his decision and hired another person, also relieving Daniel of his hiring duties. Daniel was ordered to go to an EEO seminar as a result of his actions.

Questions to consider:

1. What laws did Daniel break when asking certain questions during his interviews?
2. Why is it important to avoid specific subjects when hiring a new employee?
3. What is the purpose of EEO laws? What behaviors were they designed to curtail?
4. If you were an interviewee in this situation, how would you react to Daniel's questions?

Gender

Gender discrimination deals with unequal pay or job discrimination based on one's gender. Gender discrimination has historically been attributed to oppression of women. Currently, however, discrimination can be related to perceived gender roles (regardless of sex) and could also include how gender is performed or represented. Gender roles have transformed significantly throughout recent generations and have dramatically affected the power structure of the workplace. When anyone assigns ability to someone's gender and enforces unequal pay or hinders job opportunities in the workplace, an imbalance forms. For instance, Paul and Sally are working for a delivery company as drivers. Both have worked for the company for about a year. Their boss decides to pay Paul $2.00 more an hour because he believes Paul can lift heavier boxes and make more deliveries than Sally can. Why is this discrimination? The boss is showing gender favoritism via unequal pay, and numerous federal and state laws prohibit discrimination on the basis of sex.

It is important to note that gender discrimination does not rely exclusively on one's sex; it also encompasses examples where men are seen as "too feminine" or women as "too masculine." This type of gender discrimination is much more subtle but no less damaging in the workplace. As you navigate through your professional career, be sensitive to differences in personality and avoid harmful stereotyping regarding someone's gender.

Sexual Orientation

Sexual orientation discrimination refers to harassment or differential treatment based on someone's perceived or actual gay, lesbian, bisexual, or heterosexual orientation. Note that simple perceptions of sexuality, whether true or not, can lead to issues of sexual discrimination. In the United States, heteronormative sexual behavior dominates the business environment. Recall that **heteronormativity** is a cultural belief system that assumes that heterosexuality is the norm. "The equation 'heterosexual experience = human experience' renders all other forms of human sexual expression pathological, deviant, invisible, unintelligible, or written out of existence" (Yep, 2002, p. 167). When the workplace culture reflects a heteronormative attitude, those who do not fit into this norm are restricted from reaching a status of power and privilege. This creates friction and an unbalanced work environment. Called a heteronormative/heterosexual binary, this imbalance produces problems in organizational interactions, relationship building, and workplace friendships. Heteronormative structures can be reproduced by what is called subtle discrimination in the workplace. This includes ambiguous discrimination, which is a less visible form of discrimination that involves treating people differently based on perceived "accepted" gender behaviors. This less-visible treatment often passes under the radar of the EEO/AA guidelines.

Heteronormativity
a culture or belief system that assumes heterosexuality is the norm.

Sexual discrimination has gained more public attention in recent years and has become a sensitive issue for business professionals in the workplace.

Age

Age is another factor that can lead to discrimination. With the recent recession, businesses have been pinching every penny they can, and age discrimination has become a significant issue. Some businesses have attempted to save money by firing or laying off employees who have seniority and higher pay scales and replacing them with younger, cheaper workers.

Consider this example: Curtis is 55 years old and has been working as a supervisor for a shoe company for 15 years. He worked his way up from minimum wage to $35 an hour. Curtis is a hard worker and was surprised to learn the company was eliminating his position. After a meeting with his boss, Curtis chose "voluntary retirement due to positions being cut in the company." About 3 weeks later, Curtis heard that the same company had just hired a new person for his position. This led Curtis to believe that he had been discriminated against because the company simply did not want to continue paying him what he had earned through his years of service. Curtis also feared that he was discriminated against because he could no longer lift heavy things in the workplace and had to delegate certain jobs to younger employees.

In the above example, do you believe Curtis was the victim of age discrimination? The Age Discrimination in Employment Act (ADEA) works to prohibit employers from discriminating against employees and applicants 40 years of age and older. The Older Workers' Benefit Protection Act is another federal law prohibiting age discrimination in employment; this act makes it illegal for employers to use an employee's age as a basis for discrimination in benefits and retirement. ADEA specifically prohibits employers from discriminating on the basis of age at any stage of the employment process—including application, interview, hiring, promotion, and termination.

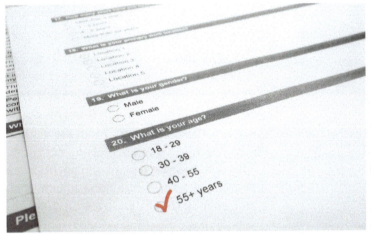

People with Disabilities

When interacting in a diverse workplace, you will need to know how to work with and include people with disabilities. Historically, society has tended to isolate and segregate individuals with disabilities (Longmore & Umansky, 2001). Some of you may have a disability or know someone who has one. In 1990, Congress passed the Americans with Disabilities Act. The purpose of this act is to prevent discrimination against people with disabilities in the workforce (as well as in most businesses and other places open to the public) by requiring that "reasonable accommodations" be made for many types of disability. Looking beyond reasonable accommodations, learn to keep open communication with everyone, including those who live with disabilities. What are some negative stereotypes regarding people with disabilities? Have you ever worked with someone who has a disability? As you encounter fellow students or coworkers with disabilities, try to engage in communication practices that are accommodating but not condescending.

Age discrimination can have severe consequences for older workers transitioning in the workforce.

IN YOUR *life*

Have you ever been discriminated against based on your age, either because you were too young or too old? How would you approach a situation where your age kept you from landing a desired job?

Activists participate in the first-ever New York City Disability Pride Parade in 2015.

Family Status

Multiple challenges of discrimination and social barriers arise for single parents, sibling guardians, and many others in different family situations. Family is an aspect of home that shouldn't be discussed in the interview process; you do not need to consider family status in deciding employment. As people join your employment team, you will have an opportunity to learn more about their family status as they share more about themselves in the workplace. Each workplace should have basic rules regarding questions about family status. A person's family status has no reflection on what type of worker he or she is; while many individuals may have to utilize sick time or vacation time to care for a loved one, their right to do so is protected by law. As with any challenge toward eliminating discrimination, it is important for the employer to be sensitive to employees' needs.

Take Jane, for example. Jane is a single mother of a 2-year-old and a 5-year-old. She has kept her marital status private from her company since she began 4 months ago. She has proved to be a positive team player and a good employee. One day, she received an emergency call from her children's day care. Jane was assisting her boss at the time, and her boss said she was not allowed to leave. Faced with a difficult dilemma, Jane chose to check on her children because there was no one else to address the emergency. The next day, Jane was reprimanded for her absence and informed that she would be excluded from the management training program that quarter.

How could the employer have been more sensitive to Jane's situation? In an ideal work environment, when Jane needed to leave for an emergency, the employer would have discussed why she needed to leave and made appropriate arrangements to complete the job in her absence. Many of you will find yourselves in a situation like Jane's or her boss's in your career. It is important for you to learn how to navigate these situations effectively while respecting the rights of your coworkers and employees.

Discrimination laws such as EEO/AA are important to understand because they create the basic ground rules of any professional environment. Beyond simply understanding the laws, it is important to use professional discretion when dealing with difficulties that may be unfamiliar to you.

Hostile work environment

when an employee experiences workplace harassment and fears going to work because of an offensive, intimidating, or oppressive atmosphere.

Another important aspect of creating a healthy work environment requires employers to ensure the safety and security of their employees. When an employee experiences workplace harassment and fears going to work because of an offensive, intimidating, or oppressive atmosphere, this is known as a **hostile work environment**. Hostile work environments can discourage employees from voicing their opinions and lead to instances of workplace bullying. It is important for employers to provide appropriate channels for employees to voice their grievances about other workers without fear of reprisal. This helps ensure a fair and accommodating work environment that allows the free exchange of diverse opinions and viewpoints.

Now that we have reviewed discrimination laws, let's see how communicative approaches in the workplace can provide either a productive or a hostile work environment.

POWER IN THE WORKPLACE

The previous sections addressed discrimination; now let's look at how prejudice, along with a passion for power, can lead to workplace bullying. **Workplace bullying** is commonly defined as a repetitive pattern of mistreatment in which the enacted behaviors are perceived by targets as an intentional effort to harm, control, or drive them from the workplace. Workplace bullying is generally emotional and psychological, and can hinder a person's performance or drive him or her out of the company entirely (Lutgen-Sandvik & McDermott, 2011). Workplace bullying takes many different forms:

- **Verbal bullying:** Slandering, ridiculing, or maligning a person or his or her family; persistent name calling that is hurtful, insulting, or humiliating; making a person the butt of jokes; abusive and offensive remarks
- **Physical bullying:** Pushing, shoving, kicking, poking, tripping, assault or threat of physical assault, or damage to a person's work area or property
- **Gesture bullying:** Nonverbal, threatening gestures; glances that convey threatening messages
- **Exclusion:** Socially or physically excluding or disregarding a person in work-related activities
- **Cyber-bullying:** Use of communications technology to make deliberate and hostile attempts to hurt, upset, or embarrass a person; harassing and abusive e-mails or phone calls; posting harassing or embarrassing comments on social networking sites; hacking into other people's accounts and sending viruses

The workplace is an environment where individuals gain and lose power daily. Many people refer to work as a "rat race," where everyone is searching for success and monetary gain. With this ever-present demand for success in the workplace, many people abuse or manipulate workplace relationships for their own professional gain.

These actions can create a rift in productive work relationships and lead to hostile work environments. Such environments are created through the use of aggressive communication and intimidation. Consider the following example about Lee.

Workplace bullying
a repetitive pattern of mistreatment in which the enacted behaviors are perceived by targets as an intentional effort to harm, control, or drive them from the workplace.

Verbal bullying
slandering, ridiculing, or maligning a person or his or her family; persistent name calling that is hurtful, insulting, or humiliating; making a person the butt of jokes; abusive and offensive remarks.

Physical bullying
pushing, shoving, kicking, poking, tripping, assault or threat of physical assault, or damage to a person's work area or property.

Gesture bullying
nonverbal, threatening gestures; glances that convey threatening messages

Exclusion
socially or physically excluding or disregarding a person in work-related activities.

Cyber-bullying
use of communications technology to make deliberate and hostile attempts to hurt, upset, or embarrass a person; harassing and abusive e-mails or phone calls; posting harassing or embarrassing comments on social networking sites; hacking into other people's accounts and sending viruses.

Lee was on the fast track to success. After graduating at the top of her class, she quickly entered the professional workplace. Landing her first job as a secretary for a local marketing firm, she thought she would work her way up the ladder quickly. Each day, however, Lee's boss would make a hurtful comment about the way she dressed or how her hair looked. Lee lost confidence because she felt that her work efforts were overshadowed by her appearance. In an attempt to look more professional, Lee began to straighten her hair and wear different clothing that seemed to fit the company culture. But her boss would still find things to "tease" her about. One day, Lee needed to take a break. Her boss—in a loud, boisterous voice—told her to get back in her place, directing Lee back to her desk. Lee was shocked and overwhelmed by her boss's aggressive tone. Each day, this tone grew harsher. Lee eventually resigned from her position because she didn't think she could ever escape the harassment. How is this story connected to workplace bullying?

Emotional tyranny

the use of emotion to be destructive, controlling, unjust, and even cruel. This form of tyranny is ascribed not only to people who already have power but also to people who use this tactic to gain power.

These types of workplace bullying are closely related to the idea of workplace tyranny or, more specifically, abuse of authority. **Emotional tyranny** is the use of emotion to be destructive, controlling, unjust, and even cruel. This form of tyranny is ascribed not only to people who have power but also to people who use this tactic to increase their power. Organizations can become hotbeds for emotional anguish, and social interactions can evoke profound feelings of humiliation, powerlessness, rage, and despair (Lutgen-Sandvik & Sypher, 2009). It is important not only to understand the laws surrounding workplace discrimination but also to treat all members of the organization (regardless of their cultural background) with respect.

Finding a healthy work/life balance is key to your success as a business professional. "Within this changing employment context, workers are challenged in their efforts to satisfactorily manage the relationship between work and life" (Wieland, 2011). In a diverse workplace, you will find many unique people with different priorities and responsibilities. When work/life imbalances occur, they can bring major power/authority struggles into the workplace. Take Kenny's story for example.

Kenny's career was a consuming aspect of his life. For 10 years, he had been CEO of a theater company. He lived by the motto, "The show must go on." With early mornings and late nights spent in the theater, he had very little time for his family. They would often drop in to say hello and tried to keep the relationship strong, but Kenny steadily allowed his work to dominate more and more of his life. After years of neglect, Kenny's wife decided she wanted a divorce. Kenny fell into a deep depression, which was evident in his lack of enthusiasm at work. Kenny could not understand how being a hard worker had driven his family away. He began to engage in more and more aggressive communication with his employees, lashing out in anger at minor details he had previously handled with poise and understanding.

He began to behave negatively toward many of the women in the company. What once ran as a well-oiled machine had become a hostile work environment.

What went wrong in Kenny's story? Why did his demanding work life end up negatively affecting both his family and career? What happened in Kenny's story is a prime example of careerism. **Careerism** is devotion to a successful career, often at the expense of one's integrity, personal life, and ethics. Performance-enhancing drugs, shady ethical dealings, and outright plagiarism are extreme examples of unhealthy career practices, but they are by no means the only negative aspects of having a disproportionate work/life balance. The three spheres of life (i.e., personal, work, and public) are represented in Figure 11.4. The first image portrays a healthy balance among the spheres. The second image shows the consequences of careerism. Careerism provides a platform for corporate colonization to take place.

Careerism
devotion to building and maintaining a successful career, often at the expense of one's integrity, personal life, and ethics.

The presence of corporate culture is also a significant factor in the professional world. The ethical implications of **corporate colonization** have to do with an organization's influence on the "formation or deformation" of human character. This phenomenon deals with cultural domination by corporate organizations in a professional and social setting. So how does corporate colonization affect workplace culture, as well as the community the organization serves? It can be attributed to the politics of the personal—the political process by which meaning, identities, and experience are formed (Littlejohn & Foss, 2009). In 2001, Paige P. Edley argued that technology was fostering corporate colonization in the lives of employed mothers. Simply put, professional women were allowed to telecommute and work flexible schedules, with the goal of making their lives easier. Women could choose when and where to work, but they were also expected to increase their professional productivity levels.

FIGURE 11.4

© Kendall Hunt Publishing Co.

Corporate colonization
an organization's influence on the "formation or deformation" of human character; the encroachment of work life on one's private and social activities.

Fast-forward to the present. With the advent of highly portable technology such as the iPad, escaping work has become very difficult. We constantly check e-mails on our smartphones and give out our personal numbers as the easiest method of contact. Wi-

Fi hotspots have become the norm in many coffee shops, restaurants, and public areas, making work even more accessible. In many ways, these handy tools make production in the workplace easier, but when it comes to identity and work/life balance, where do we draw the line? In an age of exponential technological advancement and corporate colonization, corporations are able to shape decision-making processes and ways of life more powerfully than in the past. Personal identity is now more often derived from the workplace (Littlejohn & Foss, 2009). This is true for those who work within the corporation as well as for those in the community it serves.

Corporate colonization has affected home life by creating tension between roles performed at work and those performed at home. Without thought or intention, workers automatically give the workplace the best part of their day.

Are workers in the current economy further removed from their communities, forced to spend most of their time at work with coworkers rather than home with their families? This is not necessarily a terrible phenomenon; when practiced in moderation, the drive for success is still strong within many Americans. This passion is reflected in family planning—when to have children, how to educate them, and in what communities to raise them. Corporate colonization has played a major role in the modern family, as well as in the diversity of neighborhoods. When a corporation makes the effort to foster a more diverse workplace, the communities it serves will also be more diverse. How is this beneficial for the organization? What does this mean for the employees?

WHAT YOU'VE LEARNED

From reading this chapter, you overviewed diversity and its relation to workplace and professional contexts. You began by learning to define diversity—the representation of various differences in a shared space. You then learned about the importance of cultural competence in the workplace, and you overviewed how discrimination can be related to your study of intercultural communication. Next, you were shown how cultural competence applies to the requirements of professional excellence in the workplace. Finally, you learned how power in the workplace can be both good and bad; you learned how power can lead to a hostile work environment, discrimination, and workplace bullying. As you finish your study of intercultural communication, think about the importance of diversity in both your current and future work environments. Why is diversity important, and how can you help to make sure your own workplace fosters an environment that both encourages and strives for diversity?

REVIEW

1. The piece of legislation that protects the rights of applicants and employees by monitoring to make sure that promotions, benefits, classifications, and referrals are not withheld due to discrimination associated with color, race, religion, sex, or national origin is called the _____.

2. _____ is a set of public policies and initiatives designed to help reverse and eliminate past and present discrimination based on race, color, region, sex, or national origin.

3. The underlying, shared values that provide employees with behavioral norms in the workplace are referred to as _____.

4. _____ is prejudicial treatment of an individual based on his or her actual or perceived membership in a certain group, based on age, ethnicity, gender/sex, national origin, sexual orientation, religion, or other characteristics.

5. _____ deals specifically with a person's place of origin or national affiliation through birth or naturalization, whereas _____ is a generalized categorization of people based on physical characteristics.

6. What is *heteronormativity*?

7. Which piece of legislation works to prohibit employers from discriminating against employees and applicants 40 years of age and older?

8. List some different types of workplace bullying.

9. What is *emotional tyranny*?

10. How has highly portable technology, such as the iPad, impacted *corporate colonization*?

Review answers are found on the accompanying website.

REFLECT

1. You are at work when you overhear two of your managers saying they have no plans to promote your coworker, Heather, because she's a woman and "women can't help lead a professional organization." Which law are your

managers violating, and what are some potential actions you could take to make sure Heather's rights do not continue to be violated?

2. Think of a job you currently have or have had in the past. How would you describe its *organizational culture*? What were some of the workplace's behavioral norms? Did it foster a sensitive and inclusive environment?

3. Susan enjoys getting to know her coworkers, and she often uses pictures her coworkers put on their desks of their families to start conversations with them. She notices one of her coworkers, Jacob, has a wedding ring, but he doesn't have any photos of himself and his spouse in his office. One day, Susan approaches Jacob and asks him what his wife's name is. Jacob immediately looks uncomfortable. Why do you think Jacob may have looked uncomfortable? Using the terminology from the text, discuss what was problematic about Susan's question.

4. Karen and Elise are coworkers. One day, Elise wears a dress that Karen doesn't like. Karen takes a picture of Elise without her knowing, and she later posts it to Facebook with the following caption: "This is what I had to look at all day—my coworkers have no sense of style!" Which type of *workplace bullying* is Karen participating in? Pretend you work with Karen and Elise; how might you help to stop Karen's bullying of Elise?

5. Think about all the issues surrounding diversity in the workplace. What are the pros and cons of diversity in the workplace? How does diversity shape a successful work environment?

KEY TERMS

diversity, 306
The Equal Employment Act, 307
Affirmative Action, 307
worldview, 308
culture shock, 308
cultural diversity awareness, 308
globalization, 309
cultural competence, 312
organizational culture, 312
ethnocentrism, 313
interviewing, 314
discrimination, 317
race, 319

nationality, 319
heteronormativity, 321
hostile work environment, 324
workplace bullying, 325
verbal bullying, 325
physical bullying, 325
gesture bullying, 325
exclusion, 325
cyber-bullying, 325
emotional tyranny, 326
careerism, 327
corporate colonization, 327

glossary

Ability EQ – assumes that emotions can be useful tools in understanding the meaning of a situation.

Abstract conceptualization – learning style that reveals a preference for solitary investigation and working alone rather than in groups.

Accommodating – represents the combination of active experimentation (AE) and concrete experience (CE), which implies preferences for doing and feeling.

Accommodation – a conflict style that is on the low end of concern for self but on the high end of concern for other; accommodation implies that one shows little or no assertiveness, but, rather, gives in to the other party.

Acculturation - the progression through which individuals adapt their own cultural identities and norms to fit into another culture, which is often the dominant or mainstream culture of a region or country.

Achievement - the result of individual effort or merit; examples include running a financially successful business, earning a college degree, and receiving a promotion in any professional environment.

Active experimentation (AE) – learning style where individuals like to try different solutions to see which one works best.

Actuality – the distinction we make between characteristics we possess and those we aspire to have.

Adapters – gestures we use to release tension or fulfill some other emotional need.

Adaptation – a long-term response or process that prompts someone to evolve to fit into an environment.

Adjustment – a short-term state of reducing an uncertainty to meet a more immediate need.

Affect displays – nonverbal gestures, postures, and facial expressions that communicate emotions.

Affirmative Action - a set of public policies and initiatives designed to help reverse and eliminate past and present discrimination based on race, color, region, sex, or national origin.

Agency - the ability to generate change in a culture's thoughts, beliefs, and actions, and to communicate interculturally with others while simultaneously being communicated to by them.

Analogic code - represents things through likeness or similarity.

Androgyny – a blend of both feminine and masculine traits.

Anticipatory socialization – forming expectations of what it is like to be a member of the group.

Ascribed identity – one given or assigned by others.

Ascription – conditions at birth, such as family background, race, sex, and place of birth.

Assimilating – learning style that puts ideas above people and relationships; good at working with abstract concepts; assimilators help the group organize and present information in a clear format.

Assimilation - the process of adaptation that allows one to fit into or conform in some way to a group or culture.

Authority – the "testimonial" form of persuasion, whereby a person is persuaded by a famous or well-respected person's endorsement.

Automated structure - the view that digital technology serves as the structure for the intercultural experience. In this sense, mass interpersonal communication on Facebook takes place through the automation of computer technology, such as the delivery of e-mail, requests, and links promoting ideas or events.

Autonomy – freedom.

Avoidance – also called withdrawal; a conflict style that reflects a low concern for both the self and the other person's goals.

Avowed identity – one you claim for yourself.

Biomedical model – states that doctors operate much like mechanics and scientists, looking for physical signs and symptoms of what is wrong. Once the problem is identified, physical means are used to heal the illness or injury or address the medical issue.

Biopsychosocial model – a holistic approach that states that ill health is caused by many physical, social, and environmental factors. Also, the health of the entire person is considered, not just the physical body.

Body weight – perception varies from culture to culture.

Bourgeoisie – one of the two major social classes related to economy and production; these owned the means of production.

Capital - a person's, family's, or business's accumulated goods and their overall value.

Careerism - devotion to building and maintaining a successful career, often at the expense of one's integrity, personal life, and ethics.

Categorization – helps an individual decide which characteristics represent the group of which he or she is a member.

Centrality – the extent to which a self-aspect is crucial or central to how we describe ourselves.

Certainty-uncertainty dialectic – the balance between predictability and spontaneity.

Chronemics - the study of the ways people use time to structure interactions.

Co-cultural communication - refers to interactions between underrepresented and dominant group members.

Codes of ethics - all different sets of principles that people hold themselves to or are held to by multiple organizations or groups.

Coherence – refers to something that appears to hold together and make sense.

Collaboration – the conflict style that is on the high end of concern both for self and the other; both parties reach a mutually agreeable solution that satisfies both sides completely; most desirable but difficult to enact.

Collectivism – the desire for connection and conformity with others.

Commitment and consistency - a principle of influence that refers to feeling obligated to act in ways that are reliable and constant.

Communal frame – reflected in identity shared with members of the group to which one belongs.

Communication - the collaborative process of using messages to create and participate in social reality and to achieve goals. The most important aspects of our lives—our individual identities, relationships, organizations, communities, and ideas—are accomplished through communication.

Communication accommodation theory - explains the extent to which a person in conversation *converges* with or *diverges* from the other person's verbal and nonverbal behavior, especially to accommodate perceived differences.

Communication activism - direct energetic action in support of needed social change for individuals, groups, organizations, and communities.

Communication differences tradition – presents separate and distinct conflict behaviors attributed to men and women.

Communication predicament of aging model – explains how age identity and perceptions of older adults can lead to communicated stereotypes.

Communication theory of identity - illustrates how individuals make assumptions about each other based on their backgrounds, and helps explain how misunderstandings occur in the medical context. Identity is often communicated through *identity salience* and *identity intensity*

Competition – a conflict style that reflects a high level of concern for the self's goals while ignoring the goals of the other; individuals who use this style likely want to "defeat" the other person or force him or her to acquiesce.

Compromise – a conflict style that assumes that both parties give and take a little in reaching their goals, which represents a moderate level of concern both for self and the other.

Compromise style – to handle power imbalances, each partner gives and takes to bring power in the relationship back to equilibrium.

Concern for other – having a certain level of consideration for what the other person wants from the conflict.

Concern for self – showing a level of concern for one's own goals and desired outcomes.

Concrete experience (CE)– learning style that exhibits a preference for doing and participating.

Conflict – an expressed struggle that occurs when diverse identities converge and complete agreement is not always possible. Characteristics of conflict include perceived incompatible goals and scarce resources.

Confrontational model – values forceful pursuit of individual goals, open engagement in conflict, and expression of emotions during conflict.

Connection – power of communication to link and relate you to people, groups, communities, social institutions, and cultures.

Consensus style – to resolve power issues by negotiation and mutual agreement.

Constitutive rules - what counts as what and how our messages and behavior can be interpreted (i.e., texting at dinner can be considered "rude").

Contact cultures – cultures that are characterized by frequent touching.

Contact Hypothesis – contact in itself is not necessarily a means of bringing about perception change among groups in conflict, which can be a pre-requisite to relationship building.

Contamination – a type of intrusion in which someone's territory is marked with noise or pollution.

Content - the actual information contained in a spoken or written message.

Convergence – refers to the way people use symbols to come together, overlap on ideas, or express common ground.

Convergent – learning style that solves problems, gravitates toward technical tasks, and is less concerned with relationships. Convergent learners can convert ideas and theories into practical solutions and they like to experiment with new ideas.

Coordinated management of meaning theory - focuses on how we coordinate our actions with others to make and manage meaning.

Coordination – the establishment of rules that help guide people through the communication interaction.

Core – central, most important aspect.

Corporate colonization - an organization's influence on the "formation or deformation" of human character; the encroachment of work life on one's private and social activities.

Crisis – an unlikely event—natural or human-made—that can lead to uncertainty and threaten the safety and security of individuals and organizations

Cultural capital - specialized skills and knowledge, including linguistic and cultural competencies passed down through family or personal experiences in social institutions.

Cultural competence - the ability to interact effectively with people of different cultural or ethnic backgrounds.

Cultural diversity awareness – being aware of the diversity present in any working or social environment.

Cultural identity - a dynamic production in and through intercultural contact and interaction with a cultural other.

Cultural-Individual dialectic – the extent to which one communicates in ways that stand in opposition to a person's culture, especially if that person's wishes are different from what her or his culture might prescribe.

Cultural influences - ways of understanding and interpreting the world that arise from the unique features of various social groups.

Cultural rituals - practices, behaviors, celebrations, and traditions common to people, organizations, and institutions.

Cultural studies theory - argues that media are powerful tools of the elite and serve to keep powerful people in control.

Culture - the set of shared attitudes, values, goals, and practices that characterizes an institution, organization, or group. The way you talk, behave, dress, and think have all been shaped by the way others have socialized you into various cultural groups.

Culture shock - a state of confusion, anxiety, stress, or loss felt when one encounters a culture that has little in common with one's own.

Curandero – a neighborhood healer who utilizes what some might call "folk medicine," often relying on religious tradition and natural remedies.

Currency – a perceptual concept that refers to how we see certain aspects fitting in time.

Cyber bullying - Use of communications technology to make deliberate and hostile attempts to hurt, upset, or embarrass a person; harassing and abusive e-mails or phone calls; posting harassing or embarrassing comments on social networking sites; hacking into other people's accounts and sending viruses.

Deculturation – occurs when we unlearn certain aspects of our cultures to fit into a new one.

Dedication – committing to do what is right no matter the situation.

Dialogical perspectives - those that deal with sense making that occurs through cognition and communication.

Dialogue - a conversation between two or more people.

Differences-Similarities dialectic – acknowledges that relational partners share both similarities and differences but that the key is not to let the differences overshadow the similarities.

Digital code - represents things through the use of symbols.

Digital divide- economic inequality between groups based on the access to information and new media.

Discrimination - the verbal and nonverbal communication behaviors that foster prejudiced attitudes, including the act of excluding people from or denying them access to products, rights, and services based on race, gender, religion, age, sexual identity, or disability.

Disequilibrium – a state of imbalance or disorder.

Display rules – prescriptions for what kinds and amounts of emotional expression are appropriate.

Distinguish – the ability to decide what's right and wrong.

Divergence – occurs when a person acts differently from the other, such as facing one's body away when the other person is trying to face forward.

Divergent – learning style where one can look at one issue from multiple perspectives, willing to gather outside information for the group. Divergents are sensitive, good at brainstorming and like to work in groups, and to receive feedback.

Diversity - a term used to describe the unique differences among people. These differences are based on a variety of factors such as ethnicity, race, heritage, religion, gender, sexual identity, age, social class, and the like.

Duration – how long a touch lasts.

Dyadic conflict – conflict that occurs between two people.

Dysfunctional system – a system in which an individual's needs are not met.

Eastern medicine – describes disease as a signal that the body is out of balance and it should be viewed as a reminder to slow down and take better care of ourselves.

Economic capital - a person's total financial assets.

Economic imperative – associated with the economic needs of all nations in matters of trade relations, international business ventures, and the like.

Ectomorphs – thin and tall people, without much muscle, which makes them look fragile.

Effective decision-making theory – focuses on self-construals as a way to explain cultural differences.

Electronic aggression - a form of aggressive communication in which people interact on topics filled with emotionality and aggression.

Electronic tradition - also referred to as the Electronic Age or electronic media, refers to media that require users to make use of electronics to access content.

E-mail dialogues - exchanges of messages about a particular topic using e-mail, blog space, and other electronic tools to encourage participation that will ideally lead to new ideas, planning, and sound decision making.

Emblems – specific, widely understood meanings in a given culture that can actually substitute for a word or phrase.

Emotion – a physiological and affective reaction to some circumstance or event that compels a person to interpret a meaning for it.

Emotion work – the amount of effort we expend to engender feelings we think are appropriate for a situation.

Emotional intelligence (EQ) - the ability to understand and identify the emotions one is experiencing, handle stress, empathize with others, and manage emotions in positive ways.

Emotional resources - the endurance to withstand difficult and uncomfortable emotional situations or feelings.

Emotional tyranny - the use of emotion to be destructive, controlling, unjust, and even cruel. This form of tyranny is ascribed not only to people who already have power but also to people who use this tactic to gain power.

Enactment frame – reflects the communicative behavior symbolic of one's identity

Encounter – learning more about the group and becoming more acquainted with the written rules and unwritten norms.

Enculturation – how we learn our own culture as we grow up.

Endomorphs – individuals who typically have rounded, oval, or pear-shaped bodies.

Engagement – the act of sharing in the activities of the group

Environment - our physical, social, and contextual surroundings that shape the communication context.

Episode – a broader situation created by conversational partners.

Ethical communication – symbolic verbal and nonverbal behavior that reflects perceptions and attitudes about what is right or wrong.

Ethical communicator – one who values truthful information and cultural sensitivity.

Ethical considerations - the variety of factors important when considering what is right or wrong.

Ethical dilemmas - situations that do not seem to present clear choices between right and wrong or good and evil.

Ethical imperative – guides you in doing what is right versus wrong in various communication contexts.

Ethics - a system of accepted principles that make up an individual's or group's values and judgments as to what is right and wrong.

Ethnic belonging – the level of comfort one has with one's ethnic group, as well as the sense of attachment.

Ethnic identity - an individual's commitment to communication patterns, beliefs, and philosophies shared by a particular cultural group.

Ethnicity - a social group that may be joined together by factors such as shared history, shared identity, shared geography, and shared culture.

Ethnocentrism - placing your own cultural beliefs in a superior position, which leads to a negative judgment of other cultures.

Ethnorelativism – the ability to see behaviors as culturally bound and relative, rather than universal.

Ethnorelativism model – the journey from being closed-minded about a culture to being more appreciative of the differences and willing to adapt accordingly.

Exclusion - socially or physically excluding or disregarding a person in work-related activities.

Expressive conflict – differences in how people think feelings and emotions should be expressed and released.

Extrinsic religious orientation – a person who does not necessarily put importance on the faith tradition itself but sees it as a means to an end.

Face - the image of self that we project to others.

Face-threatening acts – behaviors that insults, embarrasses, or question another person's face .

Facework -the portrayal of one's face is an inherently communicative act that is an extension of one's identity.

False consciousness – the idea that individuals are unknowingly exploited by a social system they support.

Fantasy chains – a series of symbolic cues that represent an exchange, conversation, ora series of connected thoughts or themes.

Fantasy theme – the content of the dramatizing message that sparks the fantasy chain.; an observable record of the nature and content of the shared imagination.

Feeling rules – refer to what people should feel or have the "right" to feel in a given situation.

Feminine orientation – reflects the extent to which one is task oriented or relationally oriented; generally, coming from a more feminine culture might mean that you prefer that masculine and feminine roles overlap or that the group foster a sense of community and relationship maintenance.

Fidelity – matches beliefs and expectations.

Fields of experience - collections of attitudes, perceptions, and personal backgrounds.

Financial resources - the money to purchase goods and services. When people talk about poverty, they typically discuss it in terms of financial resources only.

Framing rules – the standards taught to us by society or culture that help us define what certain situations are supposed to mean to us emotionally.

Fringe – describes the clarity (or confusion) one has about his or her ethnic identity.

Functional perspective – stipulates that the group dynamic must emphasize both the tasks and the relationships among members to be successful.

Gender - a range of social behaviors that reflect biological, mental, and behavioral characteristics used to portray oneself as masculine, feminine, or any combination of the two. When individuals refer to the behaviors associated with a particular sex (e.g., male, female), they are referring to gender.

Gender discrimination - unequal pay or job opportunities based on one's gender. Gender discrimination, historically, has been attributed to oppression of women.

Generational poverty - poverty that spans two or more generations.

Gestures – the movements we make with our hands and arms.

Gesture bullying - Nonverbal, threatening gestures; glances that convey threatening messages

Globalization - an integration of economy and technology that creates a worldwide and interconnected work environment.

Group fantasy - a collection of accounts and experiences that form a general social reality in the group.

Group faultlines – subgroups; situations in which group members—intentionally or unintentionally—align themselves according to their diversity dimensions.

Groupthink – the tendency for a group to strive for harmony and agreement at the expense of productivity and growth.

Haptics - the study of touch as nonverbal communication.

Harmony model – often seen in cultures that see the importance of maintaining relationships, avoid open communication of conflict, rely on third parties to help resolve conflict, and strive to maintain honor and pride.

Hate speech - insulting discourse, phrases, terms, cartoons, or organized campaigns used to humiliate people based on age, gender, race, ethnicity, culture, sexual identity, social class, and more.

Health - a state of physical, mental, spiritual, and social well-being, as well as the absence of illness.

Health communication - the construction and sharing of meanings about the provision of health care delivery and the promotion of public health through mediated channels.

Health literacy – understanding and being able to act on medical and health information.

Hegemony - sustained based on two main ideas: *false consciousness*, or the idea that individuals are unknowingly exploited by a social system they support, and *out-of-control bodies*, or the representation of lower-class individuals as out of control and dangerous.

Height and status – both play a huge role in perceptions of wh is attractive and who is not.

Heteronormativity - a culture or belief system that assumes heterosexuality is the norm.

Heterosexist – assuming that everyone is heterosexual.

High-context cultures – members rely on features of the context or situation to get their ideas across.

History/past-present/future dialectic – the extent to which one feels compelled to change or alter its values, beliefs, or traditions if its overall goals change or it wants to adapt to the changing times.

Homeostasis – making adjustments and achieving conformity and adapting to a new culture.

Homophobia – a fear of being perceived or labeled as gay.

Honeymoon – the time of enjoyment or euphoria.

Hostile work environment – when an employee experiences workplace harassment and fears going to work because of an offensive, intimidating, or oppressive atmosphere.

Huge social graph - an intercultural experience's ability to reach millions of people through a network.

Human nature perspective - states that our ability to judge, reason, and comprehend far exceeds that of any other species. Therefore, we hold ourselves accountable to make good judgments and decisions.

Hypermedia - allows the sender and receiver to interact in real time using new media technologies.

Identity – the representation of how you view yourself and how others may see you.

Identity intensity – the degree to which we express or communicate our identity.

Identity salience – the importance of one aspect of a person's identity in relation to other aspects.

Illustrators – gestures that complement, enhance, or substitute for the verbal message.

Inclusive language – employs expressions and words that are broad enough to include all people and avoids expressions and words that exclude particular groups.

Independent self-construal – reflects group members who see their thoughts and beliefs as uniquely their own; they are goal driven and thrive on concreteness and low uncertainty.

Individualism – the search for individual autonomy and independence

In-group distinction – a group with which one identifies as a member.

In-group member - one who is perceived as belonging to the group.

Input – the features a person brings to the new culture.

Instrumental conflict – differences in how people articulate goals and understand how tasks should be completed.

Integration-separation dialectic – a tension that acknowledges the dual needs of being connected to people and at the same time enjoying a certain level of autonomy and independence.

Intensity – the degree to which one expresses their identity or the power, force, or concentration of bodily contact.

Interdependent self-construal – people who see themselves as they are connected or related to others and the world around them; they like fitting in and acknowledge the role that others play in goal achievement.

Intercultural transformation – learning a new set of behaviors, thoughts, and feelings about the culture.

Interference – a perceived obstacle or barrier that prevents you from accomplishing a goal; perceived interference from others is a characteristic of conflict.

Intergroup interaction – reflects how much one is oriented toward communicating with members of other ethnic groups.

Interdependence – the actions of one party will affect the other and vice versa.

Interviewing – conversation between two parties that provides a platform for cultural inclusion; provides an opportunity for intimate conversation with individuals who may be from different cultural backgrounds.

Intrapersonal conflict – internal strain that can create feelings of resentment and ambivalence, and can often prevent resolution from occurring.

Intrinsic religious orientation – characterized by a strong commitment to one's faith.

Invasion – an intense and typically permanent intrusion that involves an intention to take over a given territory.

Kinesics - the study of body movement, including both posture and gestures.

Language – words that carry meanings that coordinate what we are able to think, imagine, and express.

Leakage cues - signs that information the speaker wishes to conceal verbally is spilling out nonverbally.

Learning style – the way people learn and process information.

LGBTQ – lesbian, gay, bisexual, transgender, queer, and other individuals questioning their gender or sexual orientation.

Liking – principle that explains that we prefer to say yes to people whom we enjoy or feel are similar to us.

Linguistic relativity hypothesis - the view that language helps shape perception.

Literacy – refers to the ability to read or write at a functional level or calculate basic math.

Location – where on the body contact is made or the setting within which touch occurs.

Low-context cultures – being direct and concrete is highly valued, and the words spoken convey more meaning than does the context or situation in which they occur.

Marginalization – health disparity influenced by variations in SES, such as income, amount of debt, education, occupation, and property; lower SES relates to more negative emotions and thoughts, which in turn relate to poorer health.

Masculine orientation – reflects the extent to which one is task oriented or relationally oriented. In general, coming from a more masculine culture might like to see masculine and feminine roles clearly defined, with very little or no overlap.

Mashed up – traditional media converged into new media technologies

Mass interpersonal communication - the practice of creating a message that can be consumed by a large amount of people by means of new media.

Measured impact – observing and measuring the effects of communication on thoughts, attitudes, and behavior.

Media - the variety of message delivery formats, such as print news, radio, television, and the Internet, that have evolved over time.

Media convergence - the blending or collapse of print, radio, electronic, and digital formats into one dominant medium.

Mental resources- the mental abilities and acquired skills (e.g., reading, writing, computing) needed to deal with everyday life.

Mesomorphs – a triangular body shape; broad shoulders and muscular, with a good balance between height and weight.

Metamorphosis – new members alter their behaviors and even come to accept such changes.

Mindful reframing - "the mindful process of using language to change the way each person or party defines or thinks about experiences."

Monologue - typically a performance or speech by a single person.

Myers-Briggs Type Indicator – an inventory of personality characteristics; it outlines four dimensions, and according to the inventory, we all fall on some point of each dimension or continuum.

Nationality - a person's place of origin or national affiliation through birth or naturalization.

Negative cultural transfer - when people take an ethnocentric view when engaging in intercultural communication, thereby measuring or assessing their communication based on their own cultural understanding of truth, morality, and values.

Negotiation – involves a conversation or discussion between people or parties in conflict who wish to reach an agreement.

Networking - the ability to use one's personal social connections to achieve goals.

New media – because the Internet allows the consumer to become the producer, many believe the Internet is a part of a different tradition of technology.

New media tradition – also known as the digital tradition; a classification for technological advancements such as the smartphone.

Noncontact cultures – cultures characterized by infrequent touching.

Nonverbal communication - all the ways we communicate without the use of words.

Object conflict – typically a misunderstanding or disagreement about something or about whether something is true or false, such as a fact or what some people hold as common knowledge. Concerns whether something is factual, not moral or proper (e.g., right or wrong).

Obliteration style – a couple might abandon their own traditions and norms and come together to form a new "culture" to resolve power issues.

Openness-closedness dialectic – the extent to which we disclose our feelings, intentions, or desires to the other person in the relationship.

Oral tradition - cultural messages or traditions verbally transmitted across generations.

Organizational culture – underlying, shared values that provide organization members with behavioral norms in the workplace.

Out-group distinction – those groups to which one does not feel one belongs.

Out-group member - one who does not belong to the group.

Out-of-control bodies – the representation of lower-class individuals as out of control and dangerous.

Output – resulting behavior that is learned and adopted by the new member.

Patient role – helps emphasize the dissimilarity between patient and provider; it often places the patient in a lower-status role relative to the healthcare provider.

Partnership perspective – suggests that gendered communication during conflict can be about equal collaboration; neither gender is limited to a certain group of behaviors.

Peace imperative – essential in understanding the foundations of communication, culture and diversity.

Peep culture - the entertainment derived from peeping into the real lives of others.

Perception - the process of being aware of and understanding the world around us. Perception plays an important part in tying our language to our culture.

Perception checking - the practice of verifying our perceptions with others to gain a more informed sense of understanding.

Peripheral – refers to an aspect of characteristic that appears unimportant or hardly noticeable.

Personal artifacts – objects we use to represent our identities, interests, and backgrounds.

Personal-contextual dialectic – acknowledges that we do not communicate the same way with all people.

Personal frame – an identity construction based on how one views himself or herself

Physical appearance - observable traits of the body and its accessories and extensions.

Physical bullying – Pushing, shoving, kicking, poking, tripping, assault or threat of physical assault, or damage to a person's work area or property

Physical resources - having a body that works and is capable and mobile.

Poverty - the extent to which an individual does without resources.

Power distance – the extent to which a culture maximizes or minimizes status and power differences among people.

Prejudice - the dislike or hatred one feels toward a particular group.

Primary orality - a culture that has no knowledge of technology beyond the spoken word.

Principled negotiation – puts forth four principles: 1) separate the problem from the people involved in the negotiation, 2) focus not on positions but interests, 3) create options for mutual gain, and 4) insist on objective criteria.

Print tradition - embodies the creation and dissemination of printed text.

Printing press - a mechanical device that applies pressure from an inked surface to a print medium.

Privilege-disadvantage dialectic – especially prevalent between individuals who come from cultures that do not enjoy the same level of privilege or power in the larger society.

Proletariat – one of the two major social classes related to economy and production; these formed the working class and instruments of production.

Proxemics - the study of how we use space and distance to communicate.

Race - a generalized categorization of people based on physical characteristics such as skin color, dimensions of the face, and hair texture and color.

Racial slurs - derogatory or disrespectful nicknames for racial groups. These slurs can make intercultural communication and understanding virtually impossible because of their inflammatory and belligerent nature.

Rapid cycle - the time separating interactions between individuals.

Rapport talk – attributed to women's style, which is more feminine, collaborative, and empathetic, and focuses on maintaining the relationship between conversational partners.

Razzing – used to test another person's legitimacy; similar to verbal dueling.

Reciprocation – returning a kindness that another has offered us; also refers to returning symbolic behavior that is similar in degree and kind to the behavior that was received.

Recovery – a flexible response to the environment that entails ways of working with the culture to embrace some of its aspects.

Reflective observation (RO) – people who prefer this learning style gain perspective about an experience by reflecting on it; they feel more comfortable watching how others do things or observing how something works.

Reflexive Ethics Cycle – using an unethical tactic to get something from someone else.

Regulative model – emphasizes reliance on rules and codes of conduct, procedural justice during negotiation, and downplaying the personal issues involved; also promotes the involvement of third parties during conflict resolution.

Regulative rules - guide how individuals respond or behave in interactions (i.e., "Always raise your hand before you speak in class").

Regulators – gestures used to control the turn-taking in conversations.

Relational conflict – rights, responsibilities, and roles people hold or are expected to hold in a given situation (e.g., a relationship, the workplace). Often involve disagreements in power distribution and expression.

Relational dialectics -describe how relationships are fraught with coexisting, yet opposing tensions.

Relational frame - represents the identity constructed through interactions with others.

Relational issues – the group's maintenance concerns, such as how people use or abuse power, give one another encouragement, relieve tension, and manage conflict.

Relational learning – the insights and new ways of thinking that result from the people with whom we are in relationships, especially when we have interesting dissimilarities with our relational partners.

Relationship – how people are connected to one another, such as worker and coworker, teacher and student, boyfriend and girlfriend or strangers.

Religious perspective – examines the relationship between us as humans and a higher power.

Report talk – task oriented and focuses on direct expression of ideas; typically attributed to men's style of communication.

Responsibility - the elements of fulfilling duties and obligations, being accountable to other individuals and groups, adhering to agreed-on standards, and being accountable to one's own conscience.

Salience – the importance of one identity in relation to others

Scarcity - limiting the availability of a product, offer, or membership.

Schema - a mental structure that contains various bits of information that define who a person is and guides how he or she communicates with others.

Secondary orality - verbal communication is sustained through use of other technologies, such as the telephone or Internet.

Self - a complex set of beliefs about one's attributes, as well as memories and recollections of episodes that confirm such beliefs.

Self-aspects model of identity - the self encompasses several different facets, including perceived abilities (or deficiencies), personality traits, physical features, behavioral characteristics, ideologies or belief systems, social roles, languages, and group memberships.

Self-awareness imperative – communicators learning about other cultures

Self-categorization Theory – an extension of social identity theory which takes a more psychological approach to capturing the self.

Self-enhancement – assumes that people want to see the positive aspects of themselves in relation to their groups.

Self-in-relationship movement – this body of theories focused on mutual interdependence of parties (rather than one having power over the other), constructive conflict rather than use of authority, and achieving understanding through reciprocal empathy.

Sex - biological; refers to the chromosomal combinations that produce males, females, and the other possible, but rarer, sexes.

Sexual identity - refers to one's identity based on whom one is attracted to sexually.

Sexual orientation – a romantic or sexual attraction to others.

Sexual orientation discrimination - refers to harassment or differential treatment based on someone's perceived or actual gay, lesbian, bisexual, or heterosexual orientation.

Situational perspective - examines every situation we encounter related to intercultural communication. This perspective involves being critical of your everyday communication.

Situational poverty- a shorter amount of time than generational poverty and is generally caused by circumstances (death, illness, divorce, etc.).

Small group - a collection of 3-20 individuals who share mutual influence, have one or more common goals, and are interpersonally aware of one another.

Social capital - networks or connections among people who can help one another.

Social categorization – taking extra measures to be part of social groups to which individuals from your ethnic group belong.

Social distribution – intercultural experience shared between friends.

Social identity – a group's social identity is based on common attributes held by its members and serves as a way to categorize people as well as provide an identity common to everyone in the group.

Social identity theory - takes the perspective that identity is a function of one's social groups. Humans are innately social beings, and they establish aspects of the self through social interactions with influential others and self-categorization.

Social networking - web networks specifically created to allow users to create and exchange content of mutual interest and to communicate directly with one another.

Social penetration theory – proposes that as relationships progress, non-intimate communication decreases and deeper, more intimate communication increases

Social proof - a form of influence that argues that determining whether a behavior is acceptable occurs through observing others to find out how they feel about that behavior.

Social stratification - the ranking of groups according to various criteria, with higher positions given more value, respect, status, and privilege than lower positions.

Socialization - how members learn the values, norms, and behaviors needed to fulfill their roles within a group or organization. Socialization can help one assimilate into a group.

Socioeconomic status - determined by the combination of income, education, and occupation.

Sojourning – the move from one's own culture to a new one.

Solidarity symbol – a name or logo that gives the group a unifying image or theme.

Somatotyping – classifies people according to body type.

Speech act - the various actions we perform through speech.

Spiritual resources- the belief that help can be obtained from a higher power and that one has a purpose for living.

Standpoint theory - asserts that our points of view arise from the social groups we belong to and influence how we socially construct the world.

Static-dynamic dialectic – recognizes that some aspects of a person are trait-like, but other characteristics are more adaptable and might change according to circumstances, age, experience, or the people with whom one associates.

Stereotypes - popular beliefs about groups of people. These preconceived notions can be positive, neutral, or negative, but when it comes to individuals, each one forms an incomplete picture and is potentially harmful.

Stigma – a social rejection in which the stigmatized people are ignored and/or dishonored.

Stress-adaptation-growth model – a fluctuation between adaptation and stress over time.

Submission style – most common way couples handle power imbalance; one partner abdicates power to the other partner's culture or cultural preferences.

Support systems - safety nets that help people take care of themselves in situations where they would otherwise be unable.

Sustained dialogue - promotes change in intercultural group relationships by moving the communication dynamics from negative to positive.

Symbolic convergence theory - provides a framework for group members to use communication to achieve common ground or commonly shared experiences.

Symbol - an object that stands for something else. Symbols are arbitrary, which means there is no natural likeness between a symbol and what it represents. The symbol represents what a culture agrees it should mean.

System - a set of interdependent parts that relate to each other at various levels.

Task concerns – contribute to the group's productivity and might include whether or not to have a meeting, what kind of decision must be made, the leadership style used for running the meeting, and how much members are expected to participate.

Team - a type of group that requires a higher standard of performance and commitment from its members, tends to be more structured and coordinated than a small group, and serves to empower its members. In addition, the team's goals are clear and specific to the overall objective, as well as to each member's role.

Technological imperative – technological advances make the world more accessible and continue to gain more importance in today's society.

Territoriality - the study of how people use space and objects to communicate occupancy or ownership of space.

The Equal Employment Act - protects the rights of applicants and employees by monitoring to make sure that promotions, benefits, classifications, and referrals are not withheld due to discrimination associated with color, race, religion, sex, or national origin.

Throughput --the symbols and cues that are exchanged during a communication process.

Touch ethic – people's beliefs about and preferences for touch.

Trait EQ – a construct claiming that emotions occupy a lower level of one's personality.

Transformational leadership – leadership that taps into the higher-order needs of followers, motivates followers to perform beyond their expectations, and seeks to create change in a person for the better.

Turn repair – the identification of a disruption or misunderstanding in conversation and the conversation is brought back on track with the turn-taking sequence restored.

Turn taking – one person says something that triggers a thought or memory in the other person, who then makes an utterance that follows up on that of the first person.

Unethical communicator – one who is an insensitive, insulting, and ultimately ineffective communicator because of a lack of understanding and caring for other or cultural differences.

Valence – positive and negative feelings.

Values - beliefs and attitudes we hold about what is important or worthwhile .

Verbal bullying - Slandering, ridiculing, or maligning a person or his or her family; persistent name calling that is hurtful, insulting, or humiliating; making a person the butt of jokes; abusive and offensive remarks.

Verbal communication - both our words and our verbal fillers (e.g., *um*, *like*).

Violation – the use of or intrusion into primary territory without permission.

Western medicine – relies on the scientific method and the principle of verification to understand what causes ill health.

Workplace bullying - a repetitive pattern of mistreatment in which the enacted behaviors are perceived by targets as an intentional effort to harm, control, or drive them from the workplace.

Worldview - a culture's orientation toward supernatural, human, and natural entities in the cosmological universe, and other philosophical issues influencing how its members see the world.

Written tradition - early forms of written communication such as scribe and hieroglyphics, and immediately follows the oral tradition.

references

CHAPTER 1

Bloomfield, S. (2006, January 16). The face of the future: Why Eurasians are changing the rules of attraction. *Independent on Sunday* (London), p. 3.

Braithwaite, D. O. (1991). "Just how much did that wheelchair cost?": Management of privacy boundaries by persons with disabilities. *Western Journal of Speech Communication, 55*, 254–274.

Braithwaite, D. O., & Braithwaite, C. A. (2009). "Which is my good leg?" Cultural communication of persons with disabilities. In L. W. Samovar, R. Porter, & E. R. McDaniel (Eds.), *Intercultural communication: A reader* (9th ed., pp. 207–218). Belmont, CA: Wadsworth.

Braithwaite, D. O., & Thompson, T. L. (2000). *Handbook of communication and people with disabilities: Research and application.* Mahwah, NJ: Erlbaum.

Burkard, A. W., Boticki, M. A., & Madson, M. B. (2002). Workplace discrimination, prejudice, and diversity measurement: A review of instrumentation. *Journal of Career Assessment, 10*, 343–361.

Carter, F. (2010, October 14). Why Twitter influences cross-cultural engagement. *Mashable.* Retrieved from http://mashable.com/2010/10/14/twitter-cross-cultural/

Christian, J., Porter, L. W., & Moffit, G. (2006). Workplace diversity and group relations: An overview. *Group Process & Intergroup Relations, 9*, 459–466.

Coates, J. (1993). *Women, men and language.* London: Longman.

Cruikshank, L. (2010). Digitizing race: Visual cultures of the Internet. *Information, Communication & Society, 13*(2), 278–280.

DeAndrea, D. C., Shaw, A. S., & Levine, T. R. (2010). Online language: The role of culture in self-expression and self-construal on Facebook. *Journal of Language & Social Psychology, 29*(4), 425–442.

Driscoll, K., & Wiebe, E. (2007). Technical spirituality at work: Jacques Ellul on workplace spirituality. *Journal of Management Inquiry, 16*, 333–348.

Eadie, W. F. (2009). In plain sight: Gay and lesbian communication and culture. In L. W. Samovar, R. Porter, & E. R. McDaniel (Eds.), *Intercultural communication: A reader* (9th ed., pp. 219–231). Belmont, CA: Wadsworth.

Edwards, A., Edwards, C., Wahl, S.T. & Myers, S.A). (2016). *The communication age: Connecting and engaging.* (2nd ed.). Thousand Oaks, CA: Sage.

Edwards, C., Edwards, A., Qing, Q., & Wahl, S. T. (2007). The influence of computer-mediated word-of-mouth communication on student perceptions of instructors and attitudes toward learning course content. *Communication Education, 56,* 255–277.

Fisher, W. R. (1984). Narration as human communication paradigm: The case of public moral argument. *Communication Monographs, 51,* 1–22.

Frey, L. R., & Carragee, K. M. (Eds.). (2007). *Communication activism: Volume 1. Communication for social change.* Cresskill, NJ: Hampton Press.

Guiller, J., & Durndell, A. (2007). Students' linguistic behaviour in online discussion groups: Does gender matter? *Computers in Human Behavior, 23,* 2240–2255.

Habermas, J. (1979). *Communication and the evolution of society.* Boston: Beacon Press.

Herring, S. C. (1993). Gender and democracy in computer-mediated communication. *Electronic Journal of Communication, 3*(2). Retrieved November 9, 2011, from http://www.cios.org/EJCPUBLIC/003/2/00328.HTML

Henry, E. (2010, January 18). Obama's first 'tweet' makes presidential history. *CNN Politics.* Retrieved from http://politicalticker.blogs.cnn.com/2010/01/18/obamas-first-tweet-makes-presidential-history/

Ivy, D. K. (2012). *Genderspeak: Personal effectiveness in gender communication* (5th ed.). Boston: Allyn & Bacon.

Ivy, D. K., & Wahl, S. T. (2009). *The nonverbal self: Communication for a lifetime.* Boston: Allyn & Bacon.

Ivy, D., & Wahl, S.T. (2014). *Nonverbal communication for a lifetime.* (2nd ed.). Dubuque, IA: Kendall Hunt

Jandt, F. (2010). *An introduction to intercultural communication.* Los Angeles: Sage.

Japp, P. M., Meister, M., & Japp, D. K. (2005). *Communication ethics, media, & popular culture.* New York: Peter Lang.

Johannesen, R. L., Valde, K. S., & Whedbee, K. E. (2008). *Ethics in human communication* (6th ed.). Prospect Heights, IL: Waveland Press.

Kapidzic, S., & Herring, S. C. (2011). Gender, communication, and self-presentation in teen chatrooms revisited: Have patterns changed? *Journal of Computer-Mediated Communication, 17,* 39–59.

Lakoff, R. T. (1975). *Language and woman's place.* New York: Harper & Row.

Magnuson, M. J., & Dundes, L. (2008). Gender differences in "social portraits" reflected in MySpace profiles. *CyberPsychology & Behavior, 11,* 239–241.

Nelson, L. (2017, June 6). Defiant Trump claims media trying to push him off Twitter. *Politico.* Retrieved from http://www.politico.com/story/2017/06/06/trump-twitter-mainstream-media-239177

Quan, Z. (2010). The multilingual Internet: Language, culture, and communication online. *Journal of Business & Technical Communication, 24*(2), 249–252.

Quintanilla, K.M., & Wahl, S.T. (2016). *Business and professional communication: Keys for workplace excellence.* (3rd. ed.). Thousand Oaks, CA: Sage.

Riessman, C. (1990). *Divorce talk: Women and men make sense of personal relationships.* New Brunswick, NJ: Rutgers University Press.

Ruben, B. D. (1976). Assessing communication competency for intercultural adaptation. *Group & Organization Studies, 1*, 334–354.

Ruben, B. D. (1977). Guidelines for cross-cultural communication effectiveness. *Group & Organization Studies, 2*, 470–479.

Ruben, B. D., & Kealey, D. J. (1979). Behavioral assessment of communication competency and the prediction of cross-cultural adaptation. *International Journal of Intercultural Relations, 3*, 15–47.

Samovar, L., Porter, R. E., & McDaniel, E. R. (2009). *Communication between cultures* (7th ed.). Belmont, CA: Wadsworth.

Seelye, K. Q., & Bidgood, J. (2017 June 16). Guilty verdict for young woman who urged friend to kill himself. *New York Times*. Retrieved from https://www.nytimes.com/2017/06/16/us/suicide-texting-trial-michelle-carter-conrad-roy.html

Tannen, D. (1990). *You just don't understand: Women and men in conversation*. New York: HarperCollins.

Tannen, D. (1991). *You just don't understand: Women and men in conversation*. London: Virago Press.

Tannen, D. (1994). *Gender and discourse*. New York: Oxford University Press.

Thomson, R., & Murachver, T. (2001). Predicting gender from electronic discourse. *British Journal of Social Psychology, 40*, 193–208.

Ting-Toomey, S., & Chung, L. (2005). *Understanding intercultural communication*. New York: Oxford University Press.

Wahl, S. T. (2013). *Persuasion in your life*. Boston: Allyn & Bacon.

Wahl, S. T. & Morris, E. (2018). *Persuasion in your life*. (2nd ed.). New York: Routledge.

Wood, J. T. (2009). *Gendered lives: Communication, gender, and culture*. Boston: Wadsworth.

CHAPTER 2

Allport, G. W. (1954). *The nature of prejudice*. Cambridge, MA: Perseus Books.

Amir, Y. (1969). Contact hypothesis in ethnic relations. *Psychological Bulletin, 71*, 319–342.

Capurro, R. (2011). The Dao of the information society in China and the task of intercultural information ethics. In *CEPE 2011: Crossing Boundaries* (pp. 39–45). Milwaukee: University of Wisconsin.

Guilherme, M., Keating, C., & Hoppe, D. (2010). Intercultural responsibility: Power and ethics in intercultural dialogue and interaction. In M. Guilherme, C. Keating, & D. Hoppe (Eds.), *The intercultural dynamics of multicultural working* (pp. 77–94). Bristol, UK: Multilingual Matters.

Hesson, T. (2012, December 17). A quarter of deportations are of parents of U.S. citizens. *ABC News*. Retrieved from http://abcnews.go.com/ABC_Univision/News/quarter-deportations-parents-us-citizens/story?id=18000783#.UWyBmrXCaSo

Ishii, S. (2009). Conceptualising Asian communication ethics: A Buddhist perspective. *Journal of Multicultural Discourses, 4*(1), 49–60.

Johannesen, R. L., Valde, K. S., & Whedbee, K. E. (2008). *Ethics in human communication* (6th ed.). Prospect Heights, IL: Waveland Press.

Mollov, M., & Schwartz, D. G. (2010). Towards an integrated strategy for intercultural dialog: Computer-mediated communication and face to face. *Journal of Intercultural Communication Research, 39*(3), 207–224.

Oetzel, J. (2009). *Intercultural communication: A layered approach.* New York: Vango Books.

Quintanilla, K.M., & Wahl, S.T. (2016). *Business and professional communication: Keys for workplace excellence.* (3rd. ed.). Thousand Oaks, CA: Sage.

Riccio, M. (2011). Democracy as a "universal value" and an intercultural ethics. *Cultura: International Journal of Philosophy of Culture and Axiology, 8*(2), 73–84.

Richmond, K. (2016, June 11). Valedictorian declares she is an undocumented immigrant in graduation speech. CNN. Retrieved from http://www.cnn.com/2016/06/10/us/texas-undocumented-valedictorian-trnd/index.html

Ting-Toomey, S. (2010). Intercultural communication ethics: Multiple layered issues. In G. Cheney, S. May, & D. Munshi (Eds.), *The ICA handbook of communication ethics* (pp. 335–352). Mahwah, NJ: Lawrence Erlbaum.

Ting-Toomey, S., & Chung, L. C. (2005). Understanding intercultural communication. Los Angeles: Roxbury.

Wei, X. (2009). On negative cultural transfer in communication between Chinese and Americans. *Journal of Intercultural Communication, 21.* Retrieved from http://www.immi.se/intercultural/nr21/wei.htm

Zhang, X. (2012). Internet rumors and intercultural ethics: A case study of panic-stricken rush for salt in China and iodine pill in America after Japanese earthquake and tsunami. *Studies in Literature & Language, 4*(2), 13–16.

CHAPTER 3

Akande, A. (2008). Comparing social behavior across culture and nations: The 'what' and 'why' questions. *Social Indicators Research, 92,* 591–608. doi:10.1007/s11205-008-921-9

Associated Press. (2017, July 5). Oregon is first state to allow gender-neutral driver's licenses. *New York Post.* Retrieved from http://nypost.com/2017/07/05/oregon-is-first-state-to-allow-gender-neutral-drivers-licenses/

Boellstorff, T. (2011). But do not identify as gay: A proleptic genealogy of the MSM category. *Cultural Anthropology, 26*(2), 287–312. doi:10.1111/j.1548-1360.2011.01100.x

Brewer, M. B., & Gardner, W. (1996). Who is this "we"? Levels of collective identity and self representations. *Journal of Personality and Social Psychology, 71*(1), 83–93.

Campbell, J., Assenand, S., & Di Paula, A. (2000). Structural features of the self-concept and adjustment. In A. Tesser, R. B. Felson, & J. M. Suls (Eds.), *Psychological perspectives on self and identity* (pp. 67–87). Washington, DC: American Psychological Association.

Canary, D. J., Emmers-Sommer, T. M., & Faulkner, S. (1997). *Sex and gender differences in personal relationships.* New York: Guilford Press.

Chan, S., & Lee, J. (2009, September 9). Law bans use of "Oriental" in state documents. *New York Times.* Retrieved from http://cityroom.blogs.nytimes.com/2009/09/09/law-bans-use-of-oriental-in-state-documents/

Collier, M. J. (1988). A comparison of conversations among and between domestic culture groups: How intra- and intercultural competencies vary. *Communication Quarterly, 36*(2), 122–144.

Collier, M. J., & Thomas, M. (1988). Cultural identity: An interpretive perspective. In Y. Y. Kim & W. B. Gudykunst (Eds.), *Theories in intercultural communication* (pp. 99–120). Thousand Oaks, CA: Sage.

Coupland, N., Coupland, J., & Giles, H. (1989). Telling age in later life: Identity and face implications. *Text, 9,* 129–151.

Cross, S. E., Bacon, P. L., & Morris, M. L. (2000). The relational-interdependent self-construal and relationships. *Journal of Personality and Social Psychology, 78*, 791–808.

Doi, T. (1986). *The anatomy of the self.* Tokyo: Kodansha.

Geertz, C. (1975). On the nature of anthropological understanding. *American Scientist, 63*, 47–53.

Goffman, E. (1967). *Interaction ritual: Essays on face-to-face behaviour.* New York: Pantheon.

Grinberg, E. (2017, June 28). You can now get a gender neutral driver's license in D.C. *CNN.* Retrieved from http://www.cnn.com/2017/06/27/health/washington-gender-neutral-drivers-license/index.html

Gudykunst, W. B., & Hammer, M. R. (1987). The influence of ethnicity, gender, and dyadic composition on uncertainty reduction in initial interactions. *Journal of Black Studies, 18*(2), 191–214.

Gudykunst, W. B., & Kim, Y. Y. (1992). *Communicating with strangers: An approach to intercultural communication* (2nd ed.). New York: McGraw-Hill.

Hecht, M. L. (1993). 2002—A research odyssey: Toward the development of a communication theory of identity. *Communication Monographs, 60*, 76–82.

Hecht, M. L., Collier, M. J., & Ribeau, S. A. (1993). *African American communication: Ethnic identity and cultural interpretation.* Newbury Park, CA: Sage.

Hecht, M. L., Warren, J. R., Jung, E., & Krieger, J. L. (2005). A communication theory of identity: Development, theoretical perspective, and future directions. In W. B. Gudykunst (Ed.), *Theorizing about intercultural communication* (pp. 257–278). Thousand Oaks, CA: Sage.

Hegde, R. S. (1998). Swinging the trapeze: The negotiation of identity among Asian Indian women in the United States. In D. V. Tanno & A. González (Eds.), *Communication and identity across cultures: International and intercultural communication annual* (Vol. 21, pp. 34–55). Thousand Oaks, CA: Sage.

Hogg, M. A., & Abrams, D. (1988). *Social identifications: A social psychology of intergroup relations and group processes.* London: Routledge.

Hogg, M. A., Terry, D. J., & White, K. M. (1995). A tale of two theories: A critical comparison of identity theory with social identity theory. *Social Psychology Quarterly, 58*(4), 255–269.

Hughes, P. C., & Baldwin, J. R. (2002a). Black, white, and shades of gray: Communication predictors of "stereotypic impressions." *Southern Communication Journal, 68*(1), 40–56.

Hughes, P. C., & Baldwin, J. R. (2002b). Communication and stereotypical impressions. *Howard Journal of Communications, 13*, 113–128.

Hummert, M. L., & Nussbaum, J. F. (2001). *Communication, aging, and health.* Mahwah, NJ: Erlbaum.

Hummert, M. L., & Ryan, E. B. (2001). Patronizing. In W. P. Robinson & H. Giles (Eds.), *The new handbook of language and social psychology* (pp. 253–270). Chichester, UK: John Wiley.

Imahori, T. T., & Cupach, W. R. (2005). Identity management theory: Facework in intercultural relationships. In W. B. Gudykunst (Ed.), *Theorizing about intercultural communication* (pp. 195–210). Thousand Oaks, CA: Sage.

Jung, E., & Hecht, M. L. (2004). Elaborating the communication theory of identity: Identity gaps and communication outcomes. *Communication Quarterly, 52*(3), 265–283.

Lim, T. (1994). Facework and interpersonal relationships. In S. Ting-Toomey (Ed.), *The challenge of facework* (pp. 209–229). New York: State University of New York Press.

Lippa, R. A. (2002). *Gender, nature, and nurture.* Mahwah, NJ: Erlbaum.

Lu, X. (2001). Bicultural identity development and Chinese community formation: An ethnographic study of Chinese schools in Chicago. *Howard Journal of Communications, 12*, 203–220.

McCornack, S. (2013). *Reflect and relate: An introduction to interpersonal communication* (3rd ed.). Boston: Bedford/St. Martin's.

Mead, G. H. (1962). *Mind, self, and society.* Chicago: University of Chicago Press.

Pratt, S. B. (1998). Ritualized uses of humor as a form of identification among American Indians. In D. V. Tanno & A. González (Eds.), *Communication and identity across cultures: International and intercultural communication annual* (Vol. 21, pp. 56–79). Thousand Oaks, CA: Sage.

Robinson, J. D., Skill, T., & Turner, J. W. (2004). Media usage patterns and portrayals of seniors. In J. F. Nussbaum & J. Coupland (Eds.), *Handbook of communication and aging research* (2nd ed., pp. 423–450). Mahwah, NJ: Erlbaum.

Ryan, E. B., Giles, H., Bartolucci, G., & Henwood, K. (1986). Psycholinguistic and social psychological components of communication by and with the elderly. *Language and Communication, 6,* 1–24.

Scholl, J. C., Wilson, J. B., & Hughes, P. C. (2011). Expression of patients' and providers' identities during the medical interview. *Qualitative Health Research, 21*(8), 1022–1032. doi:10.1177/1049732310393748

Scollon, R., & Scollon, S. W. (1995). *Intercultural communication.* Oxford, UK: Blackwell.

Shaver, L. D. (1998). The cultural deprivation of an Oklahoma Cherokee family. In D. V. Tanno & A. González (Eds.), *Communication and identity across cultures: International and intercultural communication annual* (Vol. 21, pp. 80–99). Thousand Oaks, CA: Sage.

Simon, B. (2004). *Identity in modern society: A social psychological perspective.* Oxford, UK: Blackwell.

Spencer-Oatey, H. (2007). Theories of identity and the analysis of face. *Journal of Pragmatics, 39,* 639–656. doi:10.1016/j.pragma.2006.12.004

Stampler, L. (2015, February 12). New York Fashion Week's first-ever model with Down syndrome owned the runway. *Time.* Retrieved from http://time.com/3708150/carrie-hammer-jamie-brewer-new-york-fashion-week/

Tajfel, H., & Turner, J. C. (1979). An integrative theory of intergroup conflict. In W. G. Austin & S. Worchel (Eds.), *The social psychology of intergroup relations* (pp. 33–47). Monterey, CA: Brooks/Cole.

Tannen, D. (1990). *You just don't understand: Women and men in conversation.* New York: Morrow.

Tanno, D. V., & González, A. (1998). Sites of identity in communication and culture. In D. V. Tanno & A. González (Eds.), *Communication and identity across cultures: International and intercultural communication annual* (Vol. 21, pp. 3–7). Thousand Oaks, CA: Sage.

Ting-Toomey, S. (1981). Ethnic identity and close friendship in Chinese-American college students. *International Journal of Intercultural Relations, 5,* 383–406.

Ting-Toomey, S. (1988). A face negotiation theory. In Y. Kim & W. Gudykunst (Eds.), *Theories in intercultural communication* (pp. 213–235). Newbury Park, CA: Sage.

Ting-Toomey, S., Yee-Jung, K. K., Shapiro, R. B., Garcia, W., Wright, T. J., & Oetzel, J. G. (2000). Ethnic/cultural identity salience and conflict styles in four US ethnic groups. *International Journal of Intercultural Relations, 24,* 47–81.

Trenholm, S., & Jensen, A. (2013). *Interpersonal communication* (7th ed.). New York: Oxford University Press.

Turner, J. C. (1985). Social categorization and the self-concept: A social cognitive theory of group behaviour. In E. J. Lawler (Ed.), *Advances in group processes: Theory and research* (Vol. 2, pp. 77–122). Greenwich, CT: JAI.

Turner, J. C. (1987). *Rediscovering the social group.* Oxford, UK: Blackwell.

Turner, J. C. (1991). *Social influence.* Milton Keynes, UK: Open University Press.

Turner, J. C., Hogg, M., Oakes, P., Reicher, S., & Wetherell, M. (1987). *Rediscovering the social group: A self-categorization theory.* Oxford, UK: Blackwell.

Adler, P. S. (1987). Culture shock and the cross-cultural learning experience. In L. F. Luce & E. C. Smith (Eds.), *Toward internationalism* (pp. 24–35). Cambridge, MA: Newbury House.

Anderson, L. E. (1994). A new look at an old construct: Cross-cultural adaptation. *International Journal of Intercultural Relations, 18*(3), 293–328.

Bennett, M. J. (1993). Towards ethnorelativism: A developmental model of intercultural sensitivity. In R. M. Paige (Ed.), *Education for the intercultural experience* (pp. 21–71.). Yarmouth, ME: Intercultural Press.

Cheney, G., Christensen, L. T., Zorn, T. E., & Ganesh, S. (2011). *Organizational communication in an age of globalization* (2nd ed.). Long Grove, IL: Waveland Press.

Cuellar, I., Harris, L., & Jasso, R. (1980). An acculturation scale for Mexican Americans, normal and clinical populations. *Hispanic Journal of Behavioral Science, 2*, 199–217.

Diao, W. (2014). Between ethnic and English names: Name choice for transnational Chinese students in a US academic community. *Journal of International Students 4*(3), 205-222.

Eisenberg, E. M., Goodall, H. L., & Trethewey, A. (2010). *Organizational communication: Balancing creativity and constraint* (6th ed.). Boston: Bedford/St. Martin's.

Furnham, A., & Bochner, S. (1986). *Culture shock: Psychological reactions*. New York: Nethuen.

Galliard, B. M., Myers, K. K., & Seibold, D. R. (2010). Organizational assimilation: A multidimensional reconceptualization and measure. *Management Communication Quarterly, 24*, 552–578.

Gudykunst, W. B., & Hammer, M. R. (1988). Strangers and hosts: An uncertainty reduction based theory of intercultural adaptation. In Y. Y. Kim & W. G. Gudykunst (Eds.), *Cross-cultural adaptations* (pp. 106–139). Newbury Park, CA: Sage.

Gudykunst, W. B., & Kim, Y. Y. (1992). *Communicating with strangers: An approach to intercultural communication* (2nd ed.). New York: McGraw-Hill.

Gullahorn, J., & Gullahorn, J. (1963). An extension of the U-curve hypothesis. *Journal of Social Issues, 19*, 33–47.

Heuman, A. N., Scholl, J. C., & Wilkinson, K. (2013). Rural Hispanic populations at risk in developing diabetes: Sociocultural and familial challenges in promoting a healthy diet. *Health Communication, 28*(3), 260–274.

Hoffenburger, K., Mosier, R., & Stokes, B. (1999). Transition experience. In J. H. Schuh (Ed.), *Educational programming and student learning in college and university residence halls*. Columbus, OH: ACUHO-I.

Hopkins, D. J. (2012). Flooded communities: Explaining local reactions to the post-Katrina migrants. *Political Research Quarterly, 65*(2), 443–459. doi:10.1177/1065912911398050.

Jablin, F. M. (1982). Organizational communication: An assimilation approach. In M. E. Roloff & C. R. Berger (Eds.), *Social cognition and communication* (pp. 255–286). Newbury Park, CA: Sage.

Jablin, F. M. (1987). Organizational entry, assimilation, and exit. In F. M. Jablin, L. L. Putnam, K. H. Roberts, & L. W. Porter (Eds.), *Handbook of organizational communication: An interdisciplinary perspective* (pp. 679–740). Newbury Park, CA: Sage.

Kiang, P. N. (2004). Voicing names and naming voices: Pedagogy and persistence in an Asian American studies classroom. In Zamel, V., & Spack, R. (Eds.), Crossing the curriculum: Multilingual learners in college classrooms (pp. 207-220). Mahwah, NJ: Lawrence Erlbaum Associates.

Kim, Y. Y. (1977). Communication patterns of foreign immigrants in the process of acculturation. *Human Communication Research, 4*, 66–77.

Kim, Y. Y. (1979). Toward an interactive theory of communication-acculturation. In D. Nimono (Ed.), *Communication yearbook 3* (pp. 435–453). New Brunswick, NJ: Transaction-International Communication Association.

Kim, Y. Y. (1988). *Communicating and cross-cultural adaptation: An integrative theory.* Clevedon, UK: Multilingual Matters.

Kim, Y. Y. (1989). Intercultural adaptation. In M. Asante & W. Gudykunst (Eds.), *Handbook of international and intercultural communication* (pp. 275–294). Newbury Park, CA: Sage.

Kim, Y. Y. (1994). Interethnic communication: The context and the behavior. In S. Deetz (Ed.), *Communication yearbook* (Vol. 17, pp. 511–538). Thousand Oaks, CA: Sage.

Kim, Y. Y. (2002). Cross-cultural adaptation: An integrative theory. In J. M. Martin, T. K. Nakayama, & L. A. Flores (Eds.), *Readings in cultural contexts* (2nd ed., pp. 237–245). Mountain View, CA: Mayfield.

Kimbro, R. T. (2009). Acculturation in context: Gender, age at migration, neighborhood ethnicity, and health behaviors. *Social Science Quarterly, 90*, 1145–1160.

Laham, S., Koval, P., & Alter, A. (2011). The name-pronunciation effect: Why people like Mr. Smith more than Mr. Colquhoun. *Journal of Experimental Psychology, 48*, 752-756.

Lewis, T. J., & Jungman, R. E. (Eds.). (1986). *On being foreign: Culture shock in short fiction.* Yarmouth, ME: Intercultural Press.

Lysgaard, S. (1955). Adjustment in a foreign society: Norwegian Fulbright grantees visiting the United States. *International Social Science Bulletin, 7*, 45–51.

Mainous, A. G., Diaz, V. A., & Geesey, M. E. (2008). Acculturation and healthy lifestyle among Latinos with diabetes. *Annals of Family Medicine, 6*, 131–137.

Marin, G., Sabogal, F., Marin, B. V., Otero-Sabogal, R., & Paerez-Stable, E. (1987). Development of a short acculturation scale for Hispanics. *Hispanic Journal of Behavioral Science, 9*, 183–205.

Mendoza, R. H. (1989). An empirical scale to measure type and degree of acculturation in Mexican-American adolescents and adults. *Journal of Cross-Cultural Psychology, 20*, 372–385.

Myers, K. K., & Oetzel, J. G. (2003). Exploring the dimensions of organizational assimilation: Creating and validating a measure. *Communication Quarterly, 51*(4), 438–457.

Oberg, K. (1960). Culture shock: Adjustment to new cultural environments. *Practical Anthropology, 7*, 177–182.

Padilla, A. M. (1980). The role of cultural awareness and ethnic loyalty in acculturation. In A. Padilla (Ed.), *Acculturation: Theory, models and some new findings* (pp. 47–84). Boulder, CO: Westview.

Ruben, B. D., & Kealey, D. J. (1979). Behavioral assessment of communication competency and the prediction of cross-cultural adaptation. *International Journal of Intercultural Relations, 3*, 15–47.

Spitzberg, B., & Cupach, W. R. (1984). *Interpersonal communication competence.* Newbury Park, CA: Sage.

Stillar, S. (2007). Shocking the cultureless: The crucial role of culture shock in racial identity transformation. *Electronic Journal of Sociology*, 1–16.

Stoller, G. (2012). Foreign etiquette for Americans: Tips for traveling abroad. *USA Today*. Retrieved from http://www.usatoday.com/story/travel/2012/09/27/business-travel-foreign-etiquette/1597617/

Vazquez, L. A. (1997). Skin color, acculturation, and community interest among Mexican American students: A research note. *Hispanic Journal of Behavioral Sciences, 9*(3), 377–386.

Wiemann, J. M., & Backlund, P. (1980). Current theory and research in communicative competence. *Review of Educational Research, 50,* 185–199.

CHAPTER 5

Armour, W. (2011). Learning Japanese by reading 'manga': The rise of 'soft power pedagogy.' *RELC Journal, 42*(2), 125–140.

Baron, N. S., & Af Segerstad, Y. (2010). Cross-cultural patterns in mobile-phone use: Public space and reachability in Sweden, the USA and Japan. *New Media & Society, 12*(1), 13–34.

Burgoon, J. K., & Jones, S. B. (1976). Toward a theory of personal space expectations and their violations. *Human Communication Research, 2,* 131–146.

Chen, L. (2011). Cultural identity as a production in process: Dialectics in Hongkongers' account. *Journal of Asian Pacific Communication, 21*(2), 213–237.

Cillizza, C. (2017, July 14). A second-by-second analysis of the Trump-Macron handshake. *CNN Politics.* Retrieved from http://www.cnn.com/2017/07/14/politics/a-second-by-second-analysis-of-the-trump-macron-handshake/index.html

CNN. (2017, July 17). Experts evaluate Trump/Macron handshake. Retrieved from http://www.cnn.com/videos/tv/2017/07/17/etiquette-experts.cnn

Croom, A. M. (2011). Slurs. *Language Sciences, 33,* 343–358.

Danesi, M. (2010). The forms and functions of slang. *Semiotica, 182*(1–4), 507–517.

De Fina, A., & King, K. A. (2011). Language problem or language conflict? Narratives of immigrant women's experiences in the US. *Discourse Studies, 13*(2), 163–188.

DePaulo, B. M., Lindsay, J. L., Malone, B. E., Muhlenbruck, L., Charlton, K., & Cooper, H. (2003). Cues to deception. *Psychological Bulletin, 129,* 74–118.

Dolinski, D. (2010). Touch, compliance, and homophobia. *Journal of Nonverbal Behavior, 34*(3), 179–192.

Domenici, K., & Littlejohn, S. W. (2006). *Facework: Bridging theory and practice.* Thousand Oaks, CA: Sage.

Ekman, P., & Friesen, W. V. (1969a). Nonverbal leakage and clues to deception. *Psychiatry, 32,* 88–106.

Ekman, P., & Friesen, W. V. (1969b). The repertoire of nonverbal behavior: Categories, origins, usage, and coding. *Semiotica, 1,* 49–98.

Ekman, P., & Friesen, W. V. (1975). *Unmasking the face: A guide to recognizing emotions from facial cues.* Englewood Cliffs, NJ: Prentice Hall.

Goffman, E. (1967). *Interaction ritual: Essays on face-to-face behavior.* New York: Pantheon.

Goffman, E. (1971). *Relations in public: Microstudies of the public order.* New York: Harper Colophon Books.

Gordon, M. E., & Newburry, W. E. (2007). Students as a resource for introducing intercultural education in business schools. *Intercultural Education, 18*(3), 243–257.

Gosselin, P., Gilles, K., & Dore, F. Y. (1995). Components and recognition of facial expression in the communication of emotion by actors. *Journal of Personality and Social Psychology, 68*, 83–96.

Guéguen, N. (2010). The effect of a woman's incidental tactile contact on men's later behavior. *Social Behavior & Personality: An International Journal, 38*(2), 257–266.

Guerrero, L. K., & Floyd, K. (2006). *Nonverbal communication in close relationships.* Mahwah, NJ: Erlbaum.

Hall, E. T. (1963). A system for the notation of proxemic behavior. *American Anthropology, 65*, 1003–1026.

Hall, E. T. (1966). *The hidden dimension.* Garden City, NJ: Doubleday.

Hall, E. T. (1981). *Beyond culture.* New York: Doubleday.

Halualani, R. (2010). Intercultural interaction at a multicultural university: Students' definitions and sensemakings of intercultural interaction. *Journal of International & Intercultural Communication, 3*(4), 304–324.

Han, C.-P. (2012). Empirical study on the integration of native culture in English language teaching for non-English majors in China. *English Language & Literature Studies, 2*(2), 116–124.

Harris, P., & Sachau, D. (2005). Is cleanliness next to godliness? The role of housekeeping in impression formation. *Environment and Behavior, 37*, 81–99.

Henry, J. S. (2009). Beyond free speech: Novel approaches to hate on the Internet in the United States. *Information & Communications Technology Law, 18*(2), 235–251.

Heslin, R. (1974). *Steps toward a taxonomy of touching.* Paper presented at the meeting of the Midwestern Psychological Association, Chicago.

Hickson, M., III, Stacks, D. W., & Moore, N.-J. (2004). *Nonverbal communication: Studies and applications* (4th ed.). Los Angeles: Roxbury.

Ivy, D. K., & Wahl, S. T. (2009). *The nonverbal self: Communication for a lifetime.* Boston: Allyn & Bacon.

Ivy, D., & Wahl, S.T. (2014). *Nonverbal communication for a lifetime.* (2nd ed.). Dubuque, IA: Kendall Hunt

Jackson, H. (2005). Sitting comfortably? Then let's talk! *Psychologist, 18*, 691.

Johnson, D. W. (2006). *Reaching out: Interpersonal effectiveness and self-actualization.* Boston: Allyn & Bacon.

Judge, T., Hurst, C., & Simon, L. S. (2009). Does it pay to be smart, attractive, or confident (or all three)? Relationships among general mental ability, physical attractiveness, core self-evaluations, and income. *Journal of Applied Psychology, 94*, 742–755.

Knapp, M. L., & Hall, J. A. (2006). *Nonverbal communication in human interaction* (6th ed.). Belmont, CA: Thomson/Wadsworth.

Larrea Espinar, Á. A., Raigón Rodríguez, A. R., & Gómez Parra, M. E. (2012). ICT for intercultural competence development. *Pixel-Bit: Revista de Medios y Educación,* (40), 115–124.

Lingel, J., & Naaman, M. (2012). You should have been there, man: Live music, DIY content and online communities. *New Media & Society, 14*(2), 332–349.

Lohmann, A., Arriaga, X. B., & Goodfriend, W. (2003). Close relationships and placemaking: Do objects in a couple's home reflect couplehood? *Personal Relationships, 10*, 437–449.

Lyman, S. M., & Scott, M. B. (1967). Territoriality: A neglected social dimension. *Social Problems, 15*, 237–241.

McCarthy, A., & Lee, K. (2009). Children's knowledge of deceptive gaze cues and its relation to their actual lying behavior. *Journal of Experimental Child Psychology, 103*(2), 117–134.

Montagu, M. F. A. (1978). *Touching: The human significance of the skin* (2nd ed.). New York: Harper & Row.

Morris, D. (1985). *Body watching*. New York: Crown.

Muslim businessman 'terror suspect' after he texts staff he's going to 'blow away' the competition. (2012, February 3). *Mail Online*. Retrieved from http://www.dailymail.co.uk/news/article-2096323/Muslim-businessman-terror-suspect-texts-staff-hes-going-blow-away-competition.html

Nelson, A., & Golant, S. K. (2004). *You don't say: Navigating nonverbal communication between the sexes.* New York: Prentice Hall.

Pearce, W. B., & Cronen, V. (1980). *Communication, action, and meaning: The creation of social realities.* New York: Praeger.

Qingchao, G. (2011). Mobile phone: A specific representation of individual space constructing (English). *China Media Report Overseas, 7*(3), 83–86.

Quintanilla, K. M., & Wahl, S. T. (2014). *Business and professional communication: Keys for workplace excellence* (2nd ed.). Thousand Oaks, CA: Sage.

Richmond, V. P., McCroskey, J. C., & Johnson, A. D. (2003). Development of the Nonverbal Immediacy Scale (NIS): Measures of self- and other-perceived nonverbal immediacy. *Communication Quarterly, 51*, 502–515.

Ritts, V., Patterson, M. L., & Tubbs, M. E. (1992). Expectations, impressions, and judgments of physically attractive students: A review. *Review of Educational Research, 62*, 413–426.

Scollon, R., & Scollon, S. (2000). *Intercultural communication: A discourse approach.* Beijing: Foreign Language Teaching and Research Press.

Sharifabad, M., & Vali, S. (2011). A comparative study of native and non-native body language: The case of Americans' kinesics vs. Persian English speakers. *Journal of Intercultural Communication*, (26), 6.

Sheldon, W. H., Stevens, S. S., & Tucker, S. (1942). *The varieties of temperament: A psychology of constitutional differences.* New York: Harper & Row.

Singh, P., & Rampersad, R. (2010). Communication challenges in a multicultural learning environment. *Journal of Intercultural Communication*, (23), 4.

Whorf, B. L. (1956). The relation of habitual thought and behaviour to language. In J. Carrol (Ed.), *Language, thought and reality: Selected writings of Benjamin Lee Whorf.* Cambridge: MIT Press.

Wittgenstein, L. (1922). *Tractatus logico-philosophicus* [Logical-philosophical treatise]. New York: Harcourt.

Wong, S.-L. C. (2004). Middle-class Asian American women in a global frame: Refiguring the Statue of Liberty in Divakaruni and Minatoya. *Melus, 29*(3–4), 183–210.

Wood, J. T. (1992). Gender and the moral voice: Moving from woman's nature to standpoint epistemology. *Women's Studies in Communication, 15*, 1–24.

Adler, R. B., & Towne, N. (2002). *Looking out looking in* (10th ed.). Fort Worth, TX: Harcourt Brace.

Altman, I., Vinsel, A., & Brown, B. (1981). Dialectic conceptions in social psychology: An application to social penetration and privacy regulation. In L. Berkowitz (Ed.), *Advances in experimental social psychology* (Vol. 14, pp. 107–160). New York: Academic Press.

Barnlund, D. C. (1989). *Communicative styles of Japanese and Americans: Images and realities.* Belmont, CA: Wadsworth.

Baxter, L. A. (1988). A dialectical perspective on communication strategies in relationship development. In S. W. Duck, D. F. Hay, S. E. Hobfoll, W. Ickes, & B. Montgomery (Eds.), *A handbook of personal relationships* (pp. 257–273). New York: John Wiley.

Baxter, L. A., & Montgomery, B. (1992). *Relating: Dialogues and dialectics.* New York: Guilford Press.

Bloom, K., Russell, A., & Wassenberg, K. (1987). Turn taking affects the quality of infant vocalizations. *Journal of Child Language, 14*(2), 211–227.

Bradberry, T. (2012, August 21). Caffeine: The silent killer of emotional intelligence. *Forbes.* Retrieved from www.forbes.com/sites/travisbradberry/2012/08/21/caffeine-the-silent-killer-of-emotional-intelligence/

Collier, M. J. (1996). Communication competence problematics in ethnic friendships. *Communication Monographs, 63*, 314–336.

Cools, C. A. (2006). Relational communication in intercultural couples. *Language and Intercultural Communication, 6*(3–4), 262–274.

Ekman, P., & Davidson, R. (Eds.). (1994). *The nature of emotions: Fundamental questions.* New York: Oxford University Press.

Foster, K. (2013, February 4). Cross-cultural conversations. *University of Saskatchewan.* Retrieved from http://news.usask.ca/2013/02/04/cross-cultural-conversations/

Gao, G. (1991). Intimacy, passion, and commitment in Chinese and U.S. American romantic relationships. *International Journal of Intercultural Relations, 25*(3), 329–342.

Goleman, D. (1997). *Emotional intelligence: Why it can matter more than IQ.* New York: Bantam Books.

Goleman, D. (2002). *Working with emotional intelligence.* New York: Bantam Books.

Griffin, E. (2006). *A first look at communication theory* (6th ed.). Boston: McGraw-Hill.

Gross, J. J., Richards, J. M., & John, O. P. (2006). Emotion regulation in everyday life. In D. K. Snyder, J. A. Simpson, & J. N. Hughes (Eds.), *Emotion regulation in couples and families: Pathways to dysfunction and health* (pp. 13–35). Washington, DC: American Psychological Association.

Gross, T. (2017, March 15). 'Get Out' sprang from an effort to master fear, says director Jordan Peele. *NPR: Code Switch.* Retrieved from http://www.npr.org/sections/codeswitch/2017/03/15/520130162/get-out-sprung-from-an-effort-to-master-fear-says-director-jordan-peele

Gudykunst, W. B., & Kim, Y. Y. (1995). *Communicating with strangers* (2nd ed.). New York: McGraw-Hill.

Gullekson, N. L., & Vancouver, J. B. (2010). To conform or not to conform? An examination of perceived emotional display rule norms among international sojourners. *International Journal of Intercultural Relations, 34*(4), 315–325.

Hall, E. T., & Hall, M. R. (1987). *Understanding cultural differences*. Yarmouth, ME: Intercultural Press.

Hochschild, A. (1979). Emotion work, feeling rules, and social structure. *American Journal of Sociology, 85*, 551–575.

Hughes, P. C. (2004). The influence of religious orientation on conflict tactics in interfaith marriages. *Journal of Communication and Religion, 27*, 245–267.

Hughes, P. C., & Dickson, F. C. (2005). Communication, marital satisfaction, and religious orientation in interfaith marriages. *Journal of Family Communication, 5*(1), 25–41.

Human Rights Campaign (2014). Marriage center. Retrieved from http://www.hrc.org/campaigns/marriage-center.

Hwang, H. S., & Matsumoto, D. (2012). Ethnic differences in display rules are mediated by perceived relationship commitment. *Asian American Journal of Psychology, 3*(4), 254–262. doi:10.1037/a00266627

Kemper, T. (1987). How many emotions are there? Wedding the social and autonomic components. *American Journal of Sociology, 93*, 263–289.

Lampe, P. E. (1982). Interethnic dating: Reasons for and against. *International Journal of Intercultural Relations, 6*(2), 115–126.

Lee, S. (2003). How to understand intercultural conversation: A conversation analysis of non-native speakers in the United States. *International Area Review, 6*(2), 65–83.

Lehrer, E. L., & Chiswick, C. U. (1993). Religion as a determinant of marital stability. *Demography, 30*, 385–441.

Lin, Y., Chen, A. S., & Song, Y. (2012). Does your intelligence help to survive in a foreign jungle? The effects of cultural intelligence and emotional intelligence on cross-cultural adjustment. *International Journal of Intercultural Relations, 36*(4), 541–552. doi:10.1016/j.ijintrel.2012.03.001

Lofland, L. (1985). The social shaping of emotion: The case of grief. *Symbolic Interaction, 8*, 171–190.

Martin, J. N., & Nakayama, T. K. (1999). Thinking dialectically about culture and communication. *Communication Theory, 9*(1), 1–25.

Martin, J. N., & Nakayama, T. K. (2007). *Intercultural communication in contexts* (4th ed.). New York: McGraw-Hill.

Martin, J. N., Nakayama, T. K., & Flores (Eds.). (1998). *Readings in cultural contexts*. Mountain View, CA: Mayfield.

Martines, D., Fernández-Berrocal, P., & Extremera, N. (2006). Ethnic group differences in perceived emotional intelligence within the United States and Mexico. *Ansiedad y Estrés, 12*(2–3), 317–327.

McCornack, S. (2013). *Reflect and relate: An introduction to interpersonal communication* (3rd ed.). Boston: Bedford/St. Martin's.

Mendelson, S. (2017, April 14). Box office: Jordan Peele's 'Get Out' is the second-biggest R-rated horror movie ever. *Forbes*. Retrieved from https://www.forbes.com/forbes/welcome/?toURL=https://www.forbes.com/sites/scottmendelson/2017/04/14/box-office-jordan-peeles-get-out-is-the-second-biggest-r-rated-horror-movie-ever/&refURL=https://www.google.com/&referrer=https://www.google.com/

Metts, S., & Planalp, S. (2002). Emotional communication. In M. L. Knapp & J. A. Daly (Eds.), *Handbook on interpersonal communication* (pp. 339–373). Thousand Oaks, CA: Sage.

Naito, M., & Seki, Y. (2009). The relationship between second-order false belief and display rules reasoning: The integration of cognitive and affective social understanding. *Developmental Science, 12*(1), 150–164. doi:10.1111/j.1467-7687.2008.00748.x

Petrides, K. V., & Furnham, A. (2000). Gender differences in measured and self-estimated trait emotional intelligence. *Sex Roles, 42*(5–6), 449–461. doi:10.1032/A:1007006523133

Petrides, K. V., & Furnham, A. (2003). Trait emotional intelligence: Behavioural validation in two studies of emotion recognition and reactivity to mood induction. *European Journal of Personality, 17*(1), 39–57. doi:10.1002/per.466

Rivera Cruz, B. V. (2004). *Across contexts comparison of emotional intelligence competencies: A discovery of gender differences.* Unpublished doctoral dissertation, Case Western Reserve University.

Romano, D. (2008). *Intercultural marriage: Promises and pitfalls* (3rd ed.). Boston: Intercultural Press.

Ross, K., Scholl, J. C., & Bell, G. C. (in press). Shaping self with the doctor: How trans patients' experiences of discrimination and communication with providers help construct identity. In V. Harvey & H. Ousel (Eds.), *Health issues among the LGBTQ community.*

Russell, J. A. (1991). Culture and the categorization of emotions. *Psychological Bulletin, 110*(3), 426–450.

Sadfar, S., Friedlmeier, W., Matsumoto, D., Yoo, S. H., Kwantes, C. T., Kakai, H., et al. (2009). Variations of emotional display rules within and across cultures: A comparison between Canada, USA, and Japan. *Canadian Journal of Behavioural Science, 41*(1), 1–10. doi:10.1037/a0014387

Schegloff, E. A. (1992). Repair after next turn: The last structurally provided defense of intersubjectivity in conversation. *American Journal of Sociology, 97*, 1295–1345.

Schegloff, E. A., Jefferson, G., & Sacks, H. (1977). The preference for self-correction in the organization of repair in conversation. *Language, 53*, 361–382.

Shaver, P. R., Wu, S., & Schwartz, J. C. (1992). Cross-cultural similarities and differences in emotion and its representation. In M. S. Clark (Ed.), *Emotion* (pp. 175–212). Newbury Park, CA: Sage.

Snow, C. E. (1977). The development of conversation between mothers and babies. *Journal of Child Language, 4*(1), 1–22.

Soto, J. A., Levenson, R. W., & Ebling, R. (2005). Cultures of moderation and expression: Emotional experience, behavior, and physiology in Chinese Americans and Mexican Americans. *Emotion, 5*, 154–165.

Sumaryono, K., & Ortiz, F. W. (2004). Preserving the cultural identity of the English language learner. *Voices From the Middle, 11*(4), 16–19.

Tsai, J. L., & Levenson, R. W. (1997). Cultural influences of emotional responding: Chinese American and European American dating couples during interpersonal conflict. *Journal of Cross-Cultural Psychology, 28*, 600–625.

Wheeless, L. R., Preiss, R. W., & Gayle, B. M. (1997). Receiver apprehension, informational receptivity, and cognitive processing. In J. A. Daly, J. C. McCroskey, J. Ayres, T. Hopf, & D. M. Ayers (Eds.), *Avoiding communication: Shyness, reticence, and communication apprehension* (pp. 151–187). Cresskill, NJ: Hampton Press.

Whorf, B. L. (1950). An American Indian model of the universe. *Etc., 8*, 27–33.

Wood, J. T. (2013). *Interpersonal communication: Everyday encounters* (7th ed.). Belmont, CA: Wadsworth/Thompson Learning.

Wu, D. Y. H., & Tseng, W. (1985). Introduction: The characteristics of Chinese culture. In W. Tseng & D. Y. H. Wu (Eds.), *Chinese culture and mental health* (pp. 3–13). Orlando, FL: Academic Press.

Zapf, D., Vogt, C., Seifert, C., Mertini, H., & Isic, A. (1999). Emotion work as a source of stress: The concept and development of an instrument. *European Journal of Work and Organizational Psychology, 8*(3), 371–400. doi:10.1080/135943299398230

CHAPTER 7

Abrams, D., Hogg, M. A., Hinkle, S., & Otten, S. (2005). The social identity perspective on small groups. In M. S. Poole & A. B. Hollingshead (Eds.), *Theories of small groups: Interdisciplinary perspectives* (pp. 99–137). Thousand Oaks, CA: Sage.

Adams, K., & Galanes, G. J. (2009). *Communicating in small groups: Applications and skills* (7th ed.). Boston: McGraw-Hill.

Adler, R. B., & Elmhorst, J. M. (2010). *Communicating at work: Principles and practices for business and the professions* (10th ed.). New York: McGraw-Hill.

Bales, R. F. (1970). *Personality and interpersonal behavior.* New York: Holt, Rinehart & Winston.

Bass, B. M. (1985). *Leadership and performance beyond expectations.* New York: Free Press.

Beebe, S. A., & Masterson, J. T. (2003). *Communicating in small groups* (7th ed.). Boston: Allyn & Bacon.

Borisoff, D., & Merrill, L. (1992). *The power to communicate: Gender differences as barriers.* Prospect Heights, IL: Waveland.

Bormann, E. G. (1982). The symbolic convergence theory of communication and the creation, raising, and sustaining of public consciousness. In J. Sisco (Ed.), *The Jensen lectures: Contemporary communication studies* (pp. 71–90). Tampa: University of South Florida, Department of Communication.

Bormann, E. G. (1996). Symbolic convergence theory and communication in group decision making. In R. Y. Hirokawa & M. S. Poole (Eds.), *Communication and group decision making* (2nd ed., pp. 81–113). Thousand Oaks, CA: Sage.

Bormann, E. G., Bormann, E., & Harty, K. C. (1993). Using symbolic convergence theory and focus group interviews to develop communication designed to stop teenage use of tobacco. In L. Frey (Ed.), *Innovations in group facilitation techniques applied to research in naturalistic settings* (pp. 203–208). Cresskill, NJ: Hampton Press.

Bunderson, J. S., & Sutcliffe, K. M. (2002). Comparing alternative explanations of functional diversity in management teams: Process and performance effects. *Academy of Management Journal, 45*(5), 875–893.

Canary, D. J., & Hause, K. S. (1993). Is there any reason to research sex differences in communication? *Communication Quarterly, 41,* 129–144.

Devine, D. J., Clayton, L. D., Phillips, J. L., Dunford, B. B., & Melner, S. B. (1999). Teams in organizations: Prevalence, characteristics, and effectiveness. *Small Group Research, 30,* 678–711.

Dindia, K. (1997, November). *Men are from North Dakota, women are from South Dakota.* Paper presented at the Speech Communication Association Conference, Chicago, IL.

Ellis, D. G. (1979). Relational control in two group systems. *Communication Quarterly, 46*, 153–166.

Fisher, B. A. (1979). Content and relationship dimensions of communication in decision-making groups. *Communication Quarterly, 27*, 3–11.

Frey, L. R. (1994). The call of the field: Studying communication in natural groups. In L. R. Frey (Ed.), *Group communication in context* (pp. ix–xiv). Hillsdale, NJ: Erlbaum.

Frey, L., & Sunwolf. (2005). The symbolic-interpretive perspective of group life. In M. S. Poole & A. B. Hollingshead (Eds.), *Theories of small groups: Interdisciplinary perspectives* (pp. 185–239). Thousand Oaks, CA: Sage.

Gouran, D. S., & Hirokawa, R. Y. (1983). The role of communication in decision-making groups: A functional perspective. In M. S. Mander (Ed.), *Communication in transition* (pp. 168–185). New York: Praeger.

Gouran, D. S., & Hirokawa, R. Y. (1996). Functional theory and communication in decision-making and problem-solving groups: An expanded view. In R. Y. Hirokawa & M. S. Poole (Eds.), *Communication and group decision making* (2nd ed., pp. 55–80). Thousand Oaks, CA: Sage.

Greer, L. L., Homan, A. C., De Hoogh, A. H. B., & Den Hartog, D. N. (2012). Tainted visions: The effect of visionary leader behaviors and leader categorization tendencies on the financial performance of ethnically diverse teams. *Journal of Applied Psychology, 97*(1), 203–213. doi:10.1037/a0025583

Gudykunst, W. B. (1991). *Bridging differences: Effective intergroup communication.* Newbury Park, CA: Sage.

Gudykunst, W. B., & Ting-Toomey, S. (1988). *Culture and interpersonal communication.* Newbury Park, CA: Sage.

Hall, E. T. (1959). *Beyond culture.* New York: Doubleday.

Hare, A. P. (2003). Roles, relationships, and groups in organizations: Some conclusions and recommendations. *Small Group Research, 34*, 123–154.

Harris, T. E., & Sherblom, J. C. (1999). *Small group and team communication.* Boston: Allyn & Bacon.

Henry, K. B., Arrow, H., & Carini, B. (1999). A tripartite model of group identification: Theory and measurement. *Small Group Research, 30*, 558–581.

Hicks, R., & Hicks, K. (1999). *Boomers, X-ers, and other strangers.* Wheaton, IL: Tyndale House.

Hofstede, G. (1983). National cultures in four dimensions. *International Studies of Management and Organization, 13*(2), 53–74.

Hui, C. H., & Triandis, H. C. (1986). Individualism-collectivism: A study of cross-cultural researchers. *Journal of Cross-Cultural Psychology, 17*, 225–247.

Inagaki, Y. (1985). *Jiko hyogen no gijutsu* [Skills in self-expression]. Tokyo: PHP Institute.

Kanisin-Overton, G., McCalister, P., Kelly, D., & MacVicar, R. (2009). The practice-based small group programme: Experiences of learners in multi-professional groups. *Journal of Interprofessional Care, 23*(3), 262–272.

Katzenbach, J. R., & Smith, D. K. (1993). *The wisdom of teams: Creating the high-performance organization.* Boston: Harvard Business School Press.

Kearney, E., & Gebert, D. (2009). Managing diversity and enhancing team outcomes: The promise of transformational leadership. *Journal of Applied Psychology, 94*(1), 77–89. doi:10.1037/a0013077

Kelley, T., & Littman, J. (2001). *The art of innovation.* New York: Doubleday.

Keyton, J. (2006). *Communicating in groups: Building relationships for group effectiveness* (3rd ed.). New York: Oxford University Press.

Kim, M., & Sharkey, W. F. (1995). Independent and interdependent construals of self: Explaining cultural patterns of interpersonal communication in multicultural organizational settings. *Communication Quarterly, 43,* 20–38.

Kinlaw, D. C. (1991). *Developing supervised work teams: Building quality and the competitive edge.* Lexington, MA: Lexington Books.

Kirchmeyer, C. (1993). Multicultural task groups: An account of the low contribution level of minorities. *Small Group Research, 24,* 127–148.

Kirchmeyer, C., & Cohen, A. (1992). Multicultural groups: Their performance and reactions with constructive conflict. *Group and Organization Management, 17,* 153–170.

Kolb, D. A. (1984). *Experiential learning: Experience as the source of learning and development.* Englewood Cliffs, NJ: Prentice Hall.

LaFasto, F., & Larson, C. (2001). *When teams work best: 6,000 team members and leaders tell what it takes to succeed.* Thousand Oaks, CA: Sage.

Larkey, L. K. (1996). The development and validation of the workforce diversity questionnaire: An instrument to assess interactions in a diverse workplace. *Management Communication Quarterly, 9,* 296–337.

McDaniel, E. (1993). *Japanese nonverbal communication: A review and critique of literature.* Paper presented at the Annual Convention of the Speech Communication Association, Miami Beach, FL.

Mudrack, P., & Farrell, G. (1995). An examination of functional role behavior and its consequences for individuals in group settings. *Small Group Research, 26,* 542–571.

Myers, I. B. (1987). *Introduction to type: A description of the theory and application of the Myers–Briggs Type Indicator.* Palo Alto, CA: Consulting Psychologists Press.

Oetzel, J. G. (1995). Intercultural small groups: An effective decision-making theory. In R. L. Wiseman (Ed.), *Intercultural communication theories* (pp. 247–270). Newbury Park, CA: Sage.

Oetzel, J. G. (1998a). Culturally homogeneous and heterogeneous groups: Explaining communication processes through individualism–collectivism and self-construal. *International Journal of Intercultural Relations, 22*(2), 135–161.

Oetzel, J. G. (1998b). Explaining individual communication processes in homogeneous and heterogeneous groups' individualism–collectivism and self-construal. *Human Communication Research, 25*(2), 202–224.

Oetzel, J. G., & Bolton-Oetzel, K. (1997). Exploring the relationship between self-construal and dimensions of group effectiveness. *Management Communication Quarterly, 10*(3), 289–315.

Patterson, C. (2007). The impact of generational diversity in the workplace. *Generational Diversity, 15*(3), 17-22.

Polzer, J. T., Milton, L. P., & Swann, W. B. (2002). Capitalizing on diversity: Interpersonal congruence in small work groups. *Administrative Science Quarterly, 47,* 296–324. doi:0001-8392/02/4701-0296

Poole, M. S., Hollingshead, A. B., McGrath, J. E., Moreland, R., & Rohrbaugh, J. (2005). Interdisciplinary perspectives on small groups. In M. S. Poole & A. B. Hollingshead (Eds.), *Theories of small groups: Interdisciplinary perspectives* (pp. 1–20). Thousand Oaks, CA: Sage.

Reich, N. M., & Wood, J. T. (2003). Sex, gender and communication in small groups. In R. Y. Hirokawa, R. S. Cathcard, L. A. Samovar, & L. D. Henman (Eds.), *Small group communication: Theory and practice* (8th ed., pp. 218–229). Los Angeles: Roxbury.

Rothwell, J. D. (2004). *In mixed company: Communicating in small groups and teams* (5th ed.). Belmont, CA: Wadsworth.

Saleh, M., Lazonder, A. W., & Tong, T. (2007). Structuring collaboration in mixed-ability groups to promote verbal interaction, learning, and motivation of average-ability students. *Contemporary Educational Psychology, 32*(3), 314–331.

Samovar, L., & Porter, R. (2001). *Communication between cultures*. Belmont, CA: Wadsworth.

Schullery, N. (2013). Workplace engagement and generational differences in values. *Business Communication Quarterly, 76*(2), 252-265.

Shulruf, B., Hattie, J., & Dixon, R. (2007). Development of a new tool for individualism and collectivism. *Journal of Psychoeducational Assessment, 25*(4), 385–401.

Stewart, L. P., & Stewart, A. D. (1985). *Communication between the sexes: Sex differences and sex role stereotypes*. Scottsdale, AZ: Gorsuch Scarisbrick.

Stewart, L. P., Stewart, A. D., Friedley, S. A., & Cooper, P. J. (1990). *Communication between the sexes: Sex differences and sex role stereotypes* (2nd ed.). Scottsdale, AZ: Gorsuch Scarisbrick.

Tajfel, H. (1970). Experiments in intergroup discrimination. *Scientific American, 223*, 96–102.

Tajfel, H. (1974). *Social identity and intergroup behavior, 13*(2), 65–93. doi:10.1177/053901847401300204

Tajfel, H., Billig, M., Bundy, R. P., & Flament, C. (1971). Social categorization and intergroup behavior. *European Journal of Social Psychology, 1*(2), 149–178. doi:10.1002/ejsp.2420010202

Tajfel, H., & Turner, J. C. (1979). An integrative theory of intergroup conflict. In W. G. Austin & S. Worchel (Eds.), *The social psychology of intergroup relations* (pp. 33–47). Monterey, CA: Brooks/Cole.

Tanikawa, M. (2012, November 12). Japanese firms try new hiring strategies. *New York Times*. Retrieved from http://www.nytimes.com/2012/11/13/world/asia/13iht-sreducjapan13.html?pagewanted=all&_r=1&

Tannen, D. (1990). *You just don't understand: Women and men in conversation*. New York: Ballantine Books.

Thomas, R. R., Jr. (1995). A diversity framework. In M. M. Chambers, S. Oskamp, & M. A. Ostanzo (Eds.), *Diversity in organizations: New perspectives for a changing workplace* (pp. 245–264). Thousand Oaks, CA: Sage.

Trezzini, B. (2006). Probing the group faultline concept: An evaluation of measures of patterned multi-dimensional group diversity. *Quality & Quantity, 42*, 339–368. doi:10.1007/s11135-006-9049-z

Triandis, H. C. (1995). A theoretical framework for the study of diversity. M. M. Chambers, S. Oskamp, & M. A. Costanzo (Eds.), *Diversity in organizations: New perspectives for a changing workplace* (pp. 11–36). Thousand Oaks, CA: Sage.

van Leeuwen, E., & Mashuri, A. (2012). When common identities reduce between-group helping. *Social Psychological and Personality Science, 3*(3), 259–265. doi:10.1177/1948550611417315

Wellins, R. S., Byham, W. C., & Wilson, J. M. (1991). *Empowered teams: Creating self-directed work groups that improve quality, productivity, and participation*. San Francisco: Jossey-Bass.

Wilson, G. L. (2002). *Groups in context: Leadership and participation in small groups* (6th ed.). Boston: McGraw-Hill.

Wong, C. L., Tjosvold, D., & Lee, F. (1992). Managing conflict in a diverse workforce: A Chinese perspective in North America. *Small Group Research, 23*, 302–321.

CHAPTER 8

Black, K. A. (2000). Gender differences in adolescents' behavior during conflict resolution tasks with best friends. *Adolescence, 35*(139), 499–512.

Blake, R. R., & Mouton, J. S. (1964). *The managerial grid*. Houston, TX: Gulf.

Choi, Y. (2013). The influence of conflict management culture on job satisfaction. *Social Behavior and Personality, 41*(4), 687–692.

Christensen, A., & Heavey, C. L. (1993). Gender differences in conflict: The demand/withdraw interaction pattern. In S. Oskamp & M. Costanzo (Eds.), *Gender issues in contemporary society* (pp. 113–141). Thousand Oaks, CA: Sage.

Collier, M. J. (1991). Conflict competence within African, Mexican, and Anglo-American friendships. In S. Ting-Toomey & F. Korzenny (Eds), *Cross-cultural interpersonal communication* (pp. 132–154). Newbury Park, CA: Sage.

Collier, M. J. (1996). Communication competence problematic in ethnic friendships. *Communication Monographs, 63*, 314–336.

Croucher, S. M., Bruno, A., McGrath, P., Adams, C., McGahan, C., Suits, A., et al. (2012). Conflict styles and high–low context cultures: A cross-cultural extension. *Communication Research Reports, 29*(1), 64–73. doi:10.1080/08824096.2011.640093

Fisher, R., & Ury, W. (1981). *Getting to yes: Negotiating agreement without giving in*. Boston: Houghton Mifflin.

Fisher, R., Ury, W., & Patton, B. (1991). *Getting to yes: Negotiating agreement without giving in* (2nd ed.). New York: Penguin Books.

Folger, J. P., Poole, M. S., & Stutman, R. K. (2009). *Working through conflict: Strategies for relationships, groups, and organizations* (2nd ed.). Boston: Allyn & Bacon.

Gudykunst, W. B. (2004). *Bridging differences: Effective intergroup communication* (4th ed.). Thousand Oaks, CA: Sage.

Hall, B. J. (2005). *Among cultures: The challenge of communication* (2nd ed.). Stamford, CT: Cengage.

Hayle, S., Wortley, S., & Tanner, J. (2016). Race, street life, and policing implications for racial profiling. *Canadian Journal of Criminology & Criminal Justice, 58*(3), 322-353. doi: 10.3138/cjccj.2014.E32

Hocker, J. L., & Wilmot, W. W. (1995). *Interpersonal conflict* (4th ed.). Madison, WI: Brown & Benchmark.

Hofstede, G., & Bond, M. (1984). Hofstede's culture dimensions. *Journal of Cross-Cultural Psychology, 15*, 417–433.

Ivy, D. K., & Backlund, P. (1994). *Exploring genderspeak: Personal effectiveness in gender communication*. New York: McGraw-Hill.

Janis, I. L. (1972). *Victims of groupthink*. New York: Houghton Mifflin.

Janis, I. L. (1982). *Groupthink* (Rev. ed.). Boston: Houghton Mifflin.

Janis, I. L. (1989). *Crucial decisions: Leadership in policymaking and crisis management*. New York: Free Press.

Kilmann, R., & Thomas, K. (1975). Interpersonal conflict-handling behavior as reflections of Jungian personality dimensions. *Psychological Reports, 37,* 971–980.

Kozan, M. K. (1997). Culture and conflict management: A theoretical framework. *International Journal of Conflict Management, 8,* 338–360.

Krauss, E. S., Rohlen, T. P., & Steinhoff, P. G. (1984). *Conflict in Japan.* Honolulu: University of Hawaii Press.

Lewicki, R. J., Barry, B., Saunders, D. M., & Barry, B. (2011). *Essentials of negotiation* (5th ed.). New York: McGraw-Hill.

Lowery, W. (2017, January 17). Black Lives Matter: Birth of a movement. *The Guardian.* Retrieved from https://www.theguardian.com/us-news/2017/jan/17/black-lives-matter-birth-of-a-movement

Nicotera, A. M., & Dorsey, L. K. (2006). Individual and interactive processes in organizational conflict. In J. G. Oetzel & S. Ting-Toomey (Eds.), *The SAGE handbook of conflict communication* (pp. 293–326). Thousand Oaks, CA: Sage.

Oetzel, J. (1998). The effects of ethnicity and self-construal on self-reported conflict styles. *Communication Reports, 11,* 133–144.

Quintanilla, K. M., & Wahl, S. T. (2014). *Business and professional communication: Keys for workplace excellence* (2nd ed.). Thousand Oaks, CA: Sage.

Rogan, R. G. (2006). Conflict framing categories revisited. *Communication Quarterly, 54,* 157–173.

Roloff, M. E., & Miller, C. W. (2006). Social cognition approaches to understanding interpersonal conflict and communication. In J. G. Oetzel & S. Ting-Toomey (Eds.), *The SAGE handbook of conflict communication* (pp. 97–128). Thousand Oaks, CA: Sage.

Rothbart, M. (2003). Category dynamics and the modification of outgroup stereotypes. In R. Brown & S. Gaertner (Eds.), *Blackwell handbook of social psychology: Intergroup processes* (pp. 45–64). Oxford, UK: Blackwell.

Ruble, T. L., & Thomas, K. W. (1976). Support for a two-dimensional model of conflict behavior. *Organizational Behavior and Human Performance, 16,* 143–155.

Scholl, J. C., & Hughes, P. C. (2011, October). *Relational and instrumental patient-centeredness among Hispanic families who utilize end-of-life care.* Paper presented at the International Conference on Communication in Healthcare (American Academy on Communication in Healthcare), Chicago, IL.

Shenkar, O., & Ronen, S. (1987). The cultural context of negotiations: The implication of Chinese interpersonal norms. *Journal of Applied Behavioral Science, 23,* 263–275.

Tajfel, H., & Turner, J. (1979). An integrative theory of intergroup conflict. In W. G. Austin & S. Worchel (Eds.), *The social psychology of intergroup relations* (pp. 33–48). Monterey, CA: Brooks/Cole.

Tannen, D. (1990). *You just don't understand: Women and men in conversation.* New York: William Morrow.

Ting-Toomey, S. (1988). Intercultural conflict styles: A face-negotiation theory. In Y. Y. Kim & W. B. Gudykunst (Eds.), *Theories in intercultural communication* (pp. 213–235). Newbury Park, CA: Sage.

Ting-Toomey, S. (2002). Intercultural conflict competence. In J. N. Martin, T. K. Nakayama, & L. A. Flores (Eds.), *Readings in intercultural communication: Experiences and contexts* (2nd ed., pp. 323–336). Boston: McGraw-Hill.

Ting-Toomey, S. (2005). Identity negotiation theory: Crossing national boundaries. In W. B. Gudykunst (Ed.), *Theorizing intercultural communication* (pp. 211–233). Thousand Oaks, CA: Sage.

Ting-Toomey, S., & Kurogi, A. (1998). Facework competence in intercultural conflict: An updated face-negotiation theory. *International Journal of Intercultural Relations, 22,* 187–225.

Ting-Toomey, S., & Oetzel, J. (2003). Cross-cultural face concerns and conflict styles: Current status and future directions. In W. B. Gudykunst & B. Mody (Eds.), *Handbook of international and intercultural communication* (2nd ed., pp. 143–163). Thousand Oaks, CA: Sage.

Yarbrough, E., & Wilmot, W. (1995). *Artful mediation: Constructive conflict at work.* Boulder, CO: Cairns.

CHAPTER 9

Allen, B. J. (2010). *Difference matters: Communicating social identity* (2nd ed.). Portland, OR: Waveland Press.

Ameli, S., & Motahari, Z. (2010). Analyzing the relationship between baseball and social capital in the United States: Professional sport as a medium of Americanization. *Global Media Journal: Persian Edition,* 1–21.

Artz, L., & Murphy, B. O. (2000). *Cultural hegemony in the United States.* Thousand Oaks, CA: Sage.

Bourdieu, P. (1987). What makes a social class? On the theoretical and practical existence of groups. *Berkeley Journal of Sociology, 22,* 1–18.

Bridgewater, M. J., & Buzzanell, P. M. (2010). Caribbean immigrants' discourses: Cultural, moral, and personal stories about workplace communication in the United States. *Journal of Business Communication, 47*(3), 235–265.

Dworkin, A. G., & Dworkin, R. J. (Eds.). (1999). *The minority report: An introduction to racial, ethnic, and gender relations* (3rd ed.). Fort Worth, TX: Harcourt Brace.

Feeny, K., & Qi, W. (2010). Success through a cultural lens: Perceptions, motivations, and attributions. *China Media Research, 6*(2), 56–66.

Funke, P. N., Robe, C., & Wolfson, T. (2012). Suturing working class subjectivities: Media mobilizing project and the role of media building a class-based social movement. *Triplec (Cognition, Communication, Co-Operation): Open Access Journal for a Global Sustainable Information Society, 10*(1), 16–29.

hooks, b. (2000). *Feminist theory: From margin to center.* Cambridge, UK: South End Press.

Kennedy, M. (2016, April 20). Lead-laced water in Flint: A step-by-step look at the makings of a crisis. *NPR.* Retrieved from http://www.npr.org/sections/thetwo-way/2016/04/20/465545378/lead-laced-water-in-flint-a-step-by-step-look-at-the-makings-of-a-crisis

Lachlan, K. A., & Spence, P. R. (2007). Hazard and outrage: Developing a psychometric instrument in the aftermath of Katrina. *Journal of Applied Communication Research, 35,* 109–123.

Lewis, O. (1971). The culture of poverty. In E. Penchef (Ed.), *Four horsemen: Pollution, poverty, famine, violence* (pp. 135–141). San Francisco: Canfield Press.

Lucas, K. (2011). The Working Class Promise: A communicative account of mobility-based ambivalences. *Communication Monographs, 78*(3), 347–369.

Lwin, M. O., Stanaland, A. S., & Williams, J. D. (2010). American symbolism in intercultural communication: An animosity/ethnocentrism perspective on intergroup relations and consumer attitudes. *Journal of Communication, 60*(3), 491–514.

Martinez, M. (2016). Flint, Michigan: Did race and poverty factor into water crisis? *CNN*. Retrieved from http://www.cnn.com/2016/01/26/us/flint-michigan-water-crisis-race-poverty/index.html

Mazer, J. P., & Thompson, B. (2011). Student academic support: A validity test. *Communication Research Reports, 28*(3), 214–224.

Paul, R. (2012). Introduction: Culture and class. *Nordic Journal of English Studies, 11*(2), 1–4.

Payne, R. K. (2005). *A framework for understanding poverty* (4th ed.). Highlands, TX: aha Process.

Pishghadam, R., & Zabihi, R. (2011). Parental education and social and cultural capital in academic achievement. *International Journal of English Linguistics, 1*(2), 50–57.

Ramzan, M., Perveen, H., & Gujjar, A. (2011). Influence of the head teacher's role on student behavior management in a primary school. *Language in India, 11*(12), 465–476.

Sands, D. (2016). U.N. says U.S. racism, class discrimination to blame for Flint water scandal. *The Washington Times*. Retrieved from http://www.washingtontimes.com/news/2016/may/3/un-racism-class-discrimination-blame-flint-crisis/

Sei-Hill, K., Carvalho, J. P., & Davis, A. G. (2010). Talking about poverty: News framing of who is responsible for causing and fixing the problem. *Journalism & Mass Communication Quarterly, 87*(3–4), 563–581.

Sei-Hill, K., Shanahan, J., & Boo-Hun, G. (2012). TV news framing supports societal poverty solutions. *Newspaper Research Journal, 33*(1), 101–112.

Snedeker, G. (2012). Culture, alienation and social classes. *Nordic Journal of English Studies, 11*(2), 189–200.

Song, Z. (2012). In retranslating Sun Tzu: Using cultural capital to outmatch the competition. *Translation & Interpreting Studies: Journal of the American Translation & Interpreting Studies Association, 7*(2), 176–190.

Southwell, B. G., Hamilton, J. T., & Slater, J. S. (2011). Why addressing the poor and underinsured is vexing. *Health Communication, 26*(6), 583–585.

Spade, J. Z. (2001). Gender and education in the United States. In D. Vannoy (Ed.), *Gender mosaics: Social perspectives* (pp. 85–93). Los Angeles: Roxbury.

Sumner, W. G. (1906). *Folkways*. Boston: Ginn.

Tilson, D. (2011). Public relations and religious diversity: A conceptual framework for fostering a spirit of communitas. *Global Media Journal: Canadian Edition, 4*(1), 43–60.

U.S. Census Bureau. (2007). *2007 economic census*. Retrieved from http://www.census.gov/econ/census07/

Wilkinson, R., & Pickett, K. (2010). *The spirit level: Why equality is better for everyone*. London: Penguin Books.

World Health Organization. (2001). Water sanitation hygiene. *World Health Organization*. Retrieved from http://www.who.int/water_santition_health/diseases-risks/diseases/lead/en/

Young, E. (2009). Memoirs: Rewriting the social construction of mental illness. *Narrative Inquiry, 19*(1), 52–68.

Agency for Healthcare Research Quality. (2000, February). *Addressing racial and ethnic disparities in health care: Fact sheet.* Retrieved July 11, 2012, from http://www.adhrq.gov/research/disparit.htm

Agency for Healthcare Research Quality. (2004). *National health disparities report.* Retrieved July 17, 2012, from http://www.arhq.gov/qual/nhdr03/nhdrsum03.htm

Ahmad, N. N. (2004, April 15). *Arab-American culture and health care.* Retrieved July 3, 2012, from http://www.cwru.edu/med/epidbio/mphp439/Arab-Americans.htm

Andrews, T.M., & Bever, L. (2016, November 22). Kanye West hospitalized in Los Angeles, placed on psychiatric hold. *The Washington Post.* Retrieved from https://www.washingtonpost.com/news/morning-mix/wp/2016/11/21/kanye-west-reportedly-hospitalized-in-los-angeles/?utm_term=.c2cd8f18c044

Andrulis, D. P. (2003). Reducing racial and ethnic disparities in disease management to improve health outcomes. *Disease Management & Health Outcomes, 11*(12), 789–800. doi:1173-8790/03/0012-0789

Beck, C. S. (1997). *Partnership for health: Building relationships between women and health caregivers.* Mahwah, NJ: Erlbaum.

Belle, D. (1990). Poverty and women's mental health. *American Psychologist, 45*(3), 385–389. doi:10.1037/0003-066X.45.3.385

Braithwaite, D. O., & Thompson, T. L. (Eds.). (2000). *Handbook of communication and people with disabilities: Research and applications.* Mahwah, NJ: Erlbaum.

Brown, J. D., & Scholl, J. C. (2006, August). A qualitative comparison of patients' and providers' ethnic identity displays. In *Proceedings of the Annual Congress of the Americas, Lima, Peru.*

Brunner, B. (2009). *The Tuskegee syphilis experiment: The US government's 40-year experiment on black men with syphilis.* Retrieved July 13, 2012, from http://www.tuskegee.edu/global/story.asp?s=1207586&ClientType=Printable

Centers for Disease Control and Prevention. (2011). *Health literacy: Accurate, accessible and actionable health information for all.* Retrieved July 10, 2012, from http://www.cdc.gov/healthliteracy/

Charmaz, K. (1999). "Discoveries" of self in illness. In K. Charmaz & D. A. Paterniti (Eds.), *Health, illness, and healing: Society, social context, and self* (pp. 72–82). Los Angeles: Roxbury.

Chew, L. D. (2009, February 29). *Self-report measures of health literacy.* Institute of Medicine. Retrieved from iom.edu/~/media/Files/Activity%2520Files/PublicHealth/HealthLiteracy/Chew.pdf

Chiu, L. (2004). Minority ethnic women and cervical screening: A matter of action or research? *Primary Health Care Research and Development, 5,* 104–116. doi:10.1191/1463423604pc172oa

Cline, R. J., & McKenzie, N. J. (1998). The many cultures of health care: Difference, dominance, and distance in physician–patient communication. In L. D. Jackson & B. K. Duffy (Eds.), *Health communication research: A guide to developments and directions* (pp. 57–74). Westport, CT: Greenwood Press.

Colón, M. (2005). Hospice and Latinos: A review of the literature. *Journal of Social Work & End-of-Life in Palliative Care, 1*(2), 27–43.

Coscarelli, J. (2016, November 20). Kanye West calls out Beyoncé and praises Trump in onstage tirade. *The New York Times*. Retrieved from https://www.nytimes.com/2016/11/21/arts/music/kanye-west-beyonce-donald-trump-speech.html

Coupland, N., Coupland, J., & Giles, H. (1991). *Language, society and the elderly*. Oxford, UK: Blackwell.

Cristancho, S., Garces, D. M., Peters, K. E., & Mueller, B. C. (2008). Listening to rural Hispanic immigrants in the Midwest: A community-based participatory assessment of major barriers to health care access and use. *Qualitative Health Research, 18*, 633–646. doi:10.1177/1049732308316669

Douki, S., Zineb, S. B., Nacef, F., & Halbreich, U. (2007). Women's mental health in the Muslim world: Cultural, religious, and social issues. *Journal of Affective Disorders, 102*(1–3), 177–189.

Du Pré, A. (2010). *Communicating about health: Current issues and perspectives* (3rd ed.). New York: Oxford University Press.

Duval, S. (2011, March 22). Culture and stigma affect mental health care for Latinos. *Center for Advancing Health*. Retrieved from http://www.cfah.org/hbns/archives/getDocument.cfm?documentID=22372

Evans, G. W., & Kantrowitz, E. (2002). Socioeconomic status and health: The potential role of environmental risk exposure. *Annual Review of Public Health, 23*, 303–331. doi:10.1146/annurev.publhealth.23.112001.112349

Fisher, S., & Groce, S. B. (1990). Accounting practices in medical interview. *Language in Society, 19*, 225–250.

Freimuth, V. S. (1990). The chronically uninformed: Closing the knowledge gap in health. In E. B. Ray & L. Donohew (Eds.), *Communication and health: Systems and applications* (pp. 171–186). Hillsdale, NJ: Erlbaum.

Gallo, L. C., & Matthews, K. A. (2003). Understanding the association between socioeconomic status and physical health: Do negative emotions play a role? *Psychological Bulletin, 129*(1), 10–51. doi:10.1037/0033-2909.129.1.10

Gaziano, C. (1983). The knowledge gap: An analytical review of media effects. *Communication Research, 10*(4), 447–486.

Giles, H., Ballard, D., & McCann, R. M. (2002). Perceptions of intergenerational communication across cultures: An Italian case. *Perceptual and Motor Skills, 95*, 583–591.

Giles, H., & Wiemann, J. M. (1987). Language, social comparison and power. In C. R. Berger & S. H. Chaffee (Eds.), *The handbook of communication science* (pp. 350–384). Newbury Park, CA: Sage.

Goffman, E. (1963). *Stigma: Notes on the management of spoiled identity*. Englewood Cliffs, NJ: Prentice Hall.

Gouin, J. P., Hantsoo, L., & Kiecolt-Glaser, J. K. (2008). Immune dysregulation and chronic stress among older adults: A review. *Neuroimmunomodulation, 15*(4–6), 251–259.

Greene, M. G., Adelman, R. D., Friedmann, E., & Charon, R. (1994). Older patient satisfaction with communication during an initial medical encounter. *Social Science and Medicine, 38*(9), 1279–1288.

Harris, C. R., Jenkins, M., & Glaser, D. (2006). Differences in risk assessment: Why do women take fewer risks than men? *Judgment and Decision Making, 1*(1), 48–63.

Health literacy: A simple question identifies patients with low health literacy. (2011). Agency for Healthcare Research and Quality. Retrieved January 4, 2013, from www.ahrq.gov/research/jul11/0711RA35.htm

Hecht, M. L. (1978). The conceptualization and measurement of interpersonal communication satisfaction. *Human Communication Research, 4*, 253–264.

Hecht, M. L. (1993). 2002—A research odyssey: Toward the development of a communication theory of identity. *Communication Monographs, 60*, 76–82.

Hecht, M. L., Collier, M. J., & Ribeau, S. A. (1993). *African American communication: Ethnic identity and cultural interpretation.* Newbury Park, CA: Sage.

Hecht, M. L., Jackson, R. L., & Pitts, M. (2005). Culture: Intersection of intergroup identity theories. In A. Reyes (Ed), *Intergroup communications: Multiple perspectives* (pp. 121–132). Newbury Park, CA: Sage.

Hecht, M. L., Jackson, R. L., & Ribeau, S. (2003). *African American communication: Exploring identity and culture* (2nd ed.). Mahwah, NJ: Erlbaum.

Hecht, M. L., Ribeau, S., & Alberts, J. K. (1989). An Afro-American perspective on interethnic communication. *International Journal of Intercultural Relations, 14*, 31–55.

Heuman, A. N., Scholl, J. C., & Wilkinson, K. (2013). Rural Hispanic populations at risk in developing diabetes: Sociocultural and familial challenges in promoting a healthy diet. *Health Communication, 28*(3), 260–274.

Hummert, M. L., & Shaner, J. L. (1994). Patronizing speech to the elderly as a function of stereotyping. *Communication Studies, 45*, 145–158.

Iezzoni, L. I., Ramanan, R. A., & Drews, R. E. (2005). Teaching medical students about communicating with patients who have sensory or physical disabilities. *Disability Studies Quarterly, 25*(1). Retrieved July 16, 2012, from http://dsq-sds.org/article/view/527/704

Institute of Medicine. (2004). *Health literacy: A prescription to end confusion.* Washington, DC: National Academic Press.

Irish, J. T., & Hall, J. A. (1995). Interruptive patterns in medical visits: The effects of role, status and gender. *Social Science and Medicine, 41*, 873–881.

Kreps, G. L. (1990). A systematic analysis of health communication with the aged. In H. Giles, N. Coupland, & J. M. Wiemann (Eds.), *Communication, health, and the elderly* (pp. 135–154). Manchester, UK: Manchester University Press.

Kreps, G. L., & Thornton, B. C. (1992). *Health communication: Theory and practice* (2nd ed.). Prospect Heights, IL: Waveland Press.

Kundrat, A. L., & Nussbaum, J. F. (2000). The impact of invisible illness on identity and contextual age. *Health Communication, 15*(3), 331–347.

LaVeist, T. A., Nickerson, K. J., & Bowie, J. V. (2000). Attitudes about racism, medical mistrust, and satisfaction with care among African American and White cardiac patients. *Medical Care Research Review, 57*(4), 146–161. doi:10.1177/1077558700574007

Lillie-Blanton, M., Martinez, R. M., Taylor, A. K., & Robinson, B. G. (1999). Latina and African American women: Continuing disparities in health. In K. Charmaz & D. A. Paterniti (Eds.), *Health, illness, and healing: Society, social context, and self* (pp. 395–414). Los Angeles: Roxbury.

Management Sciences for Health, Office of Minority Health and Bureau of Primary Health Care. (2005). *Reducing health disparities in Asian American and Pacific Islander populations: Communicating across cultures.* Retrieved July 2, 2012, from http://erc.msh.org/aapi/ca6.html

Martin, E. (1999). Medical metaphors of women's bodies: Menstruation and menopause. In K. Charmaz & D. A. Paterniti (Eds.), *Health, illness, and healing: Society, social context, and self* (pp. 291–301). Los Angeles: Roxbury.

Mechanic, D. (1999). Conceptions of health. In K. Charmaz & D. A. Paterniti (Eds.), *Health, illness, and healing: Society, social context, and self* (pp. 8–17). Los Angeles: Roxbury.

Mensah, G. A., Mokdad, A. H., Ford, E. S., Greenlund, K. J., & Croft, J. B. (2005). State of disparities in cardiovascular health in the United States. *Epidemiology, 111*, 1233–1241. doi:10.1161/01.CIR.0000158136.76824.04

Mull, J. D., & Mull, D. S. (1983). A visit with a curandero. *Western Journal of Medicine, 139*, 730–736.

Murphy, R. F. (1999). The damaged self. In K. Charmaz & D. A. Paterniti (Eds.), *Health, illness, and healing: Society, social context, and self* (pp. 62–71). Los Angeles: Roxbury.

National Institute for Literacy. (2008). *National Institute for Literacy: Stats and resources.* Retrieved July 10, 2012, from http://www.caliteracy.org/nil/

National Patient Safety Foundation. (2007). *Ask Me 3: Good questions for your good health.* Retrieved July 9, 2012, from http://www.ihs.gov/healthcommunications/AskMe_8-pg_NatAmer.pdf

National Patient Safety Foundation. (2011). *Health literacy: Statistics-at-a-glance.* Retrieved July 10, 2012, from http://www.npsf.org/wp-content/uploads/2011/12/AskMe3_Stats_English.pdf

Ndiwane, A., Miller, K. H., Bonner, A., Imperio, K., Matzo, M., McNeal, G., et al. (2004). Enhancing cultural competencies of advanced practice nurses: Health care challenges in the twenty-first century. *Journal of Cultural Diversity, 11*, 118–121.

Nemeth, S. A. (2000). Society, sexuality, and disabled/able-bodied romantic relationships. In D. O. Braithwaite & T. L. Thompson (Eds.), *Handbook of communication and people with disabilities: Research and applications* (pp. 37–48). Mahwah, NJ: Erlbaum.

Olson, T., & Anders, R. L. (2000). Ethnicity, marginalization, and mental illness in Hawaii. *Disability & Society, 15*(3), 463–473.

Orr, R. D. (1996). Transcultural medical care. *American Family Physician, 53*, 2004–2007.

Pear, R. (2012, March 19). Gender gap persists in cost of health insurance. *New York Times.* Retrieved July 16, 2012, from http://www.nytimes.com/2012/03/19/health/policy/women-still-pay-more-for-health-insurance-data-shows.html

Perron, R. (2010, February). African American experiences in the economy: Recession effects more strongly felt. Retrieved July 17, 2012, from http://www.aarp.org/money/budgeting-saving/info-02-2010/economyaa.html

Purnell, L. D. (2008, February). Traditional Vietnamese health and healing. *Urologic Nursing, 28*(1), 63–67.

Safeer, R., & Keenan, J. (2005). Health literacy: The gap between physicians and patients. *American Family Physician, 72*(3), 463–468.

Scholl, J. C. (2013). Persuasive elements of health and wellness. In S. T. Wahl (Ed.), *Persuasion in your life* (pp. 221–248). New York: Pearson.

Scholl, J. C., & Hughes, P. C. (2011, October). *Relational and instrumental patient-centeredness among Hispanic families who utilize end-of-life care.* Poster session at the International Conference on Communication in Healthcare (American Academy on Communication in Healthcare), Chicago, IL.

Scholl, J. C., Wilson, J. B., & Hughes, P. C. (2011). Expression of patients' and providers' identities during the medical interview. *Qualitative Health Research, 21*(8), 1022–1032. doi:10.1177/1049732310393748

Shaw, S. J., Huebner, C., Armin, J., Orzech, K., & Vivian, J. (2008). The role of culture in health literacy and chronic disease screening and management. *Journal of Immigrant and Minority Health, 11,* 460–467. doi:10.1107/s10903-008-9135-5

Skloot, R. (2010). *The immortal life of Henrietta Lacks.* New York: Crown/Random House.

Smith, J. M. (1992). *Women and doctors.* New York: Atlantic Monthly.

Street, R. L., & Giles, H. (1982). Speech accommodation theory: A social cognitive approach to language and speech behavior. In M. Roloff & C. R. Berger (Eds.), *Social cognition and communication* (pp. 193–226). Beverly Hills, CA: Sage.

Talamantes, M., Gomez, C., & Braun, K. (2000). Advance directives and end-of-life care: The Hispanic perspective. In K. Braun, J. H. Pietsch, & P. L. Blanchette (Eds.), *Cultural issues in end-of-life decision making* (pp. 83–100). Thousand Oaks, CA: Sage.

Teliska, H. (2005). Obstacles to access: How pharmacist refusal clauses undermine the basic health care needs of rural and low income women. *Berkeley Journal of Gender, Law, & Justice, 20,* 229.

Tichenor, P. J., Donohue, G. A., & Olien, G. N. (1970). Mass media flow and differential growth in knowledge. *Public Opinion Quarterly, 34*(2), 158–170.

Tichenor, P. J., Donohue, G. A., & Olien, G. N. (1980). Conflict and the knowledge gap. In P. J. Tichenor (Ed.), *Community conflict and the press* (pp. 175–203). Beverly Hills, CA: Sage.

Todd, A. D. (1999). Robust resistance. In K. Charmaz & D. A. Paterniti (Eds.), *Health, illness, and healing: Society, social context, and self* (pp. 337–346). Los Angeles: Roxbury.

U.S. Census Bureau. (2012). *U.S. Census Bureau projections show a slower growing, older, more diverse nation a half century from now.* Retrieved September 10, 2013, from http://www.census.gov/newsroom/releases/archives/population/cb12-243.html

Van Ryn, M., & Fu, S. S. (2003). Paved with good intentions: Do public health and human service providers contribute to racial/ethnic disparities in health? *American Journal of Public Health, 93*(2), 248–255. Retrieved from http://ajph.aphapublications.org/doi/pdf/10.2105/AJPH.93.2.248

Van Servellen, G. (2009). *Communication skills for the health care professional: Concepts, practice, and evidence* (2nd ed.). Boston: Jones & Bartlett.

Verbrugge, L. M. (1999). Pathways of health and death. In K. Charmaz & D. A. Paterniti (Eds.), *Health, illness, and healing: Society, social context, and self* (pp. 377–394). Los Angeles: Roxbury.

Wachtler, C., Brorsson, A., & Troein, M. (2005). Meeting and treating cultural difference in primary care: A qualitative interview study. *Family Practice, 23*(1), 111–115. doi:10.1093/fampra/cmi086

Ward, E. C., Clark, L., & Heidrich, S. (2009). African American women's beliefs, coping behaviors, and barriers to seeking mental health services. *Qualitative Health Research, 19,* 1589–1601. doi:10.1177/1049732309350686

Wenger, D. C. K. (2003, October). Improving cross-cultural communications between physicians and patients. *Academic Physician & Scientist,* 1–5.

West, S. (1994). *The hysterectomy hoax.* New York: Doubleday.

Williams, D. R., & Collins, C. (1999). U.S. socioeconomic and racial differences in health: Patterns and explanations. In K. Charmaz & D. A. Paterniti (Eds.), *Health, illness, and healing: Society, social context, and self* (pp. 349–376). Los Angeles: Roxbury.

Willies-Jacobo, L. (2007, August). Susto: Acknowledging patients' beliefs about illness. *Virtual Mentor, 9*(8), 532–536.

Witte, K., & Morrison, K. (1995). Intercultural and cross-cultural health communication: Understanding people and motivating healthy behaviors. In R. Wiseman (Ed.), *Intercultural communication theory* (pp. 216–246). Thousand Oaks, CA: Sage.

WomenHeart. (2012). *Women and heart disease fact sheet.* Retrieved July 13, 2012, from http://www.womenheart.org/resources/cvdfactsheet.cfm

World Health Organization. (2003). *WHO definition of health.* Retrieved July 18, 2012, from http://www.who.int/about/definition/en/print.html

Wright, K. B., Sparks, L., & O'Hair, H. D. (2013). *Health communication in the 21st century* (2nd ed.). Malden, MA: Blackwell.

Young, C. M. (2004). *Health literacy a national epidemic.* Louisville, KY: University of Louisville. Retrieved July 17, 2012, from http://www.louisville.edu/~cmyoun02/firstpage.htm

Zoucha, R., & Broome, B. (2008, April). The significance of culture in nursing: Examples from the Mexican-American culture and knowing the unknown. *Urologic Nursing, 28*(2), 140–142.

CHAPTER 11

Allen, B. J. (1995). "Diversity" and organization communication. *Journal of Applied Communication Research, 23*, 143–155.

Archer, D. (1997). Unspoken diversity: Cultural differences in gestures. *Qualitative Sociology, 20*, 79–95.

Baird, K., Harrison, G., & Reeve, R. (2007). The culture of Australian organizations and its relation with strategy. *International Journal of Business Studies, 15*, 15–41.

Barile, N. (n.d.). Chrysler and Fiat: Understanding cultural differences. *Global HR News.* Retrieved from http://www.globalhrbusiness.com/story.asp?sid=1194

Brach, C., & Fraser, I. (2000). Can cultural competency reduce racial and ethical racial health disparities? A review and conceptual model. *Medicare Care Research and Review, 57*(1), 181–217.

Chatman, J. A., & Jehn, K. A. (1994). Assessing the relationship between industry characteristics and organizational culture: How different can you be? *Academy of Management Journal, 37*, 522–553.

Civil Rights Act. (1964). Washington, DC: U.S. Federal Government.

De Anca, C., & Vega, A. V. (2007). *Managing diversity in the global organization* (A. Goodall, Trans.). New York: Palgrave Macmillan.

Deshpandé, R., & Farley, J. U. (1998). Measuring market orientation: Generalization and synthesis. *Journal of Market Focused Management, 2*(3), 237–239.

Donnelly, G. (2017, June 29). Google's 2017 diversity report shows progress hiring women, little change for minority workers. *Fortune.* Retrieved from http://fortune.com/2017/06/29/google-2017-diversity-report/

Edley, P. P. (2001). Technology, employed mothers, and corporate colonization of the lifeworld: A gendered paradox of work and family balance. *Women & Language, 24*(2), 28–35.

Fine, M. G. (1996). Cultural diversity in the workplace: The state of the field. *Journal of Business Communication, 33*, 485–502.

Hamilton, C., Parker, C., & Smith, D. (1982). *Communicating for results*. Belmont, CA: Wadsworth.

Hickman, J. (2002). America's 50 best companies for minorities. *Fortune, 148*(1), 110–114.

Holmes, J., & Marra, M. (2005). Narrative and the construction of professional identity in the workplace. In J. Thornborrow & J. Coates (Eds.), *The sociolinguistics of narrative* (pp. 193–213). Amsterdam: John Benjamins.

HR World Editors. (2013). 30 interview questions you can't ask and 30 sneaky, legal alternatives to get the same info. *HR World*. Retrieved from http://www.hrworld. com/features/30-interview-questions-111507/

Jablin, F. M. (2001). Organization entry, assimilation and exit. In F. Jablin & L. Putnam (Eds.), *The new handbook of organizational communication* (pp. 732–818). Thousand Oaks, CA: Sage.

Kienzle, N., & Husar, S. (2007). How can cultural awareness improve communication in the global workplace? *Journal of the Communication, Speech & Theatre Association of North Dakota, 20*, 81–85.

King, A. S. (1995). Capacity of empathy: Confronting discrimination and managing multicultural workforce diversity. *Business Communication Quarterly, 58*(4), 46–50.

Kirby, J. (2005, December 15). See, yo hablo Español! *Review of Optometry*, 28–30.

Ling, C. W. (1997, March). Crossing cultural boundaries. *Nursing, 45*, 32d–32f.

Littlejohn, S. W., & Foss, K. A. (2009). Corporate colonization theory. In S. W. Littlejohn & K. A. Foss (Eds.), *Encyclopedia of communication theory* (Vol. 1, pp. 208–210). Thousand Oaks, CA: Sage.

Longmore, P. K., & Umansky, L. (2001). Disability history: From the margins to the mainstream. In P. K. Longmore & L. Umansky (Eds.), *The new disability history: American perspectives* (pp. 1–24). New York: New York University Press.

Lutgen-Sandvik, P., & McDermott, V. (2011). Making sense of supervisory bullying: Perceived powerlessness, empowered possibilities. *Southern Communication Journal, 76*(4), 342–368.

Lutgen-Sandvik, P., & Sypher, B. D. (2009). *Destructive organizational communication: Processes, consequences, and constructive ways of organizing*. New York: Routledge.

McGirt, E. (2017, February 1). Inside the search giant's effort to get more diverse – and to change the way we all see the world. *Fortune*. Retrieved from http://fortune.com/ google-diversity/

Myers, K. K., & McPhee, R. D. (2006). Influences on member assimilation in workgroups in high-reliability organizations: A multilevel analysis. *Human Communication Research, 32*, 440–468.

Narver, J. C., & Slater, S. F. (1998). Additional thoughts on the measurement of market orientation: A comment on Deshpandé and Farley. *Journal of Market Focused Management, 2*(3), 233–236.

Patrick, H. A., & Kumar, V. R. (2012). Managing workplace diversity: Issues and challenges. *SAGE Open*, 1–15.

Point, S., & Singh, V. (2003). Defining and dimensionalising diversity: Evidence from corporate websites across Europe. *European Management Journal, 21*, 750–761.

Prieto, L. C., Phipps, S. T. A., & Osiri, J. K. (2009). Linking workplace diversity to organizational performance: A conceptual framework. *Journal of Diversity Management, 4*(4), 13–21.

Quintanilla, K. M., & Wahl, S. T. (2014). *Business and professional communication: Keys for workplace excellence* (2nd ed.). Thousand Oaks, CA: Sage.

Ragins, B. R. (1995). Diversity, power, and mentorship in organizations: A cultural, structural, and behavioral perspective. In M. M. Chemers, S. O. Kamp, & M. A. Castanzo (Eds.), *Diversity in organization: New perspective for a changing workplace* (pp. 91–132). Thousand Oaks, CA: Sage.

Redfield, R. (1953). *The primitive world and its transformation.* Ithaca, NY: Cornell University Press.

Samovar, L., Porter, R. E., & McDaniel, E. R. (2009). *Communication between cultures* (7th ed.). Belmont, CA: Wadsworth.

Soni, V. (2001). A twenty-first century reception for diversity in the public sector: A case study. *Public Administration Review, 60*(5), 395–408.

Thomas, D. C., & Inkson, K. (2005, March). Cultural intelligence: People skills for a global workplace. *Consulting to Management, 16,* 5–9.

Ting-Toomey, S., & Chung, L. (2005). *Understanding intercultural communication.* New York: Oxford University Press.

Triana, M. D. C., Garcia, M. F., & Colella, A. (2010). Managing diversity: How organizational efforts to support diversity moderate the effects of perceived racial discrimination on affective commitment. *Personnel Psychology, 63,* 817–843.

U.S. Census Bureau. (2012, May 17). *Most children younger than age 1 are minorities, Census Bureau reports* [Press release]. Retrieved from http://www.census.gov/newsroom/releases/archives/population/cb12-90.html

Wanguri, D. M. (1996). Diversity, perceptions of equality, and communicative openness in the workplace. *Journal of Business Communication, 33*(4), 443–457.

Webster, C., & White, A. (2010). Exploring the national and organizational culture mix in service firms. *Journal of the Academy of Marketing Science, 38,* 691–703.

Wieland, S. M. B. (2011). Struggling to manage work as a part of everyday life: Complicating control, rethinking resistance, and contextualizing work/life studies. *Communication Monographs, 78*(2), 162–184.

Witherspoon, P., & Wohlert, K. (1996). An approach to developing communication strategies for enhancing organizational diversity. *Journal of Business Communication, 33*(4), 375–399.

Yep, G. (2002). From homophobia and heterosexism to heteronormativity: Toward the development of a model of queer interventions in the university classroom. *Journal of Lesbian Studies, 6,* 163–176.

index